Web Site Construction Kit
for
Windows® NT

Web Site Construction Kit
for
Windows® NT

Christopher L. T. Brown
and Scott Zimmerman

201 West 103rd Street
Indianapolis, Indiana 46290

To my wife Bobbie Sue, a true believer in all that I do. CB

To my wife Hershey, a ray of sunshine—and to our playful dog Boston. SZ

FIRST EDITION

International Standard Book Number: 1-57521-047-9

Library of Congress Catalog Card Number: 95-71198

99   98   97   96   4   3   2   1

Interpretation of the printing code: the rightmost double-digit number is the
year of the book's printing; the rightmost single-digit, the number of the book's
printing. For example, a printing code of 96-1 shows that the first printing of
the book occurred in 1996.

Composed in AGaramond and MCPdigital by Macmillan Computer Publishing

Printed in the United States of America

President, Sams Publishing: Richard K. Swadley

Publisher, Sams.net Publishing: George Bond

Publishing Manager Mark Taber

Managing Editor: Cindy Morrow

Marketing Manager: John Pierce

Acquisitions Editor
Mark Taber

Development Editor
Fran Hatton

Software Development Specialist
Merle Newlon

Production Editor
Mary Inderstrodt

Technical Reviewer
David Schriffin

Editorial Coordinator
Bill Whitmer

Technical Edit Coordinator
Lynette Quinn

Formatter
Frank Sinclair

Editorial Assistant
Carol Ackerman

Cover Designer
Tim Amrhein

Book Designer
Alyssa Yesh

Production Team Supervisor
Brad Chinn

Production
*Mary Ann Abramson,
Georgiana Briggs, Gina
Brown, Mike Dietsch, Jason
Hand, Ayanna Lacey, Steph
Mineart, Nancy Price,
Bobbi Satterfield, Craig
Small, Andrew Stone, Susan
Van Ness, Todd Wente,
Colleen Williams*

Overview

Contents

Preface

The World Wide Web is a very powerful tool for communicating. The Web has become the avenue of choice for people who need to travel on the information superhighway. This popularity results from the ease with which information (the merchandise of the Information Age) can be obtained on the Web. As more and more people use personal computers at home or work, the Web could become as commonplace as the telephone or the television.

If you've had a chance to use the Web, perhaps you have wondered how it all got there in the first place. The answer is that anyone can help build it. Parts of it are being torn down, and new parts are going in every day. Anyone with a computer and a message can start a Web site.

Setting up a Web site can be beneficial, whether for business, education, research, or pleasure. This book will show you how to do it. It is up to you to determine your message to the rest of the world.

One little-known fact about the Web (also called WWW or W3) is that it not only works on the global Internet, but it is also a great idea for an Intranet. In other words, Web forms and databases are a terrific way for a company to communicate and deliver data across a LAN or WAN. In this respect, Web pages can replace or supplement multiuser databases or products such as Lotus Notes. We will have more to say about these exciting possibilities in Chapter 15 and Chapter 18.

Web Site Construction Kit for Windows NT goes way beyond the basics of using the Internet, and into the realm of actually being a part of the Internet! Until now, setting up a Web site has required deep knowledge of several Internet protocols and lots of experience. Many people still assume that you need to be a UNIX system administrator to run an Internet server. Not only is this untrue, but we believe that no other book will show you how easy and inexpensive it really is.

Our goal in writing this book was to make it work like a blueprint works for a carpenter. It will guide you through the entire process of setting up and managing a Web site on Windows NT. In addition, the accompanying CD includes the complete suite of software you will need. We believe this to be the most comprehensive Web publishing guide available.

The World Wide Web changes extremely fast. We have made every effort to verify that the information in this book is accurate at the time of printing. We have also endeavored to pack this volume with the most useful information you are likely to need. We hope you will find that our cross-referencing to other sections in the book and to the Internet itself is a valuable aid to furthering your understanding. Unfortunately, some books about the Web offer a lot more fluff than details. Please don't buy another book about the Web until you compare it head-to-head with ours.

Good luck in your efforts. Perhaps we will be among the many who will visit your home page someday soon.

Christopher L. T. Brown, Scott Zimmerman

San Diego, November 1995

About the Authors

Christopher L. T. Brown (clbrown@netcom.com) is a Senior Chief in the U.S. Navy. For the past 15 years, he has worked in the Naval Command Control and Communications. Brown has written programs in several computer languages including Basic, Pascal, C, and C++. In addition to proprietary operating systems, he has worked with UNIX, Macintosh, DOS, Windows, Windows NT, and Windows 95. During the past three years, Brown has dedicated most of his time to evaluation and operation of Windows NT as an Internet platform. In addition to his Navy career, he runs a World Wide Web publishing and consulting company called Final Bit Solutions, which maintains an active Internet Web server as part of its services. Brown's interests include cryptography, surfing, skiing, and wildlife.

Scott Zimmerman (scottz@sd.znet.com) has been developing software for 15 years. He has programmed in over two dozen languages, primarily C++ and Visual Basic. Currently, he serves as Software Engineering Manager with Azron, Incorporated in San Diego. Azron produces an industry leading solution for electronic medical records on Windows 95 and Windows NT. Zimmerman's interests include nature conservation, science, and technology. In a previous career, he won the World Overall Frisbee Championships eight times. For having made an Aerobie toss of 1,257 feet, he is featured in the Guiness Book of World Records as the holder of the longest throw of any object.

Introduction

Who This Book Is For

This book is your complete guide to building a very economical presence on the Internet—quickly, professionally, and securely. It is intended for anyone who wants to publish his or her own home page on the World Wide Web using Microsoft Windows NT. Although it would be helpful if you have a basic understanding of Windows NT, that isn't essential beforehand, because this book covers all the necessary information for building your own Web site. In addition to being an extremely powerful operating system, Windows NT is also quite intuitive. Most tasks can be easily accomplished with point-and-click mouse commands.

We start at the very beginning, but in some of the later sections we assume the reader has some basic knowledge of the World Wide Web—at least from the "client" side. Given the explosive growth of the Internet, nearly everyone who works with computers has had an opportunity to "surf the net" with a Web "browser." The purpose of this book is to show you how to set up your own Web server so that the rest of the world can connect to *your* computer and see what you have to say.

If you don't yet consider yourself to be very familiar with the Web, this book shows you more about how it really works, rather than other books that only talk about *using* the Web.

If you were reading this book in a Web browser, each of the quoted words and phrases in the paragraph above would have been underlined to indicate that a mouse click would take you to further information about that topic. We can't do that in this book, but we can substitute with boxes similar to pop-up boxes, like below. As you read through the book, you will notice that we use boxes such as these to point out highlights, raise caution when appropriate, and define new terms. The following is an example.

> **Note:** What is meant by *client* and *server?* The server is the computer that serves as a repository of information or provides a service when the client computer makes a request for the information or service. Sometimes the terms are arbitrary because both computers can provide information for, and make requests of, each other. Of course, the requests are usually initiated by users. When you request to view a document on a server, the computers might actually carry out dozens of low-level client/server commands.

> **Note:** What is meant by *surfing with a Web browser?* This is a strange mutation of English that allows computer experts to think of themselves as beach jocks. Actually, although Net surfing isn't as athletically demanding as surfing at the beach, the analogy has some validity. When you use a Web client program, or browser, you begin your visual adventure at a place called the *home page* on your favorite Internet server. From there, you are able to

ride the information superhighway between it and other servers, browsing the library at each destination as you go. Whenever the feeling is right, you can latch onto a promising looking keyword, and with the click of a button, get flung to yet another server that might happen to reside on the other side of the planet.

Do I Need to Know Programming or Protocols?

HTML (HyperText Markup Language) and HTTP (HyperText Transfer Protocol) are the languages of the Web, in a sense. Despite its name, HTML isn't actually considered a programming language. After you read Chapter 4, "Up and Running Fast," you will see just how easy it is. We will continue to explore HTML throughout the book, and by the time you finish, you will be very familiar with it. But do not fear; you do not need to know a programming language before you start.

On the Web, client/server conversations take place using HTTP. You do not ordinarily need to know the low-level details of HTTP to run a Web site.

In addition to plenty of HTML code, we discuss several programs written in C, Perl, and Visual Basic. All the programs are ready to run, so the reader does not need to know programming in order to use them. However, we also include the source code so that those familiar with these languages can study the programs for further information or to make enhancements.

This book does not cover internetworking or the Internet protocols in any significant way. We expect people who have a background in this area will be able to use this book as a guide to building their Web site. For those without a background in internetworking, you still should have no trouble getting your Web site up and running with the software and examples that are provided. The Internet is a very large topic—too large to completely cover in one book. You might find that additional research into Internet protocols and security will be helpful in the long run. You will find some useful references in Appendix C and in the bibliography.

What Exactly Is a Web Site?

Good question. The brief, executive answer is "A computer, an operating system, a Web server program, some content that other people would like to see, and usually, a connection to the Internet." Perhaps the fact that this sounds so open-ended is why so many different kinds of new Web sites appear each week. What you can do with a Web site is limited only by your imagination. By the way, the Web is growing at the phenomenal rate of 50 to 100 new sites per week!

A Web site provides the world with a graphical interface to information that you have to offer. Some companies are using the Web to deliver 24-hour customer service. Some use the Web to provide electronic software distribution, advertise job openings, or sell goods and services. Some places run Web sites to collect data from remote computers, such as large-scale research projects or international sales forces. Some companies use the Web internally to publish their employee handbook or provide an electronic suggestion box. Even the White House runs a Web site.

The World Wide Web is aptly named. By analogy to a spider's web, you can think of the Internet as the strands of the spider's web and the servers on the Internet like the intersections of the strands. The World Wide Web literally covers the globe. By the time you read this, there will likely be about 15,000 servers (intersections) on the Web. Each server on the Web is considered a Web site.

Why Windows NT?

There are many reasons to use Windows NT as your Web site operating system. NT offers superior reliability and security coupled with the familiar Windows user interface. NT runs on powerful and inexpensive hardware. When buying a computer to run NT, you have many excellent options depending on the bang-for-the-buck you want and can afford because the engineers at Microsoft were savvy enough to design NT to run on several hardware platforms. Today, this includes everything from Intel 386 to IBM PowerPC to MIPS to DEC Alpha. And because of multithreading, NT will continue to deliver performance under heavy user loads better than other operating systems on the Internet.

With TCP/IP and remote access software built into the operating system, NT is one of the easiest operating systems to use on the Internet. Right out of the box, you can be surfing the Internet in no time. When you consider the other benefits of NT, such as scalability, security, performance, and manageability, you've got an ideal platform to create an Internet server that anyone can connect with. There are hundreds of commercial, freeware, and shareware client and server programs for NT, in most every category, available on the Internet.

Microsoft advertises Windows NT as *scalable*, but what does that mean? We look at it this way: NT can run on several platforms, from low-end to high-end. It can also run on SMP (Symmetric Multiprocessing) machines with up to 16 CPUs. Finally, because it is portable, you never know when they will announce a version that runs on another new platform, such as they did with version 3.51 for the PowerPC. So if you find that your server is being overstressed by an increasing user base, you have three options without dropping your existing software:

■ Move the operating system to a faster computer in the same platform family. (Any operating system can do this.)

- Move it to a machine containing multiple processors. (Few operating systems can do this.)
- Move it to another platform altogether. (Almost no other operating system can do this!)

If you are still not convinced that NT is a good choice, consider a few statistics. More than two million customers used `ftp.microsoft.com` in its first year. The original Windows NT FTP server was a dual-processor, i486-based computer with 64 MB of RAM. This server easily supported 100 simultaneous FTP users via a single T1 line.

Note: FTP stands for File Transfer Protocol. It is one of the many languages, so to speak, of the Internet. It is one way for files, regardless of their type, to be copied between two computers. The benefit from conventions like this is that it works even if the two machines are running different operating systems. We cover FTP in detail in Chapter 14, "Running FTP and Telnet Servers." We discuss T1 and other network wiring technologies in Chapter 1, "Internet Technology Primer."

Note: For more information on Windows NT and the Internet, see Microsoft's Web page, "Windows NT on the Internet" at `http://www.microsoft.com/pages/bussys/internet/in10000.htm`.

Cost-Benefit Analysis

Today, companies can ill afford not to have an Internet presence. One reason is that traditional advertising is expensive—whether you choose the Yellow Pages, newspapers, magazines, TV, or mail. We certainly don't want to guess which marketing vehicle is best for your business, but this book will show you how you can get on the Net for a lot less than some of the other options.

Another compelling reason to be on the Web is that we live in a very competitive global economy, and no business can afford to overlook an opportunity to reach a new market. With a Web site, you can reach people faster than with any other medium. People in various professional fields all over the world use the Internet on a daily basis to purchase products. Furthermore, online documents can be changed easily with instantaneous effect, eliminating the waste and potential problems of obsolete information. And if your business includes customer support by phone, having a Web site can save time and money, and deliver greater customer satisfaction.

As the number of Internet Service Providers (ISPs) continues to grow, the cost of a monthly connection continues to drop. A small company can easily get by with a standard modem connection to the Web, which some service providers offer at rates as low as $200 per month. That includes domain-naming services as well. As ISDN (Integrated Services Digital Network) continues to expand, it is also becoming a popular and cost-effective method of connecting to the Internet. You will find these terms, as well as everything else you need to know about choosing an Internet service provider, in Chapter 3, "Getting Connected to the Internet."

Risk Analysis

In the midst of all the Internet hype, you've probably heard stories about hackers and viruses. The term *hacker* has come to refer to someone who tries to break into computer systems to play, steal information, or sabotage network resources. It is true that there are risks associated with opening your network to the Internet. But none of the risks are unmanageable, and the risks of keeping a modern business staff locked up in its own world are likely to be far greater. Amazingly, the topic of Internet security risks often comes up without mention of the many risks of physical theft at the location of the computer! As the saying goes, "It only takes one hole to sink a boat."

We discuss several security measures that are controlled through the Windows NT Registry. Deep coverage of Internet security, however, is beyond the scope of this book. We encourage you to see the Bibliography for further reference. Windows NT meets the security requirements of a C2-level operating system as defined by the U.S. Department of Defense. In this respect, it is ahead of many UNIX systems.

And now, the game is afoot.

Part I

Getting Started on the World Wide Web

The next four chapters are intended to get you up and running on the Web as quickly as possible. By the end of Chapter 4, your presence on the Internet is guaranteed. Here are the highlights:

- **Chapter 1**, "Internet Technology Primer," defines essential terminology and builds the foundation. It discusses some of the popular Internet programs, and how to search the Internet.

- **Chapter 2**, "Everything You Need," describes all of the software included on the CD-ROM and provides guidelines for Web server hardware requirements.

- **Chapter 3**, "Getting Connected to the Internet," helps you decipher more buzzwords and learn how to ask the right questions when you are selecting your Internet Service Provider.

- **Chapter 4**, "Up and Running Fast," is where things really start cooking. You'll install the HTTP Server and get your first home page online.

Chapter 1

Internet Technology Primer

- FAQs on the Internet
- What is TCP/IP?
- What is the OSI Networking Model?
- What is a Listserver?
- What is a Newsgroup?
- What are FTP and Anonymous FTP?
- How Can I Find Things on the Internet?
- What is the Difference Between SLIP and PPP?
- Which is Right for Me: Switched-56, X.25, Frame Relay, ISDN, T1, T3, or ATM?
- How Fast is the Internet?
- Does C2 Security Protect Windows NT for Internet Hackers?
- What is so "Hyper" About HTML?
- How Can I Learn More About the Internet?

FAQs on the Internet

For those who are new to all the jargon of the Internet, this chapter will lay the foundation for the rest of the book. We will introduce several terms that you will hear often as you go about choosing an Internet service provider (ISP) and building a Web site. If you come across any technical terms that we didn't define here, you might want to refer to the book's glossary.

Just about everywhere you look on the Internet, there are documents called Frequently Asked Questions (FAQs). The purpose of these text files is to answer common questions for newcomers. FAQs save experienced users from having to answer questions and tell about their experiences over and over. Regardless of your level of experience, FAQs are always a good place to start whenever you are trying something new on the Internet.

Another advantage of the format of FAQs is that you can quickly scan through the questions to see what parts you are interested in, without necessarily having to read the entire document. For this reason, and because we have several miscellaneous topics to discuss in this chapter, we have borrowed the FAQ concept in our organization of this material. The questions we chose for this chapter are those that we wondered about when we first started using the Internet, and which we often get asked as we assist others coming to the Net.

In answering these questions, we have tried to go into somewhat more detail than the typical FAQ file on the Internet, but in no way do we cover each topic completely. Entire books are written about most of these subjects. What we have tried to do is provide only the fundamentals, because we know that your Web site project is waiting in the wings.

If you can't wait to get started, or if you already have some experience with the Internet, feel free to skip or skim through this chapter. You can always come back to it later.

What is TCP/IP?

If the Internet were alive, TCP/IP would be its bloodstream. This now-famous acronym stands for Transmission Control Protocol/Internetworking Protocol. TCP/IP provides a method for any computer on the Internet to send electronic packets of data reliably and efficiently to any other computer on the Internet. We are talking about millions of computers, with different CPUs and operating systems, being able to identify each other, even though they aren't directly connected. (In fact, some Internet computers aren't on a wire at all, but that's another story.) Of course, packets must be able to cross company and international borders, and still find their destination.

The only way to accomplish all of this is for each computer to have an address. An address on the Internet is called a *32-bit IP address*. The phrase *32-bit* means that 4 bytes are used to hold the data, and the *IP* refers to Internetworking Protocol, as in TCP/IP. The addresses usually appear in dotted-decimal form, like this: `123.64.12.88`. Each decimal number ranges from 0 to 255.

Most humans have better things to do than decode numbers such as those and determine who or what belongs to such an address. Therefore, the engineers and researchers who created the Internet devised several clever schemes that allow us to refer to computers by name, rather than by IP address. This way, we can let the machines do the work of translating the numbers, and we can instead refer to computer resources in a somewhat more meaningful fashion, such as `www.ibm.com` and `president@white-house.gov`.

The first example (`www.ibm.com`) is called a *fully qualified domain name*, or FQDN. By now, you most likely know that the second example is called an *e-mail address*. Even if you don't understand all the syntax, you can probably guess what these addresses refer to. `www.ibm.com` is the IBM Web page, and the second (`president@white-house.gov`) is your high-speed direct link to the White House (handy when you've got something of national importance on your mind).

Both of these sample addresses include a domain name. The *domain name* is the last part on the right, such as `com` or `gov`. The Internet is divided into several domains, or hierarchies. This is part of the solution to the problem of how to accurately deliver electronic packets among the billion (or so) computers on the Internet. Think of it this way: A domain name is similar to the name of a state or country on the envelope of a piece of regular mail. In fact, some domain names are *exactly* that. Here are just a few of the common domain names you will come across:

- `com`—Commercial businesses
- `net`—Network-related
- `gov`—Government agencies, branches, and departments
- `org`—Organizations, usually non-profit
- `mil`—Military research facilities
- `edu`—Universities and educational institutions
- `jp`—Japan
- `de`—Germany
- `ca`—Canada
- `uk`—United Kingdom
- `au`—Australia

See Figure 1.1 for an illustration of the domain name hierarchy.

When we address an electronic packet of data, perhaps to a location on the other side of the world, the computers on the Internet will take turns passing the message along until it reaches its destination. Actually, not every computer between here and there gets involved—just the gateway computers. A *gateway* (also called a *router*) is a special kind of computer that is given the job of looking at an IP packet and determining whether to keep the packet for a computer on the local network or pass it to the next network in the chain and let it figure it out. Passing it along is called *making a hop*.

What if someone turns off one of the gateways between point A and point B after a message has already begun its journey? What if a voltage spike flips a bit, which causes the address to become corrupted somewhere along the line? Or what if the data is so big that it has to be split up and sent in several partial packets? How will the recipient know when it has all arrived? These are just some of the reasons that TCP is used in conjunction with IP. IP carries the packets, and TCP is the accountant that makes sure they are all delivered. If a packet is lost or corrupted along the way, TCP will see to it that the packet is sent again.

Figure 1.1.
The domain name system.

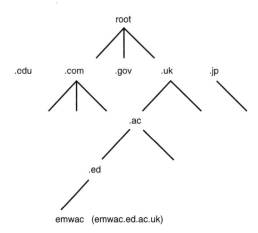

Domain Name System

What is the OSI Networking Model?

TCP/IP delivers packets in a way that fits a standard model of how networks are supposed to work. The ISO (International Standards Organization) put together the OSI (Open Systems Interconnect) reference model so a convention would exist for the interfacing of network products. (Perhaps another reason they wanted to do this was to form an acronym palindrome.)

The model consists of seven layers, but not all of the layers are used in all cases. Nonetheless, as a reference model, it still provides an invaluable theoretical basis for all discussions of networking.

Table 1.1 provides a brief description of each of the seven layers of the OSI model. Note that layer 1 is contained in hardware and layers 2 through 7 are implemented in software. The list seems to be in reverse order. Network engineers generally view the flow of data as originating at the application layer and moving downward through the layers toward the hardware.

Table 1.1. An overview of the seven layers of the OSI model.

Layer	Implemented in	Description
Layer 7	Application	The programs users interact with to initiate network data transfer
Layer 6	Presentation	Encrypts or decrypts data, packs or unpacks data, and converts data between formats
Layer 5	Session	Determines when data transmission will start and stop

Layer	Implemented in	Description
Layer 4	Transport	Concerned with the quality of data on the circuit; includes error-checking protocols
Layer 3	Network	Establishes the network route from the sender to the recipient
Layer 2	Data Link	Provides for the bundling of several bits into a data frame
Layer 1	Physical	Includes the specifications for the electrical signals and the transmission of bits

Fortunately, there is a simple analogy that might help explain all of this. Imagine that you want to send a letter by regular mail, not e-mail. In this case, the piece of paper is the application. The envelope plays the role of layer 6. The mailbox is the session (layer 5), and the postal carrier is the transport (layer 4). The mail bag emulates layer 3, the network. The mail truck is the data link (layer 2), and the road serves as the physical medium (layer 1). Figure 1.2 illustrates this analogy. If these concepts still seem fuzzy, don't worry. It usually takes lots of experience working with different network products before the layer concept becomes clear.

Figure 1.2.
The OSI reference model.

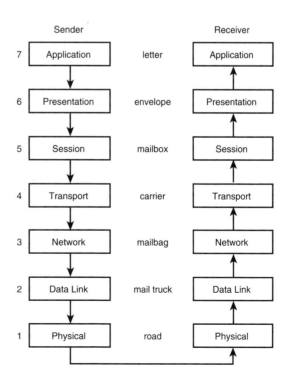

The OSI Model

The work performed by each layer on the sending side is done in reverse by the corresponding layer on the receiving side. For example, if the presentation layer performs encryption on the sending side, the decryption will be done by the presentation layer on the receiving side.

The manner in which these layers are stacked on top of each other is why you often hear TCP/IP software vendors speak of the *protocol stack*. At each level, there are several alternative or complementary protocols from which to choose. In many cases, protocols at one level can interface interchangeably with protocols at the next level.

The seven-layer structure isn't always strictly observed. In fact, TCP/IP is a very prominent example of divergence from the standard. Many experts consider these five layers to more closely reflect how TCP/IP actually works:

Layer 5   The Application layer, same as OSI, (for example, FTP). If encryption or compression is needed, it is done in the application layer, rather than the absent presentation layer.

Layer 4   The Transport layer, TCP builds or reads a packet.

Layer 3   The Internet layer, IP builds or reads a packet.

Layer 2   The Network layer, similar to the OSI model.

Layer 1   The Physical layer, same as OSI.

What is a Listserver?

Listservers (also called *listservs* and *mailing listservers*) support a group of people (called *subscribers*) who like to share e-mail with each other on a given topic. For example, the San Diego Windows NT User's Group runs a listserv that is intended for posting items of interest to NT users. Basically, when you send e-mail to the listserver, it will send it to all the other subscribers of the listserv. See Figure 1.3.

Caution: It is important to understand that a listserv has two e-mail addresses. The first address is used to start or cancel subscriptions. The second address is used for posting messages to all subscribers. Be sure to check on the details of how to subscribe to a listserv before you accidentally send your message to the wrong address. Some useful NT list servers are mentioned in Appendix D.

Figure 1.3.
How a listserver works.

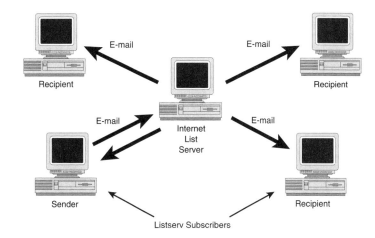

What is a Newsgroup?

Newsgroups are carried by a part of the Internet called Usenet. Like a listserver, each newsgroup is dedicated to a particular subject matter. By last count, there were more than 16,000 newsgroups on the Internet. The topics cover just about everything, ranging from discussions of computers to politics to sports to the very, very strange. Most newsgroups fall under one of the following top-level classifications:

- `alt`—Alternative topics, some of which you might find unbelievable—for example, `alt.1d`, `alt.misanthrophy`, and `alt.geek`.
- `biz`—Aspects of business
- `comp`—Computer technology, software, and protocols
- `misc`—Miscellaneous topics
- `news`—News
- `rec`—Recreation
- `sci`—Science
- `soc`—Society
- `talk`—Other miscellaneous topics, such as `talk.environment`

The classifications tell you a little bit about what kind of newsgroups you might expect to find in a certain area. Newsgroup names are organized in a hierarchy (computer scientists love tree structures) so that the nature of the topics covered gets somewhat clearer as you follow the name from left to right. For example, there are hundreds of `comp` newsgroups that discuss computers.

Underneath comp are several newsgroups that discuss protocols. One of them is called comp.protocol.tcp-ip, which, as you might expect, carries conversations (also called *articles*) about TCP/IP.

What are FTP and Anonymous FTP?

The File Transfer Protocol (FTP) was invented by the UNIX community for the simple purpose of bidirectional file transfers between computers. Like most Internet software, FTP operates in a client/server fashion. Until a couple of years ago, you had to know a little bit about UNIX to run an FTP client program. Today, there are excellent GUI versions—such as the shareware Windows FTP client included with this book—that make it as easy as drag-and-drop. Windows NT also includes a command-line FTP client and, of course, an FTP server.

> **Note:** For security reasons, Windows NT does not install the FTP Server by default. Instead, the system administrator must install it intentionally.

A server that runs FTP will usually designate a user account for each of the people it intends to grant access. Each client is required to enter his or her name and password when logging in to the FTP server. This is to protect the server from having sensitive files taken by unknown users. After you have an account with an FTP server, you can copy files to and from the server whenever you want.

The problem with this is that some sites maintain libraries of public domain software and information. Such sites like to make these files available to anyone who is interested, but they don't know beforehand who their clients will be. And even if they did know, it would be a nightmare to try and maintain such a user database, because some sites are visited by tens of thousands of users.

The answer to this dilemma is *anonymous FTP*. It works just like regular FTP, but with one simple twist. You, the client, sign in with the word anonymous for the FTP user name and, by convention, enter your e-mail address as the FTP password. (This convention was developed to permit FTP servers to track who is visiting a site, but we have never heard of a server that actually did any processing of the e-mail addresses.) After you log in anonymously, you will usually have restricted access to the file system of the server machine. It should, however, permit you to navigate to the directories you need.

FTP file transfers are always initiated by the client and can be executed in ASCII or binary mode. If you know the file you are going to upload (send to the server) or download (copy from the server) is an ASCII text file, you can actually use either method because *all* computer files are binary files—but ASCII transfers will be slightly more efficient for ASCII files. On the other hand, if the file isn't ASCII, you must transfer it using binary mode.

How Can I Find Things on the Internet?

Long before the Web, There was Gopher. Although it is still widely used, many folks consider Gopher to be the aging predecessor of the World Wide Web. Gopher servers provide menus for selecting text documents that are available online.

As with a Web browser, a Gopher client enables you to navigate deeper and deeper into the Internet until you find what you are looking for. Gopher differs from the Web in that you must follow layers of menus until you finally reach a document; whereas with the Web, the documents themselves can provide you with links to other documents.

With all the Web and Gopher servers, the Internet has gotten so enormous that no one can possibly keep track of everything it has to offer. When you want to find some information, any kind of information, it's probably a safe bet to assume that it exists on the Internet, *somewhere*. The problem is finding it. Over the years, the Internet community has developed several solutions to this problem. Each solution is a tool, and it's best to know the right tool for the job. Here are three tools for searching the Internet:

Archie	Archie searches for filenames or directory names at anonymous FTP sites that contain the word you specify. The Windows Archie client program included with this book includes a nice GUI and is preloaded with a list of Archie servers. Archie can also be invoked from a Web browser, a Gopher menu, or even through e-mail if you know the e-mail address of an Archie server.
Veronica	This stands for Very Easy Rodent-Oriented Net-wide Index to Computerized Archives. Whew! Veronica is usually run from a Gopher menu. You give it a word to search for, and it will come back with a list of Gopher menu items that contain that word. You can also search more specifically for directory names or filenames.
WAIS	This name stands for Wide Area Information Server. WAIS clients conduct searches of databases that are indexes of files contained on the server. Webmasters use WAIS to make their Web sites searchable by keyword. We will cover this topic more fully in Chapter 15, "Databases and the Web."

As you are probably aware, the Web is a great way to find things on the Internet. This is becoming even more true as the number of sites using WAIS and the number of dedicated search sites increases. For more information about Web search pages, please see the section later in this chapter titled "How Can I Learn More About the Internet?"

What is the Difference Between SLIP and PPP?

SLIP, which stands for Serial Line Internet Protocol, was invented in the early 1980s to transmit packets over a serial interface, such as a modem. It was designed for simplicity and efficiency. SLIP's lack of error-checking and flow control led to the recent development of PPP, which is a more robust protocol.

PPP stands for Point-to-Point Protocol. Among other things, PPP includes authentication, error-checking, and flow control. These features enable PPP to deliver link-layer functionality similar to that found in an Ethernet LAN. When you have a choice, PPP is the preferred way to go. Windows NT RAS supports both SLIP and PPP.

SLIP and PPP are referred to as *line protocols* because they are concerned with the reliability of the circuit, whereas TCP and IP are referred to as *data protocols* because they are designed for the purpose of application data transfer. The line protocols operate at level 2 in the OSI model, and the data protocols operate at levels 3 and 4.

Which is Right for Me: Switched-56, X.25, Frame Relay, ISDN, T1, T3, or ATM?

Before explaining each of these services separately, we'll start by laying the foundation for all of them. Other than the analog phone lines used by modems and dedicated digital lines, such as T1 (see below), there are three kinds of *switching services* offered by the phone companies for computer networks.

- *Circuit-switched*—Functions as a temporary dedicated connection, as needed.
- *Packet-switched*—Virtual network (called a *cloud*) managed by the phone company permits multiple point-to-point connections in a WAN.
- *Cell-switched*—The newest of the three, offers the greatest potential speed.

The term *switching* means that you don't own or lease a dedicated line, although you do pay for the availability of a certain minimum bandwidth. Switching technology is available thanks to high-speed computers and very sophisticated software developed by the phone companies. Because the bandwidth or resource unit is constantly switched from one customer to another based on demand, the cost to each individual is significantly reduced. Switching is similar to time-sharing.

Remember, all of these technologies transmit digital data directly, without conversion, to analog. Some of them carry voice traffic as well, but that is also digital over fiber-optic media.

Switched-56

Switched-56 is a circuit-switched technology that cannot carry voice. For several years, this has been an intermediate cost and performance point between analog lines and dedicated lines such as T1s. A connection option using this service is offered by many Internet Service Providers (ISPs.)

X.25

X.25 is a set of packet-switching protocols that include extensive error-checking designed for when networks were less reliable than they are today. It is not usually offered by Internet Service Providers. Windows NT RAS supports X.25.

Frame Relay

Frame relay is a fairly new packet-switching technology. It is much more efficient than X.25 because it avoids packet acknowledgment and error-checking, thereby saving the overhead incurred by those features. Frame relay is becoming very popular for WANs in and around a metropolitan area, because it is much less expensive than T1.

ISDN

With a modem and a phone line, you can send computer data to anyone in the world. The purpose of the modem is to convert digital data to analog so it can be carried on a standard phone line before being converted back to digital at the receiving end. If you think that process sounds somewhat convoluted, you're right.

Integrated Services Digital Network (ISDN) promises to change all that for business users and home users alike. ISDN is a set of protocols that enable the phone companies to carry computer data directly in its native digital form without having it converted back and forth between analog. Transmission of digital data provides for better performance and a significantly reduced likelihood of errors. Furthermore, ISDN can carry voice as well as data, and you can even make three calls at once!

When purchasing ISDN, there are two price points: Basic Rate Interface (BRI) and Primary Rate Interface (PRI). BRI consists of two 64-Kbps data channels and a third channel used by the phone company for call management. The two data channels are called B channels, and the call control channel is called a D channel. The D channel rate is 16 Kbps.

PRI consists of 23 B channels and one 64 Kbps D channel.

T1 and T3

These are leased-line services that provide for very high-speed dedicated connections between two points. The Internet backbone relies on T3, which has a throughput rate of 45 Mbps. T1, which runs at a rate of 1.544 Mbps, is used in regional backbones and is also offered by many ISPs for customers with the need—and the money—for a wide bandwidth connection.

ATM

Like Frame Relay and X.25, Asynchronous Transfer Mode (ATM) enables multiple logical connections to be multiplexed over a single physical interface. The information flow on each logical connection is organized into fixed-size packets, called *cells*. As with Frame Relay, there is no link-by-link error control or flow control. ATM takes full advantage of the high data rate of fiber-optics, and it allows for the dynamic selection of data rates. ATM delivers the greatest performance today and has the greatest potential performance, but it is still considered too futuristic by some.

How Fast is the Internet?

This is actually an open-ended question because there are many measures of speed. But as it turns out, there is one answer that is quite fascinating.

A program called *ping* shows that an average Internet packet travels the distance from California to Japan and back in about one second! Knowing this distance is about 6,000 miles, you can say that this happens at roughly the speed of 12,000 miles per second, give or take a smidgen. This speed is slightly slower if the packet must pass through an orbiting satellite.

Even more amazing is the fact that the packet could be picked up by perhaps 20 gateway computers along the way (as reported by the program *tracert*), each one trying to figure out where to send it next. Then another 20 gateways, not necessarily the same as those on the first leg of the journey, go to work sending the packet back to the origin—where your ping program can calculate the round-trip time.

And if that isn't mind-boggling enough, consider that each of those 40 computers had to wait until the network wire was completely clear of all traffic before they could put the packet back on the line and aim it at the next computer! Not only is this stunning speed, but that it works at all is remarkable.

> **Note:** Ping and tracert are mentioned in Chapter 12, "Maintaining and Tracking Your Web Site," and in the Windows NT TCP/IP book published by Microsoft.

To answer the question of Internet speed another way, we have prepared Table 1.2 to show the speeds of many commonly found network technologies.

Table 1.2. Data Transmission Technologies and Rates.

Network Technology	Bandwidth, or connection speed	Time (in seconds) to transfer 30K Web page
V.32 or V.42 modem	14.4 Kbps	17.067
V.34 or V.FC modem	28.8 Kbps	8.533
Switched-56	56 Kbps	4.285
ISDN BRI	56 Kbps–128 Kbps	1.875 to 4.285
Frame Relay	56 Kbps–128 Kbps	1.875 to 4.285

Network Technology	Bandwidth, or connection speed	Time (in seconds) to transfer 30K Web page
ISDN PRI	56 Kbps–1.5 Mbps	0.156 to 4.285
T1	1.544 Mbps	0.152
Ethernet LAN	10 Mbps	0.0234
T3	45 Mbps	0.0052
FDDI	100 Mbps	0.0023
Fast Ethernet	100 Mbps	0.0023
ATM	50 Mbps—622 Mbps	0.0004 to 0.0015

Because a typical Web page might consist of about 8 KB of text and 22 KB of image data, we have chosen a document size of 30 KB to estimate the time it would take to travel from the server to the client. We caution the reader that this is for illustration purposes only! This is *not* a realistic example because there are many other factors that could contribute to the total time to deliver a document on the Internet. In fact, the total time will always be slower than what is shown in the third column of Table 1.2 because other network traffic will prevent a single file transfer from owning the whole bandwidth. Also, it is usually safe to assume that there are several intermediate hosts between the server and the client, and you might not know the link speed in use between each of those hosts.

Does C2 Security Protect Windows NT from Internet Hackers?

Sorry, the short answer is "No."

The Department of Defense defines seven levels of security for computer systems: D1 (least secure) and C1, C2, B1, B2, B3, and A (most secure). DOS and Macintosh System 7.x weigh in at the D1 level. Most UNIX systems are rated C1 (below Windows NT).

The C1 level requires that users must log into the system with protected passwords. Once logged in, users are not given unlimited access to the file system unless the system administrator has chosen to configure their accounts with such a level of permission.

C2 extends the C1 level through auditing. This is an important concept because it permits the system administrator to track key events in the system and analyze them for security holes. Windows NT has excellent auditing capabilities, but this will not protect the Web site from the threats of hackers. See Chapter 16 for a further discussion of security issues.

Not every machine running Windows NT would be automatically classified as meeting the C2 standard. NT is always capable of hosting a C2-certified computer site, but many factors go into the rating—some of which are beyond the realm of the software. For example, a secure server isn't C2 if it is located in a public area.

For a detailed discussion of Internet security, see the excellent reference *Internet Firewalls and Network Security*, published by New Riders.

What Is so "Hyper" About HTML?

HyperText Markup Language (HTML) is a subset of Standard Generalized Markup Language (SGML). HTML embeds codes into a document to highlight its features and structure for subsequent display. HTML was invented in 1990 at CERN, the European Particle Physics Laboratory in Switzerland. The invention of Mosaic, the famous Web browser that runs on several different computer platforms, fueled the growth of the Web because it finally made the Internet seem more graphical than cryptic to the average user.

The purpose behind HTML is to permit documents to contain electronic links to other documents of relevancy. A document can link to another text, image, audio, or video file. HTML might have gotten the *hyper* in its name from the Asteroids video game, popular during the 1980s, which included a hyper-space button for vaulting a player in danger to some random location. It was a fascinating game because the player was never sure there would be any less danger upon his or her arrival at the surprise destination.

An electronic link from one document to another is similar to pressing hyper-space because you can be vaulted away from the file you are currently reading. Of course, you hope that you aren't going to be thrown randomly. Unfortunately, Web browsing might seem random to the newcomer. Some pages on the Web give you little help when you are considering a leap to another document. This is usually only a matter of unorganized Web page design. At its best, the Web can quickly carry you to the exact information you are looking for. The overall difficulty of Web traversal for newcomers will continue to improve as more sites incorporate search tools such as WAIS.

We should mention two other Web browsers: Lynx is a text-only browser for computers that lack graphical displays, and Netscape Navigator is generally considered king of the hill. Netscape followed in the footsteps of Mosaic and blazed new trails, such as incorporation of FTP download, newsreader capabilities, and now Java, just to name a few.

Let's get back to the point of how the Web really works with hypertext documents. The interaction between HTML and HTTP can be explained most easily with an illustration. (See Figure 1.4.)

1. The user enters the URL (Uniform Resource Locator, sort of like a symbolic name for an IP address) of a neat new Web page into their Web browser (client). Or the user clicks an underlined word that serves as a link to another Web page.

2. The request is carried through the Internet to the Web server referenced by the Fully Qualified Domain Name.

3. The HTTP server looks up the requested HTML page using the supplied pathname and sends the file back through the Internet to the client.

4. The client Web browser stores the file on the local machine temporarily, interprets the HTML contents of the file, and displays it on the screen.

Figure 1.4.
How HTML works.

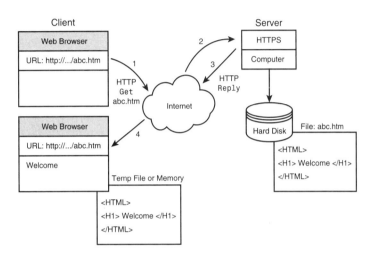

How HTML Works

How Can I Learn More About the Internet?

Actually, the Internet itself is a great way to get more information. Throughout this book we reference the URL of Web pages and FTP sites where additional information and files can be found to assist you in building a Web site.

Note: When entering a URL into your Web browser, remember that some parts of it might be case-sensitive. Also, don't follow a URL with a period. Finally, some URLs require a trailing slash at the end; and even though some don't, it never hurts to add a trailing slash.

For the technical-minded reader, the FQDN portion of a URL is not case-sensitive, but the pathname portion is case-sensitive on UNIX systems. For display purposes, the Windows NT file system (NTFS) retains the original case of directory names and filenames when they are created, but NTFS doesn't require you to use matching case to access those files subsequently. Why try to guess if the Web site you want to visit is running UNIX or NT? If in doubt, enter URLs in the exact format given in this book (without a trailing period).

Sometimes sites will move information during reorganization, and the URL will no longer work. This is often called an *expired link*. We try to list only links that are known to be stable; but if you have trouble with any of the links in this book, try using one of the online search pages to look for alternatives.

Search pages are special Web sites dedicated to helping you find anything that the Web has to offer. Here are a few good search pages:

- Yahoo—This is perhaps the best known Web site. It is so well organized and presented that anyone can use it. Try it, you'll like it.

  `http://www.yahoo.com/`

- WebCrawler—This Web site provides an excellent query program that can search for any topic on the World Wide Web. It is provided by America Online as a service to the Internet community.

  `http://www.webcrawler.com/WebCrawler/WebQuery.html`

- The Lycos Hunting WWW Information—This facility performs its own search of the Web for current information about other sites. It updates its index on a weekly basis. It is highly rated for accuracy.

  `http://lycos.cs.cmu.edu/`

- Commercial Services on the Net—This Web site provides a list of companies that are doing business on the Internet. Find out if you or your competitors are in here yet.

  `http://www.directory.net/`

Chapter 2

Everything You Need

- Web Site Hardware
- All the Server Tools to Build a Great Web Site
- Internet Client Software Recommended by the Authors
- Other Sources for Hot Software

This chapter examines the hardware and software you will need to run a professional Web site. The section on hardware discusses both a basic PC system and an enhanced PC system. We try to give specific advice on hardware when we can, but keep in mind that there are almost as many types of computers as there are computer users.

We approach the topic of software from both the client side and the server side. Although a Web site needs to run server software, any webmaster will tell you that you're also going to need good client tools to help you explore the Web and keep up with the latest developments (almost a full-time job in itself at the rate the Web is changing). The client tools discussed in this chapter (and included on the CD-ROM) will help you take advantage of all the great Internet resources that are listed throughout the book and in Appendix C, "Internet Resources for the NT Webmaster."

Please consult the glossary as necessary when unfamiliar terms are used.

Web Site Hardware

Most PC users who have been around for awhile are familiar with the excitement of having an old slow machine—which was first-class in its younger days—replaced by a new machine, costing roughly the same, offering twice the performance, and doubling the hard disk capacity. The fact is that most programs written for Windows or Windows NT a couple of years ago still run excellently on today's machines and will probably still do so two or more years from now. This level of compatibility means we are free to choose any type of PC configuration that fits our needs and our pocketbooks. We needn't be worried about losing yesterday's investment in software if we want to upgrade the performance of our hardware tomorrow.

> **Caution:** Before buying any hardware to run with Windows NT, it is always a good idea to make sure it is on the Windows NT Hardware Compatibility List. This document is published by Microsoft and can be retrieved from their Web site:
> `http://www.microsoft.com`.

This section outlines two PC configurations at opposite ends of the spectrum in terms of price and performance. At the low end, we start by simply noting that Windows NT can run on just about any kind of i386 PC with a minimum of 16 MB of RAM. Beyond that, the following guidelines will help you match your needs, whether you're buying new hardware or trying to determine whether your current computer has enough muscle to serve as your Web site.

When you shop for a new computer, think of this theory: "Buy until it hurts." In other words, go for all the performance you can get; if you don't think you need it today, you will probably want it tomorrow.

Prices for large IDE drives have dropped wonderfully in the last year or so. (IDE, EIDE, and SCSI are hardware conventions that enable many different drive types to work in many different computer types). Unless your budget is extremely tight, there is no point in buying anything less than a 1 GB (gigabyte) disk drive. Currently, street prices for 1 GB drives are around $200. If you still want to estimate the minimum disk space to run your Web site, however, try going through this list and adding up the numbers.

1. Set aside at least 70 MB for the NT Server operating system, or 50 MB if using NT Workstation. Estimate another 30 MB for pagefile.sys, which is used to swap RAM to disk.

2. Set aside at least 10 MB for the software included with this book.

3. Decide whether you plan to install other software, such as word processors or databases, on the same drive. If so, how big are those programs?

4. Estimate how big your Web pages will be. Are you going to include lots of graphics or large volumes of documentation? For more information on this subject, consult Chapter 6, "Image Mapping and Multimedia."

A Basic Platform

If some of the preceding advice strikes you as vague, you're right: This isn't an exact science. Let's take an entirely different approach. How about a sample advertisement for a very typical PC configuration that will get your Web site online, whether you're a florist or a pet shop owner?

Computer for Sale

486 33 MHz, 16MB RAM, 450MB hard disk, 3.5-inch floppy drive, CD-ROM drive, 15-inch Super VGA monitor, 1MB VLB video RAM, mouse, keyboard, 14.4 Kbps external modem. Price: $1000.

This machine will run NT reasonably well. At the time of this writing, this configuration costs about $1,300 new, $1,000 used. Although it might add a little to the cost, our preference is to get a tower case instead of a desktop case. It is usually much easier to install additional hard disk drives in a tower case.

You should also make sure the computer comes with at least a 250 Watt power supply. Some ads don't mention these items, so you need to ask. Also ask the seller if the CD-ROM is double-speed (2X) or quad-speed (4X). Quad-speed drives are faster, but double-speed is quite sufficient for installing Web site software, unless you are also planning to play multimedia games on the same computer.

With the cost of 28.8 Kbps modems now hitting $150, more and more Web clients are running at that speed. Usually, the client computer is the slowest link in the chain. Although you might be satisfied with a 14.4 Kbps modem, you wouldn't want your clients to consider your server the slowest link. Our advice: Buy at least a RAS-compatible 28.8 Kbps modem for a small Web site, or consider ISDN if you expect more visitors.

What About the Video Card?

Nearly all high-performance video cards developed within the last three years have a direct motherboard connection to the CPU (Central Processing Unit). This is usually achieved through one of two standard technologies: VLB or PCI. These two standards contrast, but also coexist, with ISA, which is the original PC bus design for adding hardware adapter cards.

VLB or VESA-LB (Video Electronics Standards Association Local Bus) was the work of an industry consortium of hardware manufacturers who were concerned about developing a standard way to boost the video display speed on PCs. Their standard was very successful for a few years, but many feel that it is now being superseded by the popularity of PCI motherboards. Intel provided the brains behind PCI (Peripheral Component Interconnect) as a way of enhancing PC performance beyond the future capabilities of VLB.

When you are buying a PC, you need to know what kind of bus design is built into the motherboard so that you will be able to choose the right kind of video card to match. Whether you choose PCI or VLB, you will get better performance. Most PCI and VLB computers have, in addition to four regular ISA slots, two or three local bus slots that let you connect to other crucial peripherals, such as hard-disk controller cards or SCSI adapters. When buying an adapter card, you can decide on a regular ISA, a PCI, or a VLB. ISA cards will work in just about any PC, but what you clearly want to avoid is buying a PCI card for a VLB computer, or vice versa.

The amount of RAM on your video card (also called Video Graphics Array card or Super VGA card) determines the maximum resolution and number of colors that can be displayed on your monitor. Most cards these days come with at least 1 MB, which means they can run 256 colors at a resolution of 1024 pixels on the x axis by 768 pixels on the y axis. As the prices of high-resolution monitors continue to drop, more and more users are buying video cards with 2 MB of RAM. With more video RAM installed, the Windows NT Control Panel offers more choices of resolution/color combinations. Most people prefer a higher resolution so that more data can appear on the screen. However, as the resolution increases, the pixel size decreases and you will need a larger monitor to avoid having to squint as you read. This author considers a 15-inch monitor suitable for 800×600 resolution and a 17-inch monitor as the minimum needed to provide nice viewing at a resolution of 1024×768. Your mileage might vary.

Tip: When choosing your display configuration in the Control Panel, don't be lured into picking a higher number of colors than you really need. Depending on the speed of your video card and its driver software, increasing the number of colors can sometimes result in a noticeable decline in screen painting performance. Unless you work with image editing software, you might need only 256 colors; that is all that NT and most programs currently use. On the other hand, if you do work with images from scanners or photo programs or from the Internet, you might want to buy a video card with more than 2 MB so you can be sure to get the highest resolution and the best color match.

A Faster Platform

If you've been around computers for awhile, you probably know that the 33 MHz computer isn't going to be a killer NT platform. Sure, it will get the job done, but the question is, "When?" If you like to have your machine ready when you are or you expect to have many Web browsers visiting your server, you are going to want a faster and more capable machine.

Listed here is a hardware configuration that is very similar to this author's typical size Web site, www.fbsolutions.com.

- Pentium 90 MHz computer in a full tower case with mouse and keyboard. Be sure it also includes a 16550 UART on the serial port for use by external modems. You probably won't need a super high-speed video card on a Web server, but you'll still want to know whether the computer supports PCI or VLB as you consider your purchase of adapter cards.

■ 250-watt power supply. This should give you enough coverage for the power draw from four disk drives, one CD-ROM drive, one tape backup, one floppy drive, VGA card, and the disk drive adapter card.

■ 32MB RAM. Windows NT runs more efficiently with 32 MB than it does with 16 MB because there is less need to temporarily store extra memory in pagefile.sys on the hard disk. Also RAM access time is much faster than hard-disk access time.

■ 15-inch or 17-inch SVGA monitor. A Web site needs to stay on all the time. If you aren't going to work at the computer all the time, you might want to turn the monitor off or get one of the new energy-saving monitors, which can reduce power usage by 90 percent.

■ Internal SCSI CD-ROM drive and SCSI adapter card. NT includes terrific support for nearly all SCSI CD-ROM drives and a handful of non-SCSI CD-ROM drives. In certain cases, it installs more easily from SCSI CD-ROM drives.

■ 512MB hard disk drive. This is the C: drive, or the *boot* drive. You can install the operating system and all utility programs on this drive. It can be either SCSI or IDE, but once you've made an investment in a SCSI adapter card for a CD-ROM drive, you won't want to buy a separate controller card for IDE drives. Find out how many internal devices your controller card can handle. You might anticipate the future need of at least four.

■ 1.2GB hard disk drive. This is the D: drive and will hold all the Web site files and FTP files. This can also be SCSI or IDE. The reasons we suggest having two physical drives are as follows: Better performance is obtained from having two platters spinning when multiple files are being loaded, and there is a gain in reliability if each drive is used less often.

■ 3.5-inch floppy drive. Hardly any currently selling systems still use the 1.2MB format of 5-1/4-inch floppy disks, so you can probably get by with just the 3.5-inch format.

■ V.34 modem or ISDN interface. You can go internal or external with these devices. External modems provide status lights and save an expansion slot inside the computer for future use. V.34 is a recent modem standard ratified by the CCITT to cover data transmission speeds up to 28.8 Kilobits per second, or Kbps. See Chapter 3 for a discussion of the monthly costs for modem and ISDN connections. Again, if your computer has a 16550 UART, you'll get the best performance out of a V.34 modem.

■ 2GB DAT backup device. Automated file backups are highly recommended.

■ Uninterruptable Power Supply, or UPS. Although optional, this is recommended for commercial Web sites so an orderly shutdown can be conducted if power is lost. See Chapter 12, "Maintaining and Tracking Your Web Site" for information about how to force NT and the Web server to completely restart when power is restored.

> **Tip:** If you're thinking that a tape backup is a luxury, we should point out that you are probably going to download a lot of software from the Internet. It is true that you can always restore shrink-wrap software products from the original media, but when you consider the amount of download time that it would take to recover all of your zipped files if they were ever lost, we think you'll agree that a backup device becomes an essential component. There are several exciting alternatives to tape backup: 100 MB zip drives from Iomega and 4.6 GB optical drives from Pinnacle. These drives function at the speed of hard drives and include replaceable media in the fashion of a huge floppy drive. The zip drives go for around $200, and three 100MB disks run about $50. The Pinnacle drive costs about $1,700 and the optical disks are about $200. This does add a lot to the cost, but there is no cheaper way to add 4.6 GB drives to your system. Also consider similar products from Bernoulli and Syquest.

All the Server Tools to Build a Great Web Site

This section provides you with a complete list of all the software you need to build a powerful and reliable Web site at the lowest possible price. All of the software mentioned here—with the exception of the Windows NT operating system—is included on the CD.

Our top concerns in selecting the software for this book were that each package had to work reliably and be economical. We chose these particular products because we know from personal experience that they do the job well. We ended up with a mixed bag of commercial, shareware, and freeware products. The Internet is loaded with other software that will assist you in setting up and running your Web site. In some cases, you can probably find a freeware product that will do the same job as one of the commercial or shareware products we selected for this book.

Please do not expect all the programs to be bug-free. Though we have been happy with their performance, they are all relatively new and have not been tested over time. Please respect the various usage and redistribution restrictions placed on each package by its authors.

We now present a brief description of each package. Further information about installing and running these programs is covered throughout the book. You will also find other useful documentation in the readme files accompanying each package. For a complete list of all the software included on the CD, see Appendix H.

Microsoft Windows NT Version 3.50 or 3.51

This is a commercial product. As of this writing (Fall 1995), version 3.51 is current. All of the software in this book will work with version 3.50 or 3.51, and almost certainly with future versions as well.

When buying Windows NT, you have a choice between the Server version and the Workstation version. Both are very capable and include FTP server software. NT Workstation is more afford-able than NT Server (street prices around $260 versus $675, respectively). Server does have sev-eral features that Workstation lacks, but most are not critical to building a Web site. Here are two key differences:

- NT Server can support 100 simultaneous LAN users, whereas NT Workstation can support up to 10 but is primarily intended for a single user.
- The microkernel in NT Server is tweaked for faster file server performance than NT Workstation.

The number of Web clients that can simultaneously connect to your server is *not* the same as the number of LAN users. With either version of NT, the number of Web client connections will be limited by the performance of the modem, the hard disk, and other factors. So the first difference listed above is not a problem. Modem speed will also be more of a bottleneck than the perfor-mance of the kernel system software, so the second difference isn't really a problem either. Therefore, we recommend NT Workstation for those who like to save a few hundred dollars.

EMWAC HTTPS Version 0.99

This is a very well-known freeware webserver from The European Microsoft Windows NT Aca-demic Center for Computing Services (EMWAC). The webserver is the main program on which a Web site is based. Chapter 4, "Up and Running Fast," discusses installing and discussing this program. For a summary of other webservers for Windows NT, including the commercial ver-sion of this program, see Appendix B. If you would like more information about EMWAC, the e-mail address is `emwac-ftp@ed.ac.uk`.

CGIKIT Version 1.2

This is a freeware C language program (and documentation) that does Web form processing in a manner compatible with the CGI specification. The original source code comes with the EMWAC HTTPS, but we have enhanced the version included with this book to do improved string pars-ing. We have also compiled it into savedata.exe, in case you don't have a C compiler. Chapter 7, "Introduction to Web Forms and CGI Scripts," covers this program extensively. Contact Chris-topher L. T. Brown, `clbrown@netcom.com`.

CGI PerForm Version 1.0

This is a shareware CGI application that will process the contents of HTML forms in many ways and includes the capability to send e-mail based on the form data. It is developed by Real Time Internet Services. Contact `webinfo@rtis.com` or `http://www.rtis.com/nat/software/`.

Blat Version 1.2

This is a public domain Windows NT console utility that e-mails a file to a user via SMTP. Blat is required by CGI PerForm for sendmail functionality. Contact: Mark Neal, `mjn@aber.ac.uk` or Pedro Mendes, `prm@aber.ac.uk`.

post.office Version 1.0

This is a demo copy of commercial SMTP and POP servers that operate together as a 32-bit NT service. These servers are configured via your Web browser. This is an interesting technique that enables you to configure and administer your mail server remotely. Contact `Software.com`, phone 805-882-2470, e-mail `sales@software.com`, or visit their Web page at `http://software.com`.

Somar ReDial Version 1.2

A shareware NT service that maintains a full-time, dial-up connection to the Internet using PPP or other RAS link. Contact `framos@somar.com`.

WebEdit Version 1.1c

This is an excellent shareware HTML editor for Windows. We will first install it in Chapter 4, "Up and Running Fast." It will be an invaluable assistant throughout Part II of the book as we write HTML code. Contact Kenn Nesbitt, `webedit@thegroup.net` or `http://wwwnt.thegroup.net/webedit/webedit.htm`.

PERL for Windows NT, Based on UNIX PERL Version 4.036.

PERL (Practical Extraction and Report Language) is an interpreted language designed for scanning arbitrary text files, extracting information, and printing reports. It's also a good language for many system management tasks. PERL for NT is distributed under the GNU General Public License, which basically means that it is freeware. Contact Intergraph Corporation.

MUSAGE Version 1.4

This is a freeware PERL script that will analyze the log files from various World Wide Web servers and produce useful summaries, including lists of the most used documents and the most active users and sites. Chapter 12, "Maintaining and Tracking Your Web Site," shows you how to use this program to track Web site statistics. For further information, contact `http://www.blpes.lse.ac.uk/misc/musage.htm`.

Map This! Version 1.0

This is a 32-bit Windows GUI program, written by Todd Wilson, to automate the creation of Imagemap *.map files. After you see this program in Chapter 6, you won't believe it's free. Contact Todd Wilson via e-mail at `tc@galadriel.ecaetc.ohio-state.edu` or via the Web, `http://galadriel.ecaetc.ohio-state.edu/tc/mt`.

SLNet Version 1.1

This is a demo of a commercial Telnet program from Seattle Lab's Telnet Service. SLNet enables up to 256 users to log into a single NT Telnet server simultaneously. These users can run any Win32, OS/2, or DOS character application or use NT's command shell. This program is optional unless you plan to administer your Web site remotely. For more information, contact `info@seattlelab.com`.

Internet Client Software Recommended by the Authors

This section covers the highlights of some major client programs found on the CD-ROM that accompanies this book. Please consult Appendix H for the CD-ROM directory structure and a brief description of all the software (some of which is described in this section). Or better yet, pop in the CD and give it a spin!

Eudora is the most popular Windows e-mail client on the Internet today. Its popularity comes from its ease of use and its price. Although Eudora is not freeware, it costs only a stamp and postcard. The author of this program states:

> If you try out Eudora and decide that you'd like to use it on a regular basis, then just send a postcard to the following address:

Jeff Beckley
QUALCOMM Incorporated
6455 Lusk Blvd.
San Diego, CA 92121-2779
USA

Eudora Light Version 1.5.2

Eudora Light lacks a few of the advanced features found in the commercial version, such as automatic uuencoding of attachments and spell checking. For more information on the commercial version, see `http://www.qualcomm.com/quest/QuestMain.html`.

WinWhois for Winsock Applications, Beta Version 1.0

This GUI utility connects to a Whois server. WinWhois enables you to gain valuable information about Internet domains from the InterNIC DNS database. For example, you could look up the point of contact at any registered Internet domain. Contact Koichi Nishitani, `njknish@mit.edu`. Also contact Larry Kahn or `71434,600`, `kahn@drcoffsite.com`.

Archie

Archie is a 16-bit GUI Archie client that enables you to search Archie servers to find the contents of published FTP directories throughout the Internet. It was written by Clifford Neuman with changes by Brendan Kehoe and George Ferguson. Contact David Woakes, `david.woakes@dial.pipex.com`.

Other Client Software Recommended by the Authors

Netscape Navigator Version 1.2

Netscape is by far the most popular Web browser. This popularity comes from the fact that Netscape has frequently updated its software and helped define the leading edge of HTML. Netscape's Web browser has always handled the HTML extensions very well, and its popularity has encouraged an increasing number of webmasters to incorporate the Netscape extensions into the design of their Web pages. HTML 3.0 is largely defined by Netscape extensions. Contact `http://www.netscape.com/`.

WS_FTP32 Version 95.08.26

While managing your Web site, you will frequently need to perform file transfers on the Internet. The FTP client is essential for uploading files; although Web browsers can also download files, many people prefer FTP for all their file transfer needs. Contact John A Junod, `junodj@css583.gordon.army.mil` or `72321.366@compuserve.com`.

WS_Ping32 Version 95.02.23

Ping is a system administrator's tool for troubleshooting network connections. WS_Ping32 is a Winsock-compliant, 32-bit GUI that also includes trace route and nslookup functions. Contact John A Junod, `junodj@css583.gordon.army.mil` or `72321.366@compuserve.com`.

Utility Programs

Paint Shop Pro Version

Paint Shop Pro is an excellent shareware image file editor for Microsoft Windows 95 and Windows NT 3.51 with NewShell. It loads and saves image files in several industry standard formats. Contact Leonardo Haddad Loureiro at `mmedia@world.std.com`. (Please mention LView in the subject of the message.)

WinZip Version 5.5a

Compressed files are often half their normal size, and therefore travel through the Internet twice as fast. It usually takes a lot less time to compress and decompress files than it does to transmit them. WinZip provides a nice drag-and-drop graphical interface on top of the ever popular PKZIP compression technology. Some of the software included on the CD-ROM is in .zip format, and WinZip will decompress those files during installation to your hard disk. It is also very handy to keep around for all of your Internet file acquisitions. Contact Nico Mak Computing, Inc., P.O. Box 919, Bristol, CT 06011 or send e-mail to `70056.241@compuserve.com`.

Other Sources for Hot Software

If you are not happy with any of the software mentioned here, there is a wide variety of other products available on the Internet. In some cases, you can download immediately with your Web browser or FTP client.

Here are a few Web pages with good information to get you started searching for Internet software available online:

- The Windows NT Resource Center

  `http://www.bhs.com/winnt/`
- Interior Alaska Windows NT Users Group

  `http://www.rmm.com/nt/`
- Rocky Mountain Windows NT Users Group

  `http://budman.cmdl.noaa.gov/RMWNTUG/RMWNTUG.HTM`
- Rick's Windows NT Info Center

  `http://137.226.92.4/rick/`

Chapter 3

Getting Connected to the Internet

This chapter attempts to cut through all the confusion about the different methods of getting on the Internet. There are so many types of Internet connections that it is impossible to say one is better than another. This chapter discusses the pros and cons of all the different options (at least all the ones we can think of). The aim is to give you enough information so that you can knowledgeably make your own determination of which plan is best for your Web site. This chapter focuses on modem and ISDN connections but also looks at LANs and leased lines.

We also discuss opening an Internet account with a service provider and registering a domain name with the InterNIC.

Types of Internet Access

If you want to establish an Internet connection for the first time, you have probably noticed a dizzying array of choices (and associated buzzwords). We hope you haven't already thrown up your hands in frustration, because now you've come to the right place.

In order to get around the big problem of how to connect to the Internet, this chapter takes the divide-and-conquer approach. Let's start by considering the many ways which Internet access can be categorized. We are going to concentrate on only the following criteria, although we recognize that there are probably other criteria that could be considered:

- Online Information Service or an Internet Service Provider (ISP)
- Dial-up connection or dedicated line
- Connection speed and hardware options
- Single computer or Local Area Network (LAN)

If some of this terminology seems strange, don't worry. We discuss all of these options shortly. The point is that you are going to see a great deal of overlap between the different ways of classifying Internet access. For example, whether you choose a dial-up connection or a dedicated line will also depend on (or you could say dictate) your choice of hardware. Okay, enough of the overview, now let's consider each category one by one.

Online Information Service Versus an Internet Service Provider

We use the phrase *online information service* to mean America Online, CompuServe, Genie, Microsoft Network, or Prodigy. Each of these services charge you a monthly subscription fee for a dial-up modem connection (which is an example of the category overlap mentioned previously). These services organize or add information content beyond what you will find on the *raw* Internet.

By contrast, ISPs usually don't add anything to your Internet access; they just give it to you straight and assume you know how to handle it. Some let you download a package of shareware Internet client programs, but then you're on your own.

The similarity between ISPs and online services is that both charge you a flat monthly rate, which gives you a certain number of "free" hours of connect time. If you go beyond your time limit, you are billed a separate rate per hour. You will always get more free hours and a lower hourly rate with ISPs than you will with the online services.

Until very recently, you could not get decent access to the Internet on most of the information services. Today, you can browse the Web or the newsgroups from all of these services. Some will even let you pay to put your own home page on their Web server. Similarly, some ISPs will also lease you disk space on their server if you want them to publish your Web pages. This is also referred to as *Web hosting*.

Leasing Web Space

Let's digress for a moment to discuss this topic. The question is bound to come up, "Why do I need my own Web site if I can pay to have it done for me?" Hiring someone with a Web server to publish your content might be the way to go if you see yourself meeting *all* of these criteria:

- You just want to test the waters on a very low budget. One word of caution if you think this sounds reasonable: If your needs expand to wanting your own server, you will have to move your home page and publish your changed URL to everyone on the Web! This could upset your business patterns while people learn your new location.

- You don't have a large amount of data to publish. You pay for your home page by the megabyte. If you need to serve large graphics or large documents, it could end up costing you more in the long run than running your own server.

- You don't plan to have any substantial database or e-mail interactions with the clients who visit your home page. In other words, you won't be doing any CGI programming to create cool customer survey forms. (Part II covers this topic in detail.) Without a direct connection to the server, your opportunities to do database queries and statistics of the server will be limited.

- You don't care if your customers have limited or slow access to the site. Keep in mind that the service providers make no guarantee of how many other home pages will be on the same server as yours. Some of their other customer sites could turn out to be very popular and bring the server to a crawl.

- You don't plan to change your content very often. It is possible to change your pages on the server remotely from your own PC using FTP, but it is less convenient.

> **Caution:** Some service providers say that they are giving you Web space and that your URL will be something like `ftp://serviceprovider.com/pub/YourUserId/file.html`. Don't fall for this one! What they are giving you is just an FTP directory to hold your HTML files. Yes, people with a Web browser could access and display your HTML files, but they would be accessing them through the FTP protocol, which requires that the client browser log on as an anonymous user. This process takes time and is the wrong way to serve an HTML document.

The point of this list is not to help you choose between ISPs and online services. It is to show you that you probably don't want to let either of them publish your home page on your behalf. We presume that you are reading this book because you want to learn how to administer your Web pages more dynamically.

If you made it through that list alive and are still thinking about leasing Web space (perhaps temporarily), you still have a lot to gain from this book. At the very least, you will be well prepared for the day you decide to take full control of your Web site.

Before you get the impression that we are down on ISPs, let us return from our digression to the question at hand: Should you open an account with an ISP or with an online service?

Remember that an ISP offers total Internet access 24 hours a day, every day of the month. You would have to stack your money pretty high to get a similar deal from an online service. Even though we have just determined that we don't want the ISP to publish our Web page for us, we still need their service to connect our Web server to the Internet.

Now that you have the basic information, we think you will see that this question is an easy issue to settle. The sample Web site that we are going to build in this book will be running 24 hours a day on our own Windows NT server, and we are going to develop our own client/interaction software. So at this point, we make the decision to go with an ISP. Appendix A should be of some help in choosing an ISP inside or outside the U.S. Please be aware that as fast as ISPs are popping up, there is no way this is a comprehensive list, but it is a good place to start.

Dial-up Connection or Dedicated Line?

We have established that we want to open an ISP account. One of the first things the ISP is going to ask us is, do we want a dial-up (also called *on-demand*) connection or a dedicated line (also called *exclusive*)?

As far as hardware options go, a dial-up account can be offered over either modem or ISDN. A dedicated line can be offered over modem, ISDN, Switched-56, Frame Relay, Fractional T1, or T1.

Fortunately, we don't need to get into all of that just yet. Deciding between a dial-up or dedicated line is not a matter of judging the anticipated performance demands on our site. Rather, it is simply a matter of cost and convenience. Recall that the Web site must run 24 hours a day. As it turns out, you can accomplish this with either a dial-up account or a dedicated line account.

We realize this terminology might sound a bit confusing. Further explanation is in order; but to keep this as simple as possible, let's agree for a moment that we are only talking about modem connections. The difference between a dial-up line and a dedicated line is that a dial-up line connects to a modem *pool* at the ISP office, whereas a dedicated line gives a private phone number to the ISP. The advantage of the dedicated line is that we don't have to worry about getting a busy signal. If the dedicated connection is lost, we can redial the ISP on our private number, without the risk of being unable to get back online immediately.

Given the higher costs of the more sophisticated connections, let's assume we decide to get a dedicated line via modem. Chapter 12, "Maintaining and Tracking Your Web Site," shows you how to keep the connection from "timing out" and how to set it up for automatic redial to recover from a disconnect.

Connection Speed and Hardware Options

This is where it gets high-tech. Just saying that we want a dedicated line didn't really narrow the field among the various types of hardware connections. Depending on your ISP, you will have a choice of connecting by modem, ISDN, Switched-56, Frame Relay, or T1. At this point, you might want to refer back to Table 1.1, which showed the relative performance of these and other transmission technologies.

This issue is mostly a matter of cost versus performance. If you are on a low budget, a modem connection is probably your best bet. And the performance is quite reasonable for most small-business needs.

When choosing a modem, make sure that it supports V.34—the preferred standard for 28.8 Kbps *data transmission* over phone lines. If your modem also supports V.42bis, which is a *data compression* standard, your throughput could run up to four times the transmission rate of the modem. We are careful to say *up to* because there are other factors that will usually prevent you from obtaining nirvana at the rate of 115 Kbps.

The first factor is line noise. The phone lines are probably over-used, and there is nothing most of us can do about this. Line noise causes errors in the packets being transmitted. TCP/IP and PPP will detect this and force those packets to be retransmitted, effectively lowering throughput. The good news is that we don't need to be concerned about this at the application layer because it is handled transparently by the lower-level protocols. Of course, we will notice it in the application layer, such as when the FTP client status bar reports that the 28.8 Kbps download is only running in the teens.

The second factor is the DTE (Data Terminal Equipment) to DCE (Data Communications Equipment) rate between your computer and your modem. (This is often called *DTE rate.*) Even if your phone line and your modem are able to scream at 115 Kbps, you have to make sure your computer will be able to process the data at that speed. This is why it is essential to have a 16550 UART. The UART is either built onto an internal modem or it is between the motherboard and the serial port connection you make to an external modem. The 16550 is able to buffer more data than its predecessors, the 8250 and the 16450. Additionally, the operating system and your application—the Web server in this case—must be running fast enough to handle the interrupts that are generated when new data arrives on the COM port. It helps if you avoid running serious number-crunching programs in the background or get a Pentium (at least). Fortunately, Windows NT is well-tuned and has a low interrupt latency within the operating system.

> **Caution:** Here's a brief word of advice about your choice of screen-savers. A Web site machine is usually not in use by its owner as often as it is by the clients who visit with their Web browsers. If this is true in your case, it means that your screen saver is going to get a lot of exercise. This is fine for avoiding damage to your monitor, but keep in mind that some screen savers (especially some of the most graphically realistic ones) use many more CPU cycles than others. If you want your server to deliver the best performance under heavy user loads, you should stay away from the Open-GL screen savers, such as 3D-Pipes, 3D-Flying Objects, and 3D-Text. These screen savers run complex algorithms, which will reduce the overall performance of your server.

Other Connection Options

If you expect your Web site to need increased bandwidth beyond 28.8 Kbps, you should consider ISDN. This book doesn't cover the other connection options such as Frame Relay or T1. These are subjects on which entire books have been written.

ISDN

In addition to standard modem connections, Windows NT Remote Access Service (RAS) supports ISDN. Integrated Services Digital Network is a set of digital transmission protocols defined by CCITT. The protocols are accepted as world-wide standards.

There are two price points with ISDN: the Basic Rate Interface (BRI) and the Primary Rate Interface (PRI). Both consist of some number of 64 Kbps B channels and a shared D channel. BRI contains two B channels, and PRI contains 23. The B channels, or bearer channels, are used for both voice and data transmission. The D channel, or data channel (referring to the data of the phone company), is used for setting up the calls and monitoring the status of all the B channels.

You are billed for your usage time of each B channel. One of the neat things about ISDN is that you can piggy-back two B channels together to increase your throughput when you need to transfer a large file.

Note: For an online primer to ISDN, see

`http://www.pacbell.com/`

`http://www.alumni.caltech.edu/~dank/isdn/`

To use ISDN, you will need a special router or adapter card. There are a growing number of ISDN hardware products available. Here is a helpful list of companies that currently make ISDN devices for personal computers and networks:

Ascend Communications, Inc., 800-621-9578
AT&T Distributor: Volt, 800-566-8658
Connective Strategies, Inc., 703-802-0023
CoSystems, Inc., 408-748-2190
DGM&S, Inc., 609-866-1212
Digiboard, 800-344-4273
Eicon Technology Corp., 514-631-2592
EuRoNis, +33-142334098, Paris
Extension Technology Corp., 415-390-8130, 508-872-7748
Fujitsu ISDN Division, 800-228-ISDN (x4736)
Hayes Microcomputer Products, Inc., 415-974-5544, 404-441-1617
Hewlett-Packard, 800-637-7740
International Business Machines Corp., 800-IBM-CALL, 919-254-0434, 507-253-7294
ISCOM, Inc., 301-779-1368
ISDN Systems Corp., 703-883-0933
Link Technology, Inc., 215-357-3354
Mitel Corp., 613-592-2122
Motorola UDS, 510-734-8820, 714-285-0824, 205-430-8902
MPR Teltech Ltd., 604-293-6047
NCR Network Products Division 612-638-7685, 612-638-7828
OST, Inc., 403-817-0400
Silicon Graphics, 415-390-2522
Sun Microsystems Computer Corp., 415-336-4433
Xyplex, 800-338-5316

Tip: Always check the Windows NT hardware compatibility list prior to purchasing any hardware to use with your Windows NT machine.

A question closely tied to your choice of connection speed and hardware options is whether you plan to run on a stand-alone PC or from a PC on a Local Area Network.

Single Computer Versus a LAN

If your company already runs an Internet server, you might be able to connect to the Internet by going through your LAN to that server. The cost and performance of this option should be favorable. The only bad news is that there are security implications. You will want to plan this carefully with a skilled network administrator or a Microsoft Certified Engineer. Here are a couple of things to consider:

- Use a firewall for increased security, in case your Web site is part of a LAN that shouldn't be exposed to the Internet.
- Consider TCP/IP addressing, in case your Web site is part of a LAN that has previously been running some other protocol. If your Windows NT LAN was running DHCP (Dynamic Host Control Protocol), you will have to arrange with your system administrator for the machine that you intend to be your Web server to have a static IP address instead of a dynamic one. This is referred to as a *reserved client,* and its configuration is beyond the scope of this book. For further information, consult the *Windows NT Resource Kit,* Volume 2; it's listed in the Bibliography.

The rest of this section briefly discusses four alternative types of Internet connections, in increasing order of expense. The first two are based on a stand-alone PC and therefore require the use of RAS; the last two are based on a LAN environment.

Type 1: NT + RAS + 28 Kbps Modem + Standard Phone Line

This connection is the simplest and least expensive. You need an NT computer for RAS and your Web server, a modem (internal or external), and a standard phone line to dial your ISP. See Figure 3.1.

Figure 3.1.
28.8 Kbps dial-up connection.

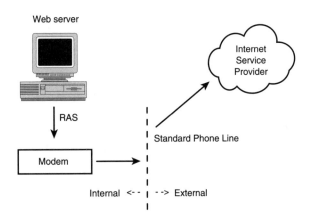

Web server

RAS

Modem

Standard Phone Line

Internal <-- | --> External

Internet Service Provider

Type 2: NT + RAS + ISDN Adapter + ISDN Line

This arrangement is one step up in cost and performance from the modem configuration shown previously. We replace the modem with an ISDN adapter card. The ISDN line installed by the phone company is plugged directly into the back of the ISDN adapter in the PC. See Figure 3.2.

Figure 3.2.
RAS ISDN connection.

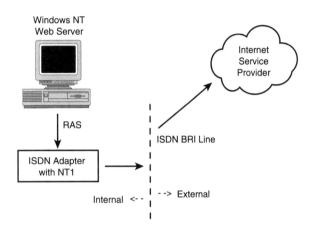

Type 3: NT + Ethernet card + ISDN Router + CSU/DSU + ISDN Line

With the addition of the Ethernet card to run on a LAN, this configuration costs more than the stand-alone diagrams shown previously. See Figure 3.3. However, this setup will give Internet access to all of your LAN users, in addition to providing you with a high-performance Web site for your clients.

A CSU/DSU is a Channel Service Unit/Data Service Unit. In this case, a CSU/DSU is to a digital line what a modem is to an analog line. Some ISDN routers, such as the Ascend Pipeline 50 HX, include the CSU/DSU.

The key advantages of this option are

- You don't have to run Somar Redial (discussed in Chapter 12) to maintain the connection.
- If there are several Internet users on the LAN, you can utilize your bandwidth more fully, as opposed to paying for bandwidth, which is often idle.
- The ISDN router can compress your data stream to the ISP up to four times.
- Finally, you gain security by using the router to do packet filtering. You can eliminate incoming traffic from certain IP addresses after using a network monitoring program to reveal a suspected hacker.

Figure 3.3.
Network ISDN connection.

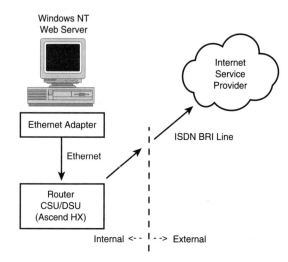

Type 4: NT + Ethernet card + Router + CSU/DSU + 56 Kbps Leased Line

This is essentially the same as the previously discussed configuration except for the change in the type of router. Your decision to go with this option depends on the leased-line pricing from the phone company and the availability of this connection to your ISP. See Figure 3.4.

Figure 3.4.
Network leased-line connection.

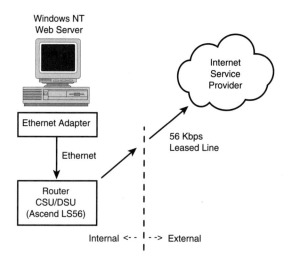

Opening Your Internet Account

Internet Services Providers (ISPs) are popping up almost everywhere. If you're like most people, you will need an ISP to serve as your intermediary to the Internet—that is, unless you are fortunate enough to have your own T-3 connection to the Internet backbone.

Most Internet providers have one or several T-1 lines, and their connectivity with the backbone is largely through T-3 lines. Internet Service Providers almost always offer standard dial-up connections via modem (14.4 Kbps–28.8 Kbps). Most also offer Frame Relay (56 Kbps–1.544 Mbps), and/or ISDN BRI (56 Kbps–128Kbps). Large, well-established ISPs even offer T-1 connections. Several major Internet Service Providers are listed in Appendix A.

There are some important things to consider when choosing an ISP. First, choose an ISP with a good reputation for customer service. After you have found a service provider in your area, call the provider and see if they are able to provide the services that you want, and at a suitable price.

Second, consider what caliber of hardware the provider is running. For example, do they have a fault-tolerant system? How many servers do they have? For that matter, how many customers and phone lines/modems do they have? This is important if you want to avoid getting a busy signal. Hopefully, their performance matches their customer needs. Most importantly, how often does their system go down (also called Mean-Time Between Failure)?

Finally, each ISP has a different list of setup and monthly costs. You might want to do some price checking with the ISPs you are considering. See the following list for a description of what you will need to ask.

This book assumes you are using a dial-up or dedicated 28.8 Kbps connection, but you will want to ensure that the ISP has the capability to provide you with higher bandwidth connections for growth—perhaps up to T1.

What You Need the ISP to Provide

Here are the services required for the sample Web site you will build in this book.

1. A dial-up 28.8 Kbps PPP (Point to Point Protocol) Internet account for business. SLIP will also work, but PPP is better.

2. A dedicated modem line and port on the service provider's machine.

3. A static IP address. Some ISPs use a dynamic IP address to conserve their own IP address pool. A dynamic IP address changes each time you log into your service provider and will not work for our purposes. You must insist on this one.

4. A DNS (Domain Naming Service) entry for your site—for example, yourco.com.

5. CNAME entries for www.yourco.com and ftp.yourco.com (if you want to provide FTP services). These CNAMEs, or canonical names, are aliases for the domain of yourco.com. This lets people use the URL http://www.yourco.com/ in their Web browsers for your Web site and the URL ftp://ftp.yourco.com for your FTP site, even though both are on the same machine.

6. Let the ISP know what protocol servers you intend to run and make sure they can support them. We will be running the following protocol servers on our sample Web site:

- SMTP—Simple Mail Transfer Protocol
- FTP—File Transfer Protocol
- HTTP—HyperText Transfer Protocol

Tip: You will also want to make sure that the ISP has a network news feed for your favorite newsgroups. This is optional, but is strongly recommended for business Web sites. You will be amazed at what you can find if you monitor key newsgroups relevant to your business. We definitely don't recommend that you run NNTP (Network News Transfer Protocol). Rather, all you need to do is subscribe to selected newsgroups. If you arrange to download only the article headers, you might be able to avoid impacting your Web site too heavily.

If you do want to run NNTP, you will need at least 9 GB of disk space, a high-speed connection, and a separate server. With 16,000 newsgroups, NNTP is resource-hungry, and you don't want to bog down the performance of your Web site.

Registering Your Domain Name

Because every interface on the Internet must have a unique IP address, there must be a central authority for allocating these addresses. That authority is the Internet Network Information Center (InterNIC). The ISP will send you a form that you fill out and e-mail to hostmaster@internic.net to register your domain. You do have the option of running your own DNS server, but that would complicate matters.

This sample form (also on the CD-ROM) is being used by InterNIC at the time of this writing. To obtain the most up-to-date form, use your Web browser and go to InterNIC Registration Services at http://rs.internic.net/rs-internic.html. There you will find all the current forms used by InterNIC.

After sending the form to InterNIC, you will get an automated reply telling you that InterNIC has received your request and how long it will take until your domain name is available for use. The last domain name this author requested took eight days to process (because of a backlog at InterNIC of 4,000 domain name requests).

What's Next?

Now that you have opened an account and applied for a domain name, you are ready to move on. Hey, you didn't think we were going to sit around for eight days just to have an official domain name, did you? That should be just enough time for you to get your server installed and all of your HTML code written. You can finish reading Chapter 4 and all of Part II before you need your domain name.

Chapter 4

Up and Running Fast

You will have a presence on the World Wide Web by the end of this chapter. There is a lot of material to cover about Windows NT, RAS, the Web server, and the Web editor. You'll also install a very handy file compression/decompression program called WinZip, which will help you install the Web server and the Web editor.

The topics are presented in order in a hands-on fashion. With so much to discuss, we try to delve into only the essential details. We want to stick to our promise of getting you up and running as quickly as possible.

Preparing Windows NT

First, you need to decide what the disk drive and directory structure will be. For the sample site you will be building in this book, the C: drive (540 MB) will be the system drive on which you install Windows NT, utilities, and other programs (Internet client applications). Although it isn't mandatory, we think it's a good idea to keep your operating system and application programs physically separated from your Web site files and directories.

If you haven't already done so, now is the time to install Windows NT. We don't have the space to discuss the details of *installing* NT, but we will cover aspects of *configuring* Windows NT, as necessary. For help in installing NT, please see the Microsoft guides that accompany the product.

> **Note:** We strongly suggest that all the hard drives are formatted using NTFS. (See the glossary if this term is unfamiliar to you.) Several of the applications included with this book (Perl and post.office to name two) require long filenames. More importantly, FTP security requires NTFS file-level security. In addition, NTFS runs more efficiently over the long haul because it doesn't generate fragmented files as easily as FAT. (See the glossary.) If you still prefer that the operating system reside on a FAT drive (C:), you can format D: using NTFS since it is the drive that we recommend for the Web server software.

The D: drive (1 GB) will be dedicated to Web files and FTP files for the Web site. A 1GB drive might seem excessive for a small company, but it should enable you room to grow. The next step is to map out a directory structure for the D: drive. We suggest you create the following subdirectories as a good way to organize your Web site:

- D:\http—holds the main HTML files and the Web server software
- D:\http\cgi-bin—holds all of the CGI scripts and applications
- D:\http\images—common directory for graphics files
- D:\http\log—for the HTTPS to put the access log files
- D:\http\pub—holds all the publicly available FTP files

These will be all of the directories needed to start out. As time goes by and the company grows, other directories can be added to logically separate additional HTML files.

Now comes the fun part: getting all your software installed and configured. The rest of this chapter assumes that you already have Windows NT installed and you are ready to set up RAS (Remote Access Service) and the Web server itself.

NT Workstation or NT Server?

If you are using NT Workstation instead of NT Server, we recommend that you change one setting to ensure the best performance. Remember that NT Workstation is primarily designed for application performance, and NT Server is intended for server software. Windows NT services are considered background applications. The Control Panel contains a setting that determines the relative performance between foreground and background programs. The default setting is Best Foreground Application Response Time. Because you won't want an application you are running to slow down the response time of your HTTP server, you can change this value as follows:

1. Double-click the System icon in Control Panel.

2. Choose the Tasking button.

3. Select Foreground and Background Applications Equally Responsive. See Figure 4.1.

Figure 4.1.
Windows NT Tasking
options.

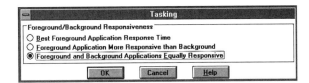

Installing RAS (Remote Access Service)

The steps after the following three assume that you have the Windows NT Network installed. If you don't, you will want to consider these next three steps first.

1. Read through this section to get an overview.

2. Go to Control Panel and double-click the Network icon.

3. You will then be prompted to install Network support. Supply the path to your distribution files and follow the prompts to install Remote Access. The procedures will be the same as what we show here; the order in which you conduct them will be different.

If you do have Windows NT Network installed, here are the steps to setting up RAS for your connection to the Internet.

1. In Control Panel, double-click the Network icon.

2. In the Network Settings dialog box, choose the Add Software button. See Figure 4.2.

3. From the Network Software drop-down list, select Remote Access Service and then choose the Continue button. When prompted for the path to the distribution files, provide the path and choose the OK button. The RAS files will be copied to your computer.

Figure 4.2
Network Settings.

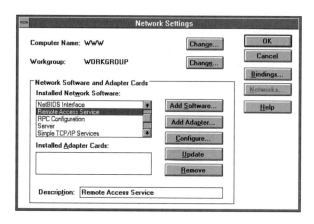

4. Remote Access Setup will offer to automatically detect the modem connected to the appropriate port. Choose Cancel to manually select a modem or choose OK to let it automatically detect the modem. A dialog box will appear announcing the modem detected. Choose OK. If Remote Access Setup does not detect your modem, you will be presented with a dialog box asking you to select a modem from a drop-down list.

5. In the Configure Port dialog box (see Figure 4.3), the modem detected will be highlighted. If RAS did not detect your modem or if you chose to manually select the modem, select the device attached to the port from the list. If your modem is on the Window NT Hardware Compatibility List, you should have no problem here. If your modem isn't detected, you might want to see if you can obtain an appropriate MODEM.INF file.

Figure 4.3.
Configure Port.

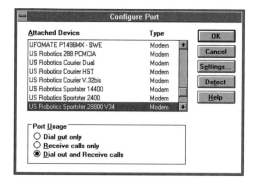

6. In the Port Usage box, choose how the port is to be used. For your purposes, select Dial out only.

7. To configure information specific to the type of device attached to the port, select the device and choose Settings. The default settings are usually ideal. Choose OK.

8. Choose Continue when you are finished setting up the port and network configurations. The Network Configuration dialog box will appear (Figure 4.4) showing the protocols installed on your computer. Remote Access Setup configures RAS, creates a Remote Access Service program group, and then confirms that the installation was successful.

Figure 4.4.
Network configuration.

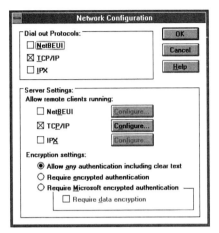

9. Choose OK in the confirmation dialog box and choose OK in the Network Settings dialog box. You might be prompted to confirm the network protocol or other settings.

Automating RAS with SWITCH.INF

Now is a good time to set up your SWITCH.INF file. This file is used by RAS to automate the login process with your service provider. The scripting language used for the file is not very well documented. We suggest that you take the sample SWITCH.INF file from the accompanying disc and modify it for your service provider with a simple ASCII text editor (such as Notepad). After you modify the file, place it in your winnt35/system32/ras directory. Here is a copy of the sample SWITCH.INF from the CD. We have marked in bold where you will need to edit the file and supply your information.

- Line 1—Insert the name of your ISP inside the brackets.
- Line 7—Insert your login name.
- Line 11—Insert your password.

```
[your service provider]
; Wait until we get the "login:" prompt
COMMAND=
ERROR_NO_CARRIER="NO CARRIER"
OK="gin:"
; Give the username and wait for "password:" prompt
COMMAND=your login name here
```

```
ERROR_NO_CARRIER="NO CARRIER"
OK="ord:"
; Give the password and ignore response (we're done)
COMMAND=your password here
ERROR_NO_CARRIER="NO CARRIER"
CONNECT="ing..."
; CONNECT response means that the connection completed fine.
; ERROR_DIAGNOISTICS response means connection attempt failed - the
; DIAGNOSTIC information will be extracted from the response and
; sent to the user.
; ERROR_NO_CARRIER means that the remote modem hung up.
; ERROR responses are for generic failures.
;----------------------------------------------
```

Now you are ready to set up the RAS Phone Book.

Setting up the RAS Phone Book

The Phone Book is used in conjunction with SWITCH.INF to automatically dial the ISP. Here are the steps for setting up the RAS Phone Book:

1. Go to the program group called Remote Access Service and double-click the Remote Access icon. You will get a dialog box that looks like the one in Figure 4.5.

Figure 4.5.
Remote Access.

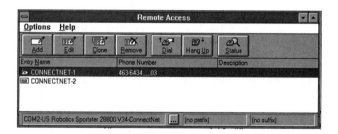

2. Choose Add and enter your service provider's information. See Figure 4.6.

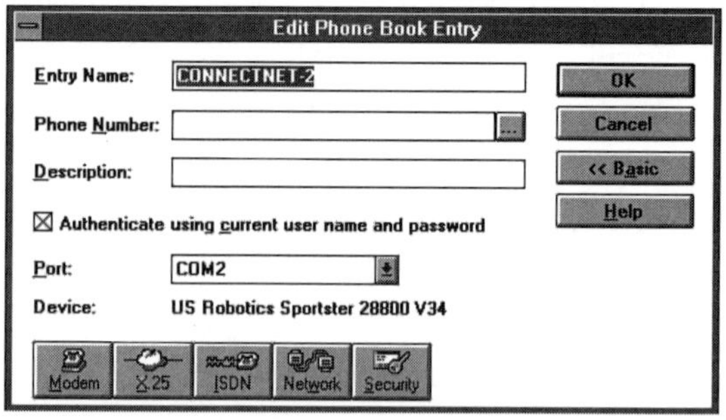

Figure 4.6.
Edit Phone Book Entry.

3. Choose the Modem button and set it up similar to Figure 4.7. Choose OK.

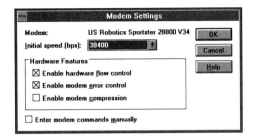

Figure 4.7.
Modem Settings.

4. Choose the Network button to see the dialog in Figure 4.8. Select the PPP radio button and check the TCP/IP checkbox.

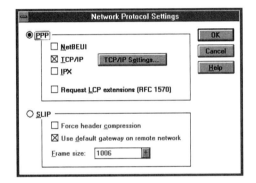

Figure 4.8.
Network Protocol Settings.

5. Choose the TCP/IP Settings button to see what is shown in Figure 4.9. Select the Server Assigned IP Address and Server Assigned Name Server Address radio buttons. Click the Use default gateway on remote network checkbox. If your service provider supports VJ header compression for PPP, check it too. Choose OK.

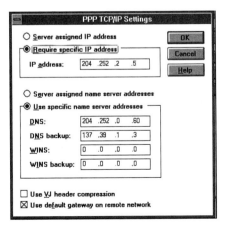

Figure 4.9.
PPP TCP/IP Settings.

6. Now choose the Security button and check the Accept any authentication including clear text radio button. See Figure 4.10. In the After Dialing drop-down box, select the name of your service provider. This is the SWITCH.INF entry that you made earlier. Choose OK.

Figure 4.10.
Security Settings.

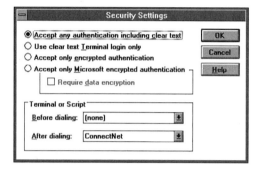

> **Caution:** Setting your server for "Clear Text" password verification puts your password in danger if your phone line is tapped, or if there is a malicious employee at the phone company or the ISP office. However, most ISPs don't seem to offer encrypted authentication, so clear text is widely used.

You now have RAS completely configured. You've come a long way and might be due for a break. This might be a good time to dial up your service provider to do a little Web surfing to unwind a bit.

More Network Configuration

Now you need to set up the Microsoft Loopback adapter. Follow these steps:

1. Go to the Control Panel and double-click the Network icon. In the dialog box that appears, choose Add Adapter. See Figure 4.11. You are already familiar with this dialog from your earlier configuration of RAS.

2. In the drop-down box that appears, select the MS Loopback Adapter and choose Continue. See Figure 4.12.

3. You will be presented with a small dialog to enter the frame type. Select 802.3 in the drop-down box and choose OK.

4. Now you will be back at the main Network configuration dialog box. Choose OK. The network bindings will start to update themselves, and the TCP/IP Configuration dialog box will appear. See Figure 4.13.

Figure 4.11.
Network Settings.

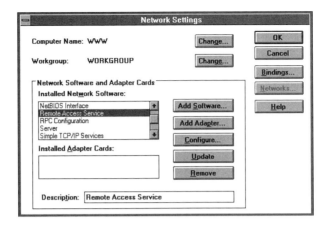

Figure 4.12
Add Network Adapter.

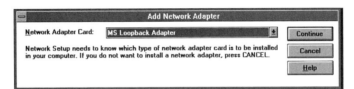

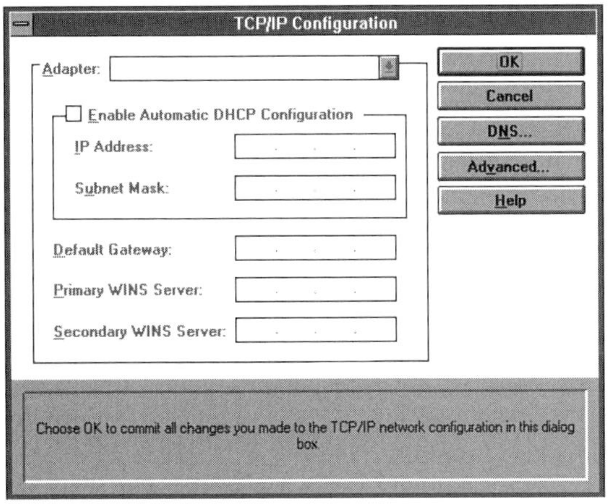

Figure 4.13.
TCP/IP Configuration.

Enter your ISP-assigned IP address in the IP address field. Don't worry about the subnet mask; NT will take care of it. Enter your ISP's domain name server in the Default Gateway field.

5. Choose DNS and you see the dialog in Figure 4.14. Enter your host name as www and your domain name, such as yourco.com, under Domain Name. Enter your ISP's primary and secondary domain name servers in the DNS Search Order box. Choose OK. Now you will be presented with a dialog box to reboot your system. Choose to reboot your system so the settings will take effect.

Figure 4.14.
DNS Configuration.

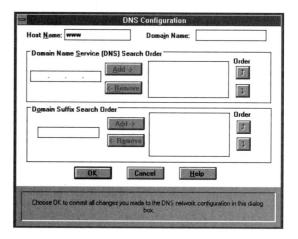

6. Now is a good time to update your host file. This step is not required for your network connections to work. However, it will enable the name-to-IP address resolution to occur locally rather than from your ISP's name server. With a standard ASCII text editor (such as Notepad), go to %systemdir%/system32/drivers/etc/host, and when you open the file you should see something like this:

```
# The IP address and the host name should be separated by at least one
# space.
#
# Additionally, comments (such as these) may be inserted on individual
# lines or following the machine name denoted by a '#' symbol.
#
# For example:
#
#      102.54.94.97      rhino.acme.com            # source server
#       38.25.63.10      x.acme.com                # x client host
127.0.0.1          localhost
Just below the localhost entry you need to make the your domain entries.
For example:
Your IP Address      yourcompany.com
Your IP Address      www.yourcompany.com
Your IP Address      ftp.yourcompany.com
```

Now save the file and exit the text editor.

Caution: If the IP address used by the RAS PPP connection collides with the IP address of any other network interface in your system, you will be unable to send network traffic over the RAS connection. Why? A RAS connection is a distinct interface. Each network interface must use a different IP address. This includes your network interface card (NIC) and the MS loopback adapter. Each interface can have several IP addresses; however, none may collide with the IP address of a different interface. A bug in Windows NT 3.5 allowed RAS to have the same IP address as your network adapter or loopback adapter. This can lead to a very mysterious malfunctioning of your network. Windows NT 3.51 corrects this problem. If you are running a stand-alone Web site that is not connected to a network, you will not need to install the loopback adapter.

Installing WinZip

WinZip is shareware developed by Nico Mak Computing, Inc. It is necessary that you use some form of a Pkunzip file decompression utility before installing the Web server and the Web editor.

WinZip is located in \WinZip95 on the CD-ROM. All you need to do to install it is to double-click SETUP.EXE in the directory and the setup program will install WinZip and start WinZip for you. You should see the main WinZip screen, which is shown in Figure 4.15.

Figure 4.15.
WinZip screen.

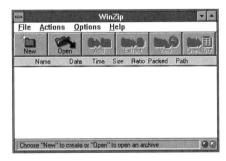

EMWAC HTTP Server Setup

Uncompress and install the EMWAC HTTPS by following these steps. These directions are also contained in the HTTPS.WRI Microsoft Write file on the CD-ROM.

1. Log into your Windows NT system as a user with administrative privileges.
2. The HTTP Server is distributed in four versions, for the Intel, MIPS, Power PC, and DEC Alpha architectures. Select the appropriate zip file for your processor.

3. Unzip the file using WinZip. You should get the following files:

HTTPS.EXE	The HTTP Server itself.
HTTPS.CPL	The Control Panel applet.
HTTPS.HLP	The Control Panel applet help file.
HTTPS.DOC	The manual in Word for Windows format.
HTTPS.PS	The manual, in postscript ready for printing.
HTTPS.WRI	The manual in Windows Write format.
EGSCRIPT.ZIP	Sample CGI script programs.
COPYRITE.TXT	The copyright statement for the software.
READ.ME	Summary of new features, etc.

4. Decide which directory you are going to put HTTPS.EXE in, and move it there. A good choice is the \WINNT\SYSTEM32 directory, which is where many other services live. Using the Security/Permissions menu option in the File Manager, verify that the SYS-TEM user has read permission for the file.

5. Move HTTPS.CPL and HTTPS.HLP to the \WINNT\SYSTEM32 directory. Start the Control Panel from the Program Manager to verify that the HTTP Server applet is represented as an icon in the Control Panel.

6. Determine which version of https you have. To do this, at the Windows NT Command Prompt, type

```
https -version
```

and the version number will be displayed. The HTTPS.WRI manual covers version 0.99. (If the program reports a later version number, you will find a corresponding later manual in the files you unpacked from the ZIP archive.) You should also check the IP address of your machine using the command:

```
https -ipaddress
```

This displays the name of your machine (for example, `emwac.ed.ac.uk`) and its IP address(es) as reported by the Windows Sockets API. If this information is incorrect, you need to reconfigure the TCP/IP software on your machine. The HTTP Server will not work if this address (or list of addresses if your machine has more than one network interface) is wrong.

7. If you have installed a previous version of the HTTP Server, you must remove it by typing

```
https -remove
```

See Section 2.4 of HTTPS.WRI for more information. You can use the old or the new version of HTTPS.EXE to perform this remove operation.

8. Install https into the table of Windows NT Services (and simultaneously register it with the Event Logger) by running the program from the Windows NT command line, specifying the `-install` flag.

For instance:

```
https -install
```

Caution: It is vital that you execute this command using the copy of HTTPS.EXE that you placed in the \WINNT\SYSTEM32 directory, and not some other copy that you plan to subsequently delete.

The program will register itself with the Service Manager and with the Event Logger, and will report success or failure. In the case of failure, see the section on Installation Problems in HTTPS.WRI.

9. To verify that the installation succeeded, start the Windows NT Control Panel and double-click the Services icon. The resultant dialog should list HTTP Server as one of the installed services. If so, see the Configuration section of HTTPS.WRI for more instructions.

HTTPS Configuration

To configure the HTTP Server, double-click the HTTPS icon in the Control Panel. See Figure 4.16.

Figure 4.16.
HTTP Server Control
Panel applet.

You can use this dialog to

- Set the root of the directory tree containing the files you want to make available on the World Wide Web. Use the Data directory: field for this. Full details of how HTTP treats the files and directories in this directory tree are given in Section 5 of HTTPS.WRI.

- Specify the TCP/IP port on which the HTTP Server listens for incoming HTTP connections. Use the TCP/IP port: field for this. The value must be a positive integer representing a legal and otherwise unused port. The default is 80.

- Specify the MIME type that corresponds to a given filename extension. This is covered in more detail in HTTPS.WRI.

- Enable and disable the logging of HTTP transactions. If this box is checked, the HTTP Server will record each HTTP request it receives in a log file. See Section 4.3 of HTTPS.WRI for more information about logging. Logging is disabled by default.

- Specify the directory in which log files are stored. Use the Log file directory: field for this purpose. This is disabled unless the Log HTTP Transactions box is checked. The default is the Windows system directory (\WINNT).

- Permit the HTTP Data Directory tree to be browsed by HTTP clients. Further details on browsing are given in Section 5 of HTTPS.WRI. Browsing is disabled by default.

- Restore the default values of all the configuration settings. Click the Defaults button to do this.

When you have finished making changes to the configuration, choose OK. The configuration will take effect the next time you start the HTTP Server. If the HTTP Server is already running, a dialog box to remind you to stop and restart it (using the Services dialog in the Control Panel) will be displayed.

Creating an HTTPS Account

After the HTTP Server is configured, set up an account for the HTTPS to run as a service. For security reasons, give this account General User privileges and don't make it a member of the Administrators group. Otherwise, anyone coming in on socket 80 (or any others you've assigned to the server) will have administrator privileges.

After you initiate an account for HTTPS, go to Control Panel, select the services applet, highlight HTTP server, and choose Startup. Set the Log On As: section of the dialog box to log on under the account name and password that you set up for HTTPS. The sample account is named https. See Figure 4.17.

Figure 4.17.
Log On As.

Installing WebEdit

In this section, you'll install and use the shareware HTML editor from the CD. This program lets you build a simple Web page with the click of one button. We'll show you how to modify the file to make it your own home page.

WebEdit was developed by KnowledgeWorks, Inc. There are a lot of other HTML editors out there, but we haven't found any to match the price and the features of this one.

To install WebEdit, copy the file from the CD-ROM to a directory on your hard disk. Then unzip the file using WinZip and run the file SETUP.EXE from the same directory.

When you run WebEdit, you will see a screen that looks similar to Figure 4.18.

Figure 4.18.
WebEdit.

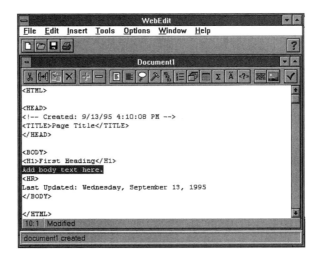

The reason we are using WebEdit is that all we need to do is press the + button to generate the basic framework of an HTML document. This results in the file shown below, which we want to save as default.htm so any Web browser that visits our site will load it automatically.

```
<HTML>
<HEAD>
<!-- Created: 9/6/95 8:47:29 PM -->
<TITLE>Page Title</TITLE>
</HEAD>
<BODY>
<H1>First Heading</H1>
Add body text here.
<HR>
Last Updated: Wednesday, September 06, 1995
</BODY>
</HTML>
```

You're There!

A sample copy of default.htm is on the CD-ROM. The last step is to modify the file in the editor to include the name of your home page. See the boldfaced lines in the preceding code. Feel free to customize it to fit your needs. When you're done, try it out in your Web browser by opening it as a local file first. If it looks good, you're ready for the big time.

Troubleshooting

Hopefully, your Web server installation went well. If you had any problems during setup, here are a few resources that will very likely be able to offer sage advice.

International Windows NT Users Group (IWNTUG) listserver: With well over a thousand members, someone on this listserver should be able to help you out. Here are the subscribing instructions:

1. Enter `join iwntug` in the body of the message and leave the subject blank. Send to `list@bhs.com`.

2. After you subscribe, send messages to the group at `iwntug@bhs.com`.

3. To leave the list, enter `leave iwntug` in the body of the message, leave the subject blank, and mail to `list@bhs.com`.

NT https listserver, `http_winnt@Emerald.NET`: This list server is a good place to get your "NT as a Web server" questions answered. Subscribing instructions: Enter `subscribe` in the subject line and leave the body blank.

In Appendix C, you will find a more comprehensive list of resources that will help you out in most any situation involving NT or the Internet.

Using RAS, call up your service provider, go to the Services applet in the Control Panel and start all the services that you installed. That's all there is to it. Your site is up and running.

If you have a second phone line, you can dial into your ISP through your Web browser and connect to your own Web server! The only caveat is that you will need to supply your IP address as part of the URL instead of your domain name. Until InterNIC has completed your Domain Name application, Web clients will only be able to access your site by using your IP address—or example, `http://201.144.128.60/` instead of `http://yourco.com/`.

What's Next?

Part II of this book is all about HTML and enhancing your home page.

Part II

HTML, the Language of the Web

In this part of the book, you'll explore HTML in depth. Getting your Web site up and running is one thing, and having it deliver meaningful and attractive pages to your audience is another.

- **Chapter 5**, "A Guided Tour of HTML," covers all the basics you need to write HTML code.
- **Chapter 6**, "Image Mapping and Multimedia," is where you add graphics, audio, and video to make your Web pages come alive.
- **Chapter 7**, "Introduction to Web Forms and CGI Scripts," gives you a hint of the unlimited capability of the Web. This is where you'll get into C programming, and all the material is precompiled on the CD-ROM ready to run.
- **Chapter 8**, "Power Programming with CGI," dives into the heart of HTML and C programming. Together, these two languages enable you to create amazingly powerful Web pages.

- **Chapter 9,** "Netscape Extensions and HTML 3.0," covers all the leading-edge developments in HTML, including Style.
- **Chapter 10,** "Putting HTML to Work Building a Sample Site," provides you with all the annotated source code for a complete Web site.

Chapter 5

A Guided Tour of HTML

- Background
- SGML and HTML
- A Basic Document
- Writing Documents
- Document Style and Organization
- Element Reference
- The Future of HTML
- Alternatives to HTML

One of the primary foundations of the World Wide Web is the HyperText Markup Language (HTML). HTML is the primary format in which documents are distributed and viewed on the Web. Many of its features, such as platform-independent formatting, structural design, and especially hypertext, make it a very good document format for the Internet and the WWW.

This chapter gives you a basic understanding of HTML and how you can create documents in this format. A brief description of the common tags and a style guide to creating good HTML documents help you on the road to getting your information onto the WWW. A few of the more advanced features, as well as a look to the future of HTML, are also covered.

Background

As one of the foundation specifications that define the Web (along with HTTP and URLs), HTML was originally developed by Tim Berners-Lee at CERN in 1989. HTML was envisioned to be a format that would enable scientists using very different computers to share information seamlessly over the network; several features were necessary. *Platform independence*, in which a document can be displayed similarly on computers with different capabilities (that is, fonts, graphics, and color) was vital to the varied audience. *Hypertext*, meaning any word or phrase in one document references another document, would allow for easy navigation between and within the many large documents on the system. Rigorously *structured documents* would allow for advanced applications such as converting documents to and from other formats and searching text databases.

SGML and HTML

Berners-Lee chose to use the Standard Generalized Markup Language (SGML) as a pattern. As an emerging international standard, SGML had the advantages of structure and platform independence. Its status also ensured its long life, meaning that documents formatted in SGML would not need to be rebuilt a few years later.

SGML is platform-independent because it focuses on encoding the *semantic structure*, or meaning, of a document—not necessarily its appearance. Thus, a chapter title would be labeled, "Chapter Title," instead of "Helvetica 18pt Centered." Although the latter style breaks down if the document is viewed on a computer that doesn't have the Helvetica typeface or support for lettering of different sizes, the former style can be displayed (intelligently) on any system. Each reader defines the appearance of chapter titles in a way that is useful on his or her computer, and any text with that style is formatted accordingly.

Another feature of this structure is that semantically encoded text can be automatically processed more intelligently by the computer. For example, if every chapter title is marked with the label "Chapter Title," perhaps with the chapter number as an attribute, a reader could request to see just Chapter 18; the SGML software would automatically look for the Chapter 18 title and the Chapter 19 title, and extract everything between them. This could not be done with the text marked with meaningless (to the computer) fonts and formatting codes.

A great advantage of SGML is its flexibility. SGML is not a format in its own right, but a specification for defining other formats. Users can create new formats to encode all the structure of certain types of documents (for example, technical manuals, phone books, and legal documents), and any SGML-capable software can understand it, simply by reading the definition first. A large number of Document Type Definitions (DTDs) have been created, both for common and very specialized documents. HTML is simply one DTD, or *application*, of SGML.

The Evolution of HTML

For several years, the use of HTML (and the WWW) grew slowly, despite these capabilities. This was primarily because it did not have enough features to do any kind of professional electronic publishing; it had some font control, but no graphics. Semantic encoding was not important to people when they couldn't make it look pretty.

Then everything changed. When NCSA first built Mosaic in early 1993, they added their own features to HTML, including inline graphics. This suddenly allowed people to attach logos, icons, photographs, and diagrams to their documents; the size and usage of the Web exploded. For the next year, the development of HTML happened on a very *ad hoc* basis. New pieces of HTML were introduced by one browser or another from time to time; some would catch on, and others would disappear. Some of the additions were poorly designed, and many were not even SGML-compliant.

By May 1994, it was apparent that HTML was growing out of control. At the first WWW conference in Geneva, Switzerland, an HTML Working Group was organized. Its primary task was to formalize HTML, as it was being used, into an SGML DTD known as HTML Level 2. (Level 1 was defined to be HTML as it was originally designed by Tim Berners-Lee.) Once standardized, it could then be safely extended to future levels, and still take advantage of the capabilities of true SGML and its formal structure. At the time of this writing, HTML Level 2 is nearing completion, having gone through several drafts, and is becoming the standard format that all WWW browsers can understand.

Even though it isn't standard, HTML 3.0 is already in wide use today and adds many needed features to the HTML 2.0 specification. Chapter 9, "Netscape Extensions and HTML 3.0," and Appendix F, "HTML Encyclopedia," give you the run-down on which features are in which versions. This chapter sticks to the basics of HTML 1.0 and 2.0 so you can ease into it.

HTML documents are in ASCII text format and can be created using most text editors. There are some Windows editors available specifically for HTML editing. We have included one on the CD that is very simple and intuitive: WebEdit.

A Basic Document

Let's first take a look at a simple HTML document to see how one normally appears. The following text is a valid HTML file:

```
<HTML>
<HEAD>
        <TITLE>Bill Jones' Document</TITLE>
</HEAD>

<BODY>
        <H1>Welcome to Bill Jones' Life</H1>
        Hi, my name is Bill Jones. Here is a picture of me:<P>
        <IMG SRC="http://foobar.hsu.edu/~jones/me.gif"><P>
        <H3>A Brief Autobiography</H3>
```

```
        <LI>Born in <A HREF="http://www.mtsmith.vt.us/">Mount Smith,
        Vermont</A>, August 26, 1965.
        <LI>Went to college at <A HREF="http://www.wyst.edu/">Wyoming
        State College</A>, earning a degree in math.
        <LI>Now work at <A HREF="http://www.hsu.edu">Horton State
        University</A> as a professor.
    </UL>
    <HR>
    <ADDRESS>Bill Jones<BR>
            285 LaSalle Ave<BR>
            Horton, NY 12645<BR>
            (615)457-3523<BR>
            <A HREF="http://foobar.hsu.edu/~jones/mailme.html">
            jones@foobar.hsu.edu</A>
    </ADDRESS>
</BODY>
</HTML>
```

It is always important to remember that HTML (as an application of SGML) encodes only the *structure* of the document. Much of the *appearance* of the document, such as type styles, color, and the window size, is under the ultimate control of the browser and the people using it. However, most browsers render things similarly; as different parts of HTML are described, their normal rendering is also given.

You can learn many things about the HyperText Markup Language from this basic document.

Basic HTML Syntax

An HTML document consists of two types of contents: normal document *text* and codes, or *tags*. Tags are text strings surrounded by a less-than and greater-than sign, such as <HTML> in the first line. Tags usually have the following structure:

```
<tagname attribute=value attribute=value . . . >
```

The `tagname` is the type of text being defined by the tag; the `attributes` (you can have none or several) give additional information about how the element should behave.

For example, in the <HEAD> tag in the second line of the sample HTML file, HEAD is the tagname and has no associated attributes. Farther down in the file is a tag with the tagname IMG and a single attribute SRC that has the value "http://foobar.hsu.edu/~jones/me.gif"). It is important to remember that the tagname and attribute are not case-sensitive. You can use uppercase and lowercase letters as you want. The values assigned to the attributes may be case-sensitive, depending on the attribute.

The tags and text combine to form *elements*. Each element represents an object in the document, such as a heading, paragraph, or picture. An element consists of one or two tags and usually some associated text.

There are two types of elements: containers and empty elements. *Container elements* represent a section of text and consist of body text (or other elements) delimited by a tag at the beginning and the end. (The end tag is identified by a / before the tagname and never carries any attributes.) For example, in the third line of the sample file, the <TITLE> and </TITLE> tags define the text between them as a title.

On the other hand, an *empty element* consists of a single tag that does not alter any text; instead, it inserts something into the document. For example, the <IMG SRC=...> tag/element places the picture in the document.

Together, container elements and empty elements completely define how a document is to be formatted and displayed. Other things normally used to format text (such as tabs, extra spaces, and carriage returns) are treated as a single space in HTML. For example, the sample HTML files could have been typed with three blank lines after every tag and ten spaces between each word, but would appear exactly the same (just as it would if the entire file had been typed on a single line). Although this might make simple formatting more difficult, it enables writers to make the HTML document more readable by using programming style techniques such as extra blank spaces and tabs (as are used in the sample file), without affecting the display of the final document.

Description of Elements in Sample Document

This section looks at the elements used in the sample document. The sample file contains the common tags used in most documents. (More thorough definitions of each element are given later in the chapter.)

First, three container elements should appear in every HTML file:

- <HTML> *text* </HTML>: This element contains the entire file (that is, the first tag appears at the beginning of the file, and the second tag appears at the end of the file) and define the enclosed *text* as an HTML document. This, the largest, container element contains the following two container elements, in order.

- <HEAD> *text* </HEAD>: This element is the *header* and contains information about the document (usually one to three lines) that is not part of the text. It plays the same role as the running head on each page of this book: It gives context and position to the text but is not part of the narrative.

- <BODY> *text* </BODY>: This element contains other elements representing the *body text* of the document, normally almost all the file's length.

Together, these three elements create a template, which all HTML documents should follow:

```
<HTML>
<HEAD>
   Header Elements
</HEAD>
<BODY>
   Body of Document
</BODY>
</HTML>
```

The <HEAD> element can contain several unique elements; however, most documents contain only the one shown in the example:

- <TITLE> *text* </TITLE>: This element is the title of the document, such as that found in the running head on each page of this book. The title is normally shown in the browser separate from the text page (for example, in the window frame or in a part of the window separate from the document).

The <BODY> element in the sample file contains several common elements:

- <H1> *text* </H1>: This element identifies the enclosed text as a *major heading* (for example, the title at the beginning of a document). You can have up to six levels of headings by using the tags <H1>, <H2>, and up to <H6>. (The lower numbers signify headings of greater importance.) Headings are normally rendered in a larger type (more important headings are in a larger type) with a blank space above and below.

- <P>: This tag marks the separation between two *paragraphs* of body text (that is, text not part of some other element).

- <IMG SRC="http://foobar.hsu.edu/~jones/me.gif">: This element places an *image* in the document, which can be found at the URL given in the SRC attribute. (See Chapter 1, "Internet Technology Primer," for an explanation of URLs.)

- <LI> *text* <LI> *text* </UL>: This construction provides an *unordered list* of items; the <LI> tag begins each item. Normally, a bullet is placed at the beginning of each entry.

- <A HREF="http://www.mtsmith.vt.us/">*text*</A>: This kind of element marks a hypertext *anchor*, also known as a *hyperlink*. The *text* is highlighted in some way on-screen (in color, with an underline or something similar); when that text is selected on-screen (that is, pointed at with the mouse), the document given by the URL in the HREF (Hypertext Reference) attribute is retrieved.

- <HR>: This element places a horizontal *rule*, or line, across the window, normally with a space above and below.

- <ADDRESS> *text* </ADDRESS>: This element marks a block of text that serves as a postal or electronic mail *address*. The address is normally rendered in a slightly different font than body text (for example, smaller, italic type) and does not use the extra space placed between body paragraphs (formatted with the <P> element).

-
: This element forces a *line break* in the text so that any succeeding text is placed on the next line.

These elements are described in more detail, along with many other valid elements, later in this chapter.

Writing Documents

Now that you have seen an HTML document in action, you're probably wondering, "How can I make one of these?" There are several options for creating HTML files, ranging from the powerful and difficult to the easy and simplistic. Most of the current HTML tools are not as useful as they could be, but the large demand for easy *and* powerful HTML tools ensures that they will become more robust in the near future.

Text Editors

Because HTML documents are really plain text files, the first (and currently most common) solution is to create them using a garden-variety text editor, such as Notepad. You create the HTML document by typing it exactly as it is to appear—including typing the tags by hand—and you finish with a file that looks just like the sample file shown earlier in this chapter.

The drawback of this approach is that because these editors are ignorant of the type of file you are entering, they cannot help you at all. They cannot correct poor syntax, offer any suggestions on element usage, or show how the finished product will appear in a WWW browser. You have to be careful to get the document right and often have to edit it many times to correct mistakes. If you decide to use a text editor to create HTML, you should also have a WWW browser available to check the document often and find any problems to be fixed.

HTML Editors

Between the two of us, we have tried over a dozen methods of HTML file creation. The one we agreed was the easiest is a simple but powerful program called WebEdit by Ken Nesbitt. WebEdit is included on the CD, and we discussed the installation process in Chapter 4, "Up and Running Fast." WebEdit is shareware. There are many other shareware and freeware HTML Editors available on the Internet, but after observing the difficulty of using other packages, we welcomed WebEdit as a companion for most of our HTML editing tasks.

Word Processor Templates

Tools in this category are not programs in their own right, but exist as macros or accessories that operate within your favorite word processor or desktop publishing program. The advantage of these templates is that they enable you to create HTML documents using the same tools and interface you use for creating normal documents; they output files in HTML instead of the program's normal format. The disadvantages are that the templates are not currently available for most word processing software and that using a large word processor to create a small, one-page document can be slow and cumbersome. However, these templates are probably very good for working on large HTML documents. Here are several currently available:

- Internet Assistant (for Microsoft Word), from Microsoft

    `http://www.microsoft.com/msoffice/freestuf/msword/download/ia/default.htm`

- GT_HTML.DOT (for Microsoft Word), from Georgia Tech University

  `http://www.gatech.edu/word_html/release.htm`
- Internet Publisher (for WordPerfect), from Novell

  `http://wp.novell.com/`

HTML Converters

Many of the documents you want to contribute to the WWW likely already exist. Most people have a large number of documents previously created using a word processor or desktop publishing program; they do not want to have to re-create the documents or convert them to HTML by hand. To assist in this process, several tools can convert existing documents to HTML. They simply take the codes from the software's internal format and convert them into HTML elements.

For these converters to work cleanly, your original document should be constructed with the same philosophy used with HTML and SGML: using a clear, semantic structure. For example, if named styles (such as Chapter Title and List Item) are used in the original document, these styles can be converted directly into corresponding HTML elements (*Chapter Title* = <H1>, *List Item* = <LI>, and so on.) On the other hand, nonsemantic markup, (such as "Helvetica 14pt centered") is difficult or impossible for the converter to interpret. Almost every word processor and desktop publishing program has a styles feature.

There are basically two types of HTML converter tools.

Word Processor Macros

These operate within the word processor or desktop publisher program, going through the document line by line and converting each code to an HTML equivalent. In the end, the user sees a raw HTML file that can be saved as plain text. Here are some available software packages:

- ANT_HTML.DOT (for Microsoft Word), by Jill Swift

  `http://www.w3.org/hypertext/WWW/Tools/Ant.html`
- WPTOHTML (for WordPerfect/DOS 5.1 through 6.0), by Hunter Monroe

  `ftp://oak.oakland.edu/SimTel/msdos/wordperf/wpt51d10.zip` or
  `ftp://oak.oakland.edu/SimTel/msdos/wordperf/wpt60d10.zip`

Stand-Alone Conversion Programs

These tools are used outside the originating software. They read the original document from the disk, converting it and saving the result as an HTML document. Here are a few of them; if your software is not represented, you can probably convert the file into a format that can be used by one of these tools. (For example, you can convert the file into RTF format and then convert that into an HTML file.)

- RTFTOHTML (for Rich Text Format files)

  `ftp://ftp.cray.com/src/WWWstuff/RTF/rtftohtml_overview.html`

- WP2X (for WordPerfect 5.1), by Michael Richardson

    `http://journal.biology.carleton.ca/People/Michael_Richardson/software/`
    `wp2x.html`

- qt2www (for Quark Xpress), by Jeremy Hylton

    `http://the-tech.mit.edu/~jeremy/qt2www.html`

Document Style and Organization

As you begin to write HTML documents, it is important that you keep in mind the following tips. Having your document obey these general style rules should make them better looking, better and more frequently used by readers, and easier for you to maintain:

- Thoroughly plan your information. The only reason people put information on the WWW is because they hope others can use it. (Often, the contributor expects to subsequently benefit from this use.) Thus, your primary goal in organizing the documents and files you place on your server is to make your information easy for users to access.

    Although this organization differs for every site, some things should be kept in mind. Use hypertext prodigiously; the more possible avenues people have to navigate through your information, the better the chance they find what they want. Create navigational pages such as directories and tables of contents to aid people in searching for information. Also, be very clear when describing links and menu choices; this decreases the number of wrong roads your users take.

- Use valid HTML. In the early days of the World Wide Web, HTML was not well-defined, and neither was the way it was to be rendered. Many tags mutated into several forms, and browsers were written to be lax in parsing documents so that they could handle the several forms in which each tag appeared. Although HTML has become more structured and stable, the browsers often still allow for variant syntaxes so that they can read the large number of old documents out there.

- Although many of these "cheater" syntaxes (for example, using `<UL>` without `<LI>` to make indented paragraphs) might produce a pleasing result on your browser, their appearance varies wildly from one browser to another (some browsers ignore the lone `<UL>` altogether) and might produce a very poor display on somebody else's screen. Although you cannot have complete control over what appears on each user's screen, your best bet for creating fairly uniform-looking documents is to use HTML as it was designed.

- Use small files. When a document is created on paper, it normally consists of one large file and is distributed as a single stack of paper. This approach is often undesirable on the World Wide Web. People generally don't like to read large quantities of text on a screen. A reader would also be very hesitant to download a 1MB file when he or she is looking for a single paragraph.

    The great advantage of hypertext is that it allows for nonlinear text: Readers can bounce around inside and between documents, reading and understanding pieces in the order and method that best suits them individually. A good document is broken into many small files, each no more than a screen or two in length, interconnected with the <A> tag to produce hyperlinks at appropriate places. Good subdocuments for a table of contents and index allow users to find and retrieve just those pieces of the document that they need.

■ Keep in mind that some users will naturally want to print certain documents. If your document is contained in many separate HTML files, the reader will have to link to each of them in order to print or save the whole topic. You can decide on a case-by-case basis what is best for each document you present.

■ Date the page. It is a good idea to include the date a document was last edited. This allows people returning to your page to know if it has been updated.

■ Don't overdo graphics. Although displaying graphics as part of a document is one of the most powerful capabilities of HTML, it is often abused. Images use much more bandwidth than normal text, so a page with many large graphics takes much longer to download than one without. In fact, many users, such as those connecting over slow telephone lines and those using text-only terminals (still a large part of the Internet audience) will not even see your graphics. Graphics also increase the space your document takes on the screen, forcing people to scroll down to see the rest of the page. Here are a few good rules of thumb when dealing with graphics:

1. Concentrate your graphics where they do the most good, such as illustrations, logos, and mastheads. (The large images that appear on the top of homepages to give the service a corporate image.)

2. Cut down the number of colors in each image. Most monitors display only 256 colors at once, so the colors of all images on the page must fit in this number. If you don't trim the images, the browser will, and it rarely does an acceptable job. If you're including photographs, they should use about 50 to 100 colors each. (You can set this limit with most graphics software.) Limiting colors also reduces the size of the file to be downloaded.

3. Make graphics as small (in memory size) as possible. For example, if you want to include a photograph, put a *thumbnail* (a smaller replica) of the photo in the document, which is linked to the full-size graphic that people can download if they really want to view it. Or link a large graphic with a text reference.

4. Never rely on the graphics to communicate your message. Any important information (titles, menu choices, and so on) that appears in the graphics should also appear in the text. This might mean using the ALT attribute in the <IMG> tag or having a duplicate page that text-only browsers can use.

5. You might supply a link to the graphic that tells the user how large it is before he or she decides to download it.

■ Test your document with multiple browsers. Browsers vary markedly in how they render HTML. Also, some browsers (such as Netscape) use additional elements that are not part of "true" HTML and which are not supported by any other browsers. The Web has many documents that were obviously written with a single browser in mind because they look awful on all the rest.

If possible, gain access to at least two browsers (preferably a graphics one and a text-only one) that you can use to view your documents. Although the documents you create with this method might not look as good on your favorite browser as they could, they will look fairly good on all browsers.

Element Reference

The following sections provide a brief guide to almost all the elements used in HTML Level 2. For a more comprehensive reference, see the official HTML 2.0 specification at `http://www.w3.org/hypertext/WWW/MarkUp/html-spec/index.html`. Remember that the tag and attribute names are not case-sensitive and can be in upper- or lowercase letters.

<HEAD> Elements

The following tags are allowed in the header part of the HTML document.

Document Title

This is the name of the document. The title is generally written in a larger type size than the current document in order to give the user a frame of reference. For example, if the document is a chapter of a book, the `<TITLE>` would probably contain the title of the book as well as the chapter title. Thus, if someone followed a hyperlink from somewhere else directly to this chapter, he or she would not be lost, but would know that this file is part of a certain book.

`<TITLE>text</TITLE>`

External Link

This establishes a relationship between the current document and another document. The `name` attribute gives the link a name, such as `Mail to Author`. The `rel` attribute describes the type of link, such as `"made"` (the author), `"parent"` (a larger document of which this is a part), `"next"` (the succeeding section of a multifile document), and `"prev"` (the previous section). The `href` attribute points to the related document. Currently, most browsers don't make use of this tag, but future browsers will likely add a new button to the screen for each `<LINK>` to allow users to easily jump to the related document.

`<LINK name="text" rel="text" href="URL">`

Document Meta-Information

This allows for extra information about a document, such as its modification data, copyright, or abstract. This is done by setting a name and value, such as `<META NAME="copyright" CONTENT="1995, Sams.Net Publishing">`. Separate `<META>` tags are included for each item of information. Currently, this tag is seldom used in browsers.

```
<META NAME="text" CONTENT="text">
```

Location of Current Document

This lets you specify the full URL of this document. Although it might seem redundant, this information is useful if you use relative URLs in the hyperlinks. Using this base, the hyperlinks are resolved correctly even if this document is requested with a different URL than you expect (for example, if users save it on their local disk and try to use it there).

```
<BASE HREF="url">
```

Searchable Document

This places a search field either in the document or elsewhere on the screen, enabling users to enter keywords to search through this document. You can't just add this tag to any arbitrary document and expect it to work. Your server must be set up to process this query, using a back-end search engine such as WAIS. For a full discussion of this topic, see Chapter 15, "Databases and the Web."

```
<ISINDEX>
```

Empty Elements

As stated earlier in this chapter, *empty elements* are elements that insert objects into the document by themselves, regardless of the surrounding text. They each consist of a single tag. For example:

```
<IMG SRC="graphic.gif">
```

Horizontal Rule

This places a horizontal line across the page, with a blank line above and below, and is normally used to separate major sections of a document (for example, before an `<H1>` or `<H2>`). Some graphical browsers give the rule a 3-D chiseled look.

```
<HR>
```

Line Break

This forces subsequent text to the next line. Unlike the `<P>` tag, the text before and after the `<BR>` tag is still considered a single paragraph. The `<BR>` tag is normally used to create tight blocks of short-line information, such as mailing addresses.

```
<BR>
```

Inline Image

This places an image within the document, as found at the URL specified in the `src` attribute (which is mandatory). The most common format for these images is CompuServe's Graphics Interchange Format, or GIF. If the browser doesn't support inline images (for example, the Lynx browser does not), the text given in the optional `alt` attribute is displayed. If no `alt` attribute is given, a default placeholder such as `[IMAGE]` may be displayed in this situation. (To ensure that nothing is displayed if the graphic cannot be shown, use the `alt =""` attribute.) The optional `align` attribute specifies how the image is to be aligned vertically with the current line of text. (The default alignment is most often `BOTTOM`, but this varies by browser.)

The `ISMAP` attribute lets you create interactive graphics, or *imagemaps*. If the syntax `<A href="http://URL1"><IMG src="URL2" ismap></A>` is used and you point to a spot on the image, the *x* and *y* coordinates are passed to the hyperlink (for example, `http://URL1?x,y`). However, the HTTP server must be able to handle imagemap queries. Chapter 6 gives step-by-step details for doing this with EMWAC. For more information on imagemaps, look for the *The World Wide Web Unleashed*, Second Edition, published by Sams.net.

```
<IMG src="URL" alt="text" align=TOP/MIDDLE/BOTTOM ISMAP>
```

Comment

Any text inside this element is ignored. This element is used to include notes that can be read by the writer but that are not part of the text of the document (which is especially useful if several writers work on the same document). The useful programming technique of temporarily commenting out sections of code cannot be done here; many older browsers use a single > as the closing character of the comment, so any tags included in the comment (such as `<BR>`) cause the comment to end early and interpret any remaining comment text as body text.

```
<!-- text -->
```

Character Containers

Character containers enable you to format or describe words and phrases within paragraphs. Although they can be used inside non-body blocks as well as in normal text, all but the `<A>` tag can produce unattractive results on some browsers.

Hypertext Links

Hypertext links are the heart of HTML. These links lets the user, with a single mouse click, move from place to place within a document or even to an entirely different document anywhere on the Internet. This use of hyperlinks is how the World Wide Web gets its name; links form a spider's web of documents that covers the globe.

Hypertext Anchor

This is used to mark the reference or the target of a hypertext link. Either the `href` or `name` attribute must be included. (Both are allowed, but they don't appear together very often.) The `href` attribute specifies a URL to which the enclosed `text` attribute is linked. (The `text` is highlighted; selecting it requests the new object.) `href` can reference another HTML document, an image, or anything else that can be addressed using a URL. The hypertext anchor can also enclose an `<IMG>` tag, allowing inline graphics (such as icons) to become links.

The `name` attribute gives a unique name to the enclosed tag, allowing users and other HTML documents to point directly to this part of the document. For example, a URL such as `http://.../thisdoc.html#part1` loads `thisdoc.html` and attempts to place the text marked with `<a name="part1">` at the top of the screen.

```
<A href="URL" name="text">text</A>
```

Logical Styles

Logical styles let you give a real meaning to sections of text. Currently, they are only used for formatting, but they can be used for more intelligent types of processing, such as automatic footnoting.

Emphasis. Used to highlight sections of text for miscellaneous reasons. Normally rendered in *italics*.

```
<em>text</em>
```

Strong emphasis. Another form of generic highlighting. Normally rendered in **bold**.

```
<strong>text</strong>
```

Citation. Used to mark a citation to another document, such as a printed book (for example, *Great Expectations*). Normally rendered in *italics*.

```
<cite>text</cite>
```

Computer code. Used to mark text from a computer (for example, `hit any key`). Normally rendered in a fixed-width font such as `Courier`.

```
<code>text</code>
```

Variable. Used to mark a variable used in a mathematical formula or computer program (for example, $z = x + y$). Normally rendered in *italics*.

```
<var>text</var>
```

Keyboard input. Used to mark text that is to be typed at the keyboard by a user (for example, `hit the enter key`). Normally rendered in a fixed-width font such as `Courier`.

```
<kbd>text</kbd>
```

Physical Styles

Originally considered *cheater* versions of the logical styles, physical style elements have become very popular because they are similar to the way people are used to highlighting text (that is, literally instead of semantically).

Bold:

`<b>text</b>`

Italics:

`<i>text</i>`

Typewriter text, rendered in a fixed-width font such as `Courier`:

`<tt>text</tt>`

Block Containers

In HTML, a *block* is defined as a piece of marked text that by itself occupies a certain amount of vertical space in a document, such as a paragraph or a heading. The following elements can be adjacent to each other, but cannot be nested (that is, you can't have a `<P>` inside an `<H1>`—because they represent different types of blocks).

Headings (1 Through 6). This acts as a title for a section of the document. The lower-number headings represent more important headings and are generally rendered in larger text. Because of a mixup in the distributed default settings, some browsers erroneously display `<H5>` and `<H6>` smaller than the body text. Until these two elements are displayed more consistently, they should probably be avoided when possible. Following is an example:

`<H#>text</H#>`

Paragraph. In most current browsers, this tag is used in the first form as a paragraph separator. Thus, it marks the boundary between two paragraphs of normal body text. You should not use this tag between body text and another element. (For example, do not use ...`<p><h1>`....) Because the second element implies a line break, some browsers put too much space between the elements. The second form (a container for each paragraph) represents a more valid SGML structure and will soon be the standard. However, the end tag `</P>` will be optional, so most documents that have been created using the first form will still work.

```
text<P>text
<P>text</P>
```

Extended quotation. Used for long quotations that exist as separate paragraphs. This is normally rendered similarly to a normal paragraph, but with both margins indented.

`<BLOCKQUOTE>text</BLOCKQUOTE>`

Mailing address. Specifically targeted to postal addresses, this tag is commonly used to mark bylines (name of the author) and e-mail addresses. It is normally rendered in a smaller font or in italics, and usually uses the `<BR>` tag to separate the individual lines of the address.

```
<ADDRESS>text</ADDRESS>
```

Preformatted text. Because extra spaces and tabs are ignored in HTML, some kinds of text, such as poetry, tables, and computer program listings, are difficult to encode. The `<PRE>` element is used with those types of text by formatting everything it contains exactly as it appears, including spaces, tabs, and line feeds. This is also useful for getting fields to line up in forms.

```
<PRE>text</PRE>
```

Lists

There are several HTML tags, which makes it convenient to display lists of items. Lists can be ordered (numbered), unordered (graphically displayed as bullet items), or appear as columns of terms and definitions. Also, list items can be hyperlinks to other documents on the Web.

Itemized List

This creates a list containing several items, each beginning with `<LI>` and normally indents each item one tab position. There are four types: `<UL>` is an *unordered list* (each entry is normally preceded by a bullet); `<OL>` is an *ordered list* (each entry is numbered); `<MENU>` is a *menu of choices* (similar to but sometimes rendered more compactly); `<DIR>` is a *directory* (designed to be a list broken into two or three columns like a disk directory; in most current browsers, the `<DIR>` element is rendered the same as `<UL>`). These lists can be nested within each other, allowing for complex list rchies such as outlines.

```
<TYPE>
        <LI>text
        <LI>text
        <LI>text
        ...
</TYPE>
```

Definition List

This syntax builds a list in which each entry has two parts, as in a glossary: a *term* (which follows the `<DT>`,) and a *definition* (which follows the `<DD>`). It is normally rendered exactly the same as this section of this chapter, with the definition indented below the term. The optional COMPACT attribute was designed to produce a more vertically compact list in which the terms and definitions are placed in side-by-side columns, but it is ignored by most current browsers.

```
<DL COMPACT>
        <DT>term text
                <DD>definition text
        <DT>term text
                <DD>definition text
        ...
</DL>
```

Forms

The forms feature of HTML is one of the things that gives the Web real power for doing live, interactive applications. The HTML form, however, is only half of this feature. After the user fills out the form, it is submitted to a specialized program, or *script*, which takes the information and does something useful with it (for example, e-mails it to you). You must either write the script yourself (that means programming) or find a prewritten script that will suit your needs. This gets into the topic of the Common Gateway Interface (CGI), which is explored in detail in Chapters 7, 8, and 15. In this chapter, we stick to the HTML side of the process.

Form

The <FORM> element encloses the entire form and gives some basic definitions. The form might take up only part of the HTML document; in fact, a single document can contain several separate forms that perform different functions. The method attribute specifies the way in which information is sent to the HTTP server; the action attribute gives the URL of the script that is to process the submitted information (usually http://.../cgi-bin/*scriptname*).

```
<FORM method="[GET¦POST]" action="URL">form body</FORM>
```

Form Input

This empty tag is used to place different fields in the form to enable users to enter information. The name attribute gives a unique name to the field; the optional value attribute gives a default value for this tag. When the form is submitted, the information is returned as a set of name-value pairs separated by ampersands, such as http://.../cgi-bin/script?*name*=*me*&*address*=*here*&*time*=*now*. The type attribute gives the style of object to be used. (See the following bulleted list.)

```
<INPUT name="text" type="" size=## value="text" CHECKED>
```

- CHECKBOX uses a simple on or off button. The value is ON or OFF.
- RADIO is similar to CHECKBOX, but allows you to pick one choice from many by having several radio tags with the same name but different values. RADIO returns the value attribute of the checked tag. (value is not optional with this type.)
- TEXT places a one-line window to allow users to type in something. The returned value is the text entered.

- IMAGE places an image in the form, allowing users to point to it, returning the *x* and *y* pixel coordinates of the selected location. IMAGE operates similarly to <IMG ISMAP>, but within a form. For this type, the SRC and ALIGN attributes from the <IMG> element are included.

- SUBMIT places a button on the form that submits the form to the action URL in the <FORM> tag. The label for the button is specified by the value attribute.

- RESET clears the form, returning all fields to their default values.

- HIDDEN does not display anything on the form. It allows you to pass nonchangeable information along with the rest of the form (using the name and value attributes).

The CHECKED attribute is used with the CHECKBOX and RADIO types to signify whether the button is selected by default or not. The size attribute is used to set the window size of a text field (in characters).

```
<SELECT name="text" multiple>
        <OPTION value="text" selected>text
        <OPTION value="text">text
        ...
</SELECT>
```

Choice Selection

This presents a list of possible values for the field, itemized by the <OPTION> tag; normally it is displayed as a pull-down menu. The name and value fields are the same as for <INPUT>. The *text* following each <OPTION> tag is displayed in the menu. If no value attribute is given, *text* is returned, if that option is selected. The multiple attribute allows more than one option to be selected, and the selected attribute identifies the default choice. For example:

```
<SELECT name="text">
        <OPTION value="OPT1" selected>Option 1
        <OPTION value="OPT2">Option 2
</SELECT>
```

Multiline Text Input

This is similar to <INPUT TYPE="text">, but allows for many lines. The name attribute is the same as for <INPUT>, whereas the number values for the rows and cols attributes define the size. The *text* contained in the element is shown in the window by default.

```
<TEXTAREA name="text" rows=## cols=##>text</TEXTAREA>
```

Entities

Many characters that appear in documents can be impossible to enter in an HTML file, including characters that have special meaning to HTML (for example, the < and > characters) and international and typographic characters not found on most keyboards.

These characters can be included in documents using *entities*, pieces of text that together signify a single character. The general syntax includes an ampersand, a unique name for the character, and a semicolon. For example, Gröning produces Gröning. There are two general types, as described in the following sections.

Reserved Characters

Reserved characters are normal characters used for other purposes in HTML that can cause confusion if entered by themselves.

Entity	Displayed As
&lt;	Less-than sign (<)
&gt;	Greater-than sign (>)
&amp;	Ampersand (&)
&quote;	Quotation mark (") (usually not necessary)

International Characters

International characters are characters used in most European languages other than English, referenced by names from the ISO Latin 1 character set. A few examples follow:

Entity	Displayed As
&Aacute;	Capital A with acute accent (Á)
&ocirc;	Small o with circumflex accent (ô)
&AElig;	Capital AE ligature (Æ)
&ccedil;	Small c with a cedilla (ç)

The Future of HTML

By the time you read this, the specification for HTML Level 2 should be complete and most browsers should be using this specification as a standard. However, Level 2 does not represent the final form of HTML. This language will continue to evolve, adding new capabilities, for years to come.

Although the current version of HTML has many powerful features, it also has its disadvantages. Suggestions are constantly being given to the HTML working group, which considers them for inclusion into the standard. Enhancements will likely allow a larger variety of documents to be put on the Web, make documents look better, and be easier to manage and use.

The Presentation Versus Structure Debate

The primary area currently evolving is in the formatting of documents. The debate is raging over how much control of the appearance of the document should rest in the hands of the user and how much should be decided by the publisher. Years of research have gone into graphic design and typography, and there are varied methods of using the appearance of text and graphics to communicate a particular message. To designers and publishers who have become experts in this art, it is important that the information contributor have a large degree of control over document appearance.

However, in the World Wide Web, the user can choose fonts, window sizes, colors, and many other presentation variables. Although this is a frustration to many publishers, it is an important part of the Web. Not all users have the same typefaces, colors, and screen area available and must be able to make the WWW page fit their constraints. In addition, physical differences in users place special needs on the appearance of pages; for example, sight-impaired people might want to use very large type; a blind user does not see anything at all and has the document read aloud by the computer.

A compromise must be reached. Information providers need the capability to dictate a large part of the appearance of the document when it is important. On the other hand, users need to be able to override or alter this appearance when necessary. The primary goal of the Web is the dissemination of information; the content of the documents should always be more important than their appearance. Whatever can be done to improve comprehension by users, including both dictated and alterable appearance, is important to that dissemination as well.

For more information about proposed solutions to some of these problems, see Chapter 9, "Netscape Extensions and HTML 3.0."

Alternatives to HTML

It is doubtful that HTML will ever be able to provide all the creative design and functionality that true electronic publishing demands; it was never intended to do so. As the battle has raged over how much HTML should expand, competitors for the online format crown have begun to appear. These file types are generally geared toward more specialized applications, and very little software currently exists for using them. However, some of them will likely become major (perhaps equal or superior to HTML) parts of the World Wide Web.

- **Portable Document Format** (Adobe). PDF, the format used in Adobe Acrobat, has almost every page layout capability that can be imagined. (It is based on PostScript.) Acrobat readers will soon become Internet-savvy and be able to include URL hyperlinks just as HTML does. The disadvantages of using PDF are these: PDF is a closed, proprietary format owned by Adobe; PDF files are much larger than the equivalent HTML file; and PDF is complex, making it difficult for automatic generation by scripts and other software. Other commercial electronic document formats, such as Folio and WordPerfect Envoy, will probably also add these capabilities. For more information, address `http://www.adobe.com/Acrobat/Acrobat0.html`.

- **Hyper-G**. This distributed hypertext system is very similar in purpose to the WWW; in fact, it is probably dumb luck that one caught on and not the other. Hyper-G has a document format called HTF that in some ways is more powerful than HTML.

- **Simple Vector Format/HyperCGM**. Many fields (including Engineering, Graphic Design, and Cartography) need a common format for distributing vector (object-based) graphics. Whether to create a new format from scratch or to alter an existing format such as CGM to allow for hyperlinks is still under debate. Conceivably, a strong vector graphics format could allow for completely graphics-based (rather than document-based) information systems on the Web. For more information, contact `http://www.niiip.org/svf/`.

- **Virtual Reality Modeling Language**. There is also a niche that would like to be able to distribute virtual reality over the Web. The specification is nearing completion and will allow for the design and distribution of "scenes" that give a 3-D look to objects and places on the Web. For information, contact `http://vrml.wired.com/`.

- **The Java Language**. This object-oriented language has been developed by Sun Microsystems to give developers a method to create interactive Web applications. The language is an extension of C++ and has been designed with network security in mind. Currently, you must run the HotJava Web browser from Sun or Netscape Navigator 2.0 to reap the benefits of the interactive capabilities of Java. For more information, see `http://java.sun.com` or *Presenting Java,* by John December, published by Sams.net.

- **Web-savvy word processors**. When you read this, there should be at least two commercial word processors with Web support: Microsoft Word (with Internet Assistant) and WordPerfect (with Internet Publisher). These add-ons will include several new capabilities:

  - HTML creation and conversion within the word processor.

  - The word processor can act as a web browser, reading HTML (so you don't need to get a separate browser like Mosaic or Netscape).

  - Small stand-alone viewers, which can be freely distributed, so that documents can be distributed in their native format (including hypertext links and all the formatting) so people can view them without buying the full word processor.

  For more information, contact the following site:

  `http://www.microsoft.com/msoffice/freestuf/msword/download/ia/default.htm`

Although few of these alternatives are available today, they will soon be around, increasing the flexibility (and confusion) of the WWW. They will probably become most popular in niche markets that require very specialized information types (such as maps, diagrams, and technical illustrations) and with professional publishers who need detailed presentation control that can't, or shouldn't, be part of HTML.

Chapter 6

Image Mapping and Multimedia

- Planning Imagemaps
- Outlining the Basic Steps
- Installing Map This
- Getting LView Pro
- Installing Paint Shop Pro
- The CERN Map File Syntax
- Creating Imagemaps
- Transparent and Interlaced GIFs
- Multimedia
- What's Next?

The World Wide Web became famous because of its capability to integrate graphics and text. This chapter is all about creating interactive Web graphics in HTML.

Chapter 5 introduced you to creating a hyperlink from one HTML file to another. As you recall, links can even reference GIF files, but the amazing thing about links is that they can reference other documents anywhere on the Web. With this capability, you can embed a picture of the Space Shuttle from NASA into your Web page, for example.

This chapter shows you how to mark regions of your Web graphics files as *hotspots*. Hotspots are the area on the GIF file that serve as hyperlinks when the user of the Web client program clicks them with a mouse.

Hotspots are also referred to as *clickable images*. The EMWAC HTTP Server you installed in Chapter 4 supports the use of clickable images. In other words, it can return different documents to the Web browser depending on where in an image the user clicks with a mouse.

Planning Imagemaps

Here are a few words of caution about images on your Web pages. First, don't go overboard with graphics. Large images will not be snappy at the typical modem speeds most Web clients are running today.

Naturally, clickable imagemaps work only with graphically oriented Web browsers. You should always provide alternate text-based methods of accessing the same information. It is a matter of style how you choose to do this. We think it is best to include text-only hyperlinks in addition to the image-mapped links on each page.

Finally, and this is probably obvious, try to choose graphics that are actually relevant to the subject of your Web page.

Outlining the Basic Steps

There are several steps involved in creating clickable imagemaps. Here's the basic plan of attack:

1. Create or obtain a GIF image file and decide where to put the *hotspots*. The graphics should be in GIF format for widest portability among all Web browsers. Use a scanner or a screen capture utility, such as LView Pro or Paint Shop Pro. You can also generate images with any drawing program that can save GIF files.

2. Develop an imagemap file that describes where each hotspot is located. The map file also specifies the URL associated with each hotspot. HTTPS uses the CERN format described below.

3. Reference the imagemap in the HTML file.

4. Always test the clickable imagemap to make sure it works the way you intended.

The sections that follow provide a more detailed view of the steps involved. But first, install Map This and LView Pro. Map This takes the drudgery out of making map files. LView Pro enables you to convert screen captures to GIF files, and to save transparent and interlaced images, which we'll talk about later.

> **Note:** For more information on GIF and other graphics file formats, see *O'Reilly and Associates' Encyclopedia Of Graphics File Formats,* by James D. Murray and William vanRyper.

Installing Map This

Map This is a program designed to create mapping files for clickable images on the World Wide Web. Follow these steps to install Map This directly from the CD-ROM:

1. Run WinZip and click the Open button on the toolbar, choose File/Open Archive, or press Control-O.

2. In the WinZip Open Archive dialog, select your CD-ROM drive, choose the \server directory, and select the file MAPTHIS.ZIP. Choose OK.

3. Click the Extract button on the toolbar, choose Actions/Extract, or press Control-E.

4. In the Extract dialog, specify the directory on your server where you would like to install the program. Choose OK. All the files will be copied from CD to the hard drive.

5. You can make an icon in Program Manager or you can run Map This from File Manager. Consult your Windows NT User's Guide if you are unfamiliar with these steps.

Here is a brief description of the files that Map This installs on your hard disk:

Map This file	Description
ReadMe.WRI	Last minute notes
ServeMe.WRI	Documentation on setting up an imagemap
MapThis.exe	Program
MapThis.hlp	Help file
examples\lake.imp	Sample lake map
examples\lake.gif	Sample GIF for said lake
examples\NSCAFISH.imp	Original map file for NSCA's map example
examples\NSCAFISH.gif	GIF for NSCA's map
examples\CERNdrag.map	Original map file for CERN's map example
examples\CERNdrag.gif	GIF for NSCA's map
examples\readme.txt	Blurb about each map

Getting LView Pro

LView Pro is an image file editor for Microsoft Windows 95 and Windows NT 3.5x. It works with image files in the following formats: JPEG, JFIF, GIF 87a/89a, TIFF, Truevision Targa, Windows and OS/2 BMP, ZSoft's PCX, PBMPLUS' PBM, PGM, and PPM.

LView Pro is an excellent shareware tool for many of the things that you will be doing in this chapter. Unfortunately, we were not able to obtain it for the CD. But don't worry about that: You can get the latest 32-bit version of LView Pro from dozens of places on the Internet. For example, `Yahoo/Computers/Software/Graphics` includes a link to LView Pro. Or you might try `http://www.tucows.com`. Either way, once you have it downloaded, you can unzip it and install it in the same manner as Map This.

Installing Paint Shop Pro

Paint Shop Pro is another very popular graphics shareware program on the Internet. Although it is not yet a Win32 application, it can also handle all the graphics chores that a webmaster is faced with. Many of the instructions we present below are specifically for LView Pro, but the procedures could also be easily applied to Paint Shop Pro.

Paint Shop Pro installs in the same manner as Map This. Just use WinZip as described in the five steps above. You may wish to choose a separate directory on your hard disk for Paint Shop Pro than the one for WinZip. On the other hand, some people like keeping all of their utility programs in one directory called "bin." It is entirely up to you.

You can obtain more information about Paint Shop Pro and Lview Pro from this Web site:

`http://dragon.jpl.nasa.gov/%7eadam/transparent.html#DOS/Windows`

Map Files, the CERN Way

In the CERN hotspot format, which is what the EMWAC HTTP server uses, each line of the map file looks like this:

shape `(x1,y1) (x2,y2) ... (xn,yn) URL`

where `shape` is one of the following:

- `circle`—a circle with two coordinate pairs: center and any edgepoint
- `poly`—a polygon with at most 100 vertices: each coordinate is a vertex
- `rect`—a rectangle with two coordinate pairs: upper-left and lower-right

Coordinates are expressed in *x,y* pairs counting in pixels from the upper-left corner of the image. The URL can point to any resource on the World Wide Web or to a file on your site.

Creating Imagemaps

Let's take a look at creating a map file for a sample image. The first step, as outlined previously, is to obtain a GIF file. You'll use LView Pro to make a screen capture and save it as GIF. Suppose the Web site will have six departments and you want your home page to contain an icon to link to each one. We created a new Program Group in Program Manager, and we dragged six icons into it, as shown in Figure 6.1. If this example doesn't seem too fascinating, you can use any GIF file that suits your needs.

Figure 6.1.
A sample clickable image.

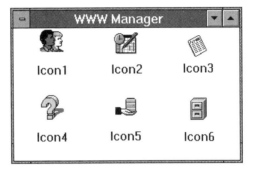

Screen Captures with LView

Here are the steps for creating a GIF file in LView Pro.

1. Load LView Pro.
2. Put the focus back to the window on your desktop that you want to make into a GIF picture. This will make it the *active* window. Position this window so that it doesn't hide the LView Pro menubar.
3. Choose Edit /Capture /Window in LView. You will see LView Pro minimize. Wait a couple of seconds while it processes the image. You will see LView Pro restore itself when the image is ready.
4. Choose File /Save As. In the Save as type: combo box, choose GIF 89a. Name the file and choose the directory in which to save it. We saved ours as window.gif. Choose OK.
5. Exit LView Pro.

Now you have a GIF file to work with in the remaining steps for creating a map file.

Screen Captures with Paint Shop Pro

Alternatively, here are the similar steps for creating a GIF file using Paint Shop Pro:

1. Run Paint Shop Pro.
2. Click the Capture menu and then click Hot Key Setup. Make a mental note of which keystroke is currently configured for making screen captures. Choose OK.

3. Click the Capture menu again and then click the menu item titled Window. This will cause Paint Shop Pro to minimize itself so that you will have an opportunity to arrange your desktop as desired before taking the screen capture. Now is the time to select the active window that you would like to make an image of.

4. Press the hot key configured for screen captures and you will notice that Paint Shop Pro immediately restores itself with a new child window showing a bitmap of the window that had the focus when you pressed the hot key.

5. Choose File/Save As. In the List Files of Type: combo box, choose GIF – Compuserve. In the File Sub-Format: combo box, choose Version 89a. Choose either Interlaced or Noninterlaced (more about that later). Name the file and choose the directory in which to save it. We saved ours as window.gif. Choose OK.

6. Exit Paint Shop Pro.

This leaves you with an image file of your own making, which you can embed in your HTML code. You could also use Paint Shop Pro or LView Pro to edit the image.

The Map File Itself

The second major step is to create the map file that references the hotspots on the GIF file. Here are the instructions to create a map file.

1. Load Map This.

2. Choose File/New.

3. The dialog tells you that you need a GIF file. Choose the button labeled Let's Go Find One.

4. Browse to the location of your GIF file. Select window.gif, which was previously saved from LView Pro. Choose OK.

5. Map This opens the GIF file as the background image on which you can create and select hotspot regions. For example, click the Rectangle tool and use the mouse to select a rectangular area of the GIF file. Repeat this step for each hotspot.

6. Choose File/Save As. It prompts you for information about the map file. Most fields are optional, but the two you must fill in are the Default URL and the Map file format. We will explain these later, but in the meantime please fill in the default URL as http:// www.yourco.com/error.htm. For now, it's fine if this isn't a valid URL. Make sure you check CERN for the Map file format. See Figure 6.2. Choose OK.

7. Now Map This should prompt you separately for each hotspot and ask you for the corresponding URL. See Figure 6.3. Fill in a complete URL like you did in the previous step. When you are finished with each region, you will see the Save As dialog.

8. Map files are usually saved in *.MAP format, so use the Save File As Type combo box to choose Generic Map Files *.Map. Give your map file a filename. You'll probably want to use the same base filename as the GIF file on which it is based. Thus, we saved ours as window.map because it is associated with window.gif. Choose OK.

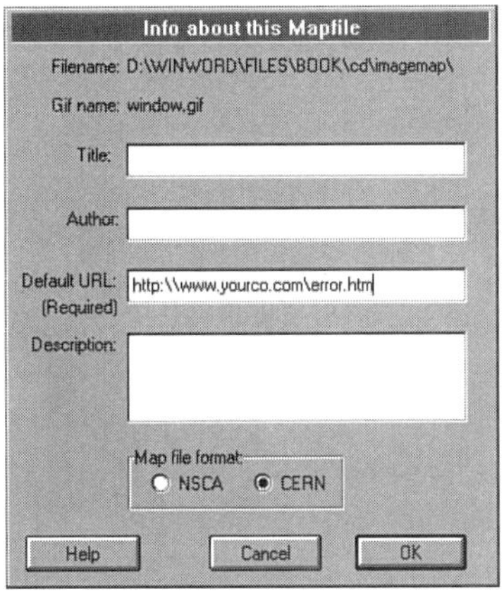

Figure 6.2.
Saving the basic information about the map file.

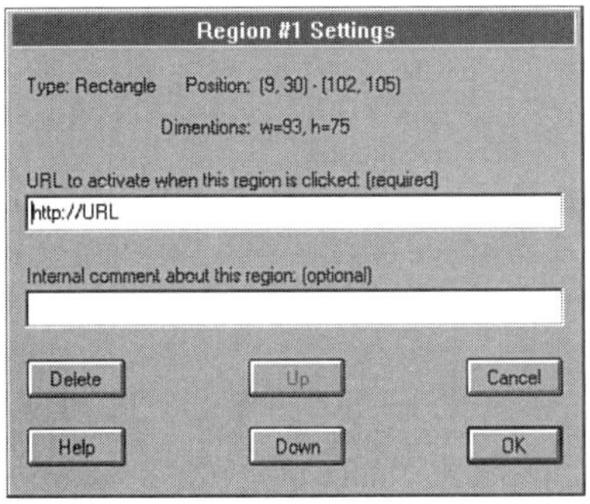

Figure 6.3.
Map This prompting for hotspot URLs.

9. Exit from the Map This program.

Now the file window.map is created by Map This. See the following code segment for the important parts of the file; we have removed the comments. If you view the file created by Map This, you can ignore the comment lines (which begin with #) automatically written by Map This at the top of the file:

```
default http://www.yourco.com/error.htm
rect (9,30) (102,105) http://URL goes here/icon1.htm
rect (110,31) (197,106) http://URL goes here/icon2.htm
rect (211,31) (297,100) http://URL goes here/icon3.htm
rect (22,110) (88,185) http://URL goes here/icon4.htm
rect (106,109) (201,196) http://URL goes here/icon5.htm
rect (214,118) (300,182) http://URL goes here/icon6.htm
```

Note that window.map contains several invalid URLs. The default URL is the one filled out in step 6 above. The URL for each hotspot will echo what you entered in step 7. If you don't know your official domain name at the time you are working through this chapter, it is OK to leave window.map as is. When you do get your official domain name and have your HTML directory structure established, you can return to the map file and edit it with a simple text editor. Either way, it is much easier than using a text editor to enter the *x,y* pixel coordinates by hand.

If the URL you want to use in a map file contains a # (indicating a location within a document), you should quote the full URL (starting with http://) in the map file so that the server issues a redirection message to the client. Note that the # we are referring to here is not the same as the # that serves to mark comment lines in the map file.

This last point is rather subtle, so perhaps a deeper explanation is in order. The # characters (some people call them pound signs, others call them sharp signs) can be used in two cases: as comments in a map file or within any URL to refer to a bookmark location within an HTML file. Because map files can contain URLs, the second usage can appear in a map file—but that usage is distinct from comment characters.

> **Tip:** In general, it is a good idea to always use the full URL (starting with http://) in the map file for all hyperlinks.

How It Works

The coordinates from a user's mouse click are passed from the client to your server. The server then searches the map file to determine whether the click is within any hotspots. If a valid match is found, the corresponding URL is used to send a document to the Web browser. If no match is found, a default URL is returned. A default URL is necessary for the times when someone clicks a spot that isn't hot, so to speak. There are a few ways to handle this. Our preference is to return an error message with a link back to the image map file so they can try again. See Listing 6.1 for an example, called error.htm.

Listing 6.1. error.htm: How to handle clicks that aren't within any hotspot.

```
<HTML>
<HEAD>
<!-- Created: 9/20/95 9:20:31 PM -->
<TITLE>Imagemap ERROR</TITLE>
</HEAD>
<BODY>
<H1>Imagemap Error</H1>
You have selected an area of the Imagemap that is not valid. Please try again.<P>
<A HREF="http://your domain/xyz.htm">[Return]</A>
<HR>
Last Updated: Wednesday, September 20, 1995
</BODY>
</HTML>
```

Referencing Clickable Imagemaps in HTML Files

The next major step in creating an imagemap is to let the Web browser know that it's accessing an HTML file with an inline image that is a clickable imagemap. This is done by adding the ISMAP qualifier to the <IMG> tag within the A HREF. For example:

```
<A HREF="image.map"><IMG SRC="image.gif" ISMAP></A>
```

It is important to understand why there are two filenames in this code. This is how mouse clicks to the image are hyperlinked to documents (via the map file URLs), which could be anywhere on the Internet.

Syntactically, you have three options when specifying either of the filenames in the preceding code above. You can use no pathname at all, in which case the files are assumed to be in the current directory; you can include a local pathname (either relative or absolute); or you can use a complete URL. Before you decide that the first answer is obviously the easiest, you should know that it doesn't work on all Web servers. Some servers require a pathname. If this describes your server or if you place the map file or the GIF file in a different directory than the HTML page, you will need to use a pathname.

The third option—using a complete URL—will always work, even for files on your own Web site. Actually, that isn't as inefficient as it seems because the URL is probably cached in the server, so it will result in a nearly instantaneous look-up.

See the following HTML code for what is needed to tie all of this together. The key lines that form the association between the map file and the GIF file are marked in bold.

```
<html>
<head><title>A Windows NT Program Group</title></head>
<body>
<h1>WWW Manager "a sample imagemap"</h1>
<hr>
Point and click on an icon:<p>
<hr>
<A HREF="window.map">
<IMG SRC="window.gif" ISMAP>
</A>
<hr>
</body>
```

Note the use of the ISMAP attribute in the <IMG> tag. This tells the client to append the mouse coordinates to the URL when it sends it to the server. The URL in the enclosing <A> anchor must refer to a map file on the HTTP Server, with the extension .map. This file contains the information that maps the image coordinates to the URL. Only the URL is returned to the client.

Testing the Imagemap

As with all HTML files, it is important to test all functions of the file, especially when you are using image mapping or CGI Scripts. Always test your imagemaps completely. It never fails that the one link you don't check will have something wrong with it.

Transparent and Interlaced GIFs

As you browse the Web, you will notice that some of the pages you come across will have inline images that blend into the background, have a fade-in effect, or both. These images are known as *transparent and interlaced GIFs.*

Transparent GIFs will appear to blend in smoothly with the user's display, even when the user has set a background color that differs from the default. If the Web browser supports transparency, the background color of the GIF will be replaced by the browser's background color.

Transparent GIFs make sense only for images that are considered to have a solid background and a foreground with some *holes* in it. For example, an image of the American flag probably wouldn't have anything in the foreground that could be made transparent. Conversely, in an image of a company logo that reads YourCo, Inc., in blue letters on a white background, the gaps between the letters could be made transparent so that the characters would show through on any background.

Interlaced GIFs, on the other hand, will appear first as a full image in low resolution and continue to gain resolution until the entire image is loaded. Normally an image will load from the top row to the bottom row. Interlaced images enable the user to get a good idea about what the image will look like (while the user is reading the text of the page). Of course, the browser must have the capability to display interlaced images for the desired effect. The good news is that browsers that do not support interlaced images will just display the image in a top-down fashion as usual.

Even more good news is that both LView Pro and Paint Shop Pro can create transparent and interlaced GIFs! Either of these programs will come in handy for many of your day-to-day graphics needs, including screen shots, graphics file format conversions, and creating transparent and interlaced GIFs.

In addition to LView Pro and Paint Shop Pro, there are a dozen or so form-based Web pages that will conduct your GIF file conversions directly from the Web. One of the best that we have found is the Image Machine, `http://www.vrl.com/Imaging/index.html`.

Making Transparent and Interlaced GIFs with LView

Here are the steps for creating transparent and interlaced GIFs using LView Pro.

1. Start LView Pro, if it is not already running.
2. Choose File/Open. Select your image and choose OK to load it.

3. Choose Retouch/Background Color.

4. Check the option titled "Mask selection using" (optional).

5. From the color palette at the top of the dialog, select the color square that corresponds to your background color. See Figure 6.4. Choose OK.

Figure 6.4.
Setting Background Color in LView.

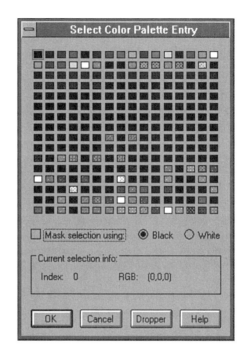

Next, set LView Pro to save your GIF in Interlaced format. This is just one step:

1. Choose File/Properties/GIF and check both options, "Save Interlaced" and "Save Transparent Color Information to GIF89a Files." Choose OK.

Finally, save the GIF in GIF89a format:

1. Choose File/Save As.

2. Select GIF 89a (*.gif) from the combo box list of file types.

3. Rename your file if you want to. Choose OK.

That's all there is to it; you now have a Transparent and Interlaced GIF.

Adding Multimedia to Your Web Pages

Chapter 18, "The Future of the Web," discusses some awesome new Web capabilities regarding multimedia. In the meantime, you can create multimedia embedded HTML pages without those advanced techniques. All you need to do is add links in your page to the multimedia file that you want presented.

Suppose you want a person browsing your page to be able to play a Windows Audio WAV recording of you welcoming them to your Web page. If the WAV file containing your welcome message is named welcome.wav, simply add the link with the <A> tag, just as you would add any other link on your page. For example:

```
<A HREF="welcome.wav">Press Here for Welcome Message</A>
```

Wow! That was easy. Well, not so fast. You can create a link to any type of file on your page, and once the person presses the hyperlink, the file will be transported to the client application (Web browser) via HTTP. The key to all of this is that the Web browser on the receiving end of this link must be configured to handle the incoming file.

Most Web browsers are configured to handle *.html, *.htm, *.txt, and *.gif files. These and other standard file types are given a MIME type. See the following sidebar for a basic discussion of MIME. For file types other than the basic ones mentioned above, you just need to configure your Web browser to handle the MIME type of that associated file.

What is MIME?

MIME stands for Multipurpose Internet Mail Extensions. MIME is a standard for Internet e-mail attachments and for Web multimedia documents sent through HTTP. The reason that this comes up in both of these applications is that both are frequently used to transfer binary files such as graphics, audio, and video. Basically, MIME encodes/decodes binary data into 7-bit ASCII using an algorithm called *base 64*. The reason it is converted to ASCII is that e-mail only supports a 7-bit word size to ensure compatibility with all computer systems on the Internet.

If you would like to know all the details, see the Request For Comments. MIME is defined by RFC 1341. See Appendix D for more information about obtaining selected RFCs.

In addition to configuring your Web browser to be aware of the file type, you will also need an application capable of displaying or playing the file. For several types of multimedia files, you already have an application that can handle this job. Windows NT includes Media Player 32, which can play AVI, MID, and WAV files. Just follow these steps to configure Netscape Navigator to use Media Player 32:

1. Run Navigator and choose Options/Preferences. Select the Helper Apps tab in the dialog box that appears.

2. Now you will see a list of all the MIME types that Navigator is configured to handle. Highlight the MIME type with the file extension .wav. Check the Launch the Application radio button. See Figure 6.5.

Figure 6.5.
Configuring Navigator MIME types.

3. Choose Browse and select mplay32.exe. It should be in the system32 directory where you installed Windows NT.

4. Choose OK.

Netscape Navigator is now configured to launch Media Player 32 any time you click a hyperlink to a file type of *.wav. Now you can go through the same steps for *.avi files.

Note that in step 2, there are other options for the Action radio button. You don't have to configure Navigator to launch an application for every MIME file type. For example, when plain text files are received by Navigator through HTTP, you can choose View in Browser or Save to Disk.

Throughout the Internet you will find Windows applications for playing a variety of multimedia formats. You can find an application capable of playing your desired multimedia format by searching through the application archives found in Appendix C.

Netscape Navigator is set up by default to handle many more MIME types than the ones mentioned here, including *.au and *.aiff files for audio.

What's Next?

The next chapter takes another brave step into the heart of HTML: CGI programming. The topics covered are not for lightweights. However, those who stick it out will see the awesome potential of the Web unveiled.

Chapter 7

Introduction to Web Forms and CGI Scripts

- How CGI Works
- Choosing a CGI Programming Language for the EMWAC Server
- CGI Environment Variables
- Understanding Input/Output with CGI
- Testing CGI Systems
- What's Next?

The Common Gateway Interface (CGI) is a standard that governs how external applications are interfaced with Web servers. The reasoning behind the invention of CGI is simple: Without it, the HTTP specification and all Web servers would have become a patchwork of ad-hoc extensions.

CGI gives a way to write programs that will run on the server when they are invoked by the client Web browser through HTML code. Naturally, these programs can be written in C language. But C is just one possibility. For a discussion of other options, see the section on "Choosing a Programming Language for CGI."

At this point, the astute reader might have noticed that there are no fewer than four areas of programming prowess needed to get this dog to hunt! Just count 'em: CGI, HTTP, HTML, and C (or some other programming language). And just for good measure, you might want to throw in the Win32 API and SQL, depending on what your Web program will actually do once you finish laying the required groundwork.

The reason we choose to run this challenging gauntlet is that CGI opens the door to great new opportunities. CGI programs are often associated with Web forms. When the user finishes filling out an HTML form and submits it, the data stream that is returned to the server is called the *form data*. Keep in mind that just because you send a blank HTML form to the client Web browser, nothing is going to happen with the form data when it is submitted—unless you make it happen. (In fact, the form data would just land in the bit bucket if not for CGI.) For example, CGI is a necessity if you want to save the form data into a database on the server. Perhaps the form data should be e-mailed to the Webmaster or some other party. Maybe the intent of the form is to have some data faxed or e-mailed back to the client. Or the form could be used to obtain a database query from the user, which is then sent to a database engine before the formatted results are finally returned to the client as an HTML file. These are just some of the possibilities available to anyone brave enough to master the details of client/server Web programming with CGI. (Actually, tools exist so that much of this can be done without programming.)

Although all of these things can be accomplished with traditional programming, doing it on the Web makes applications platform-independent, distributed, easier to update, and easier to develop.

If you prefer not to do your own programming, you might be thinking that we have gone back on one of our promises to provide everything ready to run. Although we will continue to live up to that promise, we confess that the next two chapters on CGI do contain some advanced material. So here's the plan. After giving you a background on CGI in this chapter, we will walk you through a simple sample program. This program, however, doesn't really do anything practical, so in Chapter 8 we will describe a useful CGI program that is already compiled on the CD and ready to run. You don't need to know C language or CGI to take advantage of that program. Chapter 8, "Power Programming with CGI," concludes with a discussion of several CGI programming tools, some of which also remove the burden of needing to know a programming language. If you prefer not to get into programming, you can choose to skip or skim most of these two chapters. When you are ready to tap the extended potential of your Web server, you can come back to the subject of CGI.

CGI programs are also called CGI *scripts* or *applications*. The reason they are called scripts is that they can be written in Perl or the UNIX command shell, in which case they are interpreted rather than compiled. When the C language or Visual Basic is used for CGI, the terms *CGI program* or *CGI application* are preferred to CGI script. Some people just refer to all such things as CGIs.

How CGI Works

Figure 7.1 shows a high-level overview of how CGI forms-processing works. There are many other details of HTTP and TCP/IP than what are shown here, but we omit those in order to concentrate on the basic concepts of CGI.

Figure 7.1.
How CGI processes Web forms.

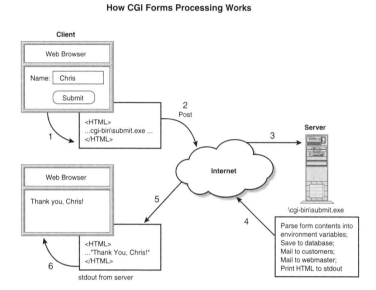

The annotated steps corresponding to Figure 7.1 follow. (We assume you are familiar with the way an HTML file gets created and displayed in the Web browser, which is where we pick up the story with step 1.)

1. After the user has completed his entry of the form data in the Web browser, he chooses the Submit button, which is coded between the <FORM> and </FORM> tags in the HTML file. The submit button is a link to a CGI application on the server. For more information about HTML Forms, see Chapter 5 and/or Chapter 10.

2. The browser uses the POST method of the HTTP protocol to send the form data to the server. The GET method could also be used, but POST is preferred for FORM data.

3. The data travels through the Internet and arrives at the server, which then passes the data to the CGI application.

4. In addition to parsing the form data and processing it as desired, the CGI application must write the HTML response that will be sent back to the client. The CGI specification says that the Web server should read the stdout device of the CGI application.

5. The server adds appropriate HTTP header information and sends the output of the CGI application back through the Internet as an HTML response file, which the Web browser receives in memory.

6. The browser interprets the HTML code and displays the results on the screen for the user. At a minimum, this file should usually contain some notification that the data was processed by the server, followed by a hyperlink to jump the user back to the HTML page he was on before choosing the link to the form page. In other words, put the client back where he was before he came to step 1 of this list. Got that?

Caution: Allowing any person with a Web browser to execute applications on your server is a security concern. It is a good idea to ensure that all the CGI applications are isolated to one directory and that no one else has access to that directory. On the Final Bit Solutions server, all CGI applications are kept in a directory called cgi-bin under the server root. Be careful about using public-domain CGI applications that have not been tested over time to be secure.

Choosing a CGI Programming Language for the EMWAC Server

The EMWAC HTTP server conforms to the Common Gateway Interface (CGI) 1.1 standard. The CGI application must be a Windows NT console-mode program and be located within the HTTP data directory tree. EMWAC CGI applications cannot be GUI programs, nor Windows NT services or DOS programs. However, as discussed in Chapter 15, "Databases and the Web," Windows NT will let you launch a GUI program from within a console-mode CGI application. The current version of EMWAC does not support WinCGI.

In UNIX, which is where the Web got its start, CGI applications are frequently written in C, Perl, or the UNIX shell command language. In Windows NT, you can use C/C++ or Perl with most servers, and Visual Basic with some. Many Windows NT webmasters run a public-domain Perl 4 interpreter for CGI and site statistics. Perl 5, which includes some nice object-oriented extensions, has just hit the scene a little too late for inclusion with this book, but you can easily find it on the Internet (by searching Yahoo, for instance).

Both Perl and C have their advocacy camps. Perl offers great file and string handling, and the code is fairly easy to write and modify. On the other hand, because C is a compiled language, it offers better efficiency, both from the optimization of the compiled code and the fact that the interpreter is not launched every time. In addition, many claim that compiled programs provide better security than scripts because hackers can more easily modify the text of a script just before its execution.

We will be using C language in this chapter and the next. The C programs have been compiled with Borland C++ and Visual C++. The makefile for Borland C++ 4.02 is on the CD. In Chapter 15, you'll construct two more CGI systems: One uses a powerful CGI tool that doesn't require programming, and the second integrates C++ and Visual Basic to talk to any Access or ODBC database.

CGI Environment Variables

The server uses environment variables to pass information to the CGI application. The environment variables are set after the HTTP GET or POST request is received (see the next section) and before the server executes the CGI application. You will find that most environment variables are fairly standard from server to server, but be aware that there are some differences. Nothing stops the maker of a Web server from adding environment variables for his or her own use.

The CGI standard specifies certain environment variables that are used for conveying information to a CGI script. The following subset of those environment variables are supported by the EMWAC HTTP server. Please don't despair; most CGI programs don't need to use all of these environment variables:

CONTENT_LENGTH—The length of the content as given by the client.

CONTENT_TYPE—For queries that have attached information, such as POST and PUT, this is the content type of the data.

GATEWAY_INTERFACE—The revision of the CGI specification to which this server complies. Format: CGI/revision.

HTTP_ACCEPT—The MIME types that the client will accept. Format: type/subtype, type/subtype.

PATH_INFO—The extra path information, as given by the client. This enables scripts to be accessed by their virtual pathname.

QUERY_STRING—The information that follows the ? in the URL that referenced this script. This is the query information.

REMOTE_ADDR—The IP address of the remote host making the request.

REQUEST_METHOD   The method with which the request was made, such as GET, HEAD, and POST.

SCRIPT_NAME—A virtual path to the script being executed.

SERVER_NAME—The server's hostname, DNS alias, or IP address.

SERVER_PROTOCOL—The name and revision of the information protocol this request came in with. Format: protocol/revision.

SERVER_PORT—The port number to which the request was sent.

SERVER_SOFTWARE—The name and version of the server software answering the request. Format: name/version.

Other HTTP headers received from the client are available in environment variables of the form HTTP_*. For instance, the User-Agent: header value is available in HTTP_USER_AGENT. Note that "-" in the header names is replaced by "_" in the corresponding environment variable names.

An understanding of the HTTP specification is probably a prerequisite to a full understanding of the purpose of some of these environment variables.

Understanding Input/Output with CGI

The CGI application accesses information about how it was invoked through the environment variables initialized by the Web server; it reads any information supplied by the client (in a POST request) via stdin and sends output to the client through stdout. It's actually pretty simple, once you get the hang of it.

GET and POST

GET and POST are two HTTP methods of sending form data to the Web server. When you write a form in HTML 2.0, you should specify which HTTP method the browser will use when the form data is sent back to the server.

Take a look at a short block of HTML code that comprises a complete form. See Listing 7.1. The line numbers are not a part of the HTML code. Note in line 2 that the form is using Method="POST". We could just as easily change it to "GET". The main difference between GET and POST is that the CGI application will receive the POST data by reading the stdin device, whereas GET data would be received on the command line and in the QUERY_STRING environment variable.

Listing 7.1. A short and sweet HTML form.

```
1. <HTML><HEAD><TITLE>Simple Form</TITLE></HEAD><BODY>
2. <FORM Method="POST"
3. Action="http://url\cgi-bin\prog.exe">
4. Your Name: <INPUT Name="user" SIZE="30"><P>
5. <INPUT Type=submit Value="Click here to send">
6. </FORM></BODY></HTML>
```

Usually, your forms will be much more complex than this one, which contains only one input field. Because many operating systems impose some limit to the length of the command line, it is usually best to use POST. On the other hand, if you know your form data is small, you can use GET.

CGI Command Lines

In the case of a GET request (or ISINDEX, discussed in Chapter 15), the form data will be on the command line and in the QUERY_STRING environment variable. The command line will contain a question mark after the application name as the delimiter that marks the beginning of the form data. For example, suppose you change the HTML code in Listing 7.1 to use Method="GET", and the user types in the string User's Name in the text field named user.

The command line of the CGI application would look like this:

```
\cgi-bin\prog.exe?user=User%27s+Name
```

The QUERY_STRING environment variable would look like this:

```
user=User%27s+Name.
```

Our first observation is that this looks pretty strange. Our second observation is that the QUERY_STRING variable is somewhat more friendly looking than the command line, so let's work with it.

Now let's try to figure out what's going on with all those funny characters. Recall from line 4 of Listing 7.1 that we named the input field user. Now that label is being sent back to us as the first word of QUERY_STRING. Everything after the equals sign in the QUERY_STRING represents the data that the user typed into that particular field. Because more than one field could be used, each one must be named uniquely in the HTML form and in the QUERY_STRING data that is sent back to the CGI application.

Remember that our example assumes the user typed User's Name with no period on the end. (If he had typed a period, that would be another story.) Checking the QUERY_STRING above, we notice that we almost have exactly what the user typed, except for the %27, which replaces the apostrophe and the plus sign, which replaces the space character.

HTTP calls for these translations because of operating system conventions for reserved characters in filenames. The same mechanism is used by HTTP to pass URLs, so the server needs to be able to distinguish between the two.

The percent sign is a hex escape character, and the two digits that follow it are used to indicate the ASCII code of a reserved character. Here, the apostrophe sign has a hex code of 27. If a period were typed by the user, it would be replaced by %2E. Not all servers encode these characters, because whether they are reserved or not depends on the operating system. For example, the apostrophe and the period are legal in some UNIX systems.

The plus sign is simply the convention for encoding space characters. Another common translation is the dash character encoded as an underscore.

Finally, if there were other input fields in the HTML form, they would follow the data of the user field. Each *name=value* pair would be separated by an ampersand (&) character.

Summary of Seven Funny Characters

Table 7.1 is a quick review of the special characters you will come across in CGI. Some of these conventions make up what is known as URL-encoding.

Table 7.1. Special characters in CGI.

+ (plus sign)	Used in place of space characters in user input.
= (equals sign)	Used to separate the field name from the field value.
? (question mark)	Used to mark the beginning of the form data on the command line.
_ (underscore)	Used to replace dash characters.
% (percent sign)	Used to encode reserved ASCII characters, followed by two hex digits.
& (ampersand)	Used as the boundary between name/value pairs for each field in the HTML form.
# (number sign)	Used in URLs to indicate a section within an HTML document, sort of like a bookmark. This is not strictly related to CGI; it can be used in any URL to an HTML document that contains an <A> tag with a Name attribute (called an anchor).

Reading from STDIN

Recall that QUERY_STRING is not used for the POST method. Because POST is probably more typical, you need to understand how to read stdin to retrieve form data.

First, the server will set the CONTENT_LENGTH environment variable to tell how many bytes to read from stdin. You should not read more than that amount.

Other than that, the POST-invoked program will read and parse the form data from the stdin device instead of the QUERY_STRING environment variable. Either way, you'll want to have some standard routines in C or Perl to help you perform standard decoding. The C programs in this chapter (as well as Chapters 8 and 15) include several useful functions for that purpose. Feel free to customize them and use them in your own programs.

Writing to stdout

When the CGI application is done parsing and processing the input data, it must send a reply to the server. The server will forward the reply to the client after applying a header as per the rules of the HyperText Transfer Protocol.

The server will be listening to the stdout device of the CGI application while the latter is executing. The CGI program can generate HTML code on the fly or refer the server to another document that it would like to have sent instead. Either you want to compose an HTML document on the fly or you want to refer to another document—via HTTP, FTP, or Gopher—anywhere on the Web.

See the section titled "A Simple CGI Example in HTML and C" for all the details about composing an HTML response document from within the CGI application.

If you wanted the server to send another document that already exists, you could use the Location code. In C, you would execute a `printf` that looks something like this:

```
printf("Location: ftp://FQDN/dir/filename.txt\n\n");
```

You must follow the header information with a blank line; thus, there are two newline characters in the example.

Tip: It is very important that your CGI program prints out an extra blank line after the HTTP header and before the document contents. This is a common source of trouble when trying to debug CGI systems.

How To Learn More About CGI

The granddaddy of all CGI information centers on the Internet is NCSA, the National Center for Supercomputing Applications at the University of Illinois. Full details of how to write CGI scripts are given in the CGI specification, which can be found online at `http://hoohoo.ncsa.uiuc.edu/cgi/`. You will find that NCSA has CGI material at all levels from beginning to advanced, as well as a CGI test suite where you can try the programs and see the code. At the time we write this, version 1.1 is the latest CGI specification. It is not available as a single document, rather it consists of several hyperlinked pages maintained at NCSA.

The subject of writing CGI programs under Windows is covered in Appendix G, "The Windows CGI 1.2 Interface." Bob Denny wrote the WinCGI specification in order to provide CGI capability in the WebSite product he developed with O'Reilly for Windows. He has kindly given his permission for this reprint. Windows programs do not access the CGI environment variables in quite the same fashion as in DOS and UNIX.

For further information about CGI, please check out these other resources:

- One of the best CGI and HTML documents available anywhere on the Internet is written by Michael Grobe at the University of Kansas. You'll find "An Instantaneous Introduction to CGI Scripts and HTML Forms" at `http://kufacts.cc.ukans.edu/info/forms/forms-intro.html`.

- For a nice introduction to HTML forms and CGI, see

  `http://www.utirc.utoronto.ca/HTMLdocs/NewHTML/htmlindex.html`. This URL is case-sensitive.

- David Robinson has written an independent and detailed version of the CGI specification. Unlike the NCSA specification, his version exists as a single document available in either HTML or Postscript format (which means it is easy to print), and it gives a fine description of all CGI environment variables. See `http://www.ast.cam.ac.uk/%7Edrtr/`.

■ Whether you want to post a question about a CGI roadblock, or you need help with or just pick up tips by reading the threads of others, the CGI newsgroup is definitely the place to be: comp.infosystems.www.authoring.cgi.

■ Last but not least, don't forget to visit www.yahoo.com. Select Computers/WWW/ CGI.

A Simple CGI Example in HTML and C

This section covers a complete CGI transaction, from server to client, back to server, and back to client. This example is not intended to be useful, except as a template from which you could build a more sophisticated CGI application.

The CGI system you are going to build here starts with an HTML file that contains a form. When the form data is submitted by the user, the server will determine that the Action attribute for the form refers to a CGI application. The server will start the application and send it the form data on stdin. Then the server will listen for stdout from the CGI application.

The CGI program is written in C. The program will show you how to retrieve the form data, parse it, and send back an HTML document. The HTML response is constructed within the CGI application because you should embed part of the form data in your response. You don't always have to create HTML on the fly from inside the CGI program, but doing so will make your Web pages more dynamic.

The Data Entry Form

In order to demonstrate CGI, we need to start with an HTML page that contains a URL to a CGI application. Listing 7.2 is the HTML code that gets the ball rolling with our sample CGI program. Figure 7.2 shows the data entry form in the browser as the user is filling it out.

Listing 7.2. The HTML code that creates the form.

```
<HTML>
<HEAD>
<!-- Created: 8/21/95 7:48:53 PM -->
<TITLE>CGI Application Example</TITLE>
</HEAD>
<BODY>
<H1>CGI Application Example</H1>
This is an example of a cgi application handling the data from a form. <BR>
<FORM ACTION="http://www.fbsolutions.com/cgi-bin/cgisamp.exe" METHOD="Post">
Please enter your first name: <INPUT NAME="name" TYPE="text"><p>
<input type=submit value="When done, click here!">
</FORM>
</BODY>
</HTML>
```

Figure 7.2.
The data entry form that the user fills out.

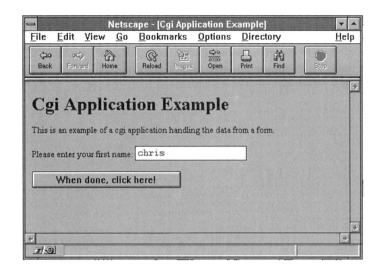

The C Code

Before we show you the C program that will process the form data, we'll discuss the output of the C program. Listing 7.3 is the HTML code that is sent back to the client after the server obtains it from stdout of the CGI application.

Listing 7.3. The HTML code that is written to stdout by cgisamp.c.

```
<HEAD><TITLE>Submitted OK</TITLE></HEAD>
<BODY><h2>The information you supplied has been accepted.<br> Thank You chris</h2>
<h3><A href="http://www.fbsolutions.com/book/cgisamp.htm">[Return]</a></h3></BODY>
```

Figure 7.3 shows the browser on the client side after the CGI application has finished processing the form data. Note in Listing 7.3 and Figure 7.3 that the HTML response sent by the CGI application is customized for each set of form data; it includes the name the user supplied.

Listing 7.4 shows the complete C program called cgisamp, which is executed by the server when the client submits the form data. Here is a quick list of the five functions in cgisamp:

- strcvrt—Converts all occurrences of one character to another within a given string.
- TwoHex2Int—Called when a percent character marks an escape code.
- UrlDecode—Expands all the escape codes by calling TwoHex2Int.
- StoreField—Retrieves field/value pairs from the form data.
- main—Reads the form data from stdin and writes the HTML response to stdout.

Figure 7.3.
The result of the CGI application as seen by the client.

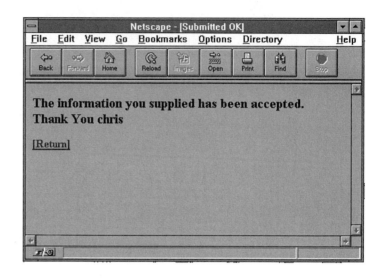

Listing 7.4. The CGI application written in C language.

```
/*****************************************************************************
 *   File: cgisamp.c
 *
 *   Use: CGI Example Script.
 *
 *   Notes: Assumes it is invoked from a form and that REQUEST_METHOD is POST.
 *   Ensure that you compile this script as a console mode app.
 *
 *   This script is a modified version of the script that comes with EMWAC
 *       HTTPS.
 *
 *   Date: 8/21/95
 *   Christopher L. T. Brown   clbrown@netcom.com
 *
 *****************************************************************************/
#include <stdio.h>
#include <stdlib.h>
#include <string.h>
#include <ctype.h>
#include <io.h>

char InputBuffer[4096];
static char * field;
static char * name;

/* Convert all cOld characters   */
/* in cStr into cNew characters. */
void strcvrt(char *cStr, char cOld, char cNew)
{
        int i = 0;

        while(cStr[i])
        {
                if(cStr[i] == cOld)
                        cStr[i] = cNew;
```

```
                i++;
        }
}

/* The string starts with two hex */
/* characters.  Return an integer */
/* formed from them.              */
static int TwoHex2Int(char *pC)
{
        int Hi, Lo, Result;

        Hi = pC[0];
        if('0' <= Hi && Hi <= '9')
                Hi -= '0';
        else if('a' <= Hi && Hi <= 'f')
                Hi -= ('a' - 10);
        else if('A' <= Hi && Hi <= 'F')
                Hi -= ('A' - 10);

        Lo = pC[1];
        if('0' <= Lo && Lo <= '9')
                Lo -= '0';
        else if('a' <= Lo && Lo <= 'f')
                Lo -= ('a' - 10);
        else if('A' <= Lo && Lo <= 'F')
                Lo -= ('A' - 10);

        Result = Lo + 16 * Hi;
        return(Result);
}

/* Decode the given string in-place */
/* by expanding %XX escapes.        */
void urlDecode(char *p)
{
        char *pD = p;

        while(*p)
        {
                if (*p == '%')          /* Escape: next 2 chars are hex          */
                {                               /* representation of the actual character.*/
                        p++;
                        if(isxdigit(p[0]) && isxdigit(p[1]))
                        {
                                *pD++ = (char)TwoHex2Int(p);
                                p += 2;
                        }
                }
                else
                        *pD++ = *p++;
        }
        *pD = '\0';
}

/* Parse out and store field=value items. */
/* Don't use strtok!                       */
void StoreField(char *f, char *Item)
```

continues

Listing 7.4. continued

```c
{
        char *p;

        p = strchr(Item, '=');
        *p++ = '\0';
        urlDecode(Item);
        urlDecode(p);
        strcvrt(p, '\n', ' ');
        strcvrt(p, '+', ' ');          /* Get rid of those nasty +'s */
        field = f;                     /* Hold on to the field just in case. */
        name = p;                      /* Hold on to the name to print*/
}

int main(void)
{
        int ContentLength, x, i;
        char *p,
                *pRequestMethod,
                *URL,
                *f;

        /* Turn buffering off for stdin.*/
        setvbuf(stdin, NULL, _IONBF, 0);

        /* Tell the client what we're going to send */
        printf("Content-type: text/html\n\n");

        /* What method were we invoked through? */
        pRequestMethod = getenv("REQUEST_METHOD");

        /* Get the data from the client       */
        if(strcmp(pRequestMethod,"POST") == 0)
        {
                /* according to the requested method.*/
                /* Read in the data from the client. */
                p = getenv("CONTENT_LENGTH");
                if(p != NULL)
                        ContentLength = atoi(p);
                else
                        ContentLength = 0;
                if(ContentLength > sizeof(InputBuffer) -1)
                        ContentLength = sizeof(InputBuffer) -1;

                i = 0;
                while(i < ContentLength)
                {
                        x = fgetc(stdin);
                        if(x == EOF)
                                break;
                        InputBuffer[i++] = x;
                }
                InputBuffer[i] = '\0';
                ContentLength = i;

                p = getenv("CONTENT_TYPE");
                if(p == NULL)
                        return(0);
```

```
        if(strcmp(p, "application/x-www-form-urlencoded") == 0)
        {
                p = strtok(InputBuffer, "&");        /* Parse the data */
                while(p != NULL)
                {
                        StoreField(f, p);
                        p = strtok(NULL, "&");
                }
        }
    }

    URL = getenv("HTTP_REFERER");                /* What url called me.*/
    printf("<HEAD><TITLE>Submitted OK</TITLE></HEAD>\n");
    printf("<BODY><h2>The information you supplied has been accepted.");
    printf("<br> Thank You %s</h2>\n", name);
    printf("<h3><A href=\"%s\">[Return]</a></h3></BODY>\n", URL);

    return(0);
}
```

Notice the calls in the main routine to the C library function getenv(). That is how the program can determine if the REQUEST_METHOD is equal to POST and how many bytes it should read by checking CONTENT_LENGTH.

Another very important point to make about the main function is that it must output a partial HTTP header to go with the HTML document that it creates. This line appears near the top of the function:

```
    printf("Content-type: text/html\n\n");
```

You might want to add error handling later, in which case you would probably create an alternative HTML response document. This HTTP header would need to be printed in any case. The CGI convention requires that the header be followed by a blank line before the HTML code that is sent. That is why the printf includes two newlines at the end. Forgive our frequent reminders, but this is an important point.

Content type indicates a MIME encoding that tells the client browser that the data stream to follow is HTML code in ASCII format. There are several standard MIME encoding types. See the CGI specification or the EMWAC HTTPS documentation for further information.

The Shortest CGI Script

There is a standard MIME type for plain ASCII text, Content type: text/plain. This is useful in a trivial but interesting example of CGI, which is often used as proof that the Web server and CGI are installed and running properly. The idea is to invoke a .cmd file that echoes the values of the CGI environment variables on the server back to the Web browser. All you need to do is save the following text into a file named test.cmd in the cgi-bin directory:

```
echo content-type: text/plain
echo.
echo script_name = %script_name%
```

Then write a line in your home page that links to test.cmd. The program should tell you its name. You could easily modify this to output other environment variables as well.

Testing CGI Systems

Getting CGI systems to work properly obviously requires the ability to integrate several sophisticated tools. And what should a good systems integrator do when faced with the challenge of building complex systems? Establish clear milestones to reach the overall goal, build the software one piece at a time (preferably as black boxes with as few interfaces as possible), and test each module as you go to prove that the milestones are met successfully.

For example, test the HTML form independently from the CGI program. You might even take the time to build a test environment for the CGI application so that you can verify its input/output completely independent of any interaction with the Web server. Doing this could yield a great payback when it comes time to debug or enhance the system, especially if it is a large application or if it interfaces with a database. The goal is to reduce the edit/compile/link/test cycle as tightly as possible. A test environment that doesn't involve running the server, launching the browser, and filling out the form will yield significant time savings.

What's Next?

Now that we have covered all the basics of CGI, Chapter 8, "Power Programming with CGI," will get into a more realistic example. The program built in Chapter 8 is already compiled on the CD and can provide you with a very useful entry into the world of CGI, even without you getting involved in programming.

We will also revisit CGI programming in the second half of Chapter 15, "Databases and the Web." There we will describe how to tie an HTML form to a server database. In our example, we use Visual Basic 4 with an Access database, but any ODBC or ISAM database could be substituted.

Chapter 8

Power Programming with CGI

- CGI Kit 1.2
- An Advanced CGI System
- C Programming with CGI
- CGI PerForm
- CGI2Shell Gateway
- CGIC
- EIT's CGI Library
- Web Developers Warehouse
- What's Next?

This chapter picks up where the last one left off. After being introduced to CGI and seeing a working but not a very practical example, you're probably eager to learn how CGI can really be put to work.

We'll start by showing you how to install and use a CGI application that is included on the CD. Then, for those of you who will want to understand the inner workings of CGI and HTML forms, we'll discuss some of the details of that program, which is written in C.

Finally, we'll introduce several CGI programming tools that are designed to make your job easier. Whether you are just counting visitors at your site, tabulating more advanced statistics, or running a customer support form, there is bound to be something here that will help you make your Web site interactive.

CGI Kit 1.2

When using forms in HTML, you need a CGI script or application to handle the contents of that form. There are several examples of CGI scripts written in C language that are included with the EMWAC HTTPS. These examples are informative but not very useful as they stand. The CGI Kit was written to give you a more useful version of the EMWAC examples. This kit contains the source code and binary for savedata.exe, a CGI application that will parse the data from your forms and save that data to a file.

This CGI application is useful if you know how to write HTML code but don't want to dive into CGI programming. It is also useful if you are taking credit card orders on a form and do not want the data mailed through the Internet. Of course, neither way is really safe, but if you only send the numbers from the client to the server to the savedata file instead of from the client to the server to the mail server to the post office to the POP3 mailbox, there are fewer links in the chain to be broken. If you plan to conduct financial transactions at your site, read Chapter 16, "Internet Robots and More Security Issues," and Chapter 17, "Commerce on the Web." Chapter 17 discusses several options for secure cash.

Installing CGI Kit

To install CGI Kit 1.2, locate the files in \cgi\cgikit\ on the appropriate directory on your hard drive.

The files listed in Table 8.1 are in CGI Kit 1.2.

Table 8.1. Files found in CGI Kit 1.2.

Filename	Description
savedata.c	C source code for savedata.exe
savedata.mak	Makefile for Borland C++ 4.02
savedata.exe	Intel binary CGI application
cw3211.dll	DLL for use with savedata.exe
feedback.htm	Sample feedback HTML document
feedback.hfo	Sample file to write saved data to

Although the kit has worked reliably for several months on the Final Bit Solutions Web site, it is not a very robust application and it certainly is not guaranteed to be bug-free. If you plan to enhance the source code yourself, ensure that you compile it as an NT console-mode application.

The CGI Kit consists of a few convenient modifications to the CGI source that comes with EMWAC HTTPS. A `Return` tag has been added to the information dialog so that after your information is written to a file, you can return to the URL from which savedata.exe was called. The nasty plus characters have been removed so strings are now separated by spaces. Newlines are now accepted. The following fields were added to the file output: posted by:, Date:, and Time.

Here are the directions for using CGI Kit:

1. Place cw3211.dll in your winnt\system32 directory.
2. Place savedata.exe in a directory for cgi binaries (for example, cgi-bin).
3. Place feedback.htm somewhere within the HTML document path of your Web server. Place feedback.HFO in the same directory as feedback.htm.
4. Provide a link to feedback.htm from your home page. You can use WebEdit to customize feedback.htm for your own purposes.
5. You are ready to go! Why don't you try out the form from your own browser. After you submit the form to the server, it should run savedata.exe. Then you can check feedback.HFO to see the results.

Recall from Chapter 7 that CGI applications can capture only the form fields that you name in the HTML document. Savedata.exe captures the form field names that you set in your HTML document (for example, feedback.htm) and write them to the file that you specify with the .HFO extension. (As currently written, the code requires .HFO to be in uppercase.)

An Advanced CGI System

This section discusses the why and how of CGI Kit. We refer to it as a CGI *system* because it requires proper integration of several languages and protocols, including HTML, C, HTTP, and CGI.

Figure 8.1 shows an example form (defined in HTML) that gathers comments from the user. When the user clicks the button labeled Submit Comments, the form is designed to run the savedata CGI application on the server, which will save the form data to a file named FEEDBACK.HFO.

Listing 8.1 shows the HTML code that creates the form and invokes the CGI application. To achieve the greatest portability, it does not take advantage of any HTML 3.0 features.

Figure 8.1.
Form Processing screen.

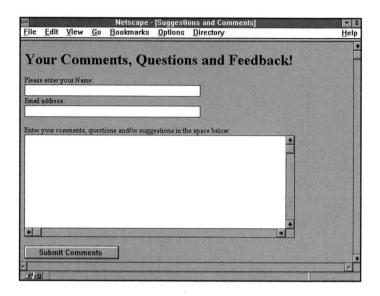

Listing 8.1. HTML code for forms processing.

```
<HEAD>
<TITLE>Suggestions and Comments</TITLE>
</HEAD>
<BODY>
<form action="http://your.ip.address.here/cgi-bin/savedata.exe/FEEDBACK.HFO"
method="POST">
<H1>Your Comments, Questions and Feedback!</H1>
Please enter your Name:
<BR><INPUT TYPE=text NAME="name" SIZE = 40 MAXLENGTH=40>
<BR>Email address:
<BR><INPUT TYPE=text NAME="email_addr" SIZE = 40 MAXLENGTH=40>
<P>
Enter your comments, questions and/or suggestions in the space below:<BR>
<TEXTAREA NAME=comments ROWS=12 COLS=60 MAXLENGTH=3000></TEXTAREA>
<P>
<input type="submit" value="Submit Comments">
</FORM>
</BODY>
</HTML>
```

The action attribute of the form is the URL of the CGI application. The action attribute of the example form is

```
http://your.ip.address.here/cgi-bin/savedata.exe/FEEDBACK.HFO
```

The cgi-bin/savedata.exe portion of the action attribute executes savedata.exe, while the /FEEDBACK.HFO component is passed to the script in the PATH_INFO environment variable.

In this example, the method attribute is POST, which means the form data will be read from stdin by the CGI application.

C Programming with CGI

Listing 8.2 is a sample CGI script written in C that will take the contents of a form and save it to a file. This file (savedata.c) and its compiled executable can be found in CGI Kit 1.2 on the accompanying CD.

Listing 8.2. Savedata.c saves the form data to feedback.HFO.

```
/***********************************************************************
*  File: savedata.c
*
*  Use: CGI Script file for use with HTTPS.
*
*  Notes: Assumes it is invoked from a form.  This script writes the
*  information to a file defined by the PATH_INFO enviroment var.  Ensure that
*  you compile this script as a console mode app. Note the file that you write *  to
*  must have the extension ".HFO" in all caps.
*  This script is a modified version of the script that comes with EMWAC
*  HTTPS.
*
*  Date: 4/4/95
*  Christopher L. T. Brown  clbrown@netcom.com
*
***********************************************************************/
#include <stdio.h>
#include <stdlib.h>
#include <string.h>
#include <ctype.h>
#include <io.h>
#include <time.h>
#define TRUE 1
#define FALSE 0
char InputBuffer[4096];

        /* Convert all cOld characters   */
        /* in cStr into cNew characters */
void strcvrt(char *cStr, char cOld, char cNew)
{
  int i = 0;
  while(cStr[i])
  {
        if(cStr[i] == cOld)
              cStr[i] = cNew;
        i++;
  }
}

        /* The string starts with two hex */
        /* characters.  Return an integer */
        /* formed from them.            */
static int TwoHex2Int(char *pC)
{
  int Hi, Lo, Result;

  Hi = pC[0];
  if('0' <= Hi && Hi <= '9')
```

Listing 8.2. continued

```
        Hi -= '0';
  else
        if('a' <= Hi && Hi <= 'f')
              Hi -= ('a' - 10);
  else
        if('A' <= Hi && Hi <= 'F')
              Hi -= ('A' - 10);

  Lo = pC[1];
  if('0' <= Lo && Lo <= '9')
        Lo -= '0';
  else
        if('a' <= Lo && Lo <= 'f')
                  Lo -= ('a' - 10);
  else
        if('A' <= Lo && Lo <= 'F')
              Lo -= ('A' - 10);

  Result = Lo + 16 * Hi;
  return(Result);
}

        /* Decode the given string in-place */
        /* by expanding %XX escapes.        */
void urlDecode(char *p)
{
  char *pD = p;

  while(*p)
  {
        if(*p == '%')         /* Escape: next 2 chars are hex          */
        {                     /* representation of the actual character.*/
              p++;
              if(isxdigit(p[0]) && isxdigit(p[1]))
              {
                  *pD++ = (char)TwoHex2Int(p);
                  p += 2;
              }
        }
        else
              *pD++ = *p++;
  }
  *pD = '\0';
}

        /* Return TRUE if the file is within or below the */
        /* current directory. It must have a .HFO ext.    */
static int FileNameIsSafe(char *FileName)
{
  char *p = FileName;

  while(*p == ' ' || *p == '\t')
        p++;
  if(*p == '\\')
        return(FALSE);
  if(strstr(p, "..") != NULL)
        return(FALSE);
```

```
  if(strchr(p, ':') != NULL)
        return(FALSE);
  if(strlen(FileName) < 5)
        return(FALSE);
  if(strcmp(".HFO", FileName + strlen(FileName) -4 )!= 0)
        return(FALSE);
  return(TRUE);
}

      /* Parse out and store field=value items. */
      /* Don't use strtok!                       */
void StoreField(FILE *f, char *Item)
{
  char *p;

  p = strchr(Item, '=');
  *p++ = '\0';
  urlDecode(Item);
  urlDecode(p);
  strcvrt(p, '\n', ' ');
  strcvrt(p, '+', ' ');                  /* Get rid of those nasty +'s */
  fprintf(f, "%s = %s\n", Item, p);
}

int main(void)
{
  int ContentLength, x, i;
  char *p, *q, *FileName, *pRequestMethod, *URL, *whocalledme;
  char datebuf[9], timebuf[9];
  FILE *f;

      /* Turn buffering off for stdin.*/
  setvbuf(stdin, NULL, _IONBF, 0);

      /* Tell the client what we're going to send */
  printf("Content-type: text/html\n\n");
  FileName = getenv("PATH_INFO");              /* Get the PATH_INFO.  */
  if(FileName == NULL)                         /* Does not exist.     */
  {
        printf("<HEAD><TITLE>Error - no filename</TITLE></HEAD>\n");
        printf("<BODY><H1>Error - no filename</H1>\n");
        printf("There is no PATH_INFO supplied.  ");
        printf("Please modify the action parameter in your form.\n");
        printf("</BODY>\n");
        exit(0);
  }

  q = FileName;                 /* Convert PATH_INFO to a filename */
  while(*q)
  {
        if(*q == '/')
              *q = '\\';
        q++;
  }
  if(*FileName == '\\')
        FileName++;
  urlDecode(FileName);

  if(!FileNameIsSafe(FileName))       /* Is it safe to use? */
```

continues

Listing 8.2. continued

```
{
      printf("<HEAD><TITLE>Error - Filename unacceptable</TITLE></HEAD>\n");
      printf("<BODY><H1>Error - Filename unacceptable</H1>\n");
      printf("The file %s is not acceptable.\n",FileName);
      printf("</BODY>\n");
      exit(0);
}

if(access(FileName, 2) < 0)        /* Does the file exist? */
{
      printf("<HEAD><TITLE>Error - cannot access file</TITLE></HEAD>\n");
      printf("<BODY><H1>Error - cannot access file</H1>\n");
      printf("The file %s could not be accessed.\n",FileName);
      printf("</BODY>\n");
      exit(0);
}

f = fopen(FileName, "a"); /* Open the file.*/
if(f == NULL)                      /* Can't open.    */
{
      printf("<HEAD><TITLE>Error - cannot open file</TITLE></HEAD>\n");
      printf("<BODY><H1>Error - cannot open file</H1>\n");
      printf("The file %s could not be opened.\n",FileName);
      printf("</BODY>\n");
      exit(0);
}

/* Indicate start of next entry in file.*/
fprintf(f, "=============================\n");

/* Who called the method action? */
whocalledme = getenv("REMOTE_ADDR");

/* Write to file which url posted data. */
fprintf(f, "Posted By: ");
fprintf(f, "%s\n", whocalledme);

_strdate(datebuf);
_strtime(timebuf);
fprintf(f, "Date: %s  Time: %s\n",datebuf,timebuf);

/* What method were we invoked through? */
pRequestMethod = getenv("REQUEST_METHOD");

if(pRequestMethod == NULL)
      return(0);

/* Get the data from the client       */
/* according to the requested method.*/

if(strcmp(pRequestMethod,"POST") == 0)
{
      p = getenv("CONTENT_LENGTH"); /* Read in the data from the client. */
      if(p != NULL)
            ContentLength = atoi(p);
      else
            ContentLength = 0;
```

```c
        if(ContentLength > sizeof(InputBuffer) -1)
                ContentLength = sizeof(InputBuffer) -1;
        i = 0;
        while(i < ContentLength)
        {
                x = fgetc(stdin);
                if(x == EOF)
                 break;
                InputBuffer[i++] = x;
        }
        InputBuffer[i] = '\0';
        ContentLength = i;

        p = getenv("CONTENT_TYPE");
        if(p == NULL)
                return(0);

        if(strcmp(p, "application/x-www-form-urlencoded") == 0)
        {
                p = strtok(InputBuffer, "&");      /* Parse the data */
                while(p != NULL)
                {
                  StoreField(f, p);
                  p = strtok(NULL, "&");
                }
        }
        else
                /* Write data to file. */
                fprintf(f, "Input = %s\n", InputBuffer);
}
else
        if(strcmp(pRequestMethod, "GET") == 0)
        {
                /* Parse the data in the search term.*/
                p = getenv("QUERY_STRING");
                if(p != NULL)
                {
                  strncpy(InputBuffer, p, sizeof(InputBuffer));
                  p = strtok(InputBuffer, "&");
                  while(p != NULL)
                  {
                        StoreField(f, p);
                        p = strtok(NULL, "&");
                  }
                }
        }

if(!ferror(f))                        /* Confirm to client. */
{
        URL = getenv("HTTP_REFERER");      /* What url called me.*/
        printf("<HEAD><TITLE>Submitted OK</TITLE></HEAD>\n");
        printf("<BODY><h2>The information you supplied has been accepted.");
        printf("  Thank You!</h2>\n");
        printf("<h3><A href=\"%s\">[Return]</a></h3></BODY>\n", URL);
}
else
{
        URL = getenv("HTTP_REFERER");      /* What url called me.*/
```

continues

Listing 8.2. continued

```
            printf("<HEAD><TITLE>Server file I/O error</TITLE></HEAD>\n");
            printf("<BODY><h2>The information you supplied could not be\n");
            printf("accepted due to a file I/O error at the server.</h2>\n");
            printf("<h3><A href=\"%s\">Return</a></h3></BODY>\n", URL);
    }

    fclose(f);                      /* Close the file.*/
    return(0);
}
```

Here is the list of functions in savedata.c:

- `strcvrt`—Converts all occurrences of one character to another within a given string
- `TwoHex2Int`—Called when a percent character marks an escape code
- `UrlDecode`—Expands all the escape codes by calling `TwoHex2Int`
- `FileNameIsSafe`—Determines whether the given filename is within the permitted directory tree
- `StoreField`—Retrieves field/value pairs from the form data
- `main`—Reads the form data from stdin, saves it to FEEDBACK.HFO, and writes the HTML response to stdout

CGI PerForm

CGI PerForm was designed to provide all the basic CGI functionality needed by a WWW site, without requiring C or Perl. With a simple command file, template file, and HTML form, you can create an e-mail feedback form, guest book, or even a ballot box—or perform all three of those operations at the same time and as many times as you want. CGI PerForm was designed to work with both Windows NT and Windows 95.

How CGI PerForm Works

You can break down an interactive WWW page into three pieces:

- The HTML form through which the data is typed in and submitted
- The Common Gateway Interface (CGI) application that receives and processes the submitted data
- The end result

CGI PerForm would be the CGI application that handles the incoming data and creates the result. A *result* can be a combination of more than one task or command. We discuss PerForm commands later in this chapter.

CGI PerForm uses a command file you create to determine what tasks it needs to perform on the data. A different command file would be created for every interactive application needed. Each command requires certain key values in order for it to perform its task. A majority of the key values are filenames. Some of these files must already exist, such as a template file or a column file. Others are created by the command, such as a data file or the output file.

CGI PerForm takes all the incoming data supplied by the HTML form and stores it into a memory block. An HTML form supplies data in *name=value* pairs—for example, `lastname=Smith`. You can supplement the data supplied by the HTML form by plugging in hard-coded *name=value* pairs in the command file. These values go into the same memory block as the submitted data. You would hard code values in your command file to hide them or to set defaults.

The next step is to use the data. You can save the data to a data file or a database—or combine the results with a template file to create a confirmation message or a form letter to be mailed.

The command can be performed as often as necessary with different key values. For example, you could save data submitted by a user into three different data files. These data files can have some of the same data as another, or two of them could be identical. You can also pass variables between command blocks to create unique files to store data in at the user's request.

Installing CGI PerForm

To install CGI PerForm, place the perform.exe file in your cgi directory. Some Web servers require you to change the extension from .exe to .cgi. You might want to put a copy of perform.exe in your path in order to run it from the command line. Note that CGI PerForm is not a Visual Basic application. Thus, Website users must place perform.exe in the cgi-dos directory for it to work.

To use the MailFile command, you must have Blat 1.2 (or greater) installed and in your path. Your NT Web server service must be logging in as a user in order for Blat to work.

Using CGI PerForm

In order to use CGI PerForm, you must create an HTML form to present the user interface and a command file to tell it what tasks to perform. Note that some commands (tasks) require you to create certain files first, such as a template file. You can use the examples supplied with CGI PerForm to get started.

Form Input

CGI PerForm recognizes both the POST and GET methods. Use the POST method if you plan to send relatively large amounts of data, such as information from a questionnaire.

You are required to send only one specific *name=value* pair in your form. You must have a line similar to this in your HTML form:

```
<input type=hidden name=CMDFile value=\path\file.cmdl>
```

where *path* is the absolute path to your command file. If your Web server data directory is `c:\web-server\`, your path should begin with `\web-server\`.

Required Fields

You can force a user to supply data in the HTML form input field by prefixing the field name with a tilde (~). For example:

```
<input name="~UserName" size=24 >
```

If the user does not type in a value in this field, he or she will be notified that the UserName is required to process the form.

URL-Encoded Output

Sometimes you might want to keep your data URL-encoded when it's placed into your template file. This would be useful when generating a list of URLs that implement the GET method to pass data to a query engine. This can be done by prefixing the name of the data field in your template file with a tilde (~). For example:

```
<a href="http://www.thesari.org/query?<!-- ~KeyWord 0 -->">Search for
<!-- KeyWord 0 --></a>
```

Removing Template Placeholders

By default, CGI PerForm leaves a template placeholder intact if a value is not found to put in its place. In some cases, this causes problems, especially when you are nesting placeholders in HTML tags. When you precede the field name in the tag with an ampersand (&), the placeholder will be deleted if the value it references is not found.

Security (Internal and External)

CGI PerForm cannot be executed without a command file. This enforces value overrides and path modifications.

There are now two versions of CGI PerForm: secure and insecure. The secure version of CGI PerForm automatically forces all paths to relative paths. For example:

```
\data\guest.dat would become data\guest.dat
```

This is done for two reasons: to be used by many forms at a time and by many users at a time. Many Web servers sell accounts to users for both commercial and private use. These users might have limited access to their files; the Web server software itself has a superset of an individual user's access rights. When a CGI application is spawned by the Web server, it inherits the rights of the Web server. If a user accidentally mistyped a path that really exists, CGI PerForm might overwrite an existing file, causing another user grief. Second, malicious Web users might create forms on the client site with the sole purpose of wiping out a file or mailing themselves another file. The command file can be used to override any values that could be passed by a malicious form. Also, variables cannot be passed from a form to CGI PerForm; they can only be created and defined in the command file. You may use the value of a specific field in a variable, but the path will be made relative.

The insecure version performs no path or drive modifications and is not recommended for use on a multiuser environment.

The CGI PerForm Command File

The command file is a simple ASCII file listing all the commands you want CGI PerForm to execute. The order of the commands is important, but you can perform any command as often as you like.

The command file is in this format:

```
[command 1]
key_name1=value
key_name2=value
...
[command 2]
key_name1=value
key_name2=value
...
```

For a real example, here are the contents of mail.cmdl, the command file used on our sample site:

```
[MakeUniqueFileName]
variable=%log
path=log\
ext=.log

[OutputFormData]
OutputFile=%log
tplFile=message.tpl

[MailFile]
FileName=%log

[OutputFormData]
TplFile=mail.tpl
BlockName=mail
```

Commands

The available commands and their associated keys are as follows. Some keys are applicable to more than one command. The keys are described in a separate list following the commands. The keys are shown in each of the following subsections.

Data

The key value pairs in this command block will override any values passed from your HTML form or will supplement those values. Place any values in this block that you do not want your users to see if they read the source of your HTML form.

DeleteFile

This is used to clean up any extraneous files generated.

> Key: `FileName`

DumpFormData

This dumps the contents of the current *Name=Value* pairs passed by your form or stored with the `Data` command.

> Key: `OutputFile`

ExportDataFile

This converts your DataFile to a more human/computer-readable format. Only a comma-delimited format is supported.

> Keys: `DataFile, OutputFile, SaveAs`

FindInDataFile

This is used to find a value in a DataFile.

The `FindInDataFile` command is used to search a DataFile for a value. If not found, the `Default` value is used.

> Keys: `DataFile, ColFile, UseColumn, GetColumn, WithValue, Default, DataType, Variable`

Note: A random value will be returned if `WithValue` and `Default` are left blank.

MailFile

By providing a filename and a few values passed by your HTML form, you can SMTP mail any file. (This function requires Blat to be installed.) The fields needed from the HTML form are mailto, mailfrom (you may also use e-mail), name, and subject. mailto is the recipient, mailfrom is the sender's e-mail address, and name is the sender's name. (If mailfrom is left blank, the value of name is used, otherwise the e-mail is sent using anonymous.)

> Keys: `FileName, CarbonCopy`

MakeUniqueFileName

This creates a unique filename in your current directory or in one of the paths specified. (The path will not be forced to be relative to your current directory because the file created is guaranteed to be unique.) This command stores the filename in the variable specified. The variable must begin with the percent (%) sign.

Keys: `Variable, Ext, Path`

MakeVariable

This creates a variable.

Keys: `Variable, UseFieldValue, Ext`

OutputDataFile

This is used to write a formatted list, including all the contents of your data file, into a single file. The `ReturnNumRec` key specifies the first number of records to be used in the data file. `LastRecOnly`, when `TRUE`, allows only the last record submitted to be used. If no `OutputFile` value is given, the output is sent directly to the client's browser.

Keys: `ColFile, DataFile, TplFile, OutputFile, BlockName, DataType, LastRecOnly, ReturnNumRec`

OutputFormData

This combines the data passed by your form with your `TplFile`. If no `OutputFile` value is given, the resulting page is sent directly to the browser.

Keys: `TplFile, OutputFile, BlockName`

PushFile

This sends a file to the browser; it works great with images.

Keys: `FileName, MimeType`

PushList

This is used to push a series of files to a Web browser. This is more commonly known as Server Pushing and currently works only with Netscape browsers. If the browser is not Netscape Navigator, only the first file in the list is sent. Otherwise, the first file is skipped and all remaining files will be sent. You can specify a delay between each file (image if used for animation) in seconds. The push list should have three columns: FileName, MimeType, and Delay (with defaults: MimeType=image/gif and Delay=1 second).

Key: `FileName`

RemoveData

This is used to delete a record from your data file. This will perform a case-insensitive search through the column specified by `UseColumn`. When found, the record is deleted and the updated `DataFile` is saved.

Keys: `DataFile, UseColumn, WithValue, ColFile`

Without the UseColumn, a full search on all columns is done. Any occurrence of the characters in the WithValue key found will cause the record to be deleted. For example, truck = firetruck.

RemoveDupData

This removes duplicate lines in your DataFile and guards against users from submitting a form more than once. For this command to work properly, each line needs to be unique. You can make each line unique by logging the user's REMOTE_ADDR and the current day of the year in your DataFile.

> Key: DataFile

ReturnURL

This forces the user's browser (such as Netscape or Mosaic) to load a page. This value must be a fully qualified URL (for example, http://foo.bar.com/). You will most likely use it to point to a file just created with the MakeOutput command. You can provide a FileName value to have the URL generated on the fly. FileName can be a variable.

> Keys: URL, FileName

SaveFormData

This saves the data passed from your HTML form to a file.

> Keys: ColFile, DataFile, DataAdd

SortDataFile

Using the column you specify, you can sort a datafile three ways: alpha, numeric, or invert.

> Keys: ColFile, DataFile, UseColumn, DataType, Sort

SumDataFile

Using the column you specify, SumData will add all of the numeric values encountered. The sumdatafile will have two columns: int and float.

> Keys: ColFile, DataFile, OutputFile, UseColumn

TallyDataFile

This summarizes data in a DataFile for a ballot box type application. Using the column you specify, TallyData will find all the occurrences of a value and count how many times it occurred. This will be repeated for all unique values. The tallydatafile will have four columns: value, total, count, and percent.

> Keys: ColFile, DataFile, OutputFile, UseColumn, IgnoreValue

UseCommandFile

Use this command to process another command file. No form data will be passed to this new process automatically. But you may create *name=value* pairs to pass data; the values may be variables.

```
Key: CmdFile
```

Description of Keys

This is a description of all the available keys and their values.

BlockName

A template file is broken up into blocks to allow you to dump more than one DataFile into it. This key tells the OutputDataFile and OutputFormData commands which block to use.

ColFile

This lists the columns used and their associated DataFiles. The order of the column names in this file correspond to the order of columns in the DataFile. The column names must be the names of the input boxes in your HTML document or names of environment variables passed by your Web server software.

DataAdd

When saving data to the DataFile, you might want recent input added to the top of the list. The values that can be used are TOP, BOTTOM, and ALPHA.

DataFile

This is the file in which the user-submitted data is stored. Each column is a different INPUT box in your HTML form or an environment variable value requested in your ColFile.

DataType

The output from SumData and TallyData do not have associated ColFiles. You can, however, tell certain commands to assume the DataFile it is using is one of these. The values can be SUM or TALLY.

ExcludeList

This is the path- and filename of an exclusion list or an absolute path so lists may be shared among applications and users. Each line of the file should contain unique words or phrases.

Ext

This is the extension you want to add to a unique filename created with `MakeUniqueFileName`. This value is not required.

IgnoreValue

This key is used by the `TallyData` command. It forces `TallyData` to skip any record with this value in the specified column. For example, users are voting for the next president using a `SELECT` box. The first item in the `SELECT` box reads Select a Candidate. You are guaranteed to have users vote on Select a Candidate. By using `IgnoreValue`, `TallyData` will not summarize data on this value, keeping your numbers accurate.

GetColumn

This specifies the column name from which to retrieve a value.

LastRecOnly

If you want to output only the last record in a `DataFile`, set this value to `TRUE`. `FALSE` is the default.

OutputFile

This is the name of a file to be generated by a command. If you use the `OutputDataFile` command, you could create a guest.htm from both the guest.tpl and guest.dat files.

Path

This is the absolute path to the location you want the new unique file created. This should point only to the directory you want to use for logging purposes, because you are not allowed to access files outside of your current directory.

ReturnNumRec

Used by `OutputDataFile`, the value of this key is the number of records returned by the command. `ReturnNumRec` can be used to limit a page to the first 50 items in the datafile, if the datafile contains a few hundred.

SaveAs

Used by `ExportDataFile`, its only value is `CSV`.

Sort

This specifies the sort type: alpha, numeric, or invert.

TplFile

This points to your template file. Template files have special placeholders in which field values from a `DataFile` are inserted. Usually an entire `DataFile` is iterated through a template file to create a guest book comments page.

UseColumn

This specifies the column name to use for certain commands. In the case of `OutputDataFile`, this key names the column to be used for filenames.

UseFieldValue

The value that this key is set to is a field name. This field name's value will be used as a filename or file variable.

Variable

This specifies the name of a filename storage space you want to create. This value must begin with the percent (%) sign.

WithValue

This is a word or phrase you want to search for. If this is used with the `UseColumn` key, an exact case-insensitive match of this value and the value of the requested column will be sought; otherwise, any case-insensitive occurrence of the `WithValue` value will be searched for. Thus, if you do not provide a column to search in (using the `UseColumn` key), the whole record will be searched. For example, `http://` will equal `http://www.whatever.com` because it contains the requested character string. If `UseColumn` is supplied, `http://` will not equal `http://www.whatever.com`.

The CGI PerForm Column File

The column file is a list of field names whose values are to be stored in a `DataFile`. The column file can contain more than just the field names returned by an HTML form. It can also be an environment variable or a time/date format specifier. A sample column file would be

```
candidate
remote_addr
fmt_tm_%j
```

In this example, we are storing the value of the candidate voted on, the user's IP address, and the current day of the year. The output `DataFile` would look like this:

```
Richard+Lugar+%28R%29 204.96.15.37 220
Bill+Clinton+%28D%29 214.46.15.3 225
Phil+Gramm+%28R%29 204.94.65.9 226
Pat+Buchanan+%28R%29 128.194.15.10 226
Select+a+Candidate 128.194.15.10 230
```

Note that the data is still URL-encoded. Use the `ExportDataFile` command to convert this to a comma-delimited format.

The CGI PerForm Template File

The template file is a standard HTML document, except that it has special comment tags acting as placeholders for the data supplied by your users.

Within this document, you are required to have both a `<!-- begin BlockName -->` and `<!-- end -->` tag. This tells `OutputDataFile` or `OutputFormData` when to start and stop replacing tags with data in your document. `BlockName` tells `OutputDataFile` or `OutputFormData` which begin/end block to use.

The comment placeholder tags have this format:

```
<!-- field_name1  min_width  -->      <!-- field_name2  min_width  -->
```

`field_name1` corresponds to a field listed in your column file (`ColFile`) or a field passed to CGI PerForm from an HTML form by a user. `min_width` is an integer specifying the number of characters required. If a field value is less than `min_width` characters, the remaining space is padded with space characters; no characters will be truncated otherwise. If width is not an issue, use `0` for `min_width`. The spaces are important to ensure that the field names and width are read correctly.

These tags can be embedded in other standard HTML tags in order to create URLs or filenames, for example:

```
<a href="http://<!-- domain 0 -->/"><!-- company 0 --></a>
```

Time Format Codes

Here are some special fields you can place in your `ColFile` file. You can also place them in your template file if you want the information displayed.

```
fmt_tm_????
```

This field allows you to construct a time/date string, where `????` can be any of the following (all times will be local server times, not user times):

- `%a`—Abbreviated weekday name
- `%A`—Full weekday name
- `%b`—Abbreviated month name
- `%B`—Full month name
- `%c`—Date and time representation appropriate for locale
- `%d`—Day of month as decimal number (01–31)
- `%H`—Hour in 24-hour format (00–23)
- `%I`—Hour in 12-hour format (01–12)

- %j—Day of year, as decimal number (001–366)
- %m—Month as decimal number (01–12)
- %M—Minute as decimal number (00–59)
- %p—Current locale's A.M./P.M. indicator for 12-hour clock
- %S—Second as decimal number (00–59)
- %U—Week of year as decimal number, with Sunday as first day of week (00–51)
- %w—Weekday as decimal number (0–6; Sunday is 0)
- %W—Week of year as decimal number, with Monday as first day of week (00–51)
- %x—Date representation for current locale
- %X—Time representation for current locale
- %y—Year without century, as decimal number (00–99)
- %Y—Year with century, as decimal number
- %z, %Z—Time-zone name or abbreviation; no characters if time zone is unknown

For example: `fmt_tm_%B+%d,+%Y` would become January 12, 1995.

CGI PerForm Environment Variables

These are the only environment variables recognized:

- CONTENT_LENGTH
- REMOTE_ADDR
- REMOTE_HOST
- REMOTE_USER
- HTTP_ACCEPT
- HTTP_USER_AGENT
- HTTP_IF_MODIFIED_SINCE
- HTTP_FROM
- SERVER_SOFTWARE
- SERVER_NAME
- SERVER_PROTOCOL
- SERVER_PORT

Variables

Variables are used to store filenames or other values created with `MakeUniqueFileName` and `MakeVariable`. These variables can be used in the command file, template files, or in your `DataFiles`. The variables will be replaced by their value where used. Variables must begin with a percent (%) sign to be recognized. They may not be passed from an HTML form.

You may also create variables in the Data command block. Note that for security reasons, these values will be forced to relative pathnames.

Note the missing slash that converts the path from absolute to relative:

```
\data\log  will become  data\log
```

Push List

The push list is used for Server Push routines that can be written to display simple animations. The push list has three columns: FileName, MimeType, and Delay.

MimeType has a default value of 'image/gif,' and the delay is set to one second. If these values are not given in the push list, the defaults will be used. If only the first (or any other) item in the push list has a MimeType and/or a Delay, those values will become the default for the rest of the list.

The first item in the push list does not get sent to the client if the client is Netscape Navigator. The first item is reserved for non-Netscape Web browsers.

You might want to make the first item a GIF file and the remaining items JPG files since Netscape can display JPG images just like GIF images. JPG images are usually smaller and can display more colors. Most other Web clients do not display JPG images the same as Netscape.

CGI2Shell Gateway

If you find yourself using a lot of CGI scripts, you'll like this little utility package from Richard Graessler of Germany.

The CGI2Shell applications are intended for Windows NT Web servers that do not support the execution of scripts without a corresponding shell in the command line of a <FORM ACTION=> or <A HREF=> tag.

The CGI2Shell Gateway is a set of programs that enable PATH_INFO to specify the name of a CGI script that will be executed with either the POST or GET method.

Currently, the shells Perl.exe and Sh.exe and the Windows NT command interpreter CMD.exe are supported.

The CGI2Shell Gateway has been tested with EMWAC HTTPS and Purveyor Web server, but it should work with all other NT Web servers.

Using CGI2Shell

The CGI2Shell Gateway includes three programs, one for each shell it supports:

```
CGI2Sh.exe for Sh.exe
CGI2Perl.exe for Perl.exe
CGI2Cmd.exe for Cmd.exe
```

All you need to do is include the script with its path in PATHINFO of the URL. For example:

`http://host.domain/progpath/CGI2xxx.exe/scriptpath/script.ext`

The shell programs must reside in the path or the same directory as CGI2*xxx*.exe.

You can find a set of examples online at `http://137.226.92.4/rick/rick/cgi2shell.html` or `http://pobox.com/~rickg/`.

CGIC

CGIC is a library of functions for CGI development with ANSI standard C, written by Thomas Boutell. You can find more information about it at `http://sunsite.unc.edu/boutell/cgic/cgic.html`.

EIT's CGI Library

Enterprise Integration Technology has created LIBCGI to assist programmers who are writing CGI systems in C language. The library consists of about 15 functions and it is freeware. Originally written for UNIX as part of their Webmaster's Starter Kit, it has been ported to several other popular platforms, including Windows NT. As with several URLs mentioned in this book, we have not tried this product and cannot endorse it other than to suggest that you visit their site and have a look for yourself: `http://wsk.eit.com`.

Web Developers Warehouse

If you program with Borland C++ and don't mind paying for CGI and HTML tools, you should definitely drop by `http://htechno.com/wdw/index.htm`. A company called Specialized Technologies has developed a suite of products they call the Web Developers Warehouse. It includes three components: TCgi, HTML Objects, and Web Wizard. TCgi is a set of C++ classes for WinCGI, which works with the WebSite server.

Visit their home page for more information. You can also try the demonstration programs and pay for the software electronically, and download it pronto.

What's Next?

If you've made it this far, the rest is easy. We're going to revisit the features of HTML in Chapter 9, "Netscape Extensions and HTML 3.0."

All of this will lead up to Chapter 10, "Putting HTML to Work Building a Sample Site," when we show you how to go online with a powerful HTML and CGI system.

Chapter 9

Netscape Extensions and HTML 3.0

- How the IETF and Netscape Have Evolved HTML
- Netscape Extensions to HTML
- The Power of HTML 3.0
- More Quick Tips on HTML Style
- What's Next?

Chapters 7 and 8 contained some advanced material. Don't feel alone if you're feeling a little brain-frazzled at this point. Fortunately, the hard stuff is mostly over and relief is in sight. If you liked Chapter 5, "A Guided Tour of HTML," you're going to like this chapter too. Because Chapter 5 was geared as an introduction for first-time Web page designers, it intentionally omitted some of the most recent advances in HTML. That's where this chapter fits in. Here, we talk about several of the hottest new things happening on the Web.

How the IETF and Netscape Have Evolved HTML

As you might have heard, Netscape Communications has frequently been a leader of new developments in HTML. Although HTML 2.0 has not been adopted at the time of this writing, it is almost entirely based on HTML 1.0 and the Netscape extensions. In other words, Netscape is trying to set the standard, and so far the Web community has looked favorably upon their suggestions.

The IETF (Internet Engineering Task Force) is responsible for writing the formal HTML specifications. Actually, the IETF (which is responsible for many other standards, such as RFCs) gives projects like this to a working group—in this case, the W3C (World Wide Web Consortium). First the W3C, and then the IETF, goes through a very careful process to ensure that new HTML standards meet the needs of the Web community and are backward-compatible (as much as possible) with existing Web documents. With HTML 2.0 now nearing the end of that process, you can look for it to be adopted sometime in early 1996.

In the meantime, Netscape isn't standing still. Their extensions have also contributed to the design of HTML 3.0, which was originally referred to as HTML +. The unofficial HTML 3.0 is already supported by several Web browsers, including Netscape Navigator (of course), and a public domain browser that the IETF is building, called Arena. If you decide to take advantage of either the Netscape extensions or HTML 3.0 in your Web pages—and you are about to see that there are many advantages to doing so— you can at least count on the fact that a good percentage of clients who visit your site will be able to see your Web pages rendered as you intended. This is true simply because of the wide popularity of Netscape. Using these extensions, however, might cause your pages to look odd on other Web browsers until HTML 2.0 and HTML 3.0 are more widely adopted.

There is a confusing aspect of this with regard to version numbers. Perhaps the map of HTML versions in Figure 9.1 will help to clear this up. Although the Netscape extensions don't really have a formal version number, people on the Net talk about them in terms of the latest version of Netscape Navigator that is available. For example, Netscape Navigator 1.2N implements the 1.2 Netscape extensions. As Netscape continues to include other HTML 3.0 ideas in Navigator, the HTML 2.0 and 3.0 drafts also evolve to include many of the Netscape ideas.

Figure 9.1.
The map of HTML versions.

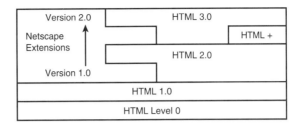

Netscape Extensions to HTML

The Netscape extensions to HTML consist of new tags and attributes. These have been built on top of the broadly adopted HTML 1.0 specification in a manner that is intended to be backward-compatible with existing WWW browsers. This way, if an older browser retrieves a page with a new tag it doesn't understand, it will just ignore it. The hope is that the page will still be displayed in readable fashion, even if not exactly as intended.

This section explains some of the major Netscape extensions. Some of these are already in the HTML 2.0 specification; a few others are in HTML 3.0.

<ISINDEX>

To the `<ISINDEX>` tag, Netscape has added the `PROMPT` attribute. `ISINDEX` indicates that a document is a searchable index. `PROMPT` has been added so the document author can specify what message is to appear before the text input field of the index. The default is that unfortunate message: `This is a searchable index. Enter search keywords:`.

<HR>

To this tag, Netscape added four new attributes to enable the document's author to describe how the horizontal rule should look.

<HR SIZE=number>

The `SIZE` attribute lets the author give an indication of how thick the horizontal rule should be.

<HR WIDTH=number|percent>

The default horizontal rule is always as wide as the page. With the `WIDTH` attribute, the author can specify an exact width in pixels, or a relative width measured as a percent of document width.

<HR ALIGN=left|right|center>

Now that horizontal rules do not have to be the width of the page, the author needs to specify whether the rules should be pushed up against the left margin, the right margin, or centered on the page.

<HR NOSHADE>

For those times you really want a solid bar, the NOSHADE attribute lets you specify that you do not want any shading on the horizontal rule.

<UL>

Netscape added a TYPE attribute to the <UL> tag so no matter what your indent level is, you can specify whether you want a TYPE=disc, TYPE=circle, or TYPE=square as your bullet.

<OL>

To the <OL> tag, Netscape added the TYPE and START attributes.

<OL TYPE=type>

This enables authors to specify whether they want their list items marked with: capital letters (TYPE=A), small letters (TYPE=a), large roman numerals (TYPE=I), small roman numerals (TYPE=i), or the default numbers (TYPE=1).

<OL START=number>

For lists that you want to start at values other than 1, you have the new START attribute. START is always specified in the default numbers and will be converted based on the TYPE attribute before display. Thus, START=5 would display either an E, e, V, v, or 5 based on the TYPE.

<LI>

To the <LI> tag they added the TYPE attribute as well. It takes the same values as either <UL> or <OL>, depending on the type of list you are in, and it changes the list type for that item and all subsequent items. For ordered lists, they have added the VALUE attribute so you can change the count for that list item and all subsequent items.

ALIGN

The additions to the ALIGN options need a lot of explanation. Images with the values *left* and *right* alignments are an entirely new floating image type. An image specified as ALIGN=left will float down and over to the left margin (into the next available space there), and subsequent text will wrap around the right side of that image. Likewise, for ALIGN=right, the image aligns with the right margin and the text wraps around the left. For example:

```
<IMG ALIGN=left¦right¦top¦texttop¦middle¦absmiddle¦baseline¦bottom¦absbottom>
```

ALIGN=top aligns itself with the top of the tallest item in the line.

ALIGN=texttop aligns itself with the top of the tallest text in the line.

ALIGN=middle aligns the baseline of the current line with the middle of the image.

ALIGN=absmiddle aligns the middle of the current line with the middle of the image.

ALIGN=baseline aligns the bottom of the image with the baseline of the current line.

ALIGN=bottom is identical to ALIGN=baseline.

ALIGN=absbottom aligns the bottom of the image with the bottom of the current line.

<IMG WIDTH=value HEIGHT=value>

The WIDTH and HEIGHT attributes were added to <IMG> mainly to speed up display of the document. If the author specifies these, the viewer of the document will not have to wait for the image to be loaded over the network and its size calculated.

*
*

Normal <BR> just inserts a line break. They added a CLEAR attribute to <BR>, so CLEAR=left will break the line and move vertically down until you have a clear left margin. CLEAR=right does the same for the right margin, and CLEAR=all moves down until both margins are clear of images.

<NOBR>

The <NOBR> tag, which stands for *no break*, means all the text between the start and end of the <NOBR> tags cannot have line breaks inserted between them.

<WBR>

The <WBR> tag stands for *word break*. This is used in the rare cases in which you have a <NOBR> section and you know exactly where you want the text to break. The <WBR> tag will not force a line break.

<FONT SIZE=value>

<FONT SIZE> enables you to change the font size. Valid values are from 1 to 7. The default font size is 3. The value given to SIZE can optionally have a + or - character in front of it to specify that it is relative to the base font of the document. The default base font is 3 and can be changed with the <BASEFONT> tag.

<BASEFONT SIZE=value>

This changes the size of the BASEFONT. The value of the SIZE attribute defaults to 3 and has a valid range from 1 to 7.

<CENTER>

This is one of the most used Netscape extensions. All lines of text between the beginning and end of <CENTER> are centered between the current left and right margins.

<BLINK>

This tag emphasizes sections your documents by causing the enclosed text to blink (no surprise).

Character Entities

Finally, these two new named entities come in handy on business pages:

®—the Registered Trademark symbol was previously only available as ®

©—the Copyright symbol; this entity works just like ©, but now you don't have to look up the magic number anymore.

> **Tip:** For a more complete discussion of Netscape extensions to HTML 2.0 and HTML 3.0, see the Netscape Home Page at `http://www.netscape.com/`.

The Power of HTML 3.0

Netscape Navigator currently supports HTML 3.0. Much of 3.0 is documented and in use on the Web today, but it is a moving target. A couple of the important additions in Netscape Navigator 1.1 that aren't in HTML 3.0 are backgrounds and dynamic updating to documents. And the Netscape support of tables goes beyond the proposed design for tables in the current draft of HTML 3.0.

Many people confuse the Netscape extensions to HTML to be HTML 3.0, but this is not the case. The IETF and Netscape cooperate, but they each play their own tunes. Although many of the Netscape extensions have made their way into HTML 3.0, there are also several that aren't in the current Internet draft. Currently, there isn't any public specification for the Netscape extensions except the information at their Web site, mentioned previously.

> **Tip:** An excellent place on the net to find information about the differences between HTML 2.0 and HTML 3.0 is "How to Tame the Wild Mozilla," `http://ic.corpnet.com/~aking/webinfo/html3andns/`.
>
> *Mozilla* is how Netscape refers to itself in the http request message. This URL also includes lots of late-breaking news about the Web. Definitely check it out!

Even though the Netscape browser is widely used (Beverly Hills Software Web site reports that 87% of all user agent requests are from Netscape clients), care must be taken when using Netscape extensions. A common practice is to include a comment on your home page saying something like "This page uses the Netscape extensions and is best viewed using a Netscape-compatible browser." Even when you use a statement such as this, it is a good idea to examine your own HTML documents with several browsers during the design stage. By doing this comparison, you will find you can reach a happy compromise that allows for Netscape-enhanced pages that don't look terrible under other browsers. We like to compare the rendering of our HTML code between Netscape, Mosaic, and the Microsoft Internet Explorer (considering it is in the hands of millions of potential Web users). If all of these browsers display your document the way you want, you know your HTML is fairly safe for the whole Web.

Tip: Note that the specification of HTML 3.0 is still a draft. Although some parts have been stable for some time, others will undoubtedly change. The best way to track the changes to HTML is to go online to any of these sites:

- Netscape Communications.

  ```
  http://www.netscape.com/
  ```

- Several papers and specifications on HyperText Markup Language.

  ```
  http://www.ietf.cnri.reston.va.us/ids.by.wg/html.html
  ```

- The HTML 3.0 Arena browser project (currently available for UNIX; stay tuned, a Windows version is being considered).

  ```
  http://www.w3.org/hypertext/WWW/Arena/Status.html
  ```

- The HTML + specification (a little dated).

  ```
  http://www.w3.org/hypertext/WWW/MarkUp/HTMLPlus/htmlplus_1.html
  ```

HTML 3.0 has several important new features. To name a few: tables, figures (`<fig>`) as a substitute for the image tag (`<img>`), support for mathematical formulae, banners, divisions, footnotes, and style sheets. You will find a complete encyclopedia of HTML in Appendix F, which shows tags that are specific to HTML 3.0 and to HTML 2.0. Here is a quick look at the major changes in 3.0.

Tables in HTML 3.0

Tables were the most requested feature for HTML 3.0. The IETF decided to stick to a powerful but simple model for creating nice looking tables. See Figure 9.2 for an example of a table created in HTML 3.0 as it appears in Netscape Navigator.

This table was created by the following short HTML code:

```
<HTML>
<HEAD>
<!-- Created: 9/26/95 9:22:11 PM -->
<TITLE>Sample table</TITLE>
</HEAD>
```

```
<BODY>
<H1>Sample Table</H1>
<TABLE BORDER>
<TR>
<TD>apples</TD>
<TD>25</TD>
</TR>
<TR>
<TD>oranges</TD>
<TD>10</TD>
</TR>
</TABLE>
<HR>
Last Updated: Tuesday, September 26, 1995
</BODY>
</HTML>
```

Figure 9.2.
A simple HTML 3.0 table in Navigator.

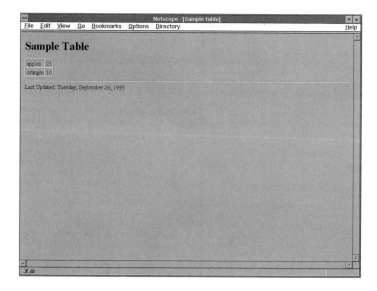

The `<TABLE BORDER>` tag begins the table. Each `<TR>` tag defines a table row. The `<TD>` tags define table data elements, as you read across the table.

Style Sheets in HTML 3.0

HTML is intended for document *content* markup on the server side. By design, it is not intended to provide direct control over the exact appearance of the document in the browser on the client side. One reason is portability. There is no way of controlling which browser and which font every client will have available. This state of affairs can be frustrating to graphic artists. Style sheets are intended to give page designers, or even the user of the browser, the opportunity to govern how the page is displayed in terms of fonts, colors, and other elements.

The IETF is still considering exactly how to implement style sheets into HTML 3.0. For the latest information, please see the URLs mentioned previously.

Writing Math in HTML 3.0

Most of us probably haven't missed being able to write the calculus integral symbol into our HTML code. Considering the Web got started in a physics lab, however, it's only natural that these features would eventually find their way into HTML. Unfortunately, these 3.0 features are just as much a moving target as style sheets. To learn more, please see Appendix F, "HTML Encyclopedia," for an introduction, and/or visit the HTML 3.0 specification at `http://www.ietf.cnri.reston.va.us/ids.by.wg/html.html`.

More Quick Tips on HTML Style

Style and style sheets are similar, but not the same. Although style sheets provide some degree of control over the appearance of Web documents, the subject of style is more a topic of what to do and what not to do in Web page design (whether style sheets are used or not).

Web purists make remarks such as, "It's the content, not the presentation." That philosophy notwithstanding, Web programmers obviously do have a great deal of control over many appearance factors, such as when to use a hyperlink, a bullet list, or a level 2 heading. You might be tempted to think that some choices are arbitrary—but be careful. If your pages demonstrate disregard for certain accepted Web standards or are hard to read, you might not get any repeat visitors. There is a lot to be said for having good style.

Here are a few resources concerning HTML style:

- *Style Guide for Online Hypertext,* by the father of the Web, Tim Berners-Lee

  `http://www.w3.org/hypertext/WWW/Provider/Style/Overview.html`

- *Web Style Manual,* by Patrick J. Lynch

  `http://info.med.yale.edu/caim/StyleManual_Top.HTML`

- *Tips for Writers and Designers,* by David Siegel

  `http://www.best.com/~dsiegel/tips/tips_home.html`

- *From Grass Roots to Corporate Image,* by Christine A. Quinn, Director Electrical Engineering Computer & Network Services, Stanford University

  `http://www.ncsa.uiuc.edu/SDG/IT94/Proceedings/Campus.Infosys/quinn/quinn.html`

What's Next?

Now that you know everything cool about HTML, it's time to get busy. Chapter 10 shows you how to put together a complete Web site based on several HTML files. The files include hyperlinks, graphics, CGI, and e-mail capability.

Chapter 10

Putting HTML to Work Building a Sample Site

- Planning Your Web Site
- Installing the Sample Web Site Files
- Configuring the Sample Web Site Files
- Review of the HTML 2.0 Form Tags
- Understanding the HTML Code, Step-by-Step
- What's Next?

You've come a long way in a short time. Your Web server is up and running and you've learned a great deal about HTML. Now it's time to put what you have learned to work by building a sample Web site from the ground up. This project will give you an opportunity to try out many of the HTML tags that you have learned along the way.

On the accompanying CD, you will find a group of files that comprise a sample Web site for a fictitious business called YourCo that sells a software product called Widget. Our imaginary Web site is designed to provide information about the products of YourCo, process orders, provide for immediate download of a demo version of Widget, and give the customer an opportunity to talk to us via a feedback form. These files are intended to give you something to experiment with and build upon. Hey, maybe your site could use some of these capabilities as-is.

Planning Your Web Site

There are many things to consider when setting up your Web site. A well-thought-out site will go online quickly and painlessly, whereas a poorly thought-out site will be a management nightmare from day one.

For example, if you were to decide to change your directory structure after establishing your site, you would have to change all the links that contained any of the affected URLs. Any non-local links would also have to be changed. And because most indexing on Web search databases takes from two to three weeks now, that could put you out of business for awhile.

As part of your planning, think about your mission. What is it that you want to do with your Web site?

Figure 10.1 is a feature map of our sample Web site for YourCo. As you can see, this site includes several links between pages, usage of the Netscape mailto feature, and a few CGI programs. See the next section for a brief description of each of the HTML files.

Figure 10.1.
Diagram of features of the YourCo Web site.

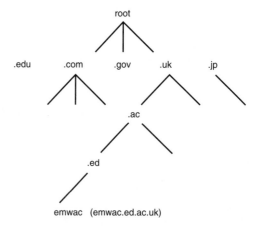

Installing the Sample Web Site Files

On the CD, you will find all the source documents for this chapter in the \site directory. Here is a brief description of the sample Web site files, in the same order as they are presented here:

- default.htm—This is the home page for YourCo.
- consult.htm—Contains information on YourCo Consulting Services.
- custreg.htm—An HTML form allowing people to sign up for the YourCo e-mail list.
- feedback.htm—An HTML form allowing people to send feedback via e-mail.
- intro.htm—Contains an introduction to YourCo products.
- order.htm—An HTML form allowing people to order YourCo products.
- product.htm—Contains further information about YourCo products and allows the user to download a demo version of Widget.
- release.htm—Contains YourCo Press Releases.
- train.htm—Contains information on YourCo Training Services.
- logo.gif—A sample logo graphic file.
- return.gif—A graphic return button.

> **Note:** All of the HTML files in this chapter were originally created using WebEdit 1.1.

To install the sample Web site on your D: drive, just copy all the files from the \site directory on the CD-ROM into the default directory of your Web server. The fact that one of the files is actually named default.htm means that it will be automatically sent by the server if any Web client specifies only the FQDN portion of your Web site. In other words, if the client doesn't specify a filename in the URL, the server tries to return a file called default.htm from the given directory. And if the URL doesn't contain a pathname either, the server looks in its default directory.

Configuring the Sample Site

There are a few places you need to edit in the sample HTML files. You can load the files into WebEdit and search for the word YourCo. Obviously, you want to change this to the real name of your organization. You might as well just search for the word your because a few of the files include text such as your IP address here or your e-mail address here. You'll see that the search for your will also turn up a few unintended hits. As we discuss the files one-by-one in the next section, we'll call your attention to the lines you need to modify.

> **Note:** If you don't have your HTTP server online yet, most browsers have an option similar to Netscape Navigator that allows you to look at the files by choosing File/Open File. This is sometimes called local mode and it is very useful for testing your pages.

Review of the HTML 2.0 Form Tags

Before diving into studying the HTML files line by line, let's recap the HTML tags that are used for creating forms on the Web. The sample files are going to show you a couple of working examples that utilize several of these tags. The possibilities for creative form development are endless. Perhaps as you study Table 10.1, your imagination will lead you to an idea about a form that you or your organization could deploy.

Table 10.1. HTML tags for creating forms.

`<FORM> ... </FORM>`	These tags appear within the `<BODY>` of the HTML file. Everything you code in between them will comprise the form. In addition to other HTML tags, the tags described in this section are valid within a `<FORM>` block.
`<TEXTAREA> ... </TEXTAREA>`	These tags cause the browser to present a multi-line text edit box on the form. You can control the width and height in character units with the ROWS and COLS properties. As with the `<INPUT>` and `<SELECT>` tags, the NAME property is used to identify the data that is returned to the server for CGI processing or sent in the e-mail body if mailto is used (more about that later).
`<INPUT> ... </INPUT>`	These tags define a single-line text box for strings or integers; a checkbox; a radio button; a pushbutton; and a few other varieties of controls. The TYPE attribute is what determines the style of `<INPUT>` control.
`<SELECT> ... </SELECT>`	These tags define a listbox of items from which the user can choose an item. You may use several `<OPTION>` tags within the `<SELECT>` block to present the available items.
`<OPTION>`	This tag indicates a selectable item within a `<SELECT>` block. You might also specify one of the values to be selected by default using the SELECTED attribute.

Understanding the HTML Code, Step-by-Step

You can browse through the HTML code and the screen shots in this chapter to get an idea of all the functionality at this site. You might be surprised at how few files are necessary to deliver such a substantial and professional business presence. You will notice that the home page contains all the necessary introductory information about YourCo, including links to more specific information on its services and products.

> **Tip:** If possible, try to keep the size of your home page down to one viewing screen. This will ensure that people can easily see your introductory information and still allow them to jump from link to link without having to use the scroll bars on their browser.

Let's go behind the scenes and see what makes the sample site tick. We are going to present each file and talk you through the highlights. We'll start off by looking at the default.htm file.

default.htm

The purpose of this file was mentioned previously; this is the YourCo home page. It is the first impression your customers will get, and it should give them an opportunity to quickly find what they are looking for. Figure 10.2 is how the page appears when loaded in Netscape Navigator.

Figure 10.2.
The appearance of the home page in Navigator.

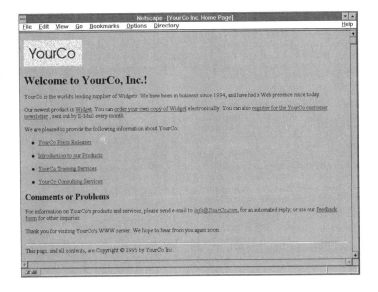

Listing 10.1 is the contents of default.htm. The annotations reference the HTML code.

Listing 10.1. The HTML code for default.htm—the home page of our sample Web site.

```
<HTML>
<HEAD>
<!-- Created: 7/30/95 8:39:28 PM-->
<!-- A comment area with file creation date and time-->

<TITLE>YourCo Inc. Home Page</TITLE>  <!-- Every file needs a TITLE-->
</HEAD>          <!-- End of the HEAD section-->

<BODY>           <!-- Begin the body of the file-->
<IMG ALT="The YourCo Logo" SRC="Logo.gif">
<!-- Display an image of YourCo's logo-->
<!-- Note the alternative text will be displayed if the browser
does not support graphics or does not have them turned on-->

<H1>Welcome to YourCo, Inc.!</H1>
<!-- A heading level one text section, no need to insert a [br] or [p] to
start next line-->

YourCo is the world's leading supplier of Widgets. We have been
in business since 1994, and have had a Web presence since today.
<P>             <!-- Note the [P] tag is not a paired tag-->

Our newest product is
<A HREF="product.htm">Widget</A>.
<!-- This is a hyperlink to the product.htm file-->

You can
<A HREF="order.htm">order your own copy of Widget</A> electronically.
You can also
<A HREF="custreg.htm">register for the YourCo customer newsletter</A>
, sent out by E-Mail every month.<P>

We are pleased to provide the following information about YourCo:<P>
<UL>
<!-- An unordered list with hyperlinks-->
<!-- note that the [LI] tag is not paired-->

<LI><A HREF="Release.htm">YourCo Press Releases</A><P>
<LI><A HREF="Intro.htm">Introduction to our Products</A><P>
<LI><A HREF="Train.htm">YourCo Training Services</A><P>
<LI><A HREF="Consult.htm">YourCo Consulting Services</A><P></UL>

<H2>Comments or Problems</H2>
<!-- Heading level 2-->

For information on YourCo's products and services, please send e-mail to
<A HREF="mailto: info@YourCo.com"><I>info@YourCo.com</I></A>,
for an automated reply,
<!-- The mailto tag used in a hyperlink will pop up a mail window in most
browsers-->

or use our <A HREF="feedback.htm">feedback form</A> for other inquiries.
<P>
```

```
Thank you for visiting YourCo's WWW server.
We hope to hear from you again soon.
<P>

<HR>This page, and all contents, are Copyright &#169; 1995 by YourCo Inc.
<!-- Insert your standard address and copyright information at the bottom of
each page. #169 is the special character entity for the copyright symbol.-->

</BODY>              <!-- End of body-->
</HTML>              <!-- End of file-->
```

Noteworthy Code in default.htm

Near the top of the file is a suggested standard comment indicating the date the file was last edited.

As per suggested style guidelines, the `<IMG>` tag includes alternative text that will display in the event the browser doesn't load the GIF file.

Remember, unlike most HTML tags that are paired, the `<P>` tag is not paired with `</P>`. As you read the comments within the code, be aware that we used the notation [tag] instead of <tag> because some browsers will be thrown off track by the occurrence of unintended HTML tags.

> **Tip:** If you ever notice that your HTML code appears strangely when you test it in local mode of your browser, be suspicious of the possibility that tags are embedded within comments.

The first interesting thing about this code is the `<A>` tag and the HREF attribute. This is called an A HREF for short. If you look at default.htm in your browser or in Figure 10.2, you'll see the line that reads, Our newest product is Widget. This snippet of code is responsible for underlining the word Widget:

```
<A HREF="product.htm">Widget</A>
```

The underlining is displayed to the user to indicate that the word is a hyperlink to another document, in this case product.htm. The absence of a pathname or a full URL on the HREF attribute means that the file product.htm must reside in the same directory on your Web server as the current file (default.htm).

Following the code further, you will see a few other A HREF hyperlinks. Then you come to the bullet list section. This bullet list starts with the `<UL>` tag, which stands for unordered list. It is unordered in the sense that it is not numbered. Numbered lists use the `<OL>` tag. (The O stands for ordered.) Within a `<UL>` or an `<OL>` section, you can include several `<LI>` tags for list items. In fact, as this example shows, you can include all kinds of other HTML code. What's interesting about the bullet list in default.htm is that it includes embedded `<A HREF>` hyperlinks!

Now you get to the `<mailto>` tag. This is an interesting critter. Netscape invented this very useful extension to HTML level 2. Most new browsers now support this feature, but some still do not. The purpose of this extension is to give the client a very convenient way to e-mail a message to you. When you think about it, this is something that you may very likely want to do while visiting a Web page. And you wouldn't want to have to bother with writing down an e-mail address, but just to type it into your mail program later. The mailto feature works by popping up a client-defined dialog box (slightly different in every browser), where the recipient list is already filled in with the e-mail address given in the HTML file, in this case *info@YourCo.com*. Typically, the client has already configured a browser with his or her own e-mail address, so all the client has to do is fill in the subject and the body text. Here are the steps of this transaction:

1. The client requests the server to send the document default.htm.

2. The server sends default.htm, and the client displays it.

3. The user clicks the mouse on the underlined text area of the screen.

4. The browser analyzes the pixel coordinates of the mouse click and determines that it is within the underlined text area of the screen formed by the `<A>` tag.

5. Because the browser understands that `<A>` tag uses HREF with mailto:, it opens a local dialog box asking the user to fill in the mail Subject and Body Text. The recipient's address is already filled in based on the HREF mailto supplied by the server. The sender's reply address and the SMTP server to use for sending mail on the client system must be preconfigured by the user of the browser.

6. When the user hits the Send button in the e-mail dialog, the mail is sent by the browser to the address that was originally specified in the HTML code written on the server side. The mail dialog closes, and the user can continue reading the Web page.

This six-step description falls somewhere in the middle of the complexity spectrum. It gets inside the HTML code but stays above the HTTP levels, and well above any analysis of the TCP/IP data stream.

If you suspect that some of your Web visitors won't have support for mailto, you do have alternatives. One method is to run a CGI application on the server side that accomplishes nearly the same thing. You might also take a look below at the file custreg.htm. It uses mailto in a slightly different fashion as part of an HTML form.

Finally, note the `<HR>` tag. This stands for horizontal rule. It draws a line across the page for decoration and readability. We use it here to separate the standard copyright or address information that shows at the bottom of the page. The copyright symbol is embedded with the special code `&#169;`. There are many other special symbols available. A Netscape HTML extension permits the use of `&copy;` to achieve the same purpose with greater readability. In any case, you must include the trailing semicolon.

You may know that HTML has an `<ADDRESS>` tag. This is often used for the same purpose as what we are doing with everything following the `<HR>` tag. Basically, it will italicize your address information.

That wraps up our basic description of default.htm. Many of the other files include several of these same features. In the sections that follow, we'll mention the areas of the code that aren't covered elsewhere.

consult.htm

This page describes our make-believe consulting services. Figure 10.3 shows the page loaded in Navigator.

Figure 10.3.
consult.htm as it appears in Navigator.

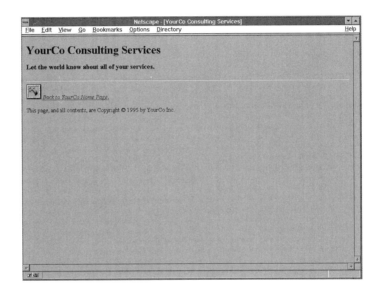

See Listing 10.2 for the HTML code.

Listing 10.2. consult.htm, the HTML code for the YourCo consulting services.

```
<HTML>
<HEAD>
<!-- Created: 7/30/95 8:39:28 PM-->
<TITLE>YourCo Consulting Services</TITLE>
</HEAD>
<BODY>
<H1>YourCo Consulting Services</H1>
<H3>Let the world know about all of your services.</H3>

<!--Give web surfers a way to return to the home page.-->
<P><HR><I><A HREF="default.htm"><IMG SRC="RETURN.GIF">
Back to YourCo Home Page.</A></I><P>
This page, and all contents, are Copyright &#169; 1995 by YourCo Inc.
</BODY>
</HTML>
```

Noteworthy Code in consult.htm

There isn't much to explain about this short page. The bottom of this page, as well as all the others except default.htm, includes a hyperlink back to the home page. This is common courtesy because readers will frequently click a link as an experiment, only to be carried to a page from which they want to return quickly.

We leave it up to you to dress up the content of this page. It is meant only as a placeholder to show where consulting services could be mentioned on a Web site.

custreg.htm

This file lets customers put themselves on the YourCo mailing list. Figure 10.4 shows custreg.htm loaded in Navigator. This form also uses mailto, but it uses it within a <FORM> tag. The difference between this and the mailto used in default.htm is that here the data in the form is automatically mailed to the address specified by the mailto element and no pop-up e-mail window is activated on the client.

Figure 10.4.
Custreg.htm in Navigator.

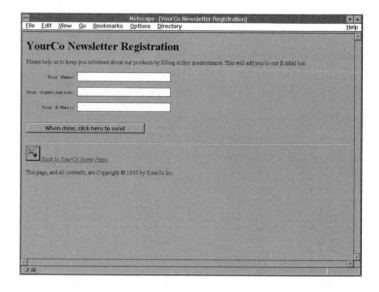

The HTML code for the customer registration form appears in Listing 10.3.

Listing 10.3. The file custreg.htm.

```
<HTML>
<HEAD>
<TITLE>YourCo Newsletter Registration</TITLE>
</HEAD>
<BODY><H1>YourCo Newsletter Registration</H1>

<FORM METHOD="POST" ACTION="mailto:register@YourCo.com">
```

```
<!-- Using "mailto" as a method in a form will mail the contents of the form
to the address stated, if the browser supports "mailto". It is more robust to
provide a CGI application to handle forms data.-->

Please help us to keep you informed about our products by filling in this
questionnaire. This will add you to our E-Mail list.
<p><PRE>
<!-- Use [PRE] tags to help you line up forms-->
<!-- INPUT data will be mailed.-->
        Your Name: <INPUT NAME="user" SIZE="30"><P>
Your organization: <INPUT NAME="org" SIZE="30"><P>
      Your E-Mail: <INPUT NAME="mail" SIZE="30"><P>
</PRE>

<input type=submit value="When done, click here to send">
<!-- Invokes the form action.-->
</FORM>

<P><HR><I><A HREF="default.htm"><IMG SRC="RETURN.GIF">
Back to YourCo Home Page.</A></I><P>
This page, and all contents, are Copyright &#169; 1995 by YourCo Inc.
</BODY>
</HTML>
```

Noteworthy Code in custreg.htm

As you can see, this HTML code is quite different than the code in the first two files. This code takes advantage of the `<FORM>` tag, a very powerful feature in HTML 2.0. Notice the line of code that reads

```
<FORM METHOD="POST" ACTION="mailto:register@YourCo.com">
```

This uses the ACTION attribute of the `<FORM>` tag to specify that the browser should perform a mailto operation on the client side after the form is submitted. It works in tandem with this line of code near the end of the form, just before the `</FORM>` tag:

```
<input type=submit value="When done, click here to send">
```

The `<INPUT>` tag specifies that a field should be drawn on the form. The TYPE attribute of this field is *submit,* which means that it will be a pushbutton. The VALUE attribute indicates what the label of the button will be. On this form, the button is called, "When done, click here to send." The browser will determine the size of the button based on the current font and the text supplied for the VALUE attribute.

When a user presses the submit button, it will cause the FORM ACTION to occur. The ACTION attribute could point to a CGI script to run on the server side, but in this case it is using built-in functionality on the client browser to cause the form data to be mailed. The recipient of the mail is automatically supplied by the HTML code on the server. Here, the form will be mailed right back to YourCo! Webmasters consider it convenient to receive form data like this in their incoming mail.

The other noteworthy code in this form determines how the screen gets drawn. The three lines containing <INPUT> tags draw text boxes for the user to fill in. Each box will accept up to 30 characters. The form data from those text boxes will be sent through e-mail formatted like this:

```
Return-Path: <bill@whitehouse.gov>
From: bill@whitehouse.gov
Date: Sat, 30 Sep 95 09:35:51 -0700
Subject: Form posted from Mozilla
Apparently-To: <register@YourCo.com>

user=Bill&org=Whitehouse&mail=bill@whitehouse.gov
```

The NAME attributes on the <INPUT> tags determine the labels that go with the form data when it is sent through e-mail or processed by CGI applications on the server. You can see the user, org, and mail labels in the last line in the form data above. The & characters are field delimiters.

feedback.htm

Figure 10.5 shows a form that enables your customers to submit feedback via e-mail. This capability is an important part of quality customer service.

Figure 10.5.
Feedback.htm in Netscape Navigator.

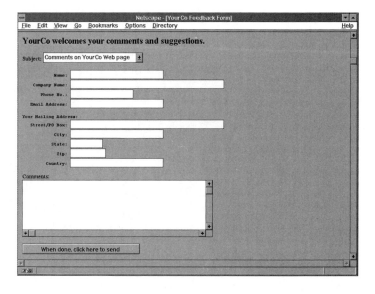

 See Listing 10.4 for the HTML code as you follow these additional comments.

Listing 10.4. The HTML code for the customer feedback form, feedback.htm.

```
<HTML>
<HEAD>
<TITLE>YourCo Feedback Form</TITLE>
</HEAD>
<BODY>
```

```
<H2>YourCo welcomes your comments and suggestions.</H2>
<P>

<!-- YOU MUST CHANGE THIS LINE TO REFLECT YOUR SERVER DOMAIN NAME-->
<FORM METHOD=POST action="http:<!--your IP address here/http/cgi-
bin/perform.exe">

<!-- Here we use a CGI application to handle the form data. The perform.exe CGI
application will handle parsing the data from the form and then mailing it.-->
<INPUT TYPE=hidden name="CmdFile" value="/http/mail.cmdl">
<INPUT TYPE=hidden name="mailto" value="your email address here">
<INPUT TYPE=hidden name="errto" value="your email address here">

<!-- These hidden values tell the mailto CGI application where to mail the
data and where to send error reports.-->

<B>Subject:</B>
  <SELECT name="subject">
  <OPTION> Comments on YourCo Web page
  <OPTION> I'd like to open an account
  <OPTION> I'd like to comment on...
  <OPTION> I need some information on...
  <OPTION> Would you please...
  <OPTION> Other
  </SELECT>
<PRE>
          <B>Name:</B> <INPUT name="name" SIZE=30>
   <B>Company Name:</B> <INPUT name="company" SIZE=50>
      <B>Phone No.:</B> <INPUT name="phoneno" SIZE=20>
  <B>Email Address:</B> <INPUT name="email" SIZE=30>
</PRE>
<P>
<PRE>
<B>Your Mailing Address:</B>
   <B>Street/PO Box:</B> <INPUT name="address1" SIZE=50>
          <B>City:</B> <INPUT name="city" SIZE=30>
         <B>State:</B> <INPUT name="state" SIZE=10>
           <B>Zip:</B> <INPUT name="zip" SIZE=11>
       <B>Country:</B> <INPUT name="country" SIZE=30>
</PRE>
<P>
<B>Comments:</B>
<BR>
<TEXTAREA name="~comments" cols=60 rows=8></TEXTAREA>
<P>
<input type=submit value="When done, click here to send">
</FORM>

<P><HR><I><A HREF="default.htm"><IMG SRC="RETURN.GIF">
Back to YourCo Home Page.</A></I><P>
This page, and all contents, are Copyright &#169; 1995 by YourCo Inc.
</BODY>
</HTML>
```

Noteworthy Code in feedback.htm

Of interest here is the `<SELECT>` ... `</SELECT>` block that includes several `<OPTION>` items. The `<SELECT>` block creates a drop-down listbox on the form, named `subject`. The item the user chooses will be sent as a text string to the CGI application on the server.

There are two separate blocks of `<INPUT>` tags. `<INPUT>` defaults to a single line text field if the `TYPE` attribute is not present. The `SIZE` attribute is used to limit the number of characters that the user is permitted to type in the field. This is an example of client/server cooperation. The CGI application on the server might be storing the form data in a relational database that has limited size fields. The HTML/CGI programmer can use the `SIZE` attribute to ask the browser to ensure proper constraints on the data that will be submitted. This represents a simple kind of fault tolerance that will prevent the user from breaking the CGI application either intentionally or accidentally. Of course, the CGI application is ultimately responsible for parsing the data and handling any error conditions.

Each `<INPUT>` tag is indented with spaces instead of tabs to line up the fields. Not all browsers will interpret tab characters the same way, so spaces are preferred.

A `<TEXTAREA>` and a submit button finish up the form. The `<TEXTAREA>` tag is used to create multi-line edit fields.

intro.htm

The purpose of this page is to introduce the YourCo products. See Figure 10.6 for the way it looks on the Web.

Figure 10.6.
Intro.htm running on the Web.

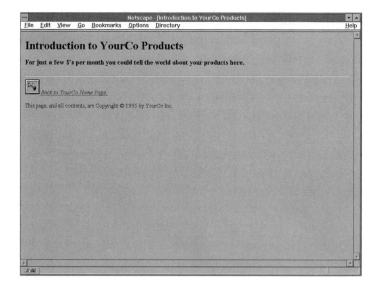

See Listing 10.5 for the HTML code of the file intro.htm.

Listing 10.5. Intro.htm.

```
<HTML>
<HEAD>
<!-- Created: 7/30/95 8:39:28 PM-->
<TITLE>Introduction to YourCo Products</TITLE>
</HEAD>

<BODY>
<H1>Introduction to YourCo Products</H1>
<H3>For just a few $'s per month you could tell the world about your
products here.</H3>

<P><HR><I><A HREF="default.htm"><IMG SRC="RETURN.GIF">
Back to YourCo Home Page.</A></I><P>
This page, and all contents, are Copyright &#169; 1995 by YourCo Inc.
</BODY>
</HTML>
```

There is nothing new to say about this file from a programming viewpoint. It is a placeholder for the actual HTML file, which you can modify to describe your products.

order.htm

The purpose of this page is to let your customers order your products. See Figure 10.7 for the way it looks on the Web.

Figure 10.7.
Order.htm running on the Web.

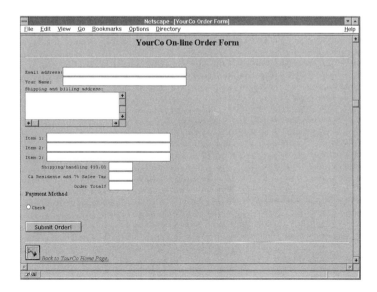

See Listing 10.6 for the HTML code of the file order.htm.

Listing 10.6. The customer order form, order.htm.

```
<HEAD>
<TITLE>YourCo Order Form</TITLE>
</HEAD>
<BODY>
<CENTER>
<!-- CENTER is an HTML 3 tag -->
<H2>YourCo On-line Order Form</H2>
<HR>
</CENTER>
<FORM METHOD=POST ACTION="http:<!--your IP address here/http/cgi-
bin/perform.exe">
<INPUT TYPE=hidden name="CmdFile" value="/http/mail.cmdl">
<INPUT TYPE=hidden name="mailto" value="your email address here">
<INPUT TYPE=hidden name="errto" value="your email address here">
<INPUT TYPE=hidden name="subject" value="demo Order">
<PRE>
<BR>Email address:<INPUT NAME=email_addr TYPE=text SIZE=40>
<BR>Your Name:    <INPUT NAME=Name TYPE=text SIZE=40 MAXSIZE40>
<BR>Shipping and billing address:
<BR><TEXTAREA NAME=address ROWS=4 COLS=30 MAXLENGTH=150></TEXTAREA>

<BR>Item 1: <INPUT NAME=Tittle TYPE=text SIZE=40>
<BR>Item 2: <INPUT NAME=Medium TYPE=text SIZE=40>
<BR>Item 3: <INPUT NAME=Edition TYPE=text SIZE=40>
<BR>       Shipping/handling $10.00 <INPUT NAME=SH TYPE=text SIZE=7>
<BR> CA Residents add 7% Sales Tax <INPUT NAME=Tax TYPE=text SIZE=7>
<BR>                  Order Total$ <INPUT NAME=Total TYPE=text SIZE=7>
<H4>Payment Method</H4>
<BR><INPUT TYPE=radio NAME=pmtmethod VALUE=M>Check
<P>
</PRE>
<INPUT TYPE=submit VALUE="Submit Order!">
</FORM>

<P><HR><I><A HREF="default.htm"><IMG SRC="RETURN.GIF">
Back to YourCo Home Page.</A></I><P>
This page, and all contents, are Copyright &#169; 1995 by YourCo Inc.
</BODY>
</HTML>
```

Noteworthy Code in order.htm

Other than the single radio button, there are no new elements to describe on this form. For the sake of simplicity, we coded only a radio button for one payment type. Strictly speaking, if you want to indicate an on/off condition of a single item, normal Windows GUI style suggests the use of a checkbox. Radio buttons are usually used to represent a group of several mutually exclusive items, which is exactly what you would want to do with this form when you add other payment methods.

Again, an <INPUT> tag using TYPE=submit is coded to send the form data to the CGI application on the server. The Web server will invoke a CGI application (perform.exe) in the cgi-bin directory each time that a client presses the submit button.

product.htm

product.htm is used to further describe the products of YourCo. See Figure 10.8 for the way it looks on the Web.

Figure 10.8.
product.htm running on the Web.

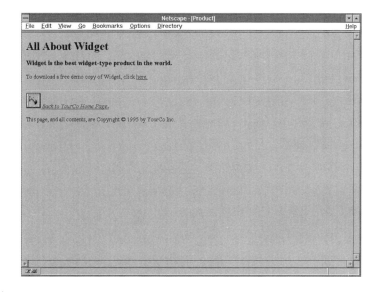

See Listing 10.7 for the HTML code of the file product.htm.

Listing 10.7. The HTML code for product.htm.

```
<HTML>
<HEAD>
<!-- Created: 7/30/95 8:39:28 PM-->
<TITLE>Product</TITLE>
</HEAD>

<BODY>
<H1>All About Widget</H1>
<H3>Widget is the best widget-type product in the world.</H3>
To download a free demo copy of Widget, click <A HREF="demo.zip">here.</A>
<P><HR><I><A HREF="default.htm"><IMG SRC="RETURN.GIF">
Back to YourCo Home Page.</A></I><P>
This page, and all contents, are Copyright &#169; 1995 by YourCo Inc.
</BODY>
</HTML>
```

Noteworthy Code in product.htm

This code contains nothing unusual, except for the fact that it permits your customer to download a free demo copy of your software product and try it out. Here's how this works. The <A HREF> refers to demo.zip. When the user clicks that screen region and the client requests the file demo.zip from the HTTP server, the client doesn't yet know exactly what type of document it really is. The server will send a header back to the client informing it that the data type is URL-encoded. The client will most likely tell the user that it is unprepared to handle that type and ask the user if he would simply like to download and save the file. Of course this is precisely what the user is hoping to do! Clicking the appropriate button in that message box will initiate the file transfer. It might take some time to download large files, so Netscape Navigator will display a progress bar as the download proceeds to 100% complete. Remember that you will often need to use WinZip to decompress files that you retrieve on the Web.

release.htm

This purpose of release.htm is to display YourCo Press Releases. See Figure 10.9 for the way it looks on the Web.

Figure 10.9.
release.htm running on the Web.

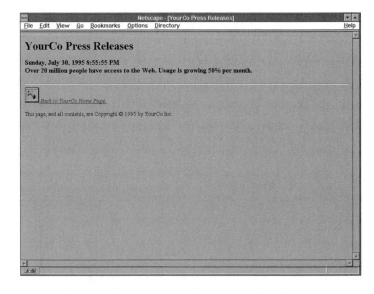

See Listing 10.8 for the HTML code of the file release.htm.

Listing 10.8. The HTML code for release.htm is very similar to the other files.

```
<HTML>
<HEAD>
<!-- Created: 7/30/95 8:39:28 PM-->
<TITLE>YourCo Press Releases</TITLE>
</HEAD>
```

```
<BODY>
<H1>YourCo Press Releases</H1>
<H3>Sunday, July 30, 1995 8:55:55 PM<BR>
Over 20 million people have access to the Web. Usage is growing 50% per
month.</H3>

<P><HR><I><A HREF="default.htm"><IMG SRC="RETURN.GIF">
Back to YourCo Home Page.</A></I><P>
This page, and all contents, are Copyright &#169; 1995 by YourCo Inc.
</BODY>
</HTML>
```

train.htm

The purpose of this page is to describe YourCo training services. See Figure 10.10 for the way it looks on the Web.

Figure 10.10.
train.htm running on the Web.

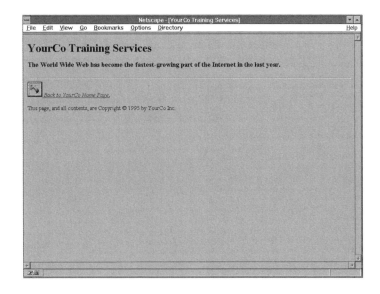

See Listing 10.9 for the HTML code of the file train.htm.

train.htm contains nothing new from a programming standpoint.

Listing 10.9. train.htm is the HTML code for YourCo training services.

```
<HTML>
<HEAD>
<!-- Created: 7/30/95 8:39:28 PM -->
<TITLE>YourCo Training Services</TITLE>
</HEAD>
```

continues

Listing 10.9. continued

```
<BODY>
<H1>YourCo Training Services</H1>
<H3>The World Wide Web has become the fastest-growing part of the
Internet in the last year.</H3>

<P><HR><I><A HREF="default.htm"><IMG SRC="RETURN.GIF">
Back to YourCo Home Page.</A></I><P>
This page, and all contents, are Copyright &#169; 1995 by YourCo Inc.
</BODY>
</HTML>
```

What's Next?

This wraps up Part II of the book. Now we can get into some of the really exciting things you can do at your Web site. Here are just a few of the topics which lay ahead of us: keeping statistics of which pages are visited most often; running mail, Telnet, and FTP servers; and connecting HTML code to relational databases.

When you are very near to having your site running officially on the Internet, you might want to take special notice of several security ideas that are going to be brought up in the remainder of the book. Several tips are presented in Part III and Part IV, which should help you to avoid some of the common threats of hackers.

Part III

Expanding Your Internet Server

This part of the book will show you how to expand your Web site way beyond the Web. We will show you how to upgrade you from a Web server to an Internet server.

Chapter 11

Announcing Your
Web Site to the World

By now, you have learned HTML, installed several Internet protocol servers, and designed a professional site. After customizing the sample files in Chapter 10, you have a real Web server on the Internet. So what's next? Let the world know that your site is there, of course!

Your data is available on the Web, but it's useless until the world knows about it. How do you publicize it so that people will read it and be able to refer to it in the future? That's what this chapter is all about.

This is a short chapter. You might be able to register your home page with all of these link clearinghouses in just a few short hours of online time.

The Top Two Places to Hit

The quickest way to bring other Web users to your window is to register with the two Web services discussed here.

First, announce your site with "Announcements of New WWW Servers." Point your browser to http://www.w3.org/hypertext/DataSources/WWW/Geographical_generation/new-servers.html. (See Figure 11.1.)

Figure 11.1.
The W3 Consortium Web page registration service.

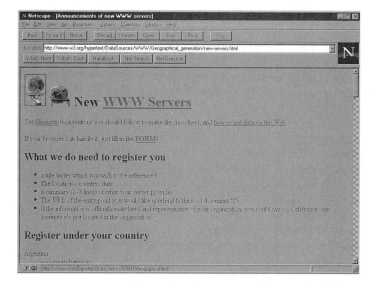

After you fill out the form, your server will be registered with the World Wide Web consortium, which maintains a database of all the Web servers on the Internet.

Next, you'll want to stop by Scott Banister's "Submit It." It's a free service designed to make the process of submitting your URLs to a variety of WWW catalogs as fast and easy as possible. Here's the URL: http://submit-it.com/.

Submit It lets you fill out one form and check off which search sites you want your site to be automatically registered with. These are the search databases that Submit It will let you register with: Yahoo, Starting Point, WebCrawler, EINet Galaxy, Lycos, Harvest, What's New Too, and Infoseek. One form or many, the choice is easy.

You might also like to browse through these other index sites, and add links to your home page and/or specific pages at your site.

General Indexes on the Web

This section lists several general resources on the Web where you might want to list your site:

- Registering with ALIWEB

  ALIWEB stands for Archie Like Searching for the Web. The idea behind ALIWEB is simple. The World Wide Web is growing by leaps and bounds on a daily basis. It is impossible for someone to keep track of all the services available because they change often and there are simply too many of them. Therefore, ALIWEB proposes that people keep track of the services they provide in such a way that programs can automatically retrieve the descriptions and combine them into a searchable database.

  `http://www.nexor.co.uk/aliweb/doc/registering.html`

- EINet Galaxy is an electronic guide to a wide array of services on the Internet.

  `http://www.einet.net`

- WebCrawler is an excellent search page on the Web. If you would like it to show your name as a result of the searches conducted by others, just fill out their URL submission form.

  `http://www.webcrawler.com/WebCrawler/WebQuery.html`

- The Lycos search page and URL registration forms work basically the same as WebCrawler mentioned previously. (See Figure 11.2.)

  `http://lycos.cs.cmu.edu/lycos-register.html`

- The Nikos Search Engine is another online search page and registration form. Nikos is provided by Rockwell. It works by sending Internet robots out to gather information about Web sites and keep it organized in a searchable database. You can have your site added to the database by submitting this form.

  `http://www.rns.com/www_index/new_site.html`

- The Otis Index links to registration forms available on each subtopic page.

  `http://www.interlog.com/~gordo/contactcom.html`

- The NetPages White Pages allows you to submit your individual or business address on the Internet. It also runs a Yellow Pages form that offers two lines of free advertising. All entries are verified every six months. You can drop your name from the service at any time. Aldea Communications also maintains an Internet Survival Guide here. (See Figure 11.3.)

```
http://www.aldea.com/
```

Figure 11.2.
The Lycos URL registration form.

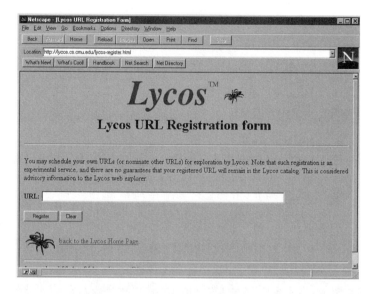

Figure 11.3.
The Aldea Communications home page.

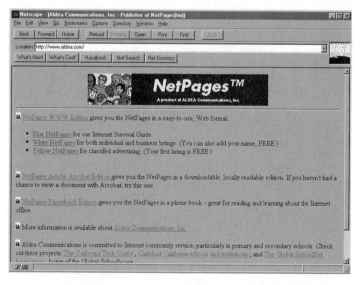

- Harvest Gatherers is another URL registration service. This one accepts home page listings only—no document-specific references. As a bonus, this Web page contains links to other interesting sites and even a query form to let you search the Web.

```
http://rd.cs.colorado.edu/Harvest/brokers/
```

Web Business Indexes

These Web resources are geared toward doing business online.

- Internet Yellow Pages Registration Form

  `http://www.yellow.com/`

- The World Wide Yellow Pages (tm) is a cost index service. Just fill out the online form, and they'll take care of the rest. Use e-mail to get more information

  E-mail: `info@yellow.com`

  Regular mail: Home Pages, Inc.
  World Wide Yellow Pages
  257 Castro Street, Suite 219
  Mountain View, CA 94041

- BizWeb Company Information Form

  This index of companies is categorized by the goods or services they provide. Click the key term that best describes the company or product you are searching for. There are currently 776 companies listed on BizWeb.

  `http://www.bizweb.com/InfoForm/infoform.html`

- Open Market, Inc., Commercial Sites Index.

  Open Market, Inc., develops and markets software and services to facilitate electronic commerce on the Internet and the World Wide Web. It also maintains the Commercial Sites Index as a service to the Internet.

  `http://www.directory.net/dir/submit.cgi`

- The Otis Business Index

  The Otis Index maintains more than 100,000 links to free software, books, magazines, newsgroups, and commercial sites.

  `http://www.interlog.com/~gordo/contactcom.html`

- WWW Business Yellow Pages

  The WWW Business Yellow Pages is a service to the Internet community provided by the University of Houston College of Business Administration.

  `http://www.cba.uh.edu/cgi-bin/autosub`

- New Riders World Wide Web Yellow Pages

  The New Riders *Official World Wide Web Yellow Pages* is a free service that lists thousands of businesses on the Web. As Figure 11.4 shows, it doesn't just list them, it also lets you search them! Electronic searching is perhaps the key advantage that the Web offers, but the information stored in this site is also used to print the annual edition of their popular paperback *Web Yellow Pages.*

Figure 11.4.
New Riders' Official World Wide Web Yellow Pages lets you register your Web site or search the database for other businesses on the Internet.

Listings in Hierarchical Indexes

These are general-purpose Web sites that cover many types of businesses.

- Yahoo

  This is perhaps the best-known Web site. Yahoo contains links to hundreds of other Web pages. Whether you choose to register here or not, you should definitely give it a try. To explore its many features, enter this URL in your Web browser: `http://www.yahoo.com/`. If you decide that your pages should be listed there too, then you can use this more specific URL: `http://www.yahoo.com/bin/add`.

- Mother of All Bulletin Board Systems

  This oddly-named site contains hundreds of links to other Web pages. It was developed by Oliver McBryan (`mcbryan@cs.colorado.edu`) of the University of Colorado. This is a very large index that permits users to automatically add new URLs.

  `http://www.cs.colorado.edu/homes/mcbryan/public_html/bb/summary.html`

Listings Submitted Through E-mail

These Web site listing centers get their input via e-mail:

- CUI W3 Catalog; catalog of catalogs

  e-mail: `www-announce@www.w3.org`

- The NCSA What's New Catalog

  The interesting thing about this is that you write the HTML code for your own submission. To get a very quick overview of the guidelines you should follow, visit their Web page at `http://www.ncsa.uiuc.edu/SDG/Software/Mosaic/Docs/submit-to-whats-new.html`. Then you can send the appropriate e-mail to `whats-new@ncsa.uiuc.edu`.

■ The Online Whole Internet Catalog

   E-mail: `wic@ora.com`

   URL: `http://nearnet.gnn.com/wic/`

Other Sites of Interest

The following list is an assortment of interesting places to check out on the Web.

■ Cool Site of the Day. This site contains a new hyperlink each day to an interesting or unique Web page. If you would like to be considered, send e-mail describing your site to `cool@infi.net`. Make sure you include your own URL. If you just want to visit an interesting Web page each day, check out

   `http://cool.infi.net/`

■ Spider's Pick of the Day. This is another site that chooses a hot Web page each day.

   E-mail: `boba@www.com`

   `http://gagme.wwa.com/~boba/pick.html`

■ Inter-Links is a great catalog of all sorts of Web resources. Every Webmaster should spend some time there just to get an idea of what's available (`http://www.nova.edu/Inter-Links/`).

■ The Clearinghouse for Subject-Oriented Internet Resource Guides. This site includes lots of links to other resources and an online submission form. It's only interested in your Web site, however, if it is a free guide to other Internet resources.

   `http://www.lib.umich.edu/chhome.html`

Newsgroups

One newsgroup is dedicated to the purpose of new Web sites coming online. Post an article here about your own site. In addition, you might want to monitor this newsgroup to see if any other sites similar to yours (shall we say, competitors) show up on the Web. Newsgroup: `comp.infosystems.www.announce`.

There are more than 15,000 other newsgroups on Usenet at the time of this writing, and if a discussion group is directly related to the topic of your page it is within netiquette to announce your Web site there.

Caution: Do not post advertisements to Usenet newsgroups that do not directly relate to your Web page, or the members of that group will not be happy with you.

What's Next?

That's it! Now that your site is running and you've announced it all over the place, you better be ready. You could be in for a flood of traffic. The next chapter is all about preparing for the growth of your site, and maintaining it. Who knows, your Web site could become famous.

Chapter 12

Maintaining and Tracking Your Web Site

By now, hopefully, you have installed the Web server and written the HTML files for your site. In addition, if you have just gone through the steps of Chapter 11, "Announcing your Web Site to the World," your home page is probably already getting some hits—perhaps hundreds (depending on how you count them; see the sidebar later in this chapter for more on this interesting question). Before it starts to get overwhelming, you should know a few things that will help you manage the growth of your site.

This chapter presents a broad collection of tips for the day-to-day maintenance of your Web site. Most of these tasks are considered system administrator responsibilities, but that doesn't mean they are difficult. In fact, we think you'll agree after reading this chapter that many of these procedures are quite easy to implement—which is a tribute to the design and simplicity of the Windows NT user interface.

Utility Programs for the Windows NT Webmaster

Let's start with a discussion of the toolbox that no NT Webmaster should be without. Each of the tools listed in this section has its place. Knowing about them is one thing, but actually being familiar with them is another. Acquaint yourself with their capabilities at your earliest convenience, and you will be rewarded day in and day out.

We can introduce you only to these tools' purpose and let you know their basic capabilities. Most of these programs have dozens of options for all kinds of different needs and situations. It is up to you to try the programs and consult the appropriate documentation for further information.

Windows NT Performance Monitor

This is a great GUI tool that is very easy to use after you get a little used to it. It gathers good statistics on IP/TCP/ICMP messages. This is your best all-around diagnostic tool for both the network (if your NT is on a LAN) and the NT system itself (for example, CPU usage and disk I/O). For more information about Performance Monitor, consult the Windows NT Resource Kit.

> **Note:** In order to get the most out of Performance Monitor, be sure to install the SNMP service along with TCP/IP. With SNMP installed (through the Control Panel Network icon) and enabled (through the Control Panel Services icon), Performance Monitor can track IP packet statistics on your site.

ping

This is used to determine whether another computer running TCP/IP is reachable and how long it takes for a packet to make the round trip back to your computer.

ipconfig

If you're running on a network, this will tell you your own IP address and let you query other interesting network statistics.

tracert

This is the NT console mode application equivalent to UNIX traceroute. This utility will display the entire route your IP packets take from your server to the host that you select.

netstat

netstat is a handy tool for looking at the status of the LAN or the Internet. You can see active connections to all ports and get a statistical breakdown of all connections over time.

WinMSD

There is not an icon added to any program group by the default installation of Windows NT for WinMSD. There is, however, a very handy utility named winmsd.exe hiding in your %systemroot%\system32 directory. You can run this program from the command line, but we use it so often that we created an icon in the Administrative Tools program group. WinMSD enables you to browse a lot of valuable system information, without having to resort to separate tools.

Although WinMSD does not let you change any system parameters, it is a handy one-stop utility for information on OS version, hardware, memory, drivers, services running, drives, devices, IRQ/port status, DMA memory, environment, and network configuration. Wow! That's a lot of capability in one program. You can print any of the information displayed or save it to a file. There is also a Tools menu bar that lets you launch Event Viewer, Registry Editor, or Disk Administrator. If you ever sit down at an NT system that you are not familiar with, WinMSD is the tool to start with. See Figure 12.1.

Figure 12.1.
*Windows NT Diagnostics
with winmsd.exe.*

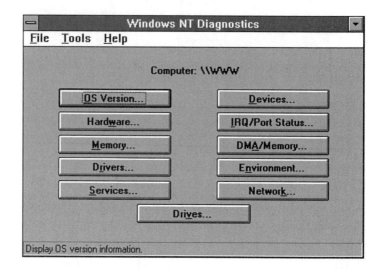

WebStone

Another Web server utility worth checking out is WebStone, developed by Silicon Graphics Incorporated. This program will benchmark the performance of your Web server by submitting HTTP GET requests repeatedly. Comparison data is available versus other Web servers on selected hardware platforms. See `http://www.sgi.com/Products/WebFORCE/WebStone/`.

Web Page Quality Assurance

As your site grows in sophistication over time and you add more and more HTML files, you will run into the problem of maintaining and checking a large body of code. Weblint is a free Web page that helps you analyze the syntax and accuracy of your HTML code. It gets its name from the C program checker called *lint,* which has been around for years.

You can download a freeware version of Weblint v1.011 or use the service online at this URL:

`http://www.unipress.com/weblint/`

Weblint was developed by Neil Bowers and Clay Webster. It is a Perl script with an HTML forms-based interface. Here are some of the notes from the Unipress Web site.

You can paste or type in HTML code and have it checked. Or you can simply supply a URL of a page anywhere on the World Wide Web to be checked.

Weblint supports HTML 3.0 tags, such as TABLE, MATH, and FIG. Weblint currently performs the following checks:

- Basic structure
- Unknown elements and element attributes

- Context checks (where a tag must appear within a certain element)
- Overlapped elements
- A TITLE in the HEAD element
- IMG elements have ALT text
- Illegally nested elements
- Mismatched tags (such as <H1> ... </H2>)
- Unclosed elements (such as <H1> ...)
- Elements that should appear only once
- Obsolete elements
- Odd number of quotes in tag
- Order of headings
- Potentially unclosed tags
- Markup embedded in comments, which can confuse some browsers
- The word *here* as anchor text (referred to as *here syndrome*)
- Tags where attributes are expected (anchors)
- Existence of local anchor targets
- Case of tags (not enabled by default)

Web Site Statistical Analysis

As a Webmaster, you want to know who's coming to your site, how often, and what they are doing there. To accomplish this we'll use the Perl programming language interpeter and the Musage CGI application.

Actually, before we get into Perl, let's mention a very interesting tool that can help you chart your Web site statistics without requiring any program customizations. It will analyze your Web page usage based on your server log files. A company called Logical Design Solutions has invented a cool program called WebTrac. If you try the program and you like it, you can get it for free. However, they are accepting donations for Save The Children, which they claim is a top-ranked charitable organization. This is a very innovative way to distribute software, and it's for a good cause. Visit their home page at http://www.lds.com.

> **Tip:** Remember that some Web server statistics tools require the Web server to close the log files before the files can be analyzed. This is true of EMWAC and Musage.

Perl

Perl is an interpreted language designed for scanning arbitrary text files, extracting information from those text files, and printing reports based on that information. It is also a good language for many system management tasks. We will use it for some of our CGI scripts. Musage is an excellent example of a powerful CGI script written in Perl.

> **Note:** Although Perl is an acronym for Practical Extraction and Report Language, like the names of many other program languages formed from acronyms, it is not often fully capitalized.

Obtaining Perl for NT

Perl currently comes in two versions: Perl 4 and Perl 5. Version 5 is the new kid on the block, and it comes with object-oriented extensions. Perl was invented on UNIX, by Larry Wall. Keep in mind that Perl has always had strong roots on UNIX platforms, and most of the Webmasters who use it and post public-domain Perl source code work on UNIX. Fortunately, some nice folks have ported Perl to Windows NT and made it available via anonymous FTP.

You can retrieve Perl 4 for Windows NT at the FTP site of Intergraph. Point your Web browser or CuteFTP to this URL: `ftp://ftp.intergraph.com/pub/win32/perl/`. You will want to download the file ntperlb.zip (if you only want the compiled version) or ntperls.zip (if you want the Visual C++ 2.0 source code).

Dick Hardt of Hip Communications has ported Perl 5 to Windows NT. If you would like to try object-oriented Perl, visit `ftp://ntperl.hip.com/ntperl/`. Here you will find source code, binary files, and documentation.

Learning Perl

As a programming language, Perl will take some time to learn. Alas, this is not a subject we can cover in this book. However, the least we can do is give you some information about where to find more information. The first thing you might want to do is check out these three text files that come with Perl.

- relnotes.txt—For general information about Perl for NT and how Perl for NT differs from Perl for UNIX.
- status.txt—For information on what features are supported.
- registry.txt—For information on using the registry access features.

To learn more about Perl, try the University of Florida's Perl Archive at `http://www.cis.ufl.edu/perl/`. Users in the UK might like to try something closer to home, such as the NEXOR Ltd Perl Page at `http://pubweb.nexor.co.uk/public/perl/perl.html`.

Here are a few other Perl resources on the Net; the last one consists of a few newsgroups dedicated to Perl topics:

```
http://www.metronet.com/perlinfo/perl5.html

http://www.perl.com/perl/faq/

http://www.ee.pdx.edu/~rseymour/perl/

comp.lang.perl
```

About Musage

As a Webmaster, you need to know how many people look at a particular section or document, and who those people are, in order to tell whether or not you are reaching your target audience. If a section is heavily used, you know it is worth developing; if it is only lightly used, maybe it isn't worth spending much time developing or maybe your menus need redesigning—because users don't realize the section is even there.

Most Web servers keep these statistics in log files—for example, every time a user looks at a document the server records the date and time, the user's IP address or DNS name, the filename of the document, and the size of the document. In order for this information to be useful, you need to analyze the log files to produce a manageable summary. Musage is a Perl script that will analyze the server log files for you and produce useful summaries, including lists of the most-used documents and the most active users and sites. Musage then generates HTML files showing a breakdown of key statistics. You can review the statistics in your Web browser.

Musage was designed to analyze the usage logs from the EMWAC HTTP and Gopher servers, but it also works with logs from any World Wide Web server that uses the common logfile format (for example, EMWAC's professional Web server, cern3 httpd).

Musage got its name because it does a monthly analysis of usage—and there is a well-known log file analyzer called *Wusage*, which does a weekly analysis. One feature of Musage not seen in other such programs is that it can separate home users from outside users, so that you can compare how users from within your organization and those from outside access your server.

Counting the Hits

Many Web sites display a counter of how many users have visited their site. These are often called *hits* instead of visitor counters because of the way in which they are calculated. No matter what you call it, it is often misleading.

For instance, some sites will say that they are getting 5,000 hits a day, when in fact they are getting 500 different Web browsers accessing 5,000 files. Hits are usually a simple count of the HTTP GET requests that are recorded by the Web server log files. This method will count a single visitor 10 times if he or she looks at 10 HTML pages. However, if a visitor navigates back and forth between two HTML pages within the Web site, this will only be recorded as two hits because the client Web browser will keep the pages in its local cache after the first retrieval. The server will not register extra hits of the same page unless the client specifically requests a reload.

What this all means is that when people talk about how many hits a site is getting, they should mean how many different visitors they have had that day; but most sites prefer to publish the inflated numbers anyway.

Obtaining and Installing Musage

This is a rather easy process. The Musage home page is http://www.blpes.lse.ac.uk/misc/musage.htm. All you have to do is click on the link to the file musage.txt. You can leave the file musage.doc on the Musage home page because musage.txt is so well-commented that you might not even need to refer to musage.doc.

Configuring Musage

You can consult musage.doc (the user's guide) and musage.txt for more details, but what follows in this section is the information you need to configure Musage to run at your Web site. You need to use a text editor to modify the Perl script Musage.txt. There are some variables you can set near the top of the script to customize it for your own site. The following examples show how the author of Musage customized it for use with the WWW server at his own site.

@homeip

All IP addresses starting 158.143 or DNS names ending lse.ac.uk belong to home users (users at the London School of Economics), therefore, @homeip=158.143, or @homeip=lse.ac.uk.

$homedomain

In the summary list showing numbers of documents accessed by each domain, all home users are lumped together as if they belong to a single domain—for the domain to be referred to as 'lse.ac.uk' in the summary list, use $homedomain=lse.ac.uk.

$homename

This is the LSE (London School of Economics), so $homename=LSE.

$servername

The part of the server that I am generating statistics for belongs to BLPES (British Library of Political & Economic Science), so $servername = BLPES.

$top

I want the summaries to show the top twenty items in each category, so `$top=20`.

$dnsnames

I want the list of DNS names that Musage has succeeded in looking up to be kept in a file called DNSNAMES.LST in the current directory, so `$dnsnames=./dnsnames.lst`.

$inputdir

The log files to analyze are in a directory called C:\LOGS, so `$inputdir=/logs/` (note trailing slash).

$outputdir

I want the report files to be written to the current directory, so `$outputdir=./`.

@ignoreip

I regularly test my server from PCs with IP addresses `158.143.104.174` and `158.143.104.209`, and if accesses from these machines were included in the analysis it would make the server seem much busier than it really is, so `@ignoreip=158.143.104.174` or `@ignoreip=158.143.104.209`.

@ignorepath

I don't want accesses to files in the directory /misc on my server to be analyzed, because they are my own private projects and not part of the server as a whole, so `@ignorepath=('/misc')`.

@focusip

I could choose to focus on accesses by specific groups of users (for example, `@focusip=158.143` or `@focusip=lse.ac.uk`) to focus on users from the LSE, but haven't done so in the example.

@focusonpath

I don't want to analyze usage of the entire server, only those parts that are set up and maintained by my department, which are in directories /blpes and /ibss on the server, so `@focusonpath=/blpes` or `@focusonpath=/ibss`.

$verbosemode

I already know it's going to take ages, so I don't need to be reassured by having Musage tell me every little thing it's doing, so `$verbosemode = 0`.

$lookupdnsnames

I want Musage to try to include the DNS name with each IP address, even though looking up DNS names slows it down badly, so `$lookupdnsnames = 1`. (Use `$lookupdnsnames = 0` if your WWW server looks up the DNS names for you.)

$commonlogformat

I'm using the EMWAC https World Wide Web server, which uses its own format for log files, rather than the professional version that uses the common logfile format, so `$commonlogformat = 0`.

$filenamestolowercase

Filenames on Windows NT are not case-sensitive, so I don't want Musage to treat the same name as two different files, so I get Musage to convert all filenames to lowercase before processing them, `$filenamestolowercase = 1`.

$logfilepattern

Most Web servers, including EMWACs, produce log files with filenames ending in .log (for example, HTTPS log files have names such as HS950227.LOG; cern3 httpd produces files called proxy.log, access.log, and cache.log), so I use `$logfilepattern = .+\.log` to tell Musage how to recognize log files. (This is the equivalent to `*.LOG` in DOS/Windows.)

$servertype

Musage identifies which type of server produced the log files from the first letter of the filenames; on my system, logfiles beginning with H are from the https WWW server and those beginning with G are from the Gopher server, so I use the lines `$servertype{"h"}= WWW` and `$servertype{"g"} = Gopher`.

Running Perl and Musage

Put copies of the HTTPS log files in the appropriate directory ready for Musage to analyze. You should be able to run Musage by typing

```
perl musage.txt
```

On an NT system you can rename MUSAGE.TXT to MUSAGE.CMD and just type `musage` to run it.

The output will consist of two files for each month called, for example, H1994-12.HTM and H1994-12.TXT. The H stands for HTTP (if it were an analysis of Gopher server logs it would be a G), 1994 is the year, and 12 is the month. The .HTM file is a summary, and the .TXT file is a complete analysis. A link to the .TXT files is embedded in the .HTM file. The first time you run Musage, it also creates an output file called HUSAGE.HTM (or GUSAGE.HTM when analyzing gopher server logs); this is the menu file that you will want to include somewhere in your home page. Each time Musage analyzes the log files for a particular month, it will update this file by adding a line.

Musage looks up the DNS names of users (as only their IP addresses are recorded in the log). This uses the `gethostbyaddr()` function. Because there may be lots of DNS lookups it's probably best to run this when the Internet is quiet, at least between your Web server and your DNS server. (It only looks each address up once, because it keeps a record of all the addresses it has looked up.)

If you get Musage to look up DNS names in this way, it is worth keeping a backup of the file DNSNAMES.LST that it creates. This keeps a list of all the DNS names Musage has looked up to save it from having to look them up again. It's worth keeping a backup of all your log files and copying them into a separate directory before running Musage on them. Musage isn't supposed to modify them, but it's better to be safe than sorry.

Musage will try to analyze all the log files it finds and won't complain if you give it half a month's worth of log files. For example, if you run it on the third of January and it finds log files for the first, second, and third, you will get a summary for January based on these days only. So copy just the files you want Musage to analyze into a separate directory first.

Here are the steps to ensure that HTTPS logging is enabled:

1. Run Control Panel and double-click the HTTPS icon.
2. Check the Log HTTP Transactions box in the HTTP Server Configuration dialog.
3. Enter the path to the directory where you want to store the log files. A new log file will be created every day. The filename is of the form HSyymmdd.LOG.

The file that is created is easy to read and can provide valuable information. Here is an excerpt of a log file (HS950606.LOG) created by EMWAC HTTPS:

```
Tue Jun 06 17:06:30 1995 204.252.2.5 128.2.110.5 GET /robots.txt HTTP/1.0
Tue Jun 06 17:06:32 1995 204.252.2.5 128.2.110.5 GET /cstudio/welcome.html HTTP/1.0
Tue Jun 06 17:36:35 1995 204.252.2.5 204.252.2.5 GET /fbs.html HTTP/1.0
Tue Jun 06 17:36:35 1995 204.252.2.5 204.252.2.5 GET /MARBLE.GIF HTTP/1.0
Tue Jun 06 17:36:36 1995 204.252.2.5 204.252.2.5 GET /LOGO2.GIF HTTP/1.0
Tue Jun 06 17:36:36 1995 204.252.2.5 204.252.2.5 GET /BLUE.GIF HTTP/1.0
```

The information is recorded in this format (reading the columns from left to right in the following order):

1. Time and date of the request
2. IP address or domain name of the server
3. IP address of the client
4. HTTP command (such as GET, POST, or HEAD)
5. URL requested
6. Version of the HTTP protocol used. (If there is no version, it means that HTTP 0.9 is in use.)

You'll notice that in the first line of this log file, the URL /robots.txt was requested. That means that the IP address 128.2.110.5 must be an Internet robot that honors the robot exclusion methods. Don't worry if you don't understand; we will explain all about Internet robots in Chapter 16.

> **Note:** The log format used by the EMWAC HTTPS is not 100-percent compliant with the CERN Common Log format used by most UNIX HTTP servers.

Keeping the Connection

After you have connected to your service provider, it is possible that your connection drops. This could happen for various reasons. For example, your service provider might allow your connection to time out after a certain period of inactivity.

Listing 12.1 shows a C program that will solve this problem. This program pings the given IP address every 15 minutes. Most service providers set their ports to time out after 20 minutes of inactivity. The source code for this program is included on the CD-ROM. You will need to insert the gateway IP address of your ISP and recompile the program as a 32-bit NT console application. If you expect that your service provider has a policy of letting inactive connections time out, you should keep this program running in the background to avoid problems.

> **Note:** You should be able to work out an arrangement with your service provider that would preclude you from needing to run hi.exe.

Listing 12.1. Hi.c is a simple hack to let your ISP know your server is still there.

```
/*  Ping host every 15 minutes
    hi.c
*/
#include <stdlib.h>
#include <process.h>
#include <dos.h>
int main(void)
{
    for(;;)
    {
        system("PING.EXE -n 1 -l 10 enter your host IP here");
        sleep(900); /* Wait 900 seconds */
    }
    return(0);
}
```

In addition to running hi.exe, you need to modify a Registry setting for Remote Access. But before you modify your Registry, here are some quick tips on how the Windows NT Registry is laid out and how you can go about editing it. It isn't as mysterious as you might have been led to believe.

Quick Tips on the Windows NT Registry

The Registry contains important Windows NT data about user preferences, and the hardware and software installed on your computer. Many of the values kept in the Registry are similar to those that you would find in the WIN.INI and SYSTEM.INI files of a machine running Windows 3.1. The Registry is a hierarchical database used to maintain configuration information for Windows NT and the users of the computer.

The Root Keys

The Registry is broken down into four subtrees. (Note: future versions of Windows NT might increase this number.) The root key names at the top of each subtree are prefixed with HKEY_ to indicate that they are handles to KEYs, or HKEYs. Windows programmers speak of a *handle* as a reference to an operating system resource. A *key* is simply a word by which you can look up an associated value (like a dictionary entry and its corresponding definition). The next sections cover the four root keys.

HKEY_LOCAL_MACHINE

This key contains information about the local computer system, including hardware and operating system data such as bus type, memory, device drivers, and startup control data. This is the subtree that you will be most concerned with.

HKEY_CLASSES_ROOT

This key contains object linking and embedding (OLE) and file-class association data.

HKEY_CURRENT_USER

This key contains the user profile for the user who is currently logged on, including environment variables, personal program groups, desktop settings, network connections, printers, and application preferences. This key always refers to a user in the subtree of HKEY_USERS.

HKEY_USERS

This key contains all actively loaded user profiles, including HKEY_CURRENT_USER, and the default profile. Users who are accessing a server remotely do not have profiles under this key on the server; their profiles are loaded into the Registry on their own computers.

Editing the Registry

Many of the program configuration changes you make through the GUI in Windows NT (such as in Control Panel) will be automatically written into the Registry for you. Whenever possible, we prefer to have the friendly interface of Control Panel and other applications write to the Registry on our behalf. Having said that, there are several advanced settings mentioned in this book that can be made only by directly editing the Registry. To make these changes, use REGEDT32.EXE as shown in Figure 12.2.

Figure 12.2.
How to use the Registry Editor to change a DWORD value.

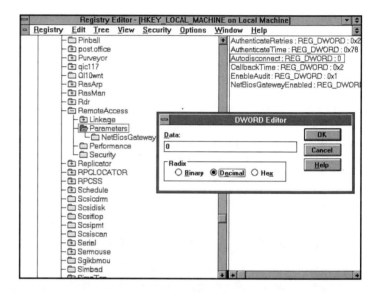

Caution: If you are not very careful, making changes directly to the Registry can sometimes prevent your computer from working properly. Windows NT has a standard warning about this, whenever you invoke the Registry editor. The warning reads "Caution: Using Registry Editor incorrectly can cause serious problems, including corruptions that may make it necessary to reinstall Windows NT."

Most of the Registry values that we change in this book are found under HKEY_LOCAL_MACHINE/ SYSTEM/CurrentControlSet.

As you navigate through the Registry with REGEDT32, you will notice that each entry in the structure is one of three things: a root key, a subtree, or a value. Value entries don't appear until you reach the end of a given subtree. Although this might sound complicated, the whole idea is to keep a huge amount of data organized. And the Registry serves that purpose very well, once you get used to it.

We've already discussed the four root keys. Think of subtrees as branches off the main trunk, assuming the root keys are the main trunk.

Each value entry has three parts: name, data type, and the actual value.

By default, the Registry recognizes the following five types of data. The Win32 API includes functions which programmers can call to add other data types as necessary.

REG_BINARY

This is used for binary data that is uninterpreted by Regedit. Such data can be interpreted either by the program that writes the entry or by a system function inside NT that will process the data at the appropriate time in the execution of the program that wrote the value. This data type can be used for values that don't fit any of the other types. Because *all* data in digital computers *always* exists in binary form, usage of the other types below is only a matter of convenience when the data can be interpreted by Regedit in a human-readable form.

REG_DWORD

This data type can contain 4 bytes of data. The basic unit of memory on Intel and many other computer architectures is 4 bytes, or 32 bits. This data type is useful for storing integers.

REG_EXPAND_SZ

The sz stands for *string zero*, which means a NULL-terminated array of characters in C or C++. This data type indicates an expandable string of text that contains a variable that will be substituted at runtime. For example, the string %SystemRoot% appears throughout the Registry. It will be replaced at runtime by the actual location of the Windows NT system directory.

REG_MULTI_SZ

This data type is used to hold several string values, each one separated by NULL bytes.

REG_SZ

This data type is used to represent a simple array of characters or byte values. As you traverse the Registry, you will come across numerous examples of its use for strings of text.

Reestablishing Dropped Connections

Even with the configuration improvements we have made, it is still possible for you to lose the connection to your service provider from time to time. When you lose the connection, versions of the EMWAC HTTPS service prior to 0.97 will need to be stopped and restarted. (This book includes version 0.99.) You might also want to stop and restart other services.

Somar Redial can help automate this process. Somar Redial is an NT service that maintains a full-time dial-up RAS connection by redialing whenever the connection is lost. It can optionally cycle the EMWAC HTTP and other services that lock up when the RAS connection is stopped and restarted. It can also throttle redialing when there is a cost to redialing. Here is a summary of how to use it:

1. Detect the loss of connection.
2. Redial the service provider.
3. Log in again.
4. After the login, restart the HTTP services.

> **Tip:** Windows NT Version 3.51 added a "Reconnect on loss of connection" feature to RAS so if you are running Windows NT 3.51 or greater and EMWAC HTTPS 0.97 or greater, you will not need to use Somar Redial unless you have other services that you want to stop and restart upon a loss of connection.

Installing Somar Redial

Here are the steps to install and configure Somar Redial. Much of this information can be found in the documentation that comes with the program on the CD-ROM.

1. Use WinZip to decompress the file redial.zip from the CD-ROM \apps directory to your hard drive. Place REDIAL.EXE, REDIAL.HLP, and REDIAL.INI together in any directory. Note that because REDIAL.INI will contain password information, a special directory should be used to which ordinary users do not have read access.

2. Modify REDIAL.INI as appropriate for your site. See the following section concerning the .INI parameters for a description of this file.

3. Normally, Somar Redial is run as a service. However, for diagnostic or evaluation purposes, it is possible to run as a console application using the following command line:

   `REDIAL.EXE /run`

4. The service must run under the Local System account if it is to stop and start other services. To install Somar Redial as a service, use the following command line:

   `REDIAL.EXE /install`

5. To uninstall Somar Redial as a service and delete the event log registry key, use the following command line:

   `REDIAL.EXE /uninstall`

6. Somar Redial must be uninstalled and reinstalled as a service if the .EXE file is ever moved to another directory.

Somar Redial adds event log entries when it is run as a service. The following event log registry key is created when Somar Redial is installed as a service:

```
HKEY_LOCAL_MACHINE\SYSTEM\CurrentControlSet\Services\EventLog
\Application\Somar ReDial
```

Somar Redial .INI Parameters

Here is an example of the file REDIAL.INI. A brief description of some parameters follows.

```
[Parms]
EntryName=DIGEX
UserName=user1
Password=pass1
MaxTrysIn1Hour=4
Service0=HTTP Server
Service1=SMTP Server
```

- `EntryName`

  Name of RAS entry.

- `UserName`

  RAS username.

- `Password`

  RAS password.

- `MaxTrysIn1Hour`

  This is the maximum number of redialing attempts to make in a one-hour period. If this limit is reached, the program waits until the next hour period before redialing. A limit of 0, which is the default, indicates that there are no limits to redialing. Dialing attempts that fail because of a busy signal are not counted.

- `Service`*NNN*

  This is the display name or internal name of service that is to be stopped and restarted whenever the connection is stopped and restarted. Up to 50 services can be specified. The *NNN* values must start at 0 and increase by 1 for each entry.

Handling System Crashes

Your site is up and running fine, and you know that if you lose the connection, Somar Redial will call your service provider and log you back in. You're set, right? Not really; what if your system crashes during the night? Here is where you have to do a little more tweaking to really automate your system. If the system crashes, you want it to reboot, start all the services you need, call your service provider, and log in.

As it turns out, NT is well-suited to do all the tasks mentioned to get you back online automatically. Here is a detailed list of what you need to do for total system automation.

1. You need to let NT know what you want it to do in case of a system crash. Run Control Panel and double-click the System icon. Choose Recovery and ensure that both the "Write an event to the system log" and "Automatically reboot" checkboxes are checked. See Figure 12.3. Choose OK.

Figure 12.3.
System Recovery settings.

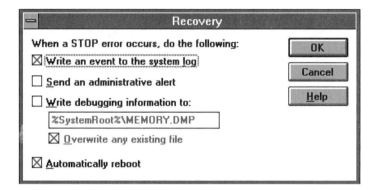

2. Make sure that Somar Redial is running as an automatic service that will initiate when NT boots. Go to Control Panel and double-click the Services icon. Select the Somar Redial service in the listbox and choose Startup. Also ensure that the Automatic radio button is enabled. See Figure 12.4. Choose OK.

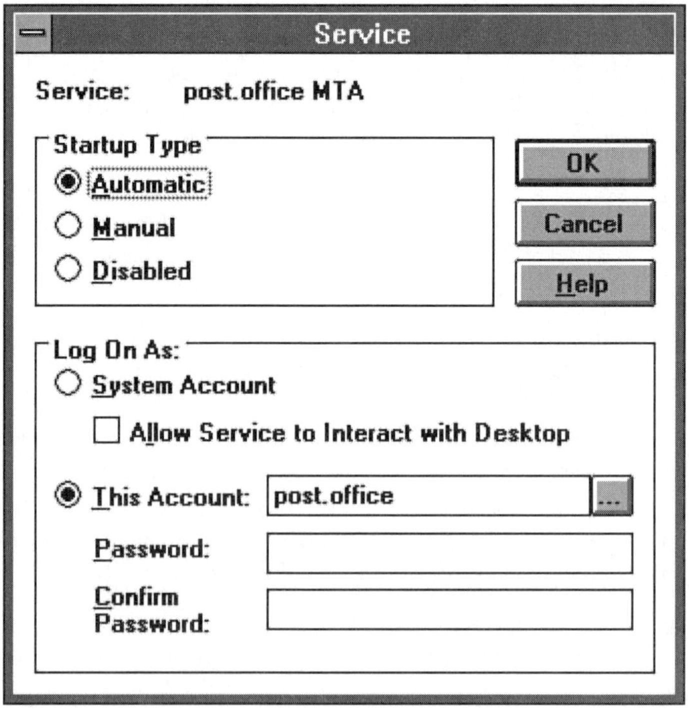

Figure 12.4.
NT Service dialog.

3. Now you need to set up NT to automatically login as a user when it reboots. This is another place you will use the Registry Editor. Before editing your Registry, you'll see the standard warnings from Microsoft about modifications. Using Regedit, make the following changes to this key:

```
HKEY_LOCAL_MACHINE\SOFTWARE\Microsoft\Windows NT\CurrentVersion\Winlogon
```

Set the `AutoAdminLogon` value to 1. This specifies automatic logon. You must also add an entry for `DefaultPassword` and give it the value of the password for the default login name.

> **Caution:** When `AutoAdminLogon` is used, Windows NT automatically logs on the specified user when the system is started, bypassing the Ctrl+Alt+Del logon dialog box. There are many security implications to setting up your system this way. This setup is only for a situation in which the physical security of the machine is not an issue. The reason you have to log on is to run a couple of applications that are not services after reboot. If security is more of a concern, it is highly recommended to look into the SRVANY.EXE utility that comes with the Resource Kit. The SRVANY.EXE utility enables you to run any Windows NT application as a service. You can also run some 16-bit applications with SRVANY. See the Resource Kit documentation for further details.

4. Set up a login script for the default login account. After NT has rebooted, you are going to want it to run two programs. You need to get RASPHONE running so after Somar Redial has called your service provider, it can log on. You may want to start the program called hi.exe, which will prevent your connection from dropping after the timeout period. If you have arranged for your service provider to ping your system, or for their port not to time out, you do not have to run hi.exe (compiled from hi.c). To do this, you need to write a little login script called login.cmd. Use any ASCII text editor (such as Notepad) to create a file with the following contents, and save it as login.cmd:

```
start rasphone.exe
start hi.exe
```

Note that the second line requires an absolute path if hi.exe is not in your system path. Move the file to the C:\systemroot\SYSTEM32\REPL\IMPORT\SCRIPTS directory. Finally, go to the User Manager's Profile of the default login account, press the profile button, enter login.cmd in the Login Script Name box, and choose OK. See Figure 12.5.

Congratulations. Your site is now completely automated and will handle connection losses, reboots, and crashes.

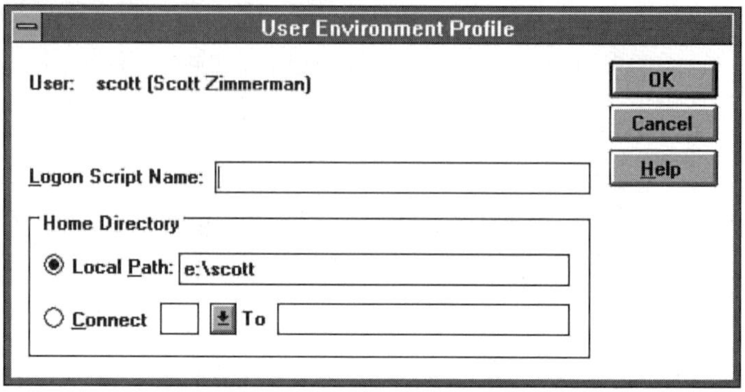

Figure 12.5.
User Environment Profile.

Being Prepared for Hardware Failures

There are two other miscellaneous topics that we must bring up in this chapter, since they are related to site maintenance: tape backups and uninterruptible power. To guard against the risks of hackers, viruses, and total hard-disk failure, you should back up your site at least once a day. To avoid forgetting a daily backup, you can schedule it to occur automatically late at night with the AT command. There is a nice graphical interface for the AT command contained in the Windows NT Resource Kit, published by Microsoft.

Now as quick as the power can go out, let's change the subject. No business Web site should be without a UPS (Uninterruptible Power Supply). Once you have announced your Web site to the world (see Chapter 11), your customers will soon start depending upon the constant up-time of your URL—even on weekends when you're not there to plug the server back in if the cleaning crew accidentally unplugs it.

There are many UPS devices available; some start at around $200. And remember, always check the NT Hardware Compatibility List before buying. For an excellent review of several UPS devices, see the November 1995 issue of *Windows NT Magazine*.

Checking on Expired Links

Expired links can be a Web management nightmare. The Web is a rapidly changing entity; thousands of pages go up and down each day. The more links your pages have to other pages, the more likelihood of having links go bad (expire). There are a few utilities that will help you check to make sure that all of your local links are good. The Purveyor 1.1 Web server by Process software includes a utility that will check both local and remote links.

Virtual Domains and Multiple EMWAC Servers

If you would like to have more than one Web site running from the same NT machine, you can run multiple instances of the HTTPS server. Each instance will have different data dictionaries, and server and domain names. Special modifications are needed to prepare HTTPS for multiple instances.

You also will need to have a distinct domain name for each Web site you want to run from the same machine—for example, www.yourco1.com and www.yourco2.com. Be aware that the InterNIC has recently changed policies and each Web site must now incur a setup fee and an annual fee. If that doesn't discourage you, however, please read this important caution before proceeding.

> **Caution:** Editing application binary files is a very advanced subject, and you should only attempt the following procedures if you are comfortable with doing hexadecimal editing of program images.

You need to install a program that will help you edit binary files.

Installing HEdit

HEdit is a hexadecimal editor for binary files on Windows NT (Intel only). It supports unlimited file sizes, drag and drop, binary and text searches, selectable fonts, clipboard, and includes a multiple document interface.

1. Use WinZip to extract all the HEdit32 files from the CD-ROM into your Windows NT directory (such as C:\WINNT). The accompanying File Manager extension will not work in any other directory.
2. Start HEDIT.EXE and follow the on-screen instructions to finish the installation.

Patch to Run Multiple EMWAC HTTP Servers

Though we have never needed to do this, it has been tried and it seemed to work fine.

> **Caution:** These patch instructions are only for EMWAC HTTPS v0. 99. See Rick's Information center for other version patches at http://137.226.92.4/rick/ or http://pobox.com/~rickg/.

> **Note:** If you ever run across version 0.97 of HTTPS, don't use it. There were several bugs introduced in that version that rendered it useless. Version 0. 99 included with this book fixes those bugs and is considered a stable version overall.

1. Copy HTTPS.EXE and HTTPS.CPL to HTTP1.EXE and HTTP1.CPL. There are several critical steps below that depend on these filenames.
2. Using HEdit, open the file HTTP1.EXE and patch the file as directed in Table 12.1. Figure 12.6 shows what some of the changes will look like in HEdit.

Figure 12.6.
The HEdit screen while patching HTTPS.

```
                                    HEdit - [http1.exe]
  File   Edit   Search   Options   Window   Help
0000CFE0  72 65 61 64 00 00 00 00  67 65 74 68 6F 73 74 6E   read....gethostn
0000CFF0  61 6D 65 00 67 65 74 68  6F 73 74 62 79 6E 61 6D   ame.gethostbynam
0000D000  65 00 00 00 4E 61 6D 65  3A 20 20 20 20 25 73 0A   e...Name:    %s.
0000D010  00 00 00 00 41 64 64 72  65 73 73 3A 20 25 73 0A   ....Address: %s.
0000D020  00 00 00 00 57 69 6E 64  6F 77 73 20 53 6F 63 6B   ....Windows Sock
0000D030  65 74 73 20 66 75 6E 63  74 69 6F 6E 20 22 25 73   ets function "%s
0000D040  22 20 66 61 69 6C 73 20  77 69 74 68 20 65 72 72   " fails with err
0000D050  6F 72 20 25 64 00 00 00  3A 0A 20 20 20 25 73 0A   or %d...:    %s.
0000D060  00 00 00 00 0A 00 00 00  57 53 41 53 74 61 72 74   ........WSAStart
0000D070  75 70 00 00 73 6F 63 6B  65 74 00 00 62 69 6E 64   up..socket..bind
0000D080  00 00 00 00 6C 69 73 74  65 6E 00 00 48 53 79 79   ....listen..HSyy
0000D090  6D 6D 64 64 2E 4C 4F 47  00 00 00 00 48 54 54 50   mmdd.LOG....HTTP
0000D0A0  31 00 00 00 45 4D 57 41  43 20 48 54 54 50 31 53   1...EMWAC HTTP1S
0000D0B0  65 72 76 65 72 00 00 00  30 2E 39 39 00 00 00 00   erver...0.99....
0000D0C0  48 54 54 50 31 3A 00 00  72 65 63 76 00 00 00 00   HTTP1:..recv....
0000D0D0  74 65 78 74 2F 68 74 6D  6C 00 00 00 57 57 57 2D   text/html...WWW-
0000D0E0  41 75 74 68 65 6E 74 69  63 61 74 65 3A 20 00 00   Authenticate: ..
0000D0F0  0D 0A 00 00 0D 0A 00 00  3C 54 49 54 4C 45 3E 25   ........<TITLE>%
0000D100  73 3C 2F 54 49 54 4C 45  3E 0D 0A 00 3C 42 4F 44   s</TITLE>...<BOD
0000D110  59 3E 0D 0A 3C 48 31 3E  25 73 3C 2F 48 31 3E 0D   Y>..<H1>%s</H1>.
0000D120  0A 00 00 00 3C 50 3E 48  54 54 50 31 73 74 61 74   ....<P>HTTP1stat
0000D130  75 73 20 63 6F 64 65 3A  20 25 64 0D 0A 3C 2F 42   us code: %d..</B
0000D140  4F 44 59 3E 0D 0A 00 00  48 54 4D 00 48 54 4D 4C   ODY>....HTM.HTML
0000D150  00 00 00 00 74 65 78 74  2F 68 74 6D 6C 00 00 00   ....text/html...
File length: 83456    Offset dec: 53408   hex: D0A0
```

Table 12.1. Hex and ASCII changes to HTTP1.EXE.

Address	https.exe	http1.exe	ASCII Equivalent
0000D0A0:	53 [change to]	31	(HTTPS [change to] HTTP1)
0000D0AE:	20 [change to]	31	(HTTP Server [change to] HTTP1Server)
0000D0C4:	53 [change to]	31	(HTTPS: [changes to] HTTP1:)
0000D12B:	20 [change to]	31	(HTTP status [change to] HTTP1status)
0000F9F4:	53 [change to]	31	(HTTPS\Parameters [change to] HTTP1\Parameters)
0000FCA8:	53 [change to]	31	(HTTPS/ [change to] HTTP1/)
0000FEEC:	53 [change to]	31	(HTTPS/ [change to] HTTP1/)

Address	https.exe	http1.exe	ASCII Equivalent
00012C78:	20 [change to]	31	(HTTP request [change to] HTTP1request)
00012E04:	20 [change to]	31	(HTTP Server [change to] HTTP1Server)
00012E28:	20 [change to]	31	(HTTP Server [change to] HTTP1Server)
00012E50:	20 [change to]	31	(HTTP Client [change to] HTTP1Client)

Any changes that you make to the hex code will be reflected in the ASCII code, and vice versa.

4. Using HEdit, open the file HTTP1.CPL and patch the file as directed in Table 12.2.

Table 12.2. Hex and ASCII changes to HTTP1.CPL.

Address	https.exe	http1.exe	ASCII Equivalent
00006ED8:	53 [change to]	31	(HTTPS\Parameters [change to] HTTP1\Parameters)
00006FE0:	53 [change to]	31	(HTTPS.CPL [change to] HTTP1.CPL)
00006FEC:	20 [change to]	31	(HTTP Server [change to] HTTP1Server)

If you need more than one additional HTTPS server, create https2.exe and http2.cpl, and replace the hex values 31 with 32 (and so on) in each of the preceding steps.

5. Copy the patched files to your %systemroot%\system32 directory.

6. Run Control Panel. You will notice an additional HTTPS icon for each patched server.

7. Configure each Server as you did in Chapter 4. Give each server a different port (for example, 80 or 8001). Give each server a document root (Data Directory). You can set the document root of each server to a different directory. You can even use the same directory, but that would probably defeat the purpose of running two servers. Remember that the server expects the directories to exist. Finally, configure a log file directory for each server if you want to log HTTPS transactions. All other options can be set as needed.

Configure the startup modes for each server in Control Panel.

Using Different Hostnames and Domain Names

If you want different hostnames and domain names, you must configure your DNS Server for this. It is best if you have a separate network interface card (NIC) for each HTTPS Server. Then you can assign a unique name for each HTTPS server in the DNS host database. See Table 12.3 for an example of this.

Table 12.3. Configuring multiple DNS names.

NIC	Hostname	WWW URL
1.	Rick.wzl.rwth-aachen.de	http://rick.wzl.rwth-aachen.de/
2.	wzl-ps4.wzl.rwth-aachen.de	http://wzl-ps4.wzl.rwth-aachen.de:8001/

Running several servers on the same machine or several domains under the same server is supported by several HTTP servers made today. For a list of HTTP servers for Windows and Windows NT, refer to Appendix B.

Chapter 13

Serving Internet Mail

- post.office and SMTP
- Blat
- Running a List Server
- Gopher and Finger
- What's Next?

This chapter is all about running your own e-mail server. E-mail is responsible for the greatest percentage of packet traffic on the Internet.

It is customary, when one is visiting a home page on the Web, that comments can be e-mailed to an address of the form webmaster@yourco.com. If you would like to carry on this tradition, you will probably want to run your own mail server.

You might also complement your Web site with a mail server if you offer leased Internet service to your clients. Think about it. With a well-built Web site (like the one in this book), a mail server, and an FTP server, you could sell Internet access. The next chapter discusses FTP servers.

The industry of e-mail server software for Windows NT is just heating up. We have only found a few such packages. All are very competitive. The one we chose to include with this book is post.office from a humbly named company called Software.com in Santa Barbara, California.

While we're on the subject of mail, we'll also show you how to install Blat. Blat is a console program that can e-mail HTML form data. The astute reader might remember why we need console programs: They are the only kind of CGI application that the current version of EMWAC can launch.

Here's an example of what you can do with Blat. Suppose you sell software over the Internet and you would like to encourage and track your customer feedback. In order to make it as simple as possible for your customers to express their opinion about your product, you provide a convenient HTML form on your home page. When a customer fills out the form, the SUBMIT action invokes a CGI Perform program to parse the data. Then it is passed to Blat to be e-mailed to your inbox.

At the end of the chapter, we'll talk briefly about listservers, Gopher servers, and Finger servers.

post.office and SMTP

Because you are going to want to have several e-mail addresses for yourco.com and possibly a list server in the future, we are going to show you how to install post.office.

post.office is a feature-rich set of utilities. It contains RFC-compliant SMTP and POP servers that operate as 32-bit services on Windows NT.

The next several sections describe pre-installation procedures for post.office.

> **Note:** post.office uses long filenames and requires the drive to be formatted using NTFS.

Creating an NT Login Account for the Service

Every process running under Windows NT operates with the privileges of an account (either local or part of a domain, if you're using NT Server). The post.office service can operate using the privileges of the built-in System account (which is the default during install) or as any local account that is preconfigured (prior to running the installation program) on the machine. This decision is primarily a security consideration. The advantage of using an account other than the built-in System account is that the default installation of post.office will set up permissions that will not allow other processes or accounts to access any of the post.office directories/files or registry information. (Additionally, the post.office service will be unable to read/modify/delete any system or user files.) The main disadvantage of using an account other than System is that you need to set up the local account and group, and ensure that they are not deleted, because post.office will not be able to run if its account is disabled.

We recommend the use of a new account and group other than the built-in System account for sites connecting to the Internet. If you choose to use the System account, you may skip the remainder of this section and proceed to the section titled "Miscellaneous Pre-Installation Planning." When prompted for the System account, please use System (with an uppercase S).

You will need to use the User Manager (as an administrator) to create an account and group for the service to use during normal operation. The new account and group should be specifically for the post.office service and should have no other members or groups. The account must have User Cannot Change Password and Password Never Expires checked, and must not have User Must Change Password at Next Login checked.

NT Workstation Installation Notes

You will be creating a local user and group. If the workstation is also part of a NT Domain, we suggest that you use a local user and local group (specific to the workstation, not a member of the NT Domain). Be sure that you include only the post.office user in the new group and that the post.office user has membership in only the new post.office group.

NT Server Notes

On a server acting as a primary or backup domain controller, we suggest that you use a global user/global group for the post.office service account. On a server that is not a PDC or BDC, use a local user/local group for the post.office service account.

After creating the post.office user and group, be sure to set the post.office group to be the primary group for the post.office user. (Under the user properties/Groups button, select the post.office group on the left side and click the Set Primary Groups button.) Then remove the domain users group from the list of groups for the post.office user. (It is added by the user manager by default.)

You must also give the account the *logon as a service* privilege. This is accomplished while still in the User Manager program. Under the Policies menu, select the User Rights option. There is a checkbox titled Show Advanced User Rights, which must be checked. Under the scrollbar titled Right:, choose Log on as a Service and add the account name (chosen above) that you created for the mail system to this privilege list. You will need to choose the Add button, Show Users, and then the post.office user account (it will be near the bottom of the list); then choose the Add button.

Setting Permissions for the System Directories

To ensure that the post.office installation program is able to give the proper permissions for operation, it is necessary that the owner of the System directories be the Administrators. You can easily determine this with the File Manager. Select the system directory (/winnt, /winnt35, or /windows, depending on your specific installation) and select Permissions under the Security menu item. The directory owner must be Administrators for the install to proceed. If this is not the case, you will need to take ownership of the directory, subdirectory, and files within—as one of the administrators. This is not a step to take lightly, so please review the online help and additional manuals to be sure that you understand this operation.

Machine Name and Internet Protocol Number

The beta installation program will request the hostname (without domain name) from the TCP Service. Please ensure that the hostname listed in the Control Panel | Network | Select TCP/IP Protocol | choose Configure | choose DNS | hostname is the name you are planning to use. In addition, the install program must do a reverse lookup to turn an IP number into a hostname. The file named HOSTS in \winnt\system32\drivers\etc has a list of IP numbers and hostnames. Please ensure that the proper hostname and IP numbers are listed. Sites using DNS may have only a local host entry in this file and don't need to create a new entry if one is not present.

A sample HOSTS entry for a machine rome, in the domain software.com, with an IP number of 198.17.234.2 is

```
198.17.234.2   rome   rome.software.com
```

There are two names here for the same machine: `rome` and `rome.software.com`, separated with a space.

> **Note:** The current version of the Windows NT TCP services is case-sensitive, so use lowercase names in the HOSTS file.

Do a final check of the machine name/IP Number configuration by running a Command window and issuing these commands:

> `> ping your-host-name` (example: `ping rome`)
> Pinging host-name [IP number]
> Reply from IP number ....
> `> ping HostName.DomainName` (example: `ping rome.software.com`)
> Pinging *HostName.DomainName* [IP number]
> Reply from IP number ....

Please verify for both cases that the IP numbers returned by ping are what you think they should be and that the pings are successful. The result of a misconfigured hostname or IP number will be the inability to request forms for adding, changing, or deleting accounts—and for configuration information.

Miscellaneous Pre-Installation Planning

There are three passwords used in the installation section: the *local account password*, the *Postmaster password*, and *your mail account password*. For security reasons, each of these should be different. The *local account password* is used by the Service Control Program (in Windows NT) to log in to the post.office service and give it access rights on the machine it is running. The *Postmaster password* is used by post.office to verify any administrative actions such as creating a new mail account. *Your mail account password* is the password assigned to your e-mail account; it allows you to retrieve your mail (as it is also your POP password), and lets you make any changes to your e-mail account (such as finger information).

Software License Number

During the installation, you will be prompted to enter a license number. If you want to proceed with the 45-day trial period, enter `trial` instead of a number. You will be able to rerun setup later and update your license information with a permanent, valid license number. You should purchase this from Software.com before the trial period expires. To order, send e-mail to `sales@software.com`.

WWW Server Port Number

The post.office mail service comes with an integrated WWW Server for remote management via a WWW browser. This module operates on a specific port (which is usually 80 by default for WWW Servers). If you do not have (and do not plan to have) a WWW Server on the machine already using port 80 (the default if you have not specified it), please choose another port such as 81. If you do not specify another port and there is another WWW Server already using port 80, either post.office's WWW Server or your existing WWW Server will not start properly and will put a message in the event log explaining this. If you do choose to operate post.office's WWW Server on a port other than 80, you will need to specify the port number you have picked when you give the browser the URL. (For example, if you choose 81, the URL will be `http://yourhost:81`.)

Installing post.office

You can use WinZip to unpack the software directly from the CD-ROM to your temp directory. From there, you can execute the setup program.

The last step in the installation, after the service is operating, is to create at least one mail account for the person who will initially be acting as the postmaster (to create new accounts and change mail system parameters). Direct your WWW browser to the post.office WWW Server management URL and answer the questions on the form.

Post-Installation Setup

The post.office services should be installed and operating. You can check this from a Command window by typing

```
> finger postmaster@hostname
```

You should see

```
[hostname]
Account Name:  Mail Administrator
Email address: Postmaster@yourhost
----------
mail system administrator.
```

Configure via Your WWW Browser

Using your WWW browser, you can configure post.office quite easily. The URL for the server is `http://hostname:Port#` (for example, `http://oslo.software.com:81`). If you used the default port during the installation, you do not need to use the `Port#` part (for example, `http://oslo.software.com`).

You will be presented with an Authentication screen. Please use `Postmaster@yourhost` as the e-mail address and the postmaster password to get to the menus. Mail users can change their individual account information by using their personal e-mail address and mail account passwords. See Figure 13.1.

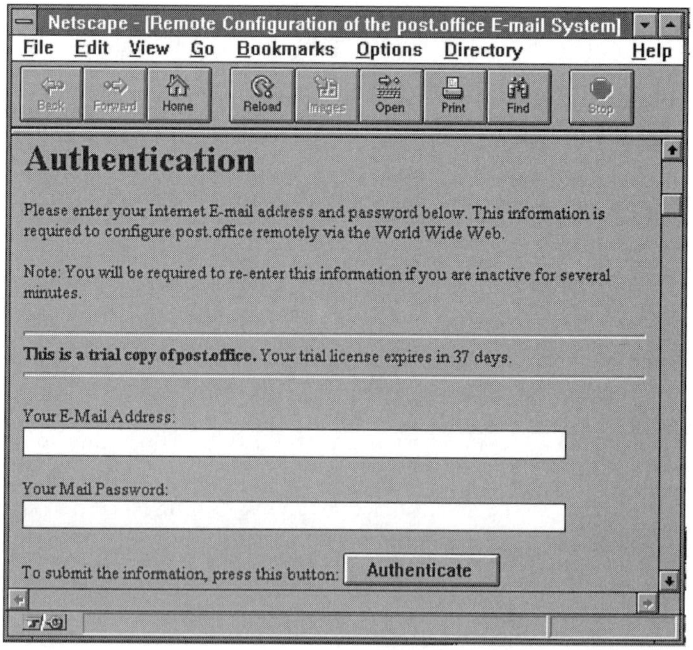

Figure 13.1.
Configuring post.office via HTML.

Upon successful authentication, you will receive a list of available forms. The first step is to ask for a blank account form and create an account for yourself (6.3) and give your new account Postmaster privileges (6.4).

Creating New Mail Accounts

After installing post.office, add `info` and `webmaster` to the root mailbox. This will allow you to log into your mail server with a mail client such as Eudora as root and get any mail addressed to `info@yourco.com` or `webmaster@yourco.com`.

To create a new account, select the Account Form (leave the field above blank) button and REQUEST selected form. You will be presented with an empty account form. Fill this out as desired and submit when finished. Here is an annotated list of the fields:

> **User's Real Name:** Your name (for example, Jane S. Doe).
> **Mail Account Password:** Used by your mail program for POP3 pickup.
> **Finger Information:** (You can skip this for now and add later.)
> **Internet Addresses:** `Name@host` (for example, `Jane@lhasa.software.com`).
> **From Address Rewrite Style:** (You can skip this for now.)
> **POP3-Delivery: Checkbox:** You will probably want POP delivery.
> **POP3-Username:** POPName for your mail program (for example, Jane).

Setting up the Default Account

You might want to configure the Default account form to set up any commonly used parameters as defaults.

Get a List of Accounts

You can get a list of mail accounts on the system with the List of Existing Accounts form. All your accounts will be listed by account name and their first Internet address (called the *primary address* for the account).

Blat

Blat is a public domain Windows NT console utility that will e-mail a file to a user via SMTP. The program requires the gensock DLL (borrowed from WinVN). A Registry entry is generated when the program is used with the `-install` flag. This stores the address of the default SMTP server and the address of the default sender. Blat is used by CGI Perform to mail the contents of an HTML form to whomever you choose.

> **Note:** The binary files for Blat require the Intel 486 platform. However, source code is included (wow!), so you can recompile the program if you need to run it on a different architecture.

Installing Blat

Use WinZip to decompress Blat directly from the CD-ROM. Then follow these steps:

1. Copy the file gensock.dll to your \WINNT\SYSTEM32 directory or to any other directory in your path. (Check if you already have this DLL; if so, copy only the DLL if the date is more recent than the existing one.)

2. Copy the file Blat.exe to your \WINNT\SYSTEM32 directory or to any other directory in your path.

3. Type: Blat -install yourco.com youremail@yourco.com.

A Registry entry is generated when the program is used with the -install flag. This stores the address of the default SMTP server and the address of the default sender (which may be over-ridden with the -f flag).

Impersonation can be done with the -i flag, which puts the value specified in place of the sender's address in the From: line of the header. When this is done, however, the real sender's address is stamped in the Reply-To: and Sender: lines. This feature can be useful when using the program to send messages from NT users who are not registered on the SMTP host.

Blat Syntax

The Blat command line has a few variations. Here are the command types, followed by a description of each of the syntax elements.

```
Blat filename -s subject -t recipient -f address -i address
```

```
Blat -install server address sender's address
```

```
Blat -h
```

`-install server address sender's address`

which sets the address of the default SMTP server.

`filename`

which is the file with the message body.

`-s subject`

which is the (optional) subject line.

`-t recipient`

which is the recipient's address.

`-c recipient`

which is the carbon copy recipient's address.

`-f sender`

which is the sender's address (must be known to the SMTP server).

`-i address`

which is a `From:` address, not necessarily known to the SMTP server.

`-h`

which displays this help.

`-server server address`

which overrides the default SMTP server to be used.

Note that if the `-i` option is used, `<sender>` is included in `Reply-to:` and `Sender:` fields in the header of the message.

Sample Blat Commands

Although we installed Blat for use with the CGI Perform CGI application, you can use Blat from the command line or implement your own CGI application that calls Blat. Here are some examples of using Blat from the command line

```
Blat -install smtphost.bar.com foo@bar.com        //
```

sets the host and userid.

```
Blat -install smtphost.bar.com foo                //
```

sets the host and userid.

```
Blat -install smtphost.bar.com                    //
```

sets the host only.

```
Blat myfile.txt -s "A file for pedro" -t foo@bar.com//
```

sends a file with subject line A file for pedro.

```
Blat myfile.txt -s "A file for mark" -t fee@fi.com -f foo@bar.com //
```

The `-f` option overrides the default sender.

```
Blat myfile.txt -s "A file for pedro" -t foo@bar.com -i "devil@fire.hell" //
```

-i replaces `From:` line address (but leaves `Reply-To:` and `Sender:` lines).

```
Blat myfile.txt -s "animals" -t fee@fi.com -c "moo@grass.edu,horse@meadow.hill"//
```

-c mails carbon copies to users moo@grass.edu and horse@meadow.hill.

The authors of Blat have very generously placed it in the public domain. This means you can use Blat free of charge, for any purpose you like. The source code is also available free of charge. The authors of Blat are Mark Neal (mjn@aber.ac.uk) and Pedro Mendes (prm@aber.ac.uk).

Running a Listserver

A listserver (also called *listserv*) is a service program that lets its groups' members broadcast e-mail messages amongst themselves. An individual user sends a single e-mail message to the server, which in turn sends it to all the other members of the listserv group.

We had hoped to include the Software.com listserver to go with post.office. Unfortunately, it was undergoing careful beta-testing at the time we went to print, so we can only mention the feature set it is expected to have. You can get further information from Software.com at the e-mail. (addresshttp://www.software.com/ is the URL, and support@software.com is the e-mail address.) If you try the post.office mail server and like it, you will probably want to contact the company and ask for the commercial release of their companion listserver.

Features of Software.com List Manager

Here is a quick look at the features of List Manager:

- Users can subscribe and unsubscribe via WWW or e-mail forms.
- List owners can maintain the mail list via WWW or e-mail forms.
- Subscription and unsubscription posting detection.
- Moderated and unmoderated subscriptions.
- Maximum message size limit per list.
- Maximum posts/day limit total or per subscriber.
- Header deletion/addition.
- Mail server delivery priority.
- Digesting (with time and message count triggers).
- Configurable posting policy.
- Unmoderated lists.
- Semi-moderated lists. Only list subscribers can post.
- Intro-moderated. Initial postings from a given user are moderated.

Gopher and Finger

You might have guessed that these topics don't belong in a chapter about e-mail. You're right. In fact, if you'll excuse us, we really didn't feel that they belonged anywhere in this book. Here in between the sections on mail servers, listservers, and the next chapter on FTP and Telnet, is as good a spot as any to tell you why we decided to leave out Gopher and Finger.

As discussed in Chapter 1, "Internet Technology Primer," Gopher has been around for a while and is a popular way to provide access to a repository of text documents on the Internet. Gopher's greatest weakness is also its greatest strength: It only provides text-based menus to the client, no hypertext. Of course, that means that it can run on just about any kind of client that can hook up to the Net. The main reason we don't bother running a Gopher server is that you can do the same thing with a Web server. All you need to do is provide an unordered list of <A HREFs> in your HTML code. Virtually all browsers can handle either text or binary documents (through MIME) by either invoking the appropriate viewer application or by prompting the user to do a download.

"What about Finger?" you ask. We'll give it to you straight: There are two reasons for us avoiding Finger. Finger has frequently been used as a back door by hackers to breach security, and we simply didn't have the time and space to include everything about the Internet in one book.

What's Next?

FTP and Telnet are up next. Installing these two servers will wrap up our grocery list of Internet servers for building a complete Web site.

Chapter 14

Running FTP and Telnet Servers

- Installing the FTP Server Service on Windows NT
- FTP Security
- Fine-Tuning FTP
- Remote Administration with Telnet
- Installing SLNet
- What's Next?

Let's take a moment for a quick review of FTP and Telnet. As you recall from Chapter 1, "Internet Technology Primer," the File Transfer Protocol governs file transfers between local and remote systems. When talking about FTP programs (and most things on the Internet), we must be careful to distinguish between the *client* and the *server*. Note that the FTP client that comes with NT is a command-line version, but this book includes a freeware FTP client with a Win32 GUI! Windows NT also includes an FTP server, which we will install in this chapter.

To understand Telnet, think client/server. A machine running a Telnet server enables other computers or terminals on the network to connect to it via remote login and issue basic commands to the file system on the server. In fact, the remote computer running the Telnet client can execute *any* Windows NT console application on the Telnet server.

If you let your imagination wander a little, you can probably think of many useful scenarios for installing these protocols on your Web site. Remote administration of your server might come to mind. For example, with FTP you could modify your Web pages when you are traveling and then upload the new files to your home directory—thus making them immediately available to the next browser that hits your site. Telnet will let you to check your free disk space, start and stop other Windows NT services, read the server logfiles, or check on other network statistics when you are on the road.

Another use for FTP is to make files on your server available for download by the public. Although this function can also be accomplished through the Web, some users might still prefer to download files via FTP. If you want users to upload files to your site, you'll need to run an FTP server because this function can't be done through a Web browser (not yet anyway, but at the rate things are changing on the Internet, somebody will probably invent a way to do this).

While we're on the subject of FTP, we'll mention Archie again. Archie is a search utility that keeps a database of FTP servers and the files that each has available. If you are planning to run an anonymous FTP site, you might consider having it cross-referenced by an Archie server. The Archie server would then be able to refer to your documents when the search string entered by the Archie client is contained within the name of one of your directories or files. We aren't going to discuss this topic further, except to say that a pretty cool Archie GUI client is included on the CD-ROM.

With that out of the way, let's get busy.

Installing the FTP Server Service on Windows NT

This section describes the steps to install the Microsoft FTP Server Service for Windows NT. It's called a *server service* because, well, it isn't a client, and it runs as a Windows NT 32-bit service, which provides both it and your system with greater protection than ordinary application programs. The Windows NT FTP server service is installed through the Network icon in Control Panel similar to the way in which we installed TCP/IP in Chapter 4. The following steps assume that you haven't already installed FTP:

1. Double-click the Network icon in Control Panel.
2. Choose Add Software. In the dialog box that appears, select TCP/IP Protocol And Related Components in the Network Software drop-down listbox. Choose Continue.
3. When the Windows NT TCP/IP Installation Options dialog box appears, check the box for FTP Server Service. Choose Continue.

4. When the warning message prompts you to confirm that you are familiar with FTP security, choose Yes to continue with the installation. The reason for the warning is that running an Internet server such as FTP will expose your machine and LAN to all sorts of new electronic villains. Later, we will show you how to protect yourself from most of these risks. When prompted for the full path to the Windows NT distribution files, provide the appropriate location (such as your CD-ROM drive) and choose Continue after inserting your Windows NT disk.

5. After the necessary files are copied to your computer, the FTP Service dialog box appears. You must decide if you want the FTP server to allow anonymous logins. If so, is that the only type of FTP user you want to allow? This depends on whether you plan to let a *secure group* of remote users, such as users who want to manage their own home page that you are hosting for them, copy files to your server or whether you plan to run FTP as a download/upload site for the Internet—in which case you don't know exactly who will be visiting, and you would not be able to create specific user accounts. If you create user accounts for people who are going to manage their own directories, you will be able to log them into their own private directories, not the Home Directory shown in Figure 14.1, which is for all anonymous users. Also, it is a good idea to let the user know that his or her ID and password are passed in the clear over the net. That's a chance that users must take if they want to manage their own Web pages remotely.

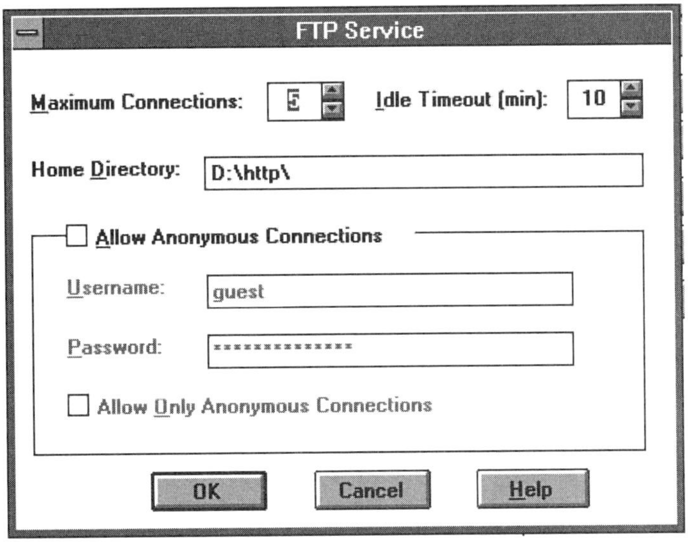

Figure 14.1.
The Windows NT FTP Service dialog.

6. The next time you start Control Panel, you will see a new icon for the FTP Server. Double-click it, and you will see the FTP User Sessions dialog. Choose Security to bring up the FTP Server Security dialog in Figure 14.2. If you have built your Web site as we did in Chapter 4, the operating system is on the C: drive and the Web site is on the D: drive. In that case, uncheck both boxes for the C: drive to ensure that no access is granted to it, and set the read-only checkbox for the D: drive. This step is very important!

Figure 14.2.
The Windows NT FTP Server Security dialog.

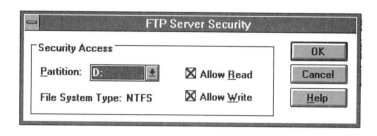

7. Be sure to read the following sections on FTP security and limiting the number of simultaneous FTP visitors. The latter section revisits the dialog in step 6.

FTP Security

If your Web site provides a hosting service for other home pages, you might want to arrange it so that those people can write their own HTML pages and manage them through FTP access. As it turns out, NT's file and directory security will help ensure that your users are restricted from remotely wandering all over your hard drive. You recall that we showed you how to limit read and write access for FTP services to one drive and directory, which the FTP server calls the home directory. Now we are going to take that one step further and show you how to set up an account for people who log into your server. These accounts will ensure that the user, once logged in, is placed in the proper directory and cannot stray from that directory. This will show you the power of the Windows NT user security system. There are many ways to set this up. What we show you here is only one example of how to use the NT security system.

> **Tip:** To employ these FTP security methods, you will need to have your drive formatted in the NTFS format.

Creating the FTP User Group

Here are the steps to create a user group that will allow its members to have the minimum file system privileges necessary for typical FTP usage.

1. Double-click the icon for User Manager (on NT Workstation) or User Manager for Domains (on NT Server) in your Administration Tools program group.

2. Select User | New Local Group.

3. In the dialog box, enter HTML Managers in the Group Name textbox and HTML Managers User Group in the Description textbox. Choose OK. (You can choose to enter a different name and description, but we will refer to these names in the steps below.)

Granting Network Access to FTP Users

Here are the steps to grant network access to the NT server for the user group that you just created.

1. If it is not already running, run User Manager or User Manager for Domains.
2. Select Policies | User Rights.
3. In the User Rights Policy dialog, highlight "Access this computer from the Network" from the Right: drop-down box. Choose Add.
4. A new dialog box called Add User and Groups will pop up. In the top window of that dialog box, highlight the HTML Managers group you created and choose Add again.
5. Choose OK to return to the User Rights Policy dialog box. Then choose OK again.

Managing the User Accounts

Here are the steps to create a sample account with limited directory browsing for a user named John. This is a very important step in a good FTP security policy.

1. If it is not already running, run User Manager or User Manager for Domains.
2. Select User | New User.
3. In the User Properties dialog that appears, enter the string john in each of these three text boxes: Username, Password, and Confirm Password. Choose Groups.
4. In the dialog that appears, highlight Users in the Member of: window. Choose Remove. (This will remove this user from the default Users group that NT provides for standard access privileges.)
5. In the Not Member of: window, highlight HTML Managers. Choose Add. Choose OK to return to the User Properties window.
6. Choose Profile. This will pop up the User Environment Profile dialog box.
7. In the Home Directory field, enter the path to the john directory that you are going to create in the next section (for example, C:\HTTP\john). Ensure that the Local Path radio button is selected. Choose OK to return to the User Properties window.
8. Choose OK again, and your account is set up.

The next section is closely related to this one. You have pointed the user account to a private directory, now you need to configure the user directory structure on the hard drive and set its file permissions.

Creating the User Directory and Setting Permissions

In the previous section, you specified where NT will deposit the FTP user named John when he logs in. In other words, NT will set his current working directory to the home directory that you chose above. Now you need to create this directory. For the purposes of this discussion, let's assume that you have set up your HTTP server's home directory to be C:\HTTP.

1. Run File Manager and select the C:\HTTP subdirectory so that it is highlighted.

2. Choose File | Create Directory. Enter john for the Directory name and choose OK.

3. Select the directory root in which your HTTP subdirectory is located. For example, D:\-NTFS should be highlighted.

4. Choose Security | Permissions. In the dialog that appears, choose Add.

5. Select HTML Managers from the Names window and choose Add. Choose OK to return to the Directory Permissions dialog box.

6. Ensure that you check the box to Replace Permissions on Subdirectories.

7. In the drop-down box labeled Type of Access, select Special Directory Access. In the dialog box that appears, select the Other radio button and check only the Execute (x) checkbox.

8. Choose OK to return to the Directory Permissions dialog. Choose OK again.

9. Return to the main window of File Manager and select the subdirectory that you created for John in step 2 (for example, C:\HTTP\john).

10. Select Security | Permissions. In the dialog that appears, choose Add.

11. Choose Show Users. Select john from the Names: window and choose Add.

12. In the Type of Access drop-down box select Full Control. Choose OK to return to the Directory Permissions dialog box.

13. Ensure that you check the Replace Permissions on Subdirectories checkbox. Choose OK.

The Outcome

Now when a user logs in using FTP, he or she will automatically be placed into his or her personal directory. The user will be able to create subdirectories underneath that directory and manage all the files that belong to him or her, but won't be able to look outside his or her directory.

Fine-Tuning FTP

Many of the values we are going to describe in this section might not be automatically entered in the Registry Parameters key following a default installation of Windows NT and FTP. There are several other registry values for FTP services that can be added to the Parameters key. For more information, see the Windows NT online help topic on "Advanced Configuration Parameters for FTP Server Service," or consult the Windows NT Resource Kit.

Limiting the Number of Simultaneous FTP Visitors

If you have popular files that a lot of people want to download, FTP could become a resource hog at your Web site. When several file transfers are in progress at once, a substantial portion of your CPU, disk I/O activity, and modem bandwidth will be eaten. You can follow the steps below to configure NT to limit the number of simultaneous FTP visitors to your site. This won't prevent other users from simultaneously downloading files via your Web page (assuming you provide that capability by including <A HREF> tags in your HTML code), but it will help preserve resources for your Web server and any other applications you choose to run.

1. Double-click the Network icon in Control Panel. Select FTP Server in the Installed Network Software list. Choose Configure.

2. Set the Maximum Connections value to an integer between 0 and 50. A value of 0 allows an unrestricted number of simultaneous FTP users (limited only by available resources). A value between 1 and 50 will limit the number of simultaneous FTP users to the given value.

3. To customize the message that will be displayed when someone tries to connect to your FTP server and the Maximum Connections have already been reached, run the Registry Editor and navigate to this key:
   HKEY_LOCAL_MACHINE...\SYSTEM\CurrentControlSet\Services\ftpsvc\Parameters.

4. Add or edit the entry for MaxClientsMessage. Data type = REG_SZ. Set the value to a custom string, such as Sorry, our FTP site is just too darn popular right now. Please try again later.

5. In order for these FTP configuration changes to take effect, stop and restart the FTP service. Because that will disconnect current users, first determine whether anyone is connected. Double-click the FTP Server icon in Control Panel. This will bring up the dialog (shown in Figure 14.3) that will tell you if anyone is connected, and how long they have been logged in. You'll recall that we went through this dialog after installing FTP. Keep this dialog running for a moment.

6. Switch back to Control Panel and run the Services icon. If anyone is currently connected (according to the User Sessions window in step 5), pause the FTP service until he or she logs out. This will prevent any new users from coming in while you wait. Assuming there are no FTP users currently connected, temporarily stop the FTP Server service and start it again. Choose Close.

Figure 14.3.
The FTP User Sessions dialog.

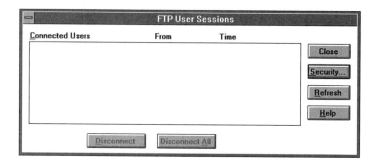

> **Tip:** There are several upcoming sections on fine-tuning FTP that also involve Registry editing. You will need to repeat steps 5 and 6 to restart the FTP service after each of the following procedures, or you can wait until you get to the section on FTP Security and then stop and restart the service just once.

Hello and Good-bye

After you've had a chance to log onto your FTP server a few times, you'll probably decide that you would like to see a message other than Welcome and Good-bye. Making these changes is easy with the Registry Editor.

> **Caution:** Before modifying your Registry, remember the standard warnings from Microsoft about editing the system configuration with the Registry Editor, which Chapter 12, "Maintaining and Tracking Your Web Site," discussed.

With that out of the way, make the following changes using the Registry editor:

1. Navigate to
   `HKEY_LOCAL_MACHINE..\SYSTEM\CurrentControlSet\Services\ftpsvc\Parameters`.
2. Add or edit the entry for `GreetingMessage` data type = REG_MULTI_SZ, `range = String, default = "Your Company's welcome message here"`.
3. Add or edit the entry for `ExitMessage`, data type = REG_SZ, `range = String, default = "Your Company's Goodbye message here"`.

Counting the Hits

You will most likely want to keep track of everyone who logs into your server using FTP. Follow these steps to turn on FTP logging.

1. Navigate the Registry Editor to this key:
   `HKEY_LOCAL_MACHINE...\SYSTEM\CurrentControlSet\Services\ftpsvc\Parameters.`

2. Add or edit the entry for `LogAnonymous` data type = REG_DWORD. Set the value to 0 or 1. A value of 1 specifies that you would like NT to note anonymous logins in the System event log.

3. Add or edit the entry for `LogNonAnonymous` data type = REG_DWORD. Set the value to 0 or 1. A value of 1 specifies that you would like NT to note non-anonymous logins in the System event log.

4. Add or edit the entry for `LogFileAccess` data type = REG_DWORD. Set the value to 0 or 1. A value of 0 means turn off logging of file accesses. A value of 1 specifies that you would like NT to note all file accesses in FTPSVC.LOG located in the `%SystemRoot%System32` directory. A value of 2 will start a new log file each day using a filename of the form: `FTyymmdd.LOG`.

5. Add or edit the entry for `LogFileDirectory` data type = REG_SZ. Set the value to the directory where you would like NT to create the logfiles from step 4. The default is `"%SystemRoot%\System32"`. This setting doesn't matter unless the value of `LogFileAccess` is non-zero.

Tip: Have you ever wondered what those percent signs are doing in the Registry default values for the pathname of the system directory? In `%SystemRoot%`, the percent signs signify that this is a variable name, which NT will fill in for you with the name of the actual directory where you installed NT. In a typical default installation of NT, this string would be replaced with C:\WINNT. If you elected to install NT on a different drive or in a different directory, the appropriate text will be substituted.

How to Make Windows NT Look Like DOS or UNIX

Why would any proud owner of Windows NT want to make it look like either of these other (insert your choice of adjective here) systems? Although the title of this section is intended as a joke, when it comes to FTP, we aren't kidding. You really do have to choose between DOS or UNIX for the style of FTP directory listings. By default, FTP directory listings appear in DOS format, and some FTP client software (the current version of Netcom's Netcruiser, for one) will not be able to parse the text stream properly. To solve this, you can put the FTP server into UNIX mode, which all FTP clients should know how to parse correctly. Just follow these steps:

1. Position the Registry editor to this key,
   `HKEY_LOCAL_MACHINE...\SYSTEM\CurrentControlSet\Services\ftpsvc\Parameters.`

2. Add or edit the entry for `MsDosDirOutput` data type = REG_DWORD. Set the value to 0.

When this value is 1, directory listings will look like MS-DOS listings, and the path will contain backslashes. If this value is 0, listings will appear as in UNIX systems and the path will contain forward slashes.

Annotating FTP Directory Listings

Because UNIX-style directory listings are not familiar to some of our users, NT has a nifty method that will let you pretty them up a bit. Follow these steps as an example of how to place a useful description at the top of the directory listing, as it is displayed in the users FTP client:

1. Run a text editor such as Notepad.

2. Create a new file and type in a string such as `John: This is your private directory`.

3. Save this file as ~ftpsvc~.ckm in the C:\HTTPS\john directory. The filename is required, and the directory name is up to you. With this directory name, you are continuing our example from the previous FTP Security section.

4. So users won't see this file as part of the directory itself, you can make this a hidden file using either File Manager or the command shell. Here's the command line you could run from a .cmd command file, or it could be typed directly into the Command Prompt window (assuming you are in the correct subdirectory, such as C:\HTTPS\john):

   `attrib +h ~ftpsvc~.ckm.`

5. Position the Registry editor to this key:

   `HKEY_LOCAL_MACHINE...\SYSTEM\CurrentControlSet\Services\ftpsvc\Parameters.`

6. Add or edit the entry for `AnnotateDirectories` data type = REG_DWORD. Set the value to 1. When this value is non-zero, the FTP server will display the contents of the file named ~ftpsvc~.ckm each time the user switches directories. The default value of 0 will cause it to bypass checking for these files.

Remote Administration with Telnet

Many people ask "Why use Telnet? Why not just log on with WfWG or Win95 from your notebook?" If you have Win95 on a notebook with a modem, you can set up a RAS connection to your server. It's true that a Win95 RAS connection would give you the benefits of a graphical interface. A Win95 login, however, does not necessarily solve all of your needs. Sometimes you might only have access to a UNIX platform or a shell account. With Telnet, you can log into your site from any platform connected to the Internet. Once connected, you'll have full access to NT's command shell, and you can run a variety of DOS, POSIX, and console applications.

In keeping with the high-quality/low-cost theme of this book, Telnet is inexpensive. If you travel anywhere in the world and want to continue monitoring your Web site without having to make a long distance call to log into your RAS server, a Telnet server is a great solution. The Telnet server will let you log into your Web site from any computer running a Telnet client—no matter how the client is connected to the Internet.

SLNet is the Telnet server that we are going to use. SLNet enables you to log into your Web site and run any Win32, OS/2, or DOS character application, or use NT's command shell. For example, one console mode application you might want to try is netstat. Among the many features of this little tool, it lets you monitor all active TCP/IP connections. For more information on netstat, see the NT online help file.

Installing SLNet

To install SLNet, run WinZip to uncompress it from the CD-ROM to your temp directory on the hard disk. Then run setup.

SLNet Features

SLNet gives Telnet clients full access to NT's command shell. With SLNet, multiple users can simultaneously access a Windows NT server and run most character-based applications.

SLNet provides a complete set of configuration options to the NT system administrator, allowing user access and permissions to be defined for individual users and groups of users. As the NT administrator, you can specify that a user or group of users will have a custom application started when they log in, rather than having them see a command-line prompt.

One of the best things about Telnet, SLNet included, is that it allows access to any Telnet clients from any TCP/IP system on the Internet. Clients can be running on any of the following platforms on either the local network or the Internet: UNIX, Macintosh, Windows, DOS, network terminal, or dumb terminal connected to Seattle Lab's SeriaLink.

When a Telnet user is connected to the NT server, he can do work without interfering with the system administrator who might be running GUI applications, or with the other Telnet clients who are running in a command shell.

In an interesting twist of technology, SLNet includes a graphical interface for the system administrator. It also maintains a log of all events and user activities.

Terminal Emulation

SLNet provides mapping sequences for the PC function keys. This allows users running terminal emulators to make use of function keys (for example, arrow keys, Alt-key sequences, and function keys), even though the keys are not directly available to users on their remote keyboards.

What's Next?

This concludes Part III of the book, and you now stand on the frontier of what we call Part IV, "Empowering Your Internet Server." At this point, you have acquired some fairly deep knowledge about the details of building and managing a Windows NT Web site. Now you're ready to move on to several more advanced topics that will help you tap the full potential of your Internet server.

Part IV

Empowering Your
Internet Server

Chapter 15

Databases and the Web

- WAIS
- ODBC
- CGI Databases with Cold Fusion
- Web Database Programming with Visual Basic 4
- The Efficiency of CGI
- Other Search Engines
- What's Next?

Databases are at the root of all business computing today. At some point you are going to want to integrate a company database with your Web site. Or, perhaps when you have a large Web site, you'll want to create a database that will let clients search the text of your HTML files.

There are several ways to achieve database and Web site integration. If you have read Chapter 7, "Introduction to Web Forms and CGI Scripts," you are no doubt thinking of writing a CGI application that will suit your needs. But what if you are not a CGI programmer and you want to connect an off-the-shelf database, such as Microsoft Access, to your Web site? Or what if you want to give people the ability to search your Web site for the page that they are looking for and you don't have the time to learn Perl? Well never fear; this chapter is going to show you how to handle both of these situations, and more, without learning complex programming languages.

And if you just can't live without programming, we're going to show you how to build a CGI system that uses C++ and Visual Basic 4 to update an Access or ODBC database through an HTML form!

WAIS

WAIS, which stands for Wide Area Information Server, is a tool for sharing information on the Internet. Because WAIS uses the Z39.50 protocol, you might hear the two terms used synonomously.

There are a couple of ways to use WAIS (pronounced *ways*). One of the techniques is extremely simple and works basically like this: You build a WAIS index of all the HTML files at your site and include the <ISINDEX> tag in your home page. It's that simple, and your users will love you for it.

EMWAC has developed the WAIS Toolkit to help you create a database of all the text at your Web site so that users can search it by keyword. The creators of HTML designed the <ISINDEX> tag with this feature in mind. <ISINDEX> will cause the Web server to invoke a program named WAISLOOK to search a WAIS database and return links to the pages containing the search keyword. (The WAIS database is also referred to as an index.)

Now we'll talk about the steps involved in turning the YourCo sample site into a searchable site. First, you need WAIS.

Installing the WAIS Toolkit

Wouldn't you know it? The EMWAC WAIS Toolkit works very well with the EMWAC HTTPS. Here are the steps to install the WAIS Toolkit.

> **Note:** There are several misguided steps in the WAIS Toolkit readme files that these instructions improve upon.

1. The WAIS Toolkit is distributed in four versions for the different architectures that Windows NT supports. From the CD \apps directory, select the appropriate ZIP file for your processor: wti386.zip for Intel, wtalpha.zip for DEC Alpha, wtmips.zip for MIPS, or wtppc.zip for Power PC.

2. Unzip the file from the CD-ROM to your hard drive. This should leave you with the following files:

   WAISINDX.EXE: The WAISINDEX program

WAISLOOK.EXE: The searching program

WAISSERV.EXE: The Z39.50 searching program

WAISTOOL.DOC: WAISTOOLKIT manual in Word for Windows format

WAISTOOL.WRI: WAISTOOLKIT manual in Windows Write format

WAISTOOL.PS: WAISTOOLKIT manual, in PostScript ready for printing

READ.ME: Summary of new features

3. If you have installed a previous version of the toolkit, remove it by deleting the old files or by moving them to another directory (which is not referred to by the PATH environment variable) for deletion after you have validated that the new version works correctly.

4. Decide which directory you are going to put the tools in and move the unzipped .EXE programs there. Ensure that the directory is on the path so that the commands may be executed from the command line. If you plan to use the WAIS Toolkit with the WAIS, Gopher, or HTTP servers, put the .EXE programs into the \WINNT\SYSTEM32 directory so that the servers can find them.

5. Determine which version of the Toolkit you have. To do this, at the Windows NT command prompt, type these commands:

```
waisindx -v

waislook -v

waisserv -v
```

and the version number for each program will be displayed. In fact, two version numbers will be shown for WAISINDX and WAISSERV; the first refers to the version of the freeWAIS code from which the programs were ported, and the second is the number of the Windows NT version. Here, we are describing version 0.7. If the programs report a later version number, you will find an updated manual in the files you unpacked from the ZIP archive.

Creating a Simple WAIS Database

Here are the steps for creating a WAIS database of the HTML files at your site. You will find additional documentation with the WAIS Toolkit and with EMWAC HTTPS.

First get into the home directory of your Web site. Assume it's d:\http.

1. Make d:\http the current directory.

2. Execute WAISINDX, giving it parameters as shown below:

```
waisindx -d index -t html *.htm*
```

3. Observe the messages from WAISINDX to check that there are no errors.

4. Do a DIR command on the d:\http directory to check that WAISINDEX has created the seven index files, named index.*.

Here is a description of the files created by WAISINDX:

- index.cat

  The catalog of the indexed files, with about three lines of information for each file indexed. This is a text file.

- index.Dct

  The dictionary of indexed words. This is a binary file.

- index.Doc

  The document table. This is a binary file. A file may contain several documents, depending on the type specified in the -t option.

- index.Fn

  The filename table. This is a binary file. The filenames stored in this table are supplied as the final parameters to WAISINDEX. Thus, if filenames are supplied relative to the current directory (for example, files/*), they will be stored in the filename table in that form, and the resulting filenames from a database search will also be in relative form.

- index.Hl

  The headline table. This is a binary file. A *headline* is (ideally) a line of descriptive text summarizing the contents of a document. The headline is normally taken from the document itself—for instance, it might be the Subject: line if the document is a mail message, the first line of the file, or the filename itself. Which it is depends on the type of the file, as notified to WAISINDEX using the -t option.

- index.Inv

  The inverted file index. This is a binary file.

- index.Src

  The source description structure. This is a text file.

Using ISINDEX with WAIS

Now that the WAIS index files are created, you need to modify your HTML code to take advantage of it. This is where the HTML `<ISINDEX>` tag enters the picture. Remember, the HTTP server is designed to invoke WAISLOOK whenever it receives an ISINDEX request from the client.

Create a new search page named index.htm with the `<ISINDEX>` tag. You can load the sample file shown in Listing 15.1. The filename is `\site\index.htm`.

Listing 15.1. Index.htm is a sample HTML file that uses `<ISINDEX>`.

```
<html><title>Search the Your Company Web Site</title>
<body>
<center>
<img alt="YourCo Logo" src="LOGO.GIF">
<h2>Search the Your Company Web Site</h2>
</center>
```

```
<p>To search the YourCo Web site just enter your search term(s) below.<isindex>
<hr size=5>
<i><a href="http://your IP address here/"><img src="RETURN.GIF">Back to YourCo Home
Page.</a></i>
<p>
<center>
This page, and all contents, are Copyright (C) 1995 by YourCompany
Inc., San Diego, California.
</center>
</BODY>
</HTML>
```

Now we need to provide a link on our sample home page to the new index file just created. Listing 15.2 is a slightly modified version of the file default.htm from the sample site created in Chapter 10. This file is also included on the CD as default2.htm in the \site directory. You can just rename it as default.htm if you wish, assuming you haven't already customized the default.htm file from Chapter 10.

Listing 15.2. Default.htm modified to link to index.htm.

```
<HTML>
<HEAD>
<TITLE>YourCompany Inc. Home Page</TITLE>
</HEAD>
<BODY>
<IMG SRC="Logo.gif">
<H1>Welcome to YourCompany!</H1>
Welcome to YourCompany!  YourCo is the world's leading supplier of
something. We have been in business since 1994, and have had a Web presence since
today.
<P>
Our newest and most exciting product is
<A HREF="product.html">Product here</A>. Select <A HREF="order.htm">here</A> to order
your own copy of Product here. You can also
<A HREF="custreg.htm">register for our customer newsletter</A>, sent out by E-Mail
every six weeks.<P>
We are pleased to provide the following additional information:<P><UL>
<LI><A HREF="Release.htm">YourCo Press Releases</A><P>
<LI><A HREF="Lit.htm">YourCo Marketing Literature</A><P>
<LI><A HREF="Intro.htm">Introduction to our Products</A><P>
<LI><A HREF="Train.htm">YourCo Training Services</A><P>
<LI><A HREF="Consult.htm">YourCo Consulting Services</A><P>
<LI><A HREF="index.htm">Search the YourCo Web Site</A><P></UL> <!-- this line is new
link -->
<H2>Comments or Problems</H2>
Again, thanks for visiting YourCompany's WWW server. We hope to hear
from you again soon.<P>
For information on YourCompany's products and services, please send
e-mail to <a href="mailto: info@YourCompany.com"><i>info@YourCompany.com</i></a>, for
an automated reply<br>
or use our <A HREF="feedback.htm">feedback form</A> for other inquiries.<P>
This page, and all contents, are Copyright (C) 1995 by YourCompany
Inc., San Diego, California.
</BODY>
</HTML>
```

Congratulations, now your site will be searchable by keyword. Use your Web browser and give it a try.

ODBC

Microsoft Open Database Connectivity (ODBC) is a standard programming interface for application developers and database systems providers. Before ODBC became a *de facto* standard for Windows programs to interface with database systems, programmers had to use proprietary languages for each database they wanted to connect to. Now, ODBC has made the choice of the database system almost irrelevant from a coding perspective, which is as it should be. Application developers have more important things to worry about than the syntax that is needed to port their program from one database to another when business needs suddenly change.

Through the ODBC Administrator in Control Panel, you can specify the particular database that is associated with a data source that an ODBC application program is written to use. Think of an ODBC data source as a door with a name on it. Each door will lead you to a particular database. For example, the data source named Sales Figures might be a SQL Server database, whereas the Accounts Payable data source could refer to an Access 2.0 database. The physical database referred to by a data source can reside anywhere on the LAN.

> **Note:** The ODBC files are not installed on your system by Windows NT. Rather, they are installed when you purchase a separate database product, such as SQL Server 6.0 or Visual Basic 4. When the ODBC icon is installed in Control Panel, it uses a file called ODBCINST.DLL. It is also possible to administer your ODBC data sources through a stand-alone program called ODBCADM.EXE. There is a 16-bit and a 32-bit version of this program, and they each maintain a separate list of ODBC data sources.

After an ODBC-compliant application begins running, it uses the same set of function calls to interface with any data source. The source code of the application doesn't change whether it talks to Oracle or SQL Server. (We only mention these two as an example. There are ODBC drivers available for several dozen popular database systems. Even Excel spreadsheets and plain text files can be turned into data sources.) The operating system uses the Registry information written by ODBC Administrator to determine which low-level ODBC drivers are needed to talk to the data source (such as the interface to Oracle or SQL Server). The loading of the ODBC drivers is transparent to the ODBC application program. In a client/server environment, the ODBC API even handles many of the network issues for the application programmer.

The advantages of this scheme are so numerous that you are probably thinking there must be some catch. The only disadvantage of ODBC is that it isn't as efficient as talking directly to the native database interface. ODBC has had many detractors make the charge that it is too slow. Microsoft has always claimed that the critical factor in performance is the quality of the driver software that is used. In our humble opinion, this is true. The availability of good ODBC drivers has improved a lot in the last year. And anyway, the criticism about performance is somewhat analogous to those who said that compilers would never match the speed of pure assembly language. Maybe not, but the compiler (or ODBC) gives you the opportunity to write cleaner programs, which means you finish sooner. Meanwhile, computers get faster every year.

CGI Databases with Cold Fusion

To write a CGI application that would interact with an off-the-shelf database would take quite a bit of programming expertise. Why take the time to write such an application or pay someone else to do it when perfectly good ones already exist? We have included a demo version of a product called Cold Fusion, which is a CGI application that will allow full Web integration with any 32-bit ODBC database application. The demo is a completely operational version; its only limitation is that it will stop working 30 days after installation.

Cold Fusion can be used to create a wide range of World Wide Web applications including customer feedback, online order-entry, event registration, searching of catalogs, directories and calendars, bulletin-board style conferencing, online technical support, and interactive training.

You create Cold Fusion applications by combining standard HTML files with high-level database commands and a powerful CGI program that is precompiled. This method of developing Web applications is an order of magnitude faster, more robust, and more flexible than first generation, code-intensive techniques.

Cold Fusion applications can be developed very rapidly because no code (beyond simple markup tags) is required. The applications are also robust because all database interactions are encapsulated in a single industrial-strength CGI script.

Cold Fusion applications are also very flexible because all formatting and presentation is done using standard HTML files that can be modified and revised at any time (as opposed to having to edit and recompile source code).

Installing Cold Fusion

Installation of the Cold Fusion demo is a snap. Just copy the file cfuseval.exe from the \apps directory on the CD to a temporary directory on your hard disk. Then execute the self-extracting install program in your temporary directory. The Cold Fusion installation process will handle the rest.

The Cold Fusion demo application includes a complete online tutorial in HTML format that will guide you through developing several examples. Now is a good time to spend some time with the Cold Fusion online tutorial and examples.

Important Notes about Installating Cold Fusion

- If you are running Windows NT, you must be running under an account with Administrator privileges in order to install the software.

- Do not attempt to install the software while running under the "technology-preview" release of the Windows 95 shell for Windows NT. (There are problems accessing the Registry when this version of the shell is running.)

- If the installation of ODBC components does not complete successfully, it is probably because an ODBC library was in use during setup. In this case, restart Windows and double-click the ODBC Setup icon in the Cold Fusion Program Group to complete the installation of ODBC.

CGI Database Access with No Programming

Let's say that you have a company mailing list and it's in the Microsoft Access *.MDB file format. You want people browsing your Web site to be able to add their names to the mailing list. With Cold Fusion you can create a form that will enable people to fill out a Web form and have the data automatically entered into your Access .MDB file. We have included all the files necessary to accomplish this on the CD in the \supp directory. Here is a description of the files:

- mlist.htm

    The .htm file that contains the form for entering information to the database

- mlist.mdb

    The Access 2.0 database

- default3.htm

    Modified home page from the sample site that adds a link to mlist.htm

Here are the steps to add the record entry functionality to the database at your sample site:

1. Create a directory named mlist under d:\http.

2. Copy the files mlist.htm and mlist.mdb to the mlist directory.

3. Copy default3.htm to the d:\http directory and rename it default.htm. It's okay if it overwrites the file by the same name from your sample site in Chapter 10, unless you have customized the latter. If so, please be sure to save it.

4. Open Cold Fusion and create one or more ODBC data sources for MS Access. See Figure 15.1. For more information on what ODBC is and how it works, see the Cold Fusion User's Guide.

Figure 15.1.
The Cold Fusion Adminis-trator.

5. Choose the Manage button to bring up the Data Sources dialog shown in Figure 15.2.

Figure 15.2.
The Cold Fusion Data Sources dialog.

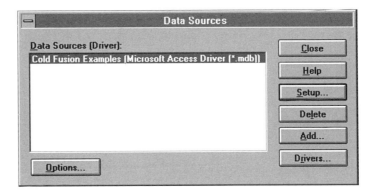

6. Choose the Add button to bring up the Add Data Source dialog as shown in Figure 15.3.

Figure 15.3.
Adding a data source.

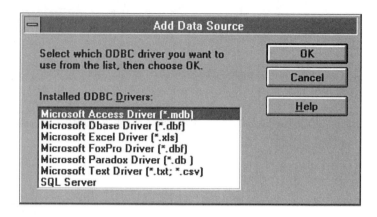

7. Select the driver for the Access 2.0 database and then choose OK. In the dialog box that appears enter MS Access for the Data Source Name. See Figure 15.4.

Figure 15.4.
Naming a data source.

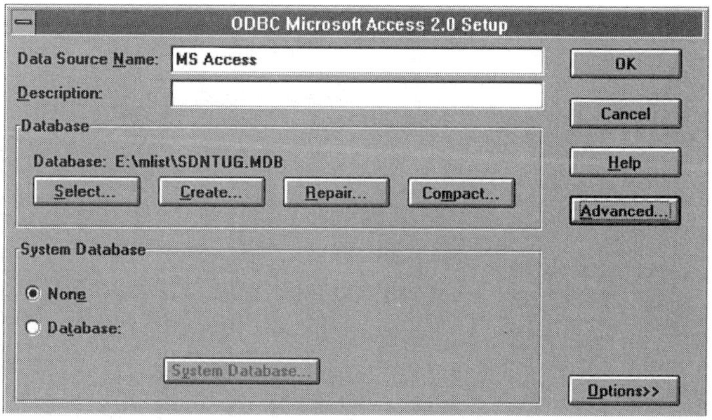

8. Choose the Select button to enter the path to the mlist.mdb file from step 2. See Figure 15.5. Choose OK to close the Select Database dialog. Choose OK again to close the ODBC Microsoft Access 2.0 Setup dialog.

9. Now the new data source is created, but it isn't available until you choose the Publish button in the main Cold Fusion Administrator dialog. See Figure 15.6.

That's all there is to it. Your sample site now has a link to a page that will automatically add people to your mlist.mdb file containing your mailing list. Now is a good time to break out your Web browser and add a few names to the list. Of course, without Microsoft Access you will not be able to view, modify, or print out any information from the .MDB file yet. The next step is to edit and search the database from the Web.

Figure 15.5.
Selecting the path to the database file.

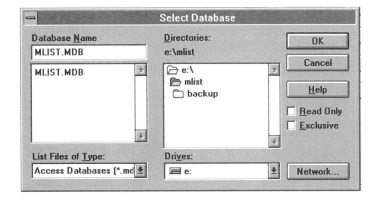

Figure 15.6.
Publishing the data source.

Inserting and Updating Data with Cold Fusion

Cold Fusion's most basic functionality (inserting form data into database tables) is implemented by the addition of hidden configuration fields to HTML forms. This technique is extremely easy to learn for anyone already familiar with HTML forms.

To insert or update data, you create an HTML form containing the fields in the database table that you want to insert or update. You then add three hidden fields to the form which indicate what you want Cold Fusion to do with the data entered by the user. These hidden fields are as follows:

Field Name	Purpose
DataSource	Name of the ODBC data source containing your table
TableName	Name of the table you want the form fields written to
NextPage	A URL indicating which page the user should be sent to if the submission is successful

Additional hidden fields can also be specified to validate the user's entries (for example, required, numeric, date, and range-checked).

When this form is submitted to the Cold Fusion CGI program (DBML.EXE), the data entered by the user is added to the specified table and the user is routed to the specified next page.

Queries and Dynamic Pages with Cold Fusion

Cold Fusion enables you to dynamically generate HTML pages based on user queries. These queries are submitted to the Cold Fusion CGI program (DBML.EXE), which then (based on a template file specified in the query) generates the output which is sent back to the user.

The key to dynamic page generation is a small (but powerful) set of database-oriented markup tags. These tags are collectively referred to as DBML (Database Markup Language). DBML tags are very similar to HTML tags except they are database-oriented. Learning to use the DBML tags is extremely simple. Almost all of the core functionality of Cold Fusion is encapsulated in these four tags:

Tag	Purpose
DBQUERY	Submits a SQL query to the database
DBOUTPUT	Displays the result of a query, freely intermixing result set fields and HTML tags
DBTABLE & DBCOL	Displays a preformatted table containing the result set of a query

Dynamic pages are created using template files, which are composed of a mix of HTML and DBML tags that define how the user's request should be processed and what type of output should be returned.

The DBML tags are used to specify how you want Cold Fusion to interact with the database, as well as where you want to display the results of your queries. For example, you might specify that you want the SQL query SELECT * FROM Customers sent to the database and the results returned as a preformatted table.

The HTML tags are used both for implementing the non-database driven parts of your output (for example, page header and footer) as well as for specifying how you want the results of your queries formatted. For example, you might specify that you want a field bolded or a horizontal rule drawn between each record displayed.

Expanding the Database Interface with Cold Fusion

To add more functionality to the mail list entry, you can search and update the mailing list from a Web browser, too. To accomplish this, you need three more files. Here are the files you need from the \supp directory of the CD:

- results.dbm

   The DBML file that passes SQL information to Cold Fusion to conduct the search
- srch.htm

   The search form to link to your sample site's default.htm file
- default4.htm

   A modified default.htm file with links added for srch.htm and mlist.htm

Here are the steps to add database search and update functionality:

1. Copy the file srch.htm to the mlist directory you created.
2. Copy default4.htm to the d:\http directory and rename it default.htm. Again, unless you have customized the previous version, it should be okay to overwrite it.
3. In the directory in which you installed Cold Fusion, create a directory named mlist under the Cold Fusion template directory. The path should be something like:
   `c:\cfusion\template\mlist`.
4. Copy the file mlist.dbm to the directory you just created.

Fire up your Web browser and go to your sample site home page to try out the new link. See if you can search and update the mailing list database.

Depending on the nature of your data, you might immediately realize that you would not want a link like this available to the general public. If this is the case, you'll want to use one of the commercial Web servers (such as Process Purveyor) that enables you to password-protect your pages.

Cold Fusion was the first to market with an ODBC database and Web integration tool for Windows NT. At the time of this writing it is still the only tool available for this task, but several others are in the works.

Web Database Programming with Visual Basic 4

Cold Fusion is obviously great for many database-oriented CGI tasks, especially for nonprogrammers. C, C++, and Perl are also popular CGI languages, but they all have a high-entry fee in terms of programming experience. And when it comes to CGI, they "don't do Windows." Nor do they have an ODBC database interface. CGI PerForm, mentioned in Chapter 8, does have a database interface, but it is a proprietary one (very powerful, but not ODBC-compatible).

If it sounds like we are heaping on the criticism to prepare you for the next pitch, here it comes. To put it simply, you have to give Visual Basic a try before you can appreciate its awesome potential. Not only is it a rapid-development environment, but it supplies all of the features we just discussed that are missing from other CGI alternatives.

Visual Basic includes very powerful capabilities for database, file, and string manipulation. These features happen to have a high correlation with a "dream" language for CGI. And once you get familiar with VB, you'll see that this list is just the tip of the iceberg of its other capabilities. For example, did you know that VB Professional will let you send and receive e-mail on the LAN using MAPI (the Mail API)? Did you know that you can use it to send a fax? VB programs are even used to control factory automation processes. Imagine using a Web form to automatically initiate a fax transmission, or beep your pager, or build a customized pizza.

Pundits claim that VB is slow, but this just isn't true. It is slower than a compiled language, but the point is *that this usually doesn't matter.* You see, as soon as you identify the segment of your code that cries out to be optimized (evidence suggests that this is often way less than one percent) and assuming your customers don't already have more important things for you to be working on instead, you can rewrite that function in C and put it in a DLL. This way, you get to retain VB for the things it does best, namely user interface construction and database connectivity, while tuning only the sections of the program that really need the boost. Isn't it better to get it working first and optimize later?

CGI with Visual Basic

As you might have noticed, the EMWAC HTTPS doesn't support WinCGI and VB doesn't build console-mode applications. This is unfortunate but—thanks to the infinite malleability of software—is not insurmountable. We have devised a clever kludge (yes, we believe in the power of positive criticism) so that you can hang on to the economical EMWAC server and still take advantage of the database power of VB.

We are going to use a C++ program (extended C, not object-oriented) to parse the form data into a temporary file before it invokes the Visual Basic application. The VB program will run invisibly while it reads the temporary file passed in by the C++ program and writes the information to the Access database.

If you read the WinCGI specification in Appendix G, you'll see that this method is very comparable in terms of efficiency. WinCGI involves file I/O to write the environment variables to WIN.INI and to write the form data to a temporary file. (Speaking of efficiency, see the sidebar below, "The Efficiency of CGI".)

There are four pieces to this puzzle: You need an HTML form that will invoke the CGI application, the CGI application written in C++ that will handle the environment variables and pass the form data to the Visual Basic program, the Visual Basic program itself, and an Access database to store the data. Using Visual Basic, you could just as easily connect to a FoxPro database, or any database for which an ODBC driver is available.

And what does this application do when it is all done? Frankly, not much more than what you have already seen. In order not to introduce too much complexity all at once, we are going to recycle the customer feedback form from Chapter 10. It presents a simple form interface on the Web to enable a customer to compliment or complain about your products or services. You'll recall that the feedback form in Chapter 10 processed the data by e-mailing it to the attention of a predetermined company representative. In this chapter, you'll insert the form data into a table in an Access database. Each record you insert includes a timestamp so that you can use a SQL query (in a separate program such as Access) to determine which records have been added within a given date range.

The main goal of this section is to show you the possibilities of CGI with VB. The sample application that you are going to build can be easily extended in any number of ways. With HTML, VB, ODBC, and the Windows API at your disposal, you are limited only by your imagination.

The Efficiency of CGI

CGI was invented from a command-line perspective in a UNIX environment. Having the Web server invoke the CGI application separately for each client request is not the most efficient means of processing form data on Windows NT.

Why is CGI efficiency important? The answer depends mostly on how large your Web site is. If you have only a few visitors per day, you don't need to worry about it. But if you are running a server with dozens of simultaneous client connections, you'll want your server to be tuned as tight as possible.

New Web servers available for Windows NT in 1996 promise to make great gains in terms of CGI efficiency. Recent announcements from Process Software and Microsoft indicate that their Web servers will be supporting a new open specification called ISAPI (Information Server Application Programming Interface). ISAPI allows developers to create 32-bit DLLs to run within the memory context of the Web server. Not only does the server avoid reloading the CGI executable, but form data is passed into the application, and the HTML response is passed back, using pointers to memory blocks—thus saving a substantial amount of file I/O.

Although Visual Basic doesn't allow pointer manipulation as easily as do C and C++, ISAPI programming in VB will probably be about as complex as WinCGI or CGI 1.1.

Another alternative to CGI is SSI+ (Server Side Includes), supported by the WebQuest server from Questar. Only time will tell which of these techniques will ultimately prove to be the most effective. In the meantime, consider many factors when choosing your server and then use the tools it offers.

The HTML Program

Listing 15.3 is the file feedbck2.htm from the \vb directory on the CD. It is a modified version of feedback.htm from Chapter 10. Notice in the <FORM> tag that this version uses the POST method to invoke a CGI application on the server named cgi_cpp.exe. Also notice the names of the input fields; you will be looking at those in the VB program.

Listing 15.3. The file feedbck2.htm gathers database input.

```
<HEAD>
<TITLE>Suggestions and Comments</TITLE>
</HEAD>
<BODY>
<form action="http://localhost/cgi-bin/cgi_cpp.exe" method="POST">
<H1>Your Comments, Questions and Feedback!</H1>
Please enter your Name:
<BR><INPUT TYPE=text NAME="name" SIZE = 40 MAXLENGTH=40>
<BR>Email address:
<BR><INPUT TYPE=text NAME="email" SIZE = 40 MAXLENGTH=40>
<P>
Enter your comments, questions and/or suggestions in the space below:<BR>
<TEXTAREA NAME=comments ROWS=12 COLS=60 MAXLENGTH=3000></TEXTAREA>
<P>
<input type="submit" value="Submit Comments">
</FORM>
</BODY>
</HTML>
```

Take another look at the <FORM> tag in Listing 15.3. Notice the URL indicates localhost. 127.0.0.1 is defined to be the loopback address for IP. The HOSTS file in your Windows directory should indicate that localhost is an alias for 127.0.0.1. This makes a convenient way to check your CGI systems on your server, even if you aren't connected to the Internet.

The C++ Program

The program we develop here is called cgi_cpp.cpp. It has been modified from savedata.c, which we presented in Chapter 8, "Power Programming with CGI." You recall that savedate.exe can be used to parse the contents of an HTML form and save them in a text file named savedata.HFO.

Our purpose for modifying the program in this chapter is to get it to parse the data slightly differently before handing it off to the Visual Basic program.

One way in which it is modified is that it creates a small temporary file each time it is invoked, rather than inserting the data into one file which increases in size. See Listing 15.4 for the code. Most of it will look very familiar to you by now. In order to save trees, we have trimmed out three functions in Listing 15.4 and marked the location with a comment. You have already seen the functions strcvrt, TwoHex2Int, and urlDecode in Chapters 7 and 8, and they remain unchanged in this program. The file cgi_cpp.cpp appears in its entirety in the \cgi\vb directory on the CD.

Listing 15.4. CGI_CPP.CPP runs between the server and the VB program.

```
/*************************************************************************
 *   File: CGI_CPP.CPP
 *
 *   Description: CGI program for use with HTTPS.
 *   Parses form data and invokes Visual Basic application.
 *
 *   Assumes it is invoked from a form. This script writes the form data
 *   to a temporary file and then invokes the Visual Basic application
 *   which serves as the interface to the database.
 *   Ensure that you compile this script as an NT console mode app.
 *   This program is a modified version of the source code that comes with
 *   EMWAC HTTPS.
 *
 *   October, 1995
 *   By: Scott Zimmerman and Christopher L. T. Brown
 *
 *************************************************************************/
#include <stdio.h>
#include <stdlib.h>
#include <string.h>
#include <ctype.h>
#include <io.h>
#include <time.h>
#define DATA_PATH "c:\\temp"        // Location of temp file for form data
char InputBuffer[4096];        // Maximum amount of data user may enter

/*** the function void strcvrt(char *cStr, char cOld, char cNew) appears here ***/
/*** the function static int TwoHex2Int(char *pC) appears here ***/
/*** the function void urlDecode(char *p) appears here ***/

/* Parse out and store field=value items into the temp file.
** DON'T use strtok here because it is ALREADY used by caller.
*/
void StoreField(FILE *f, char *Item)
{
        char *p;

        p = strchr(Item, '=');
        *p++ = '\0';
        urlDecode(Item);
        urlDecode(p);
        strcvrt(p, '\n', ' ');
```

continues

Listing 15.4. continued

```c
        /* Get rid of those nasty +'s */
        strcvrt(p, '+', ' ');
        fprintf(f, "%s=%s\n", Item, p);
}

int main(void)
{
        int  ContentLength, x, i;
        char *p, *URL, *whocalledme;
        char datebuf[9], timebuf[9];
        char FileName[_MAX_PATH];
        char cmdbuf[_MAX_PATH + 30];
        FILE *f;

        // Turn buffering off for stdin
        setvbuf(stdin, NULL, _IONBF, 0);

        // Tell the client what we're going to send back
        printf("Content-type: text/html\n\n");

        // Uses a kludgy IPC method to pass form data to VB
        for (i = 0; i <= 9999; i++)
        {
                // Make a new filename
                sprintf(FileName, "%s\\CGI%d.HFO", DATA_PATH, i);

                // If the file exists, try again. Doesn't handle errors!
                if(access(FileName, 0) == -1)
                        break;
        }

        // Open the file
        f = fopen(FileName, "a");

        // Check if open succeeds
        if(f == NULL)
        {
                printf("<HEAD><TITLE>Error: cannot open file</TITLE></HEAD>\n");
                printf("<BODY><H1>Error: cannot open file</H1>\n");
                printf("The file %s could not be opened.\n",FileName);
                printf("</BODY>\n");
                exit(0);
        }

        // Write to the file the URL which posted the form data
        whocalledme = getenv("REMOTE_ADDR");
        fprintf(f, "URL=%s\n", whocalledme);

        // Write to the file the date/time of this hit
        _strdate(datebuf);
        _strtime(timebuf);
        fprintf(f, "Date=%s\n", datebuf);
        fprintf(f, "Time=%s\n", timebuf);

        // Get the length of the client input data
        p = getenv("CONTENT_LENGTH");
```

```
if(p != NULL)
      ContentLength = atoi(p);
else
      ContentLength = 0;

// Avoid buffer overflow -- better to allocate dynamically
if(ContentLength > sizeof(InputBuffer) -1)
      ContentLength = sizeof(InputBuffer) -1;

// Get the data from the client (assumes POST method)

i = 0;
while(i < ContentLength)
{
      x = fgetc(stdin);
      if(x == EOF)
            break;
      InputBuffer[i++] = x;
}
InputBuffer[i] = '\0';
ContentLength = i;

p = getenv("CONTENT_TYPE");
if(p == NULL)
{
      fclose(f);
      return(0);
}

if(strcmp(p, "application/x-www-form-urlencoded") == 0)
{
      // Parse the data
      p = strtok(InputBuffer, "&");
      while(p != NULL)
      {
            // Write the field/value pair to the temp file
            StoreField(f, p);
            p = strtok(NULL, "&");
      }
}
else
      // Write the whole data to file
      fprintf(f, "Input = %s\n", InputBuffer);

// Confirm to client
if(!ferror(f))
{
      // What url called me
      URL = getenv("HTTP_REFERER");
      printf("<HEAD><TITLE>Submitted OK</TITLE></HEAD>\n");
      printf("<BODY><h2>Your information has been accepted.");
      printf("  Thank You!</h2>\n");
      printf("<h3><A href=\"%s\">Return</a></h3></BODY>\n", URL);
}
else
{
      // What url called me
      URL = getenv("HTTP_REFERER");
      printf("<HEAD><TITLE>Server file I/O error</TITLE></HEAD>\n");
```

continues

Listing 15.4. continued

```
                printf("<BODY><h2>Your information could not be accepted\n");
                printf("due to a file I/O error at the server.</h2>\n");
                printf("<h3><A href=\"%s\">Return</a></h3></BODY>\n", URL);
        }

        // Close the file.
        fclose(f);
        // Invoke the Visual Basic program to update the database
        sprintf(cmdbuf, "start cgi_vb.exe %s", FileName);
        system(cmdbuf);

        return(0);
}
```

The only thing that has significantly changed is the `main()` function. One of the first things that `main()` does is invent a temporary filename. It tries to use CGI0.HFO. If that filename exists, it will increment the number and try CGI1.HFO. This algorithm is very inefficient and doesn't check for errors, but it serves the purpose so we can focus on the interesting stuff.

The first item written to the temporary file is the URL from the `REMOTE_ADDR` environment variable. This tracks the client. We follow that with the date and time, on separate lines. All fields are on lines by themselves, and each field name is separated from its corresponding data by an equal sign. You need to keep these things in mind when you write the VB program. The `StoreField` function has also been modified from the savedata version in Chapter 8 so that all lines are formatted similarly, with no spaces surrounding the equals signs.

Unlike savedata.c, this program ignores some error-checking, and it blindly assumes that `REQUEST_METHOD` is `POST`.

The interesting thing about it is that two output files are being built simultaneously. Remember, the CGI application is supposed to send some HTML output back to the browser so that the user won't get stranded on the Web. This is achieved by the calls to printf, which write to stdout. The HTTP server will pick up the stdout data, apply the HTTP protocol, and send it back to the client.

Meanwhile, you still have to write the form data from the client into the temporary file before you launch the VB program. That is achieved by the `fprintf` calls.

At the end of the program, cgi_vb.exe is launched via the `system()` call in the C standard library.

The Visual Basic Program

Now you need the VB program to pick up the form data and insert it into the database. This process will execute fairly quickly, so you really don't need a user interface. In fact, you want the program to quit as soon as it's finished—with no user involvement at all. Remember, this program is only going to run on the server. You can set the `Visible` property on the main form to `False`. You could accomplish the same thing by placing the code from `Form_Load` into `Sub Main` in a .BAS file, and getting rid of the .FRM file altogether.

See Listing 15.5 for the code. This is the file cgi_vb.frm in the \cgi\vb directory on the CD. The VB 4.0 project file is cgi_vb.vbp.

> **Note:** This program was developed using the Visual Basic 4.0 Enterprise Edition. The program will also work as-is with the 4.0 Professional Edition. With very minor changes, the program could be made to work with the Visual Basic 3.0 Professional Edition.
>
> The files on the CD do not include a setup program for this application. You must have Visual Basic installed to get the proper DLLs and for OLE registration of the JET engine to take place.

Listing 15.11. The VB program, which interfaces with the database.

```
Private Function ParseField(szText As String) As String
    Dim k As Integer
    k = InStr(szText, "=")
    ' Return the substring following the equals sign
    ParseField = Mid$(szText, k + 1)
End Function

Private Sub Form_Load()
    Dim szURL       As String
    Dim szDate      As String
    Dim szTime      As String
    Dim szName      As String
    Dim szEmail     As String
    Dim szComments  As String
    Dim db          As Database
    Dim rs          As Recordset

    ' Open the temporary file with form data and read it into memory
    Open Command$ For Input As #1
    Line Input #1, szURL
    Line Input #1, szDate
    Line Input #1, szTime
    Line Input #1, szName
    Line Input #1, szEmail
    Line Input #1, szComments

    ' Close the temporary file and delete it
    Close #1
    Kill Command$

    ' Open the database and the table
    Set db = OpenDatabase(App.Path & "\cgi_vb.mdb")
    Set rs = db.OpenRecordset("table1", dbOpenTable)

    ' Add a new record to the table. Counter field is
    ' initialized automatically by Jet 3.0.
    rs.AddNew

    rs!When = ParseField(szDate) & " " & ParseField(szTime)
```

continues

Listing 15.11. continued

```
    rs!URL = ParseField(szURL)
    rs!Name = ParseField(szName)
    rs!Email = ParseField(szEmail)
    rs!Comments = ParseField(szComments)

    ' Update the table, close everything and quit
    rs.Update
    rs.Close
    db.Close
    End
End Sub
```

Almost all of the code is in the `Form_Load` event. The project only includes one form. The `command$` statement is used to retrieve the name of the temporary file passed in by the C++ CGI program.

Note that it assumes the order of the fields in the text file written by the C++ program. This isn't robust; but again, that isn't our point. If you want to modify the HTML feedback form, you will also have to modify the VB code. The C++ should be able to survive without modification if new fields are added to the HTML file, the VB code, and the database.

The temporary input file from the C++ CGI program is deleted as soon as we are through reading it. Then the database is opened, and a recordset is created using the `dbOpenTable` parameter. This will permit you to write to the table. The table is called `table1` (until you change it).

The fields in the table correspond to the data you capture on the form, as well as the URL of the client and the date/time the submission was made to the server. For each field, call the `ParseField` function to retrieve the substring following the equal sign.

If you designate a key field to use AutoIncrement in Data Manager, the JET 3.0 engine will automatically take care of incrementing it for you. Therefore, you don't need to supply the value of the key field between the calls to `AddNew` and `Update`.

Examining the Database with Data Manager

The database is named cgi_vb.mdb. We assume it lives in the same directory as the Visual Basic program itself. By the way, depending on your server, the C++ program probably needs to live in the cgi-bin directory. The VB program is not invoked with a full pathname, so it too should probably go in the cgi-bin directory.

The database is also in the \cgi\vb directory on the CD. We suggest that you copy it and the rest of the \cgi\vb directory to a location on your hard drive where you can experiment with it.

You can open the database with Access 7.0 or the Data Manager utility that comes with the VB 4.0 Professional and Enterprise editions. We won't go into the steps to create the database, because that information is readily available in the product documentation for Access and Data Manager.

Here are the fields and data types in table1 in cgi_vb.mdb:

Field Name	Data Type
Counter	Long
URL	Text:40
When	Date/Time
Name	Text:40
Email	Text:40
Comments	Text:255

The field named Counter is the key field and is also marked as a Counter type in Data Manager. This means that you don't need to calculate unique values for it, because VB will do this automatically when you execute rs.Update.

The program lacks several important error-checking features. For example, no check is made to ensure that the supplied text does not exceed the field sizes. The field sizes in the database should match the MAX attribute of the TEXT input fields in the HTML file. The VB program should probably be written to truncate longer text in case the two sizes should ever become mismatched. As it stands now, the VB program would crash if the input text exceeded the database field size.

Other Search Engines

There are several CGI applications that will work in conjunction with an HTML form, allowing you to conduct a database search. These applications are beyond the scope of this book, but you can find some examples at the Windows NT Resource Center http://www.bhs.com/winnt/.

What's Next?

This part of the book is all about turbo-charging your Internet server. We still have several progressive topics to cover, such as internet robots, advanced security, financial transactions, and future trends.

Chapter 16

Internet Robots and More Security Issues

- Internet Robots
- Excluding Robots
- Firewalls and Proxy Servers
- Software Viruses
- Miscellaneous Security Advice
- Windows NT Domains
- What's Next?

One should always be suspect of hackers who are looking to steal data or computer resources. This is true simply because the nature of digital communications permits such activities to go easily undetected. Hackers just can't be spotted—in a physical sense—as easily as, say, car jackers.

This book has brought up the topic of security whenever it has been pertinent to the other techniques or software being discussed. Chapter 12, "Maintaining and Tracking Your Web Site," discussed several settings in the Windows NT Registry relevant to security. This chapter takes a look at the bigger picture of security—from an Internet perspective.

We'll also be talking about Internet robots, or bots. Internet robots are a progressive and controversial topic on the Internet. Many people are still unaware of their existence, and lots of people are upset by their existence. We are going to tell you what these robots are doing on the Internet, how you can benefit from them, why you should be concerned, and what you can do about it.

The second part of this chapter is about using a firewall to protect your server or your LAN from outside intrusion and about using proxy servers to keep your network diagram from being reverse-engineered.

Finally, we will mention the topic of software viruses and what you should do to minimize your risk of attack.

The security information in this chapter is more concerned with the structure of the network than it is with secure commercial transactions. If you are looking for information about secure commerce on the Web, see Chapter 17, "Commerce on the Web."

Internet Robots

World Wide Web robots, sometimes called *wanderers* or *spiders,* are programs that traverse the Web automatically. The job of a robot is to retrieve information about the documents that are available on the Web and then store that information in some kind of master index of the Web. Usually, the robot is limited by its author to hunt for a particular topic or segment of the Web.

At the very least, most robots are programmed to look at the <TITLE> and <H1> tags in the HTML documents they discover. Then they scan the contents of the file looking for <A HREF> tags to other documents. A typical robot might store the URLs of those documents in a data structure called a *tree,* which it uses to continue the search whenever it reaches a dead end (more technically called a *leaf-node*). We are oversimplifying this a bit; the larger robots probably use much more sophisticated algorithms. But the basic principles are the same.

The idea behind this is that the index built by the robot will make life easier for us humans who would like a quick hop to information sources on the Internet.

The good news is that most robots are successful at this and do help make subsequent search and retrieval of those documents more efficient. This is important in terms of Internet traffic. If a robot spends several hours looking for documents, but thousands (or even millions) of users take advantage of the index that is generated, it will save all those users from tapping their own means of discovering the links, potentially saving a great amount of network bandwidth.

The bad news is that some robots inefficiently revisit the same site more than once, or they submit rapid-fire requests to the same site in such a frenzy that the server can't keep up. This is obviously a cause of concern for Webmasters. Robot authors are as upset as the rest of the Internet community when they find out that a poorly behaved robot has been unleashed. But usually such problems are found only in a few poorly written robots.

Figure 16.1 shows a hypothetical case of a tree-traversal algorithm that a robot might use. Node #1 is where the journey begins; it is considered the root of the tree. Upon inspecting the HTML code at node #1, it discovers a link to node #2. When it reaches a static document at node #3 (a leaf node), it backtracks first to node #2 and then to node #1 where it continues to node #4, and so on.

Figure 16.1.
A robot traversing the Web.

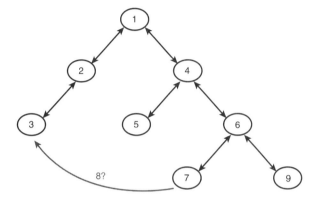

The problem that occurs is when node #7 contains an additional link back to node #3. The dynamic nature of the Web does not preclude this. If the robot isn't smart, it will revisit node #3, placing an unnecessary burden upon that server.

Fortunately, guidelines have been developed for robot authors, and most robots are compliant. An excellent online resource for information about robots, including further information on which much of this chapter is based, see "World Wide Web Robots, Wanderers, and Spiders" by Martijn Koster, http://info.webcrawler.com/mak/projects/robots/robots.html. It contains links to documents describing robot guidelines, the standard for robot exclusion, and an in-depth collection of information about known robots.

There are many active robots on the Web today. For a list of known robots at the time of printing, see Appendix E.

Tip: The Internet community puts up with robots because robots give something back to all of us. Private robots are seriously frowned upon because they take resources and offer value only to a single user in return. If you are looking for your own Internet robot, however, you can check out the Verity Inc. home page at http://www.verity.com/. Please remember that one of the guidelines of robot design is to first analyze carefully if a new robot is really called for.

A good understanding of Web robots and how to use or exclude them will aid you in your Web ventures; in fact, it could help to keep your server alive.

Excluding Robots

There are lots of reasons to want to exclude robots from visiting your site. One reason is that rapid-fire requests from buggy robots could drag your server down. Or your site might contain data that you do not want to be indexed by outside sources. Whatever the reason, there is an obvious need for a method for robot exclusion. Be aware that it wouldn't be helpful to the Internet if all robots are excluded.

Often on the Internet Web-related news groups and listservers, you will see a new Web site administrator ask the question "What is robots.txt and why are people looking for it?" This question often comes up after the administrator looks at his or her Web access logs and sees the following line:

```
Tue Jun 06 17:36:36 1995 204.252.2.5 192.100.81.115 GET /robots.txt HTTP/1.0
```

Knowing that they don't have a file robots.txt in the root directory, most administrators are puzzled.

The answer is that robots.txt is part of the Standard for Robot Exclusion. The standard was agreed to in June 1994 on the robots mailing list (`robots-request@webcrawler.com`) by the majority of robot authors and other people with an interest in robots. The information on these pages is based on the working draft of the exclusion standard, which can be found at

`http://info.webcrawler.com/mak/projects/robots/norobots.html`

Some of the things to take into account concerning the Standard for Robot Exclusion are

- It is not an official standard backed by a standards body.
- It is not enforced by anybody, and there are no guarantees that all current and future robots will adhere to it.
- Consider it a loose standard that the majority of robot authors will follow.

In addition to using the exclusion described below, there are a few other simple steps you can follow if you discover an unwanted robot visiting your site:

1. Check your Web server log files to detect the frequency of document retrievals.
2. Try to determine where the robot originates. This will enable you to contact the author. You can find the author by looking at the User-agent and From field in the request, or look up the host domain in the list of robots. Also, the originations of several robots are given in Appendix E, "Discussions of 36 Internet Robots."
3. If the robot is annoying in some fashion, let the robot author know about it. Ask the author to visit `http://info.webcrawler.com/mak/projects/robots/robots.html` so he or she can read the guidelines for robot authors and the standard for exclusion.

The Method

The method used to exclude robots from a server is to create a file on the server that specifies an access policy for robots, this file is named /robots.txt.

The file must be accessible via HTTP on the local URL, with the contents as specified here. The format and semantics of the file are as follows:

- The file consists of one or more records separated by one or more blank lines (terminated by CR, CR/NL, or NL). Each record contains lines of the form:

  `<field name>:<optional space><value><optional space>.`

- The field name is case-insensitive. Comments can be included in a file using UNIX Bourne shell conventions. The # character is used to indicate that preceding space (if any) and the remainder of the line up to the line termination are discarded. Lines containing only a comment are discarded completely and therefore do not indicate a record boundary. The record starts with one or more User-agent lines, followed by one or more Disallow lines. Unrecognized headers are ignored.

- User-agent

  The value of this field is the name of the robot for which the record is describing an access policy. If more than one User-agent field is present, the record describes an identical access policy for more than one robot. At least one field needs to be present per record. The robot should be liberal in interpreting this field. A case-insensitive substring match of the name without version information is recommended. If the value in the record describes the default access policy for any robot that has not matched any of the other records, it is not allowed to have two such records in the /robots.txt file.

- Disallow

  The value of this field specifies a partial URL that is not to be visited. This can be a full path or a partial path; any URL that starts with this value will not be retrieved. For example:

  `Disallow: /help`

  disallows both /help.htm and /help/default.htm, whereas

  `Disallow: /help/`

  disallows /help/default.htm but allows /help.htm.

Any empty value indicates that all URLs can be retrieved. At least one Disallow field needs to be present in a record. The presence of an empty /robots.txt file has no explicit associated semantics; it will be treated as if it were not present—for example, all robots will consider themselves welcome to pillage.

Examples

Here is a sample /robots.txt for `http://www.yourco.com/` that specifies no robots should visit any URL starting with /yourco/cgi-bin/ or /tmp/:

```
User-agent: *
Disallow: /yourco/cgi-bin/
Disallow: /tmp/
```

Here is an example that indicates no robots should visit the current site:

```
User-agent: *
Disallow: /
```

Firewalls and Proxy Servers

Let's face it, the very thing that made the Internet grow so large and fast is what makes it such a dangerous place. There are entire books written about Internet security, and rightly so: Internet security is a complex topic. Clearly, this section won't tell you everything you need to know about Internet security, but it will help you to understand many of the security implications of your decisions. Our motto is that it's always good to know what it is that you don't know.

> **Caution:** The threat to your site is real. We don't want to alarm you, but as the Internet grows, so does the threat. If you are running a business Web site, your risks range from annoying pranks to sabotage to industrial espionage. Regardless of whether your server is on a LAN, if you have any files at all worth protecting (financial information or even just the operating system itself), you should definitely consider building an Internet firewall.

Recently, there was an interesting thread (a sequence of several messages on the same topic) in a listserver about Web site security. The story went like this: An Internet Service Provider (ISP) was updating its Web page that contained service prices. When the ISP employee opened the document for editing, he/she noticed that all the service prices had been bumped up to outrageous levels. This is just one example of how your site can be compromised.

If you intend to maintain an Internet connection and you truly want a secure site, you will have to consider getting firewall protection. The first thing to do if you want to add a firewall to your site is to change from an RAS-based connection to an Ethernet/router-based connection.

A *firewall* can be software, hardware, or a combination of the two. Commercial firewall packages cost a lot more than loose change— a price range of anywhere from $1,000 to $100,000.

We haven't heard of a software-only firewall for Windows NT, but when it becomes available it would likely be less expensive than the hardware versions. In the meantime, you might consider running a freeware version of UNIX for the purpose of including a firewall in your network.

A firewall usually includes several software tools. For example, it might include separate proxy servers for e-mail, FTP, Gopher, Telnet, Web, and WAIS. The firewall can also filter certain outbound ICMP (Internet Control Message Protocol) packets so your server won't be capable of divulging network information.

Figure 16.2 shows a network diagram of a typical LAN connection to the Internet including a Web server and a firewall. Note that the Web server, LAN server, and firewall server could all be rolled into one machine if the budget is tight, but separating them as we show here is considered a safer environment.

Figure 16.2.
Using a firewall/proxy server on a LAN.

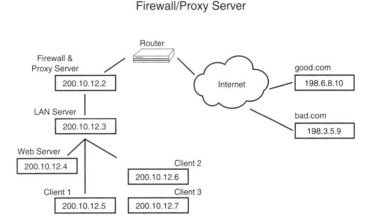

The proxy server is used to mask all of your LAN IP addresses on outbound packets so they look like they all originated at the proxy server itself. Each of the client machines on your LAN must use the proxy server whenever they connect to the Internet for FTP, Telnet, Gopher, or the Web. The reason for doing this is to prevent outside detection of the structure of your network. Otherwise, hackers monitoring your outbound traffic would eventually be able to determine your individual IP addresses and then use *IP spoofing* to feed those back to your server when they want to appear as a known client.

Another purpose of a firewall is to perform *IP filtering* of incoming packets. Let's say that you have been monitoring the log files on your Web server and you keep noticing some unusual or unwanted activity originating from 198.3.5.9. After checking the whois program (such as the GUI version included with this book), you determine the domain name is bad.com, and you don't have any business with them. You can configure the IP filter to block any connection attempts originating from bad.com while still allowing packets from the friendly good.com to proceed.

Caution: Many people think IP packet filtering is worthless if only implemented in software. They may advise that packet filtering is useful only in a router or a hardware firewall solution that includes the capability to filter at the Link layer, as opposed to the

Network or Transport layers where the TCP/IP software operates. However, even if you do packet filtering via software, the trick is to filter based on both the source IP *and* the interface. That is, if a packet with a source address that is also an internal IP shows up on the external interface of your router (such as from the Internet side), you should drop the packet and have it logged for immediate attention.

Other Firewall Configurations

Now let's return to the previous point about the need to switch your Internet connection method to an Ethernet and router combination—as opposed to an RAS modem connection. Following are a few possible firewall configurations.

Internet, CSU/DSU, Router, and NT Server

Figure 16.3 depicts one of the most simple firewall configurations. The router that resides between your server and the Internet is the key element. Of course, adding a router means also adding a CSU/DSU and takes you out of the realm of a simple modem connection.

Figure 16.3.
Server and router.

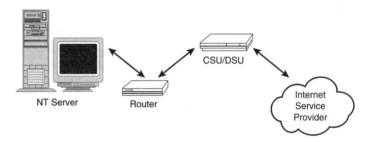

This economical network depicts a router that offers IP packet filtering. This is hardware-only firewall protection.

Internet, CSU/DSU, Router, NT Server, and Software Firewall

This scenario is only slightly more involved. Figure 16.4 shows a software firewall (perhaps just a proxy Web server) being added to the Web site.

In this case, if the router offered no IP packet filtering you would have software-only firewall protection. At the time of this writing, we had found no software-only solutions that ran natively under NT.

Figure 16.4.
The server with a built-in firewall.

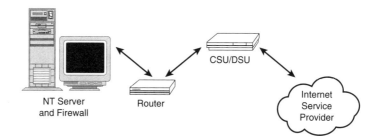

Internet, CSU/DSU, Router, Firewall Server, and NT Server

The configuration shown in Figure 16.5 is rather advanced. The addition of a separate firewall server to your network is one of the best ways to guard your resources from intruders.

Figure 16.5.
Using a firewall server to protect the rest of the LAN.

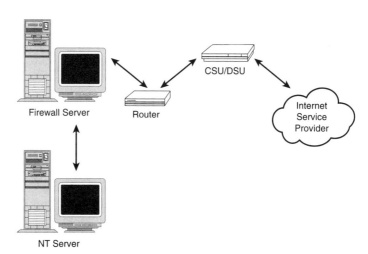

In this case, we added a separate computer running firewall/IP filtering software. This is the hardware/software solution described earlier.

> **Note:** Because of the current lack of NT-based, software-only firewall solutions, the firewall server is most likely a UNIX box. With the enormous surge of popularity that NT is undergoing, however, we can expect this situation to change very soon.

These diagrams do not show the connections beyond the server. If your situation involves a network, the server would be a multihomed host with two NICs acting as a bridge or Internet gateway.

As you can see, there are many benefits to firewalls. The choice of whether or not to implement a firewall is a complex decision that will involve factors such as

- Risk analysis
- Cost-benefit analysis
- Network security policies
- Network topology

If you decide you need to implement a firewall but don't have the cash to fork out for a 30K or 40K hardware solution, you might want to take a look at using the FWTK (Firewall Toolkit). FWTK is a freeware collection of firewall-related utilities from TIS (Trusted Information Systems, Inc.). This toolkit is distributed in source code format. It is written for UNIX, so you will need run it on a UNIX box or spend the time or money to convert the code to Windows. There are several freeware versions of UNIX that run on the PC, so this solution can be a very inexpensive one. The drawback to this method is that it requires a great deal of time, effort, and UNIX knowledge to implement. To obtain the FWTK, and read lots of other information on commercial firewalls, see `http://www.tis.com`.

Software Viruses

As if you don't already have enough trouble, alas, the risk of a virus deleting or scrambling your files is very serious.

One way to curtail the risk is to avoid downloading programs from the Internet. You must realize that you can be bitten the instant you run any kind of executable image. This includes programs, DLLs, command files, or even autostart macros in commercial applications.

Of course, life on the Net isn't too practical without access to all the cool stuff that keeps being invented everyday. So the next level of protection is to test new software on a stand-alone cheap machine before giving it access to your precious hard drive.

Virus detection programs (or virus scanners) should be used to verify that a new program appears legitimate. Virus scanners analyze your software looking for several types of red flags that would indicate danger. They are able to detect and warn you of hundreds of known viruses. The problem is that new viruses are being written by scum programmers every day.

> **Caution:** Some viruses can infect a LAN after they land on a single machine on the network. If you can't be certain about the type of software someone else might install on your LAN, you should seriously consider running a network virus scanner on an ongoing basis. This option is safer and more practical than having network police running around checking on all the employees.

At the time of this writing, we know only of three virus scanners for Windows NT. We have used NT Anti-Virus from Carmel Software Engineering and found it to be a satisfactory product. For a thorough review of this and other virus detection software, see the article titled "It's a Dangerous World Out There," by Tim Daniels, in *Windows NT Magazine*, October, 1995, pages 55-58.

Miscellaneous Security Advice

When people think about security on the Internet, they automatically think about firewalls—but there is a lot more to security than just firewalls. You will keep away most general pranksters by setting up your site with security in mind. Here are some miscellaneous pointers for running a secure Web site:

- If you allow FTP access, set restrictive FTP directory and file permissions.

- Don't let server applications run as system services. Because server applications are basically listening to a port, a hacker could pass data to the well-known port. If the application is running as a system service, the application has system privileges and could in theory be forced to run a program that you do not want it to run. It is always best to create an account for the server application to run under so that it has only the privileges necessary to do its job. Server applications running as system services on UNIX have been the source of many documented break-ins. (Granted, having public access to the UNIX source code made it easier.)

- Don't put any files in the directory of an application server that you can't afford to lose.

- Either make sure that Permit Directory Browsing is checked in the HTTPS configuration dialog or make sure that you place a file named default.htm in your server root directory. (EMWAC calls it the Data directory.) Otherwise, users who only key in your Fully Qualified Domain Name will end up with an FTP directory listing of your document root directory—and there might be files other than your home page that you don't want them to see.

- Develop a security policy for users whom you allow to log into your server. What programs are they allowed to run? How often must they change their password? Are users permitted to dial out to the Internet from a private modem?

- Monitor your system logs carefully and often. It might be your only chance to catch strange behavior as it begins to develop. If you're lucky, you'll be able to exclude a hacker before further damage is done.

Windows NT Domains

Unfortunately, we just don't have the space to get into this topic very heavily. Both the Microsoft documentation that comes with Windows NT and the NT Resource Kit (sold separately) provide several excellent chapters on this subject.

If your Web site is part of a corporate LAN, this is the granddaddy of all security issues. Make sure you understand the reasons for having *trusted* and *trusting* domains. Our experience has shown that network management in a small company is greatly simplified when all the user accounts are maintained on one machine. Through the use of global groups, those user accounts can be imported to other domains.

What's Next?

The topics of Web site security and secure commerce on the Web are frequently grouped together. In our view, they are somewhat distinct. We have intentionally left the topic of Internet credit-card transactions out of this chapter on security because we wanted to address it as part of our chapter on Web commerce. And that is only part of what the next chapter covers.

Chapter 17

Commerce on the Web

- What Businesses are Doing on the Internet
- Shopping Malls on the Web
- Internet Cryptography Standards: DES, RSA, PEM, and PGP
- Secure Transactions on the Web: SSL, S-HTTP, STT, and PCT
- Secure Digital Cash
- Internet Business Resources
- Internet Demographics
- What's Next?

This chapter is a collection of topics that every business person on the Internet should understand something about.

Like most things of a technical nature, from astronomy to zoology, learning about the Internet is mostly a matter of coming to grips with its basic terminology. This is also true when it comes to the subject of Internet commerce and cryptography. This chapter serves as a primer of the key terms and definitions in this area. As you can see from the outline above, there are enough three-letter acronyms to make your head spin. But soon you will know enough about the buzzwords to help you develop an effective business plan for the Internet (or at least get you through the day).

Finally, we'll wrap up with some terrific hotspots that you'll want to visit at least once. The following business resources were designed and selected to help you succeed in business from almost every conceivable angle. Knowing what's there could pay off for you; and all the information is right at your fingertips.

But first, let's take a look at some of the Internet features that other businesses are already taking advantage of.

What Businesses are Doing on the Internet

The number one thing that most business people do on the Internet is send and receive electronic mail—instant message delivery anywhere in the world. And having the ability on the receiving end to edit attached data in the same application that created it is what puts e-mail way ahead of the fax machine.

Research on the Web is the second most likely way a business person can utilize the Internet. The word *research* takes on a new meaning on the Web because it is so easy to do. Once you see the resources available, you might not believe your eyes. And no matter what industry you're in, there are golden nuggets waiting to be mined.

Third, read the newsgroups or subscribe to a listserver relevant to your line of business. You might find people who are asking the kinds of questions that your products or services are designed to answer. Be careful about the way you respond to the whole group; they generally don't like companies who plug their own products. You may want to consider sending e-mail directly to the person who posed the question. Also, don't underestimate the newsgroups as an extremely dynamic resource for problem solving and research.

Fourth, consider starting your own listserver for your products. This might work if you let the list take on the atmosphere of a user group, and you have enough customers who are interested in keeping each other informed of issues and workarounds in your products. Your organization can simply supply the server for their free use (and you might post an occasional newsletter or press release).

Fifth, and this is the big enchilada, establish your own presence on the Web. The book you hold in your hands has everything you need. Whether you choose to publish marketing literature about your products, take sales orders by electronic forms (*eforms*), advertise employment openings within your organization, or provide online customer support, the Web will help you advance your business.

Already, some businesses have reported that 80 percent of their sales are from the Web—although 1–10 percent is more typical. All you have to do is surf the Net to see what other businesses are doing. After awhile, you're bound to formulate some new ideas for your own Web site. If you're in the retail business, for example, you might want to start at the mall.

Shopping Malls on the Web

The terms virtual malls, cyber malls, Internet malls, virtual storefronts, and online malls all describe Web sites that give you dozens of links to the home pages of other stores. It's based on the department model found in ordinary malls—for example, appliances, sporting goods, and women's clothing.

Actually, the word *virtual* seems to be somewhat of a misnomer in describing these stores. After all, they sell real merchandise and they really will take your credit card numbers.

Here are a few of the more established ones. Pardon our lack of enthusiasm (or ignorance), but they are all similar to each other. They do have some interesting nooks and crannies, if you have the time to explore.

- The Internet Mall. `http://www.internet-mall.com/`
- Empire Mall. `http://empire.na.com/`
- The Net Mall. `http://www.ais.net/netmall/`
- iMall. `http://www.imall.com/homepage.html`

Internet Cryptography Standards: DES, RSA, PEM, and PGP

Wow, what a way to change the subject—from shopping malls to cryptography! Actually, the two are quite related.

Cryptography is an important aspect of security. Chapter 16 took the perspective of overall security at an Internet site, and this section relates more to the security of business data. The purpose of cryptosystems is to render useless the digital data containing credit card numbers and other valuable information in case hackers intercept it between a customer's modem and a business Web server. Some of the world's greatest practical mathematicians have devised these software schemes to guard our private packets on the net, and still provide us a means to have the data deciphered when it lands in the right hands. What follows is a brief overview of several prevalent standards.

DES

DES stands for the Data Encryption Standard. It was invented by IBM in the 1970s and is widely considered to be very secure. A hacker would probably have to spend a million dollars and weeks, years, or decades of computer time to break the code.

DES is considered a *symmetric* cypher because both the sender and the recipient must have the same secret key. The advantage of symmetric cryptosystems is that they are very fast and therefore are useful for large blocks of data.

According to RSA Laboratories, DES is 100 times faster than RSA when both are implemented in software, and up to 10,000 times faster when implemented in hardware.

RSA

RSA gets its name from the fact it that it was invented by Ron Rivest, Adi Shamir, and Leonard Adleman. It is a public key (or *asymmetric*) encryption system.

RSA has also been under the microscope for many years and survived as a very reliable scheme. It is also ideal for use in *digital signatures* so that the recipient of a message can be certain who sent it. RSA is most useful for small blocks of data, such as the encryption of the secret key to be used in a DES system.

For more information about RSA and a great collection of Frequently Asked Questions about cryptography, including information about digital signatures, see `http://www.rsa.com/rsalabs/`.

PEM

PEM stands for Privacy Enhanced Mail. Both PEM and PGP use RSA. These programs exist as shareware on the Internet so that you can add them to your mail client or your Web server. PEM hasn't enjoyed wide support, and it may eventually become obsolete.

PGP

Pretty Good Privacy (PGP) was invented by Phil Zimmermann. He generously put it on the Internet as a poor-man's alternative to high-priced encryption. His troubles started when someone outside the country downloaded it and the U.S. government decided that Phil had violated weapons export laws because the software used a key-length greater than the allowable limit of 40 bits. PGP is still available for use in the United States. To our knowledge, the international legal issues have not yet been resolved.

Secure Transactions on the Web: SSL, S-HTTP, STT, and PCT

If your Web site is going to take credit card orders, you will certainly want to upgrade from the EMWAC server included with this book. The Purveyor Web server by Process Software, which is the commercial version of EMWAC, is a *secure* Web server. There are many other vendors of secure servers, such as Netscape, Open Market, IBM, Internet Factory, SAIC (in beta), and Microsoft (in beta).

Today, a secure Web server features either or both S-HTTP and SSL. However, there is fierce competition among software companies to set the standard for Web servers and browsers.

Tip: The Open Market, Inc. home page includes a *security checker* to determine whether your browser or your server supports secure transactions using S-HTTP or SSL. See `http:/ /www.openmarket.com.`

SSL

SSL stands for Secure Sockets Layer. It was invented by Netscape as a way to encrypt the data that travels at the link layer (or transport layer) between the Web server and the browser. Because Netscape Navigator has been so popular, this has become a *de facto* standard.

For awhile, it looked like the Web community couldn't decide between using SSL or another standard called S-HTTP. Perhaps because they each operate in a different technical manner and each has its pros and cons, the Web community seems to be moving toward adopting both of them. In a nutshell, the essential difference is that SSL makes the wire secure, whereas S-HTTP makes the documents secure.

S-HTTP

When the HyperText Transfer Protocol and the Web were first conceived, security didn't seem to be much of an issue. Who could have foreseen the enormous potential of the Web for financial data?

S-HTTP stands for Secure-HTTP. S-HTTP builds upon the omnipresence of HTTP (see Appendix F) by adding new security features. It is a non-proprietary standard.

For more information about S-HTTP, try this URL: `http://www.commerce.net/information/stan-dards/.`

STT

Just when the Web community seemed to have chosen both SSL and S-HTTP, Microsoft and Visa decided to speak up with the announcement of Secure Transaction Technology (STT).

Although Netscape has always enjoyed the luxury of being out front on the Internet, Microsoft is a software giant probably capable of convincing everyone to adopt its standards instead. Although Microsoft and Visa claim that STT addresses several flaws in the design of SSL, most end users choose their software based on overall quality. Marketing muscle plays a heavy role too. The point is that it is too early to tell which standard, if any, will dominate. We must wait for the market reaction to Netscape Navigator 2.0 and Internet Explorer 2.0.

Internet Explorer 2.0 and a new Windows NT Web server are expected to be available from Microsoft by early 1996, both with support for STT.

Don't count Netscape out; they have Mastercard on their side.

PCT

Yet another acronym that fell out of the Microsoft/Visa partnership, PCT stands for Private Communication Technology. The Microsoft press release claims that it is a separate technology based on some of the algorithms in STT. However, PCT is designed more for the purpose of transmitting secure data of all types, as opposed to purely financial data.

Secure Digital Cash

Most Web server manufacturers offer a secure commerce version of their Web server. The secure Web servers are often an expensive solution to secure commerce. If your individual business transactions on the Web are not large ticket items, it can be expensive to buy a commercial Web server and establish an account with a major credit card company.

There are many other third-party solutions for secure money transactions on the Internet. Most of these work by having the customer make a digital deposit with the bank, before they visit your Web site to spend their *ecash*. Here is a list of just a few:

- Cybercash. `http://www.cybercash.com/`
- Digicash will give you $100 of their money for free. `http://www.digicash.com/`
- ViaCheck. `http://theyellowpages.com/viacheck/index.htm`
- First Virtual Holdings. `http://www.fv.com/`
- Netchex has an online application for merchants, and free software for end users. `http://www.netchex.com`

> **Caution:** With all the recent talk of Internet hackers breaking in and stealing credit card numbers, secure cash is a hot topic. We can't over emphasize how a good security policy and well-configured server alone will keep you out of trouble in this regard.
>
> One example: Don't allow a CGI application that takes credit card information to write that data to a file that is in any directory available to an Internet server application. Remember, the user account under which the server is running should have limited access to the machine.

Internet Business Resources

We have to mention the famous Yahoo again. Try it and you might want to make it your default home page: `http://www.yahoo.com`.

At the Internet Banking Web site, you will find a white paper that provides a very lucid overview of commerce on the Net. See `http://www.sfnb.com/wpaper.html`.

The Galaxy Catalog at `http://www.einet.net` contains very handy links to other resources grouped by category. Among the categories are business, engineering, government, law, and medicine.

The Internet Group has built an online business center that is definitely worth checking out. Their site at `http://www.tig.com` contains all of the following:

- Advice about conducting business on the Web
- Lists of companies by industry that are already on the Net
- Discussion areas about marketing, security, and so on
- News about the Internet
- Internet statistics and demographics
- Links to other business resources

For stock market quotes and analysis, as well as other business data, see `http://www.quote.com`.

The Accel Partners is a venture capital firm that has prepared informative white papers covering several areas of business financing. Every small business owner should take a look at `http://www.accel.com/entreprn.htm`.

Charm Net, Inc., has established a Web site that collects dozens of great links to other business resources all under one roof. Most of the links are to well-known resources, but unless you see them all on this page you might not have thought of visiting them. The home page is `http://www.charm.net`, but if you want to look at the business section specifically, try `http://www.charm.net/biz.html`.

Here is a brief collection of other business resources:

- The Small Business Administration: `http://www.sbaonline.sba.gov`
- Federal Government Information on the Internet: `http://www.wcs-online.com/usgovdoc`
- Stat-USA: `http://www.stat-usa.gov/`
- The World Wide Web Yellow Pages (includes a search page): `http://www.yellow.com`
- Yellowpages.com, another reference to online businesses: `http://theyellowpages.com/default.htm`
- Monster Board Classified Ads: `http://www.monster.com/`

Internet Demographics

The Georgia Tech study of the Internet has really got its act together. They conduct surveys every six months. The last study garnered more than 13,000 respondents. The best part is that they provide more than 200 graphs of the results, and it's all free! Figure 17.1 is just one example of their colorful bar graphs. It shows that there are more workers in the USA who spend less than 5 hours per week on their computer than any other amount spanning 5 to 20 hours. Hmm. Visit their Web site at `http://www.cc.gatech.edu/gvu/user_surveys/`.

Figure 17.1.
Demographic data from the
Georgia Tech survey.

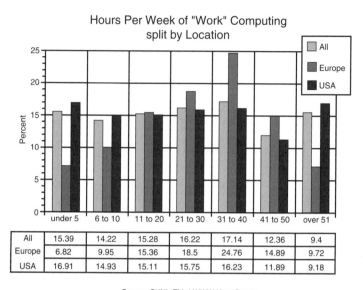

	under 5	6 to 10	11 to 20	21 to 30	31 to 40	41 to 50	over 51
All	15.39	14.22	15.28	16.22	17.14	12.36	9.4
Europe	6.82	9.95	15.36	18.5	24.76	14.89	9.72
USA	16.91	14.93	15.11	15.75	16.23	11.89	9.18

Source: GVU's Third WWW User Survey
<URL:http://www.cc.gatech.edu/gvu/user_surveys>
Contact: www-survey@cc.gatech.edu
Copyright: Permission is granted to use this material only with this notice intact

The iVALS project includes an online HTML survey so you can determine your own electronic personality demographically. You can also check out their database of the profiles of other Internet users. See `http://future.sri.com/`.

Yet another source of free Internet statistics and demographics is `http://www.survey.net/`.

> **Note:** The statistic services above are free, provided you agree to credit the source as they request.

This list is just the tip of the iceberg. Many of the business resources mentioned above also include information about Internet statistics.

What's Next?

We have tried to compile this chapter to serve as the businessperson's quick compendium to the World Wide Web. We hope that you will be able to refer back to it and explore many of the Web pages that are mentioned. It is almost guaranteed that you will find valuable resources tucked away in many of the Web sites mentioned in this chapter.

Chapter 18

The Future of the Web

- The Future of Windows NT
- The Future of HTML
- New Techniques in Web Servers
- Java and HotJava
- VRML
- The Corporate Intranet
- New Directions from Netscape and Microsoft
- Network Technology Advances
- Closing Remarks

Now that you know everything you need about putting your Web server on the Internet, the question that arises is what can you look forward to in the future?

As the saying goes, "The only thing that doesn't change is change itself." Nothing we can say about the Internet, and the Web in particular, could be more true than that. In fact, during the time that we have been working on this book, we have witnessed a barrage of news events and announcements that are certain to have massive impact on the future of the Web. Here are just a few of the things that have come about (officially or unofficially) during the fall of 1995: new Web servers, new Web browsers, new Web programming languages, new Web applications, new ISDN/modem products, headline-grabbing security setbacks, security advancements, a litany of ongoing improvements in network transmission technologies (from modems to ATM), and of course, hundreds of new Web pages from mega-corporations all the way down to the man on the street.

The only way to keep up is to read books (like this one and others mentioned in the Bibliography) and check out the online resources in Appendix C for the most timely information.

The Future of Windows NT

It doesn't take a crystal ball to see that Windows NT has a great future. Microsoft is not releasing its sales figures, but some independent sources say that during the first two years of release, Windows NT gained 8 percent of the network operating system market. We've seen speculative reports that estimate Windows NT will have 81 percent of the network operating system market by the year 1999. This might seem like a high figure, but there is no doubt that NT's market share will grow at an exponential rate.

With Microsoft putting such a great deal of effort in expanding its network communications, it is safe to say that soon the NT operating system will have an even broader implementation of rock-solid TCP/IP applications. Microsoft is currently in beta for a DNS server, a multi-protocol router, a firewall product, the Exchange server with full SMTP/POP3 support, and a secure Web server. There are also rumors that they are developing a new version of Visual Basic to suit CGI programming and take on the Java language from Sun Microsystems, but nothing has been announced yet.

One of the things always crucial to the success of an operating system is the amount of new software applications that are developed for it. With the advent of Windows 95, which is also a 32-bit Windows operating system, software producers now have an even wider market (tens of millions of potential new customers) for which to develop Win32 applications. In most cases, the software can be written to run identically on both operating systems. In fact, one of the requirements to obtain the coveted "Windows 95 compatible" logo for software packaging is that the application must run on Windows NT as well. Our prediction is that the number of applications available for Windows NT should increase dramatically during the first year of the release of Windows 95.

In addition, Windows NT isn't going to sit still. The next major version is due out during the first half of 1996. Among many enhancements, the new version is expected to include the new Windows 95 GUI, support for TAPI (Telephony API), and possibly a version of network OLE (available now in Visual Basic 4.0). The new version of NT, combined with a new Web server, and probably a new release of SQL Server also, will help Microsoft distinguish its Back Office suite as a dominant force in the industry. Microsoft is discussing plans to include clustering support (many servers mirrored together for fail-safe operation) in a future version of Windows NT. This would be further enticement for Fortune 1000 companies to run their mission-critical applications on NT.

The Future of HTML

It seems that there is a new development in HTML every day. A good place to monitor the direction of the Web is the World Wide Web Consortium. The W3 Consortium, as it's called, exists to develop common standards for the evolution of the World Wide Web. It is an industry consortium run by the Laboratory for Computer Science at the Massachusetts Institute of Technology. In Europe, MIT collaborates with CERN, the originators of the Web, and INRIA, the European W3C center.

W3C provides a repository of information about the World Wide Web for developers and users. Specifications about the Web, reference code implementations, and various sample applications can all be found on the W3 Web site.

> **Note:** For more information on W3, see its home page at `http://www.w3.org/hypertext/WWW/Consortium/`.

HTML 2.0 is widely implemented and should be standard by the time you read this. HTML 3.0 is still in the very early stages of being implemented and debated. In particular, no decision has been made yet as to which system for style sheets will find its way into the final specification.

New Techniques in Web Servers

There are several recent enhancements found in some servers that might or might not become standard. It all depends on whether the Web community (and/or Netscape) decides that these are useful techniques. Some of these are only supported by certain Web servers. Your best source for further information is the documentation that comes with your server.

Server-Side Includes

One recent development is server-side includes. This is a way of generating dynamic HTML without using CGI. Basically, the way it works is that you designate a particular file type, say .shtml, to represent files that the server will parse before sending the document to the client. When the server parses the file, it looks for comments within the HTML code, which include the text #include. Upon finding such a string, the server replaces that line of the document with the entire text from the file that is referenced.

Server-Push and Client-Pull

Server-Push and Client-Pull can both be used to accomplish similar things. Both are supported by Netscape. They are frequently mentioned in the context of doing graphic animation, such as a dynamic corporate logo, on the Web.

One difference between the two is that Server-Push is implemented through CGI on the server, whereas Client-Pull can be accomplished simply through HTML with a compatible browser.

Client-Pull uses a feature in HTML 3.0 to specify that a document should be retrieved by the browser automatically after a certain time interval, whether the user clicks a link or not. Server-Push relies on a CGI application that maintains a timer and knows when to transmit the next document to the client.

Java and HotJava

HotJava is a new Web browser, currently in alpha release, that brings multimedia to the World Wide Web. Imagine opening your Web browser to http://java.sun.com, and as the page is loading, you see the animated character Duke, the HotJava mascot on your screen waving at you.

Java is a programming language that many are already predicting will become the standard for interactive Web application programming. Sun designed Java as a derivative of C++ with modifications to simplify Web application development. The company also wanted it to include security so that a user can be confident a Web application doesn't include a virus.

Netscape has licensed Sun's Java programming language, and it is currently implemented in version 2.0 of Netscape Navigator.

> **Note:** For more information on the status of HotJava, see any of these URLs:
>
> The Sun HotJava home page: http://java.sun.com/.
>
> Dr. Dobbs Journal includes many articles on the subject of Java: http://www.dobbs.com/dddu/java.html.
>
> The Class Hierarchy of the Java Language: http://rendezvous.com/java/hierarchy/index.html.

VRML

VRML stands for Virtual Reality Modeling Language. Still in its early development stages, it is a draft specification for adding three-dimensional data to the Web. WebSpace is a freely distributed, VRML-enabled Web browser from Silicon Graphics Computer Systems.

> **Note:** To find out more about VRML and Silicon Graphics Software, go to http://www.sgi.com/Products/WebFORCE/WebSpace/.
>
> For the VRML Frequently Asked Questions document, see http://www.oki.com/vrml/VRML_FAQ.html.

The Corporate Intranet

When many people think of the World Wide Web, they think of a global network of hypertext document servers providing text and graphics pages to everyone on the Internet. What some people forget is that companies with Local Area Networks (LANs) and Wide Area Networks (WANs) need to distribute documents and information, too, even if they are not connected to the Internet.

The phrase *Intranet* has been coined to describe these companys' LANs and WANs. A Web server is a perfect information server for the Intranet. For example, what better way for a company to distribute Human Resources information such as policy manuals and company newsletters? The applications for a Web server in an Intranet environment are limitless. We have seen a college Web server that provides a Web-based form for the campus sandwich shop. Students just fill out the order form, and once the data is posted, a CGI application transfers the order to a fax server that faxes it to the shop. The sandwich is ready by the time the student gets there.

Process Software, the makers of the Purveyor Web server, tout a case study in which Tyson Foods uses the Purveyor Web server on their own Intranet, consisting of 100 remote sites worldwide.

New Directions from Netscape and Microsoft

Just when Netscape might have thought it was going to run away with the business of setting all trends on the Internet, Microsoft kicked into some kind of newly discovered Web-strategy mode. Microsoft and Netscape have emerged as the rivalry to watch in 1996. It looks as if they will be competing in all of these major areas:

- Web browsers: Microsoft Internet Explorer 2.0 versus Netscape Navigator 2.0.

- Web servers: Microsoft Gibraltar (the current code name) versus the Netscape Secure Server. One difference between the servers is that Microsoft will likely be supporting ISAPI (Internet Server Application Programming Interface) instead of CGI. ISAPI is a new standard for Web server programming, jointly developed by Microsoft and Process Software. This might require a lot of reprogramming of existing CGI applications, but the server documentation from Process Software claims that great performance gains in ISAPI will make it a worthwhile effort.

- Interactive Web programming languages: Microsoft Visual Basic versus SunSoft Java. (Sun and Netscape have an alliance concerning Java.) Microsoft has announced support for VRML in Internet Explorer 2.0 as if it hopes to ignore Java.

- Secure transactions on the Web: the Microsoft and Visa Secure Transaction Technology (STT) versus the approach of Netscape and Mastercard using the Secure Sockets Layer (SSL).

In addition, Microsoft is distributing a new software development kit named Blackbird, which is geared to get businesses and application developers to come to MSN, The Microsoft Network.

At this point, Netscape has the clear advantage in the browser battle because of the wide popularity and cross-platform support of Navigator. As if defining HTML 3.0 weren't enough, Navigator 2.0 also sets a new standard for Web browsers by including integrated e-mail, a newsreader, and FTP support. Estimates are that between 60 and 90 percent of the Web browsers in use today are built by Netscape. And it looks like Navigator 2.0 packs enough new features that it will be very hard for Netscape's competitors to bite into that market share.

Network Technology Advances

Everyday, more people use the Internet to do more things than ever before. This leads to a need for ever increasing data throughput rates—if we hope not to find ourselves going slower and slower. Fortunately, it seems that network engineers never run out of tricks to speed up the wires and the algorithms and the routers through which our data travels (not to mention there is an enormous profit motive to deliver speed improvements to the large body of customers the Internet represents).

One area of intense interest these days is ATM. It seems that every week the trade journals contain news about advances in this technology or the formation of key partnerships in this industry. Alas, as we mentioned in Chapter 1, this is a subject on which entire books are written, and many more will follow, but it is beyond our scope.

33.6 Kbps Modems

What about performance gains for the little guy? ATM, and even ISDN (although this too is changing fast), are still out of reach financially for most home users. As it turns out, two companies, AT&T and U.S. Robotics, are currently selling modems that boast a DTE rate of 33.6 Kbps. U.S. Robotics is arguably the market leader when it comes to modems. Ask about their Courier V.Everything modem if you're shopping for a speed demon. But keep in mind that the prices for low-end ISDN cards are beginning to overlap with the prices for high-end modems.

Advances in ISDN Products

Not too long ago if you wanted an ISDN connection to the Internet, you were talking about a fairly high-end piece of equipment and not very many manufacturers. With bandwidth needs increasing, ISDN has become a favored choice. This has created a boom in ISDN products.

Today you can find many ISDN boards compatible with your ISA or EISA bus. One of the newer trends for home use is a dual-purpose ISDN box that not only supports ISDN connections but also includes a 28.8 Kbps analog modem. One such product is the Pipeline 25 from Ascend Communications. Actually, it doesn't include the modem, but it gives the user two analog phone ports so that a standard phone and fax/modem can be connected using one B channel, in addition to

ISDN running on the other B channel—and the amazing thing is that you can do all of this simultaneously! Ascend Communications makes an entire line of ISDN products.

Closing Remarks

Hopefully, this book has helped you, and you have had as much fun building your Web site and learning about the World Wide Web as we have had setting up ours and writing this book. You have chosen an extremely exciting time to be involved with the Internet and with Windows NT.

Part V

Appendixes

Appendix A

Internet Service Providers

Inside the USA

Nuance Network Services	Huntsville	AL	205-533-4296	PPP, SLIP
Internet Direct, Inc.	Phoenix	AZ	602-274-0100	PPP, SLIP
Evergreen Communications	Phoenix	AZ	602-955-8315	PPP, SLIP
Primenet	Phoenix	AZ	602-870-1010	PPP, SLIP
a2i Communications	San Jose	CA	408-293-8078	PPP, SLIP
	Cupertino	CA	408-973-9111	PPP, SLIP
BARRNet	Menlo Park	CA	415-725-7003	PPP, SLIP
CONNECTnet	San Diego	CA	619-450-0254	PPP, SLIP
CRL Network Services	Larkspur	CA	415-381-2800	PPP, SLIP
CTS Network Services	San Diego	CA	619-637-3637	PPP, SLIP
HoloNet	Berkeley	CA	510-704-0160	SLIP
Beckmeyer Development	Oakland	CA	510-530-9637	PPP

IGC	San Francisco	CA	415-442-0220	PPP, SLIP
CERFnet	San Diego	CA	800-876-2373	SLIP
TL Consulting	Sunnyvale	CA	408-739-6602	PPP
CCNET Communications	Walnut Creek	CA	800-CCNET-4-U	PPP, SLIP
Caprica Telecomputing Resources	Monterey Park	CA	213-266-0822	SLIP
The Cyberspace Station	Encinitas	CA	619-634-2894	PPP, SLIP
Internet Express	Co Springs	CO	800-592-1241	PPP, SLIP
Rocky Mountain Internet, Inc.	Co Springs	CO	719-576-6845	PPP, SLIP
Old Colorado City Communications	Co Springs	CO	719-632-4848	PPP
Paradigm Communications Inc.	Cheshire	CT	203-250-7397	PPP
Systems Solutions (SSNet)	Middletown	DE	302-378-1386	PPP, SLIP
Satelnet	Davie	FL	305-434-8738	SLIP
CyberGate, Inc	Deerbeach	FL	305-428-GATE	PPP, SLIP
CFTnet	Tampa	FL	813-980-1317	PPP
MindSpring	Atlanta	GA	404-888-0725	PPP, SLIP
Internet Atlanta	Alpharetta	GA	404-410-9000	PPP, SLIP
Computing Engineers Inc.	Vernon Hills	IL	708-367-1870	PPP, SLIP
InterAccess	Northbrook	IL	800-967-1580	PPP
MCSNet	Chicago	IL	312-248-8649	PPP, SLIP
XNet Information Systems	Lisle	IL	708-983-6064	PPP, SLIP
IgLou Internet Services	Louisville	KY	502-968-8500	PPP, SLIP
The Internet Access Company	Bedford	MA	617-275-2221	PPP, SLIP
North Shore Access	Lynn	MA	617-593-3110	PPP, SLIP
Schunix	Worcester	MA	508-853-0258	PPP
Clark Internet Services, Inc. (ClarkNet)	Ellicott City	MD	410-995-0691	PPP, SLIP
Digex (Digital Express Group)	Greenbelt	MD	800-969-9090	PPP, SLIP
Msen, Inc.	Ann Arbor	MI	313-998-4562	PPP, SLIP
CICNet	Ann Arbor	MI	313-998-6700	SLIP
MRnet	Minneapolis	MN	612-342-2894	SLIP
Skypoint Communications	Plymouth	MN	612-475-2959	PPP, SLIP
Tyrell	Kansas City	MO	800-989-7351	PPP, SLIP

Vnet Internet Access, Inc.	Charlotte	NC	800-377-3282	PPP, SLIP
FXnet	Charlotte	NC	704-338-4670	SLIP
MIDnet	Lincoln	NE	402-472-7600	PPP, SLIP
MV Communications, Inc.	Manchester	NH	603-429-2223	PPP, SLIP
Global Enterprise Service, Inc.	Princeton	NJ	609-897-7309	SLIP
Engineering International, Inc.	Albuquerque	NM	505-343-1060	SLIP
The Pipeline	New York	NY	212-267-3636	PPP, SLIP
Cloud 9 Internet	White Plains	NY	914-682-0626	PPP, SLIP
Internet Access Cincinnati	Hamilton	OH	513-887-8877	PPP
APK- Public Access UNI* Site	Cleveland	OH	216-481-9428	PPP, SLIP
Freelance Systems Programming	Dayton	OH	513-254-7246	SLIP
OARnet	Columbus	OH	800-627-8101	PPP, SLIP
Teleport, Inc.	Portland	OR	503-223-4245	PPP, SLIP
Pacific Systems Group (RAINet)	Portland	OR	503-227-5665	PPP, SLIP
Telerama Public Access Internet	Pittsburgh	PA	412-481-3505	PPP, SLIP
Net Access	Glenside	PA	215-576-8669	PPP, SLIP
The IDS World Network	Greenwich	RI	401-884-7856	PPP, SLIP
SunBelt	Rock Hill	SC	803-324-6205	SLIP
Adhesive Media, Inc.	Austin	TX	800-455-EDEN	SLIP
INET Enterprises	Austin	TX	512-388-2393	PPP
The Black Box	Houston	TX	713-480-2684	SLIP
South Coast Computing Services, Inc.	Houston	TX	713-661-3301	SLIP
Texas Metronet	Irving	TX	214-705-2900	PPP, SLIP
NeoSoft's Sugar Land Unix	Houston	TX	713-438-4964	PPP, SLIP
Real Time Communications	Austin	TX	512-451-0046	SLIP
On-Ramp Technologies, Inc.	Dallas	TX	214-746-4710	PPP, SLIP
XMission	Salt Lake City	UT	801-539-0900	PPP, SLIP
Infinet, L.C.	Norfolk	VA	800-849-7214	PPP, SLIP
UUNET Technologies, Inc.	Falls Church	VA	800-488-6386	PPP
Performance Systems International, Inc. (PSI)	Herndon	VA	703-904-4100	PPP
CompuTech	Spokane	WA	509-624-6798	PPP, SLIP

WLN	Lacey	WA	800-342-5956	PPP, SLIP
Network Access Services	Bellingham	WA	206-733 9279	PPP, SLIP
Cyberspace	Seattle	WA	206-286-1600	PPP, SLIP
Olympus	Pt. Townsend	WA	206-385-0464	PPP
Northwest Nexus Inc.	Bellevue	WA	206-455-3505	PPP, SLIP
Route 66 Networks, Inc.	Mercer Island	WA	206-324-6666	PPP
NorthWestNet	Bellevue	WA	206-562-3000	PPP, SLIP
SEANET (OSD, Inc.)	Seattle	WA	206-343-7828	PPP, SLIP
FREE.ORG	Marshfield	WI	715-387-1700	PPP, SLIP
Milwaukee Internet X	Milwaukee	WI	414-228-0739	PPP
Berbee Information Networks Corporation	Madison	WI	608-233-2228	PPP, SLIP

Outside the USA

AARNet	Canberra	Australia	61-6-249 2874	PPP
connect.com.au pty Ltd.	Caulfield	Australia	61-3-528-2239	PPP, SLIP
Pegasus Networks	Broadway	Australia	61-7-257-111	SLIP
Personal InterNet Gate (PING)	Vienna	Austria	43-1-319-43-36	PPP
EUnet Austria	Wien	Austria	43-1-317-4969	PPP
EUnet Bulgaria	Varna	Bulgaria	359-52-259-135	PPP
EUnet Belguim	Leuven	Belgium	32-16-201-015	PPP, SLIP
IBASE - Alternex Access Center	Rio de Janeiro	Brazil	55-21-286-6161	PPP
ARnet (Alberta Research Network)	Edmonton	Canada	403-450-5187	PPP, SLIP
Helix	Vancouver, BC	Canada	604-689-8544	PPP, SLIP
ICE Online	Burnaby, BC	Canada	604-298-4346	PPP, SLIP
Cyberstore	New Westminster, BC	Canada	604-526-3373	PPP, SLIP
Wimsey Information Services	Burnaby, BC	Canada	604-421-4741	PPP, SLIP
MIND LINK! Communications Corp.	Langley, BC	Canada	604-534-5663	SLIP
AMT Solutions Group Inc.	Victoria, BC	Canada	604-370-4601	PPP, SLIP
MBnet	Winnipeg, Manitoba	Canada	204-474-6236	PPP, SLIP

New Brunswick's Regional Network	New Brunswick	Canada	506-694-6404	PPP, SLIP
NSTN Nova Scotia Technology Network	Nova Scotia	Canada	902-468-6786	PPP, SLIP
UUNET Canada, Inc.	Ontario	Canada	416-368-6621	PPP
HookUp Communication Corporation	Ontario	Canada	905-847-8000	PPP, SLIP
Resudox	Ontario	Canada	613-567-6925	PPP
Communications Accessibles Montreal	Quebec	Canada	514-931-0749	PPP, SLIP
RISQ	Quebec	Canada	514-398-1234	PPP, SLIP
Metrix Interlink Corp.	Montreal, Quebec	Canada	514-933-9171	PPP, SLIP
SASK#net	Saskatoon, Saskatchewan	Canada	306-966-4816	PPP, SLIP
The Direct Connection	London	England	44-(0)81-317 0100	PPP, SLIP
Demon Internet Systems	London	England	44-(0)81-349 0063	PPP, SLIP
GreenNet	London	England	44-71-713-1941	PPP, SLIP
ESDATA Ltd.	Tallinn	Estonia	372-2-527-504	PPP, SLIP
EUnet France	Paris	France	33-1-53-81-60-60	PPP
Individual Network	Frankfurt	Germany	49-69-631-12083	PPP
Contributed Software GbR	Berlin	Germany	49-30-694-69-07	PPP, SLIP
Commercial Link Systems	Kiel	Germany	49-431-979-0161	PPP, SLIP
GeoNet Mailbox Systems	Dortmund	Germany	49-231-9070-100	PPP, SLIP
Hong Kong Supernet	Kowloon	Hong Kong	852-358-7924	SLIP
ERNET	New Delhi	India	91-11-436-1329	PPP, SLIP
IEunet Ltd.	Dublin	Ireland	353-1-679-0832	PPP, SLIP
Ireland On-Line	Furbo, Galaway	Ireland	353-(0)91-92727	PPP, SLIP
Active Communications LTD	Haifa	Israel	972-4-676-115	SLIP
GulfNet Kuwait Ministry Of Communications	Sharq Area	Kuwait	956-242-6728	PPP
JARING	Malaysia		60-3-254-9601	PPP, SLIP
SURFnet	Da Utrecht	Netherlands	31-30 310-290	PPP, SLIP
Actrix Networks Ltd.	Melrose, Wellington	New Zealand	64-4-389-6316	PPP
Red Cientifica Peruana	Lima 33	Peru	51-14-368-989	PPP, SLIP
EUnet Romania	Bucharest	Romania	0040-1-312-6886	SLIP
Demos Plus Co., Ltd.	Moscow	Russia	7-095-943-4735	SLIP

GlasNet	Moscow	Russia	7-(095)-207-0704	PPP
ARNES	Ljubljana	Slovenia	386-61-126-1204	SLIP
Aztec Information Management	Cape Town	South Africa	27-21-419-2690	PPP, SLIP
EUnet Spain	Madrid	Spain	34-1-413-48-56	PPP, SLIP
SWITCH	Zurich	Switzerland	41-1-268-1520	PPP, SLIP
PIPEX	Cambridge	UK	44-223-424-616	PPP

Appendix B

Discussions of Windows NT Web Servers

SerWeb

This freeware Web server runs under Microsoft 3.1 or Windows NT. The server was written in C++ by Gustavo Estrella, and the source code is available as part of the software distribution.

`ftp://sunsite.unc.edu/pub/micro/pc-stuff/ms-windows/winsock/apps`

Web4HAM

This server was developed by Gunter Hille at the University of Hamburg. The product is in its early development (v 0.16) and offers an-easy-to-install package.

`ftp://ftp.informatik.uni-hamburg.de/pub/net/winsock`

WHTTPd

This is Bob Denny's Windows HTTP server. The operation and configuration of the Windows HTTP server closely parallels the UNIX server.

`http://www.city.net/win-httpd`

Beame & Whiteside BW Connect

Web server for DOS and Microsoft Windows 3.1.

`ftp://ftp.bws.com/pub/evaluation/nfs_dos_windows/`

ZBServer

Written by Bob Bradley, this does double duty as a Web and Gopher server for Windows 3.1 and Windows 95. It is easy to install.

`http://unix1.utm.edu/~bbradley/zbs/zbsgetit.htm`

Purveyor

Process Software Corporation, through an agreement with EMWAC, has taken the EMWACS Web server, enhanced it, and offers it as a commercial product. Windows NT and Windows 95 versions are available. This was the first commercial Web server for Windows NT.

`http://www.process.com/prodinfo/purvdata.htm`

EMWAC HTTP Server for Windows NT

An excellent WWW server written by Chris Adie of EMWAC. You can't beat the price—it's free!

`http://emwac.ed.ac.uk/html/internet_toolchest/https/contents.htm`

WebSite

An HTTP server for Windows 95 and Windows NT written by Bob Denny in cooperation with O'Reilly & Associates.

`http://gnn.com/gnn/bus/ora/news/c.website.html`

Alibaba

This is an HTTP server for Windows NT from Computer Software Manufacturer in Austria.

`http://www.csm.co.at/csm/alibaba.htm`

SAIC-HTTP Server

The status of the SAIC-HTTP Server has not yet been decided. SAIC has no current plans to market or sell this software. The software was originally developed for internal use by Don De Coteau out of SAIC's San Diego, CA Information Technology Laboratory.

```
http://wwwserver.itl.saic.com/
```

Netscape Communications and Netscape Commerce from Netscape Communications

Netscape Communications corporation, the makers of the most popular Web browser, offers a standard Web server for Windows NT and a Commerce version that supports SSL for encrypted secure operation.

```
http://www.netscape.com/comprod/netscape_commun.html
```

Ameritech Library Services' NetPublisher Demonstration Server

The NetPublisher Server provides the functionality of a Z39.50 server, a World Wide Web server, and a Gopher server all in one. The extended architecture has been designed to allow you to focus on the information you are serving, not how it is served. There is one source for all three protocols. Ameritech also offers a complete package of Web publishing tools.

```
http://netpub.notis.com/
```

INTERNET FACTORY's Commerce Builder: the Secure SSL Server for Windows NT

This is a pair of web servers for Windows NT and Windows 95: Communications Builder and Commerce Builder. Features include multiple web/domain support, authentication-based access control, a caching HTTP proxy, and an exclusive, web-based, real-time chatroom.

```
http://www.aristosoft.com/ifact/inet.htm
```

ILAR Concepts' FolkWeb WWW Server

This is a full-featured Web server for Windows NT and Windows 95 whose key feature is that it uses built-in Database connectivity, allowing you to publish your databases without writing a single line of CGI code.

```
http://www.ilar.com/default.htm
```

Folio Corporation's Folio Infobase Web Server

This is a Web server for Windows NT and Windows 95.

`http://www.folio.com/`

Reviews

We personally tested five of the servers listed above. The number of Web servers available for Windows NT has more than doubled over the past six months, and we can only assume that this number will continue to increase rapidly. You will find that most of the Web servers on the market today offer a free trial period of 30 to 60 days.

Some of the Web Servers listed here have additional features that we have not covered in this appendix; please consult the product documentation or contact the manufacturer for full information.

Of the servers that we tested, here is a list in the order that we rank them, with a brief statement of our likes and dislikes:

1. **HTTPS from European Microsoft Windows NT Academic Center (EMWAC)**

   Likes: Despite the fact that it's free, HTTPS is a very robust and simple Web server. It includes a good manual and has image mapping built into the system; so there is no need to call a CGI image mapping routine. We highly recommended this as a good starting point.

   Dislikes: It lacks the more advanced security features offered by commercial packages, such as exclusion by IP, File, or Directory. If you are connected by dial-up and lose your connection, after reconnection you will have to stop and restart the HTTPS service for it to work.

2. **Purveyor from Process Software**

   Likes: This is the server Chris uses. It is simple to install, is fast, and has all the advanced security features for password-protecting files and directories by user or group. All the configuration is done from a Control Panel applet or an additional pull-down menu and button bar added to File Manager. Purveyor has full support to run as a proxy server. This is one smooth server with a killer interface. It's available for Windows NT and Windows 95.

   Dislikes: We haven't run across any yet.

3. **Netscape Communications and Netscape Commerce from Netscape Communications**

   Likes: Both packages are very robust but take a little more time to install than the others. All server configuration and administration is done from a Web browser using forms. The Web browser approach to administering your Web server will appeal to anyone who wants to change server configuration remotely. It has a very nice server statistics viewer for monitoring server operation.

Dislikes: We prefer a Control Panel applet for server administration, instead of the Web browser approach. Setup proved to be somewhat time-consuming and hard to follow. If you use this server, do your homework prior to setup and installation.

4. **WebSite from O'Reilly and Associates**

Likes: This is packed full of features and utilities. After installation, you will have a new program group with several utilities to make your Web site maintenance easier: Home Page Wizard, What's New Wizard, Web View, Web Index, Quick Stats, and The Image Map Editor. The installation is smooth, and you have the option to run from the desktop or as an NT service. This product runs on NT and Win95.

Dislikes: We found all the utilities somewhat overwhelming and not very intuitive. Image mapping was not as straightforward as with the others servers. With the proper time invested in learning this package, it can be very powerful.

5. **SAIC-HTTP**

Still in beta, this product is expected to be freeware. It installed smoothly and was easily configured via the NT Control Panel. It also had nice file redirection and security features. It supports installing multiple HTTP servers on one NT Server. It also has a feature called External modules, which enables you to extend the functionality of the server. Modules (CGI scripts that reside in the modules directory under the server root directory) are automatically executed when the URL that is referenced matches an entry in the module mapping table.

Dislikes: This is still a little quirky but is definitely one product to keep your eye on.

Appendix C

Internet Resources for the NT Webmaster

This appendix consists of dozens of Internet locations that we have found useful. These resources, organized by the following categories, can help you too.

- World Wide Web Development
- Windows NT Download Sites
- Windows NT User Groups and Associations
- Informational Web Sites
- Internet Server Software
- Windows NT Hardware Compatibility Information
- Windows NT Newsletters & FAQs
- Newsgroups of Interest
- About ISDN and Windows NT

The number of Windows NT resources available on the Internet grows every day, so this list is by no means complete. If you have a question about running a Web server, however, you will almost certainly be able to find something in here that will lead you to the answer.

For those who don't want to type in all these URLs, we have included on the CD a bookmark.htm file for use with Netscape. You will find the file in the \supp directory.

World Wide Web Development
From these two sites you will be able to find all the WWW development information you need.

The WWW Developer's Virtual Library `http://www.stars.com/`

Bob Allisons' Web Masters `http://gagme.wwa.com/~boba/masters1.html`

Windows NT Download Sites
Microsoft's Gopher `gopher://gopher.microsoft.com/`

Microsoft's Web Server `http://www.microsoft.com`

Digital Equipment Corporation `http://www.windowsnt.digital.com/`

Windows NT Shareware `http://spectrum.ece.jhu.edu/shrindex.htm`

Microsoft Windows NT Software—PD tools, etc. `http://www.digital.com/www-swdev/pages/Home/TECH/software/sw-wnt.html`

EMWAC—Czech Republic FTP `ftp://emwac.faf.cuni.cz`

EMWAC—Czech Republic Gopher `gopher://emwac.faf.cuni.cz`

CICA Gopher Windows NT Directory—Index for CICA Gopher `gopher://ftp.cica.indiana.edu:70/11/pc/win3/nt`

The Coast to Coast Software Repository Windows NT Primary Mirror `http://www.acs.oakland.edu/oak/SimTel/SimTel-nt.html`

WWW Site for Native Alpha NT Tools & Utilities `http://www.garply.com/tech/comp/sw/pc/nt/alpha.html`

FTP Site for Native Alpha NT Tools & Utilities `ftp://ftp.garply.com/pub/pc/nt/alpha`

Somar Software—Many NT Security Type Applications & Others `http://www.somar.com/default.htm`

Tucows Winsock Utilities `http://www.tucows.com`

Windows NT User Groups and Associations

San Diego Windows NT Users Group `http://www.bhs.com/sdug/`

International Windows NT Users Group `http://www.iwntug.org/`

Los Angeles NT/Microsoft Networking Users Group `http://bhs.com/winnt/lantug.html`

Rocky Mountain Windows NT User Group `http://budman.cmdl.noaa.gov/rmwntug/rmwntug.htm`

Advanced Systems User Group, Washington D.C. (temporary home) `http://www.microsoft.com/pages/guided-tours/federal/user1.htm`

Interior Alaska Windows NT Users Group `http://rmm.com/iawntug/`

Northern California Microsoft Windows NT Users Group Information: `http://www.actioninc.com/winntug.htm`

Stuttgart Windows NT Home Page `http://www.informatik.uni-stuttgart.de/misc/nt/nt.html`

European Microsoft Windows NT Academic Center - Czech Republic `http://emwac.faf.cuni.cz/html/emwaccz.htm`

EMWAC Information Services -UK `http://emwac.ed.ac.uk/`

Informational Web Sites

The Windows NT Resource Center `http://www.bhs.com/winnt/`

Rick's Windows NT Info Center `http://137.226.92.4/rick/`

Windows NT Information `http://infotech.kumc.edu/winnt/`

iNtformaTion `http://rmm.com/nt/`

Windows NT Information—Stuttgart `http://www.informatik.uni-stuttgart.de/misc/nt/nt.html`

Windows NT and NT Advanced Server Information `http://ms-nic.gsfc.nasa.gov/Titles/WinNT.html`

Windows NT Network Specialist `http://infotech.kumc.edu/`

European Microsoft Windows NT Academic Centre—EMWAC `http://emwac.ed.ac.uk/`

Windows NT Support Center—University of Karlsruhe `http://jerusalem.windows-nt.uni-karlsruhe.de/english.htm`

Windows NT RAS Setup `http://www.mindspring.com/~ekelley/html/ntras.htm`

CSUSM—Windows NT File Archives `http://coyote.csusm.edu/cwis/winworld/nt.html`

Netherlands Windows NT `http://nt.info.nl/english/default.htm`

Yahoo Windows NT Page `http://akebono.stanford.edu/yahoo/Computers/`
`Operating_Systems/Windows_NT/`

Internet Server Software

EMWACS Freeware Gopher server `ftp://emwac.ed.ac.uk/pub/gophers/`

EMWACS Freeware WAIS server `ftp://emwac.ed.ac.uk/pub/waiss/`

EMWACS WAIS toolkit based on freeWAIS 0.202 `ftp://emwac.ed.ac.uk/pub/`
`waistool/`

EMWACS Freeware Finger Server `http://emwac.ed.ac.uk/html/internet_toolchest/`
`fingers/contents.htm`

Windows NT Hardware Compatibility Information

Windows NT 3.5 Hardware Compatibility List `ftp://ftp.microsoft.com/`
`bussys\winnt\winnt-docs\hcl\hcl35\dec94hcl.txt`.

Windows NT 3.5 Hardware Incompatibility List 4/16/95 `http://www.sparco.com:80/`
`~cheema/NT/`.

Windows NT Newsletters & FAQs

FAQ—Windows NT Administration `http://www.iftech.com/classes/admin/admin.htm`

FAQ—Windows NT by Dale Reed 4/15/95 `http://www.iea.com/~daler/nt/faq/`
`toc.html`

MS NT FAQ `http://ftp.microsoft.com/bussys\winnt\winnt-public\ntfaq.txt`

Microsoft's 32-bit Applications Catalog `http://www.microsoft.com/pages/bussys/`
`ntserver/NTS14100.htm`

Windows NT v3.5 Internet/Connectivity FAQ, by Steven Scoggins and Tom
Baltrushaytis `http://www.luc.edu/~tbaltru/faq/`

Windows NT Internet FAQ Part 1 of 2 Available via FTP download `ftp://`
`rtfm.mit.edu//pub/usenet-by-hierarchy/comp/os/ms-windows/nt/setup/`

Windows NT Internet FAQ Part 2 of 2 Available via FTP download. `ftp://`
`rtfm.mit.edu//pub/usenet-by-hierarchy/comp/os/ms-windows/nt/setup/`

Windows NT FAX software FAQ—Courtesy of Walter Arnold `http://www.mcs.net/`
`~sculptor/NTFAX-FAQ.HTML`

The Consummate Winsock Apps Page `http://cws.wilmington.net/`

Somar Software's NT Security White Paper `http://www.somar.com/security.htm`

PERL—Practical Extraction and Report Language 4/14/95 `http://www.cis.ufl.edu/cgi-bin/plindex`

Newsgroups of Interest

- `comp.os.ms-windows.nt.admin.misc`
- `comp.os.ms-windows.nt.admin.networking`
- `comp.os.ms-windows.nt.advocacy`
- `comp.os.ms-windows.nt.misc`
- `comp.os.ms-windows.nt.pre-release`
- `comp.os.ms-windows.nt.setup`
- `comp.os.ms-windows.nt.setup.hardware`
- `comp.os.ms-windows.nt.setup.misc`
- `comp.os.ms-windows.nt.software.backoffice`
- `comp.os.ms-windows.nt.software.compatability`
- `comp.os.ms-windows.nt.software.services`
- `alt.winsock`   Discusses Windows TCP/IP
- `alt.security`   Discusses computer security
- `alt.security.pgp`   Discusses the Pretty Good Privacy program
- `comp.os.ms-windows.nt.misc`   Discusses miscellaneous Windows NT topics
- `comp.os.ms-windows.nt.setup`   Discusses Windows NT configuration issues
- `comp.os.ms-windows.networking.tcpip`   Discusses running TCP/IP in Windows
- `comp.risks`   Discusses computer security

Listservers

In addition to the informational sites above, these listservers are very valuable resources of information. You will receive an auto-reply telling you how to send messages to the list after you are a member.

- NT HTTPS: `http_winnt@Emerald.NET`. Enter `subscribe` in the subject line and leave the body blank.
- The International Windows NT Users Group (IWNTUG): `list@bhs.com`. Enter `subscribe iwntug` in the first line of the body of the message.
- The Beverly Hills Software Resource Center Newsletter: `list@bhs.com`. Enter `subscribe rcnews` in the first line of the body of the message.

- NT Consultants List: `list@bhs.com`. Enter `subscribe ntconsult` in the first line of the body of the message.
- UK NT listserver: `mailbase@mailbase.ac.uk`. Enter `join windows-nt` *firstname lastname* in the body of the message and leave the subject blank.
- UK Microsoft Back Officer listservers: `mailbase@mailbase.ac.uk`. Enter `join ms-back-office` *firstname lastname* in the body of the message and leave the subject blank.
- NT Lanman listserver: `listserv@list.nih.gov`. Enter `subscribe lanman-l` *firstname lastname* in the body of the message and leave the subject blank.
- `Webserver-nt-request@DELTA.PROCESS.COM`. Enter `subscribe webserver-nt` in the body of the message.
- DEC Alpha NT Listserver: To subscribe, send an e-mail to `majordomo@garply.com` with the body text of `subscribe alphant`. After you are subscribed, send messages to `alphant@garply.com`.
- Windows NT Perl Listserver: To subscribe, send e-mail to `majordomo@mail.hip.com` with the body text of the message saying `subscribe ntperl`.

About ISDN and Windows NT

See the Microsoft KnowledgeBase article: Q133704.

For general information about the PPP Multilink protocol or ISDN, see: `http://www.almaden.ibm.com/ciug/ciug.html` or `http://alumni.caltech.edu/~dank/isdn/`

Business Resources

Here are a few sites that should be of interest to any business person. See Chapter 17 and Yahoo at `http://www.yahoo.com` for other resources.

- The Small Business Administration: `http://www.sbaonline.sba.gov`
- Federal Government Information on the Internet: `http://www.wcs-online.com/usgovdoc`
- Stat-USA: `http://www.stat-usa.gov/`
- The World Wide Web Yellow Pages (includes a search page): `http://www.yellow.com`
- Yellowpages.com, another reference to online businesses: `http://theyellowpages.com/default.htm`
- Monster Board Classified Ads: `http://www.monster.com/`

Appendix D

Selected RFCs

RFCs, or Request for Comments, are the official standards in the Internet community. Contained in this index is a partial list of relevant RFCs. A complete list of effective RFCs, as well as the RFCs themselves, is available online in various places throughout the Internet. Sending e-mail to rfc-info@isi.edu with a subject, getting rfcs, and help, ways_to_get_rfcs, in the body of the message will return a list containing current methods for obtaining RFCs. At the time of printing, that e-mail message returned the following:

Where and How to Get New RFCs

RFCs may be obtained via e-mail or FTP from many RFC Repositories. The Primary Repositories will have the RFC available when it is first announced, as will many secondary repositories. Some secondary repositories might take a few days to make available the most recent RFCs.

Primary Repositories

RFCs can be obtained via FTP from `ds.internic.net`, `nis.nsf.net`, `nisc.jvnc.net`, `ftp.isi.edu`, `wuarchive.wustl.edu`, `src.doc.ic.ac.uk`, `ftp.ncren.net`, `ftp.sesqui.net`, or `nis.garr.it`.

ds.internic.net—InterNIC Directory and Database Services

RFCs can be obtained from `ds.internic.net` via FTP, WAIS, and electronic mail. Through FTP, RFCs are stored as `rfc/rfcnnnn.txt` or `rfc/rfcnnnn.ps`, where *nnnn* is the RFC number. Log in as anonymous and provide your e-mail address as the password. Through WAIS, you can use either your local WAIS client or Telnet to `ds.internic.net` and log in as `wais` (no password required) to access a WAIS client. Help information and a tutorial for using WAIS are available online. The WAIS database to search is `rfcs`.

Directory and Database Services also provides a mail server interface. Send a mail message to `mailserv@ds.internic.net` and include any of the following commands in the message body:

- `document-by-name rfcnnnn`, where *nnnn* is the RFC number. The text version is sent.
- `file /ftp/rfc/rfcnnnn.yyy`, where *nnnn* is the RFC number and *yyy* is txt or ps.
- `help` to get information on how to use the mailserver.

The InterNIC Directory and Database Services Collection of Resource Listings, Internet Documents such as RFCs, FYIs, STDs, Internet Drafts, and Publically Accessible Databases are also now available via Gopher. All our collections are waisindexed and can be searched from the Gopher menu.

To access the InterNIC Gopher Servers, connect to `internic.net`, port 70.

`admin@dsinternic.net`

nis.nsf.net

To obtain RFCs from `nis.nsf.net` via FTP, log in with username anonymous and password guest; then connect to the directory of RFCs with `cd/internet/documents/rfc`. The filename is of the form `rfcnnnn.txt` (where *nnnn* refers to the RFC number).

For sites without FTP capability, electronic mail query is available from `nis.nsf.net`. Address the request to `nis-info@nis.nsf.net` and leave the subject field of the message blank. The first text line of the message must be `send rfcnnnn.txt`, where *nnnn* is the RFC number.

`rfc-mgr@merit.edu`

nisc.jvnc.net

RFCs can also be obtained via FTP from NISC.JVNC.NET, with the pathname `rfc/rfcnnnn.txt` (where *nnnn* refers to the number of the RFC). An index can be obtained with the pathname `rfc/rfc-index.txt`. JvNCnet also provides a mail service for those sites that cannot use FTP. Address the request to `sendrfc@nisc.jvnc.net`. In the Subject: field of the message, indicate the RFC number, as in `Subject: rfcnnnn` (where *nnnn* is the RFC number). RFCs whose numbers are less than 1000 need not place a leading 0. (For example, RFC932 is fine.) For a complete index to the RFC library, enter `rfc-index` in the Subject: field, as in `Subject: rfc-index`. No text in the body of the message is needed.

`rfc-admin@nisc.jvnc.net`

ftp.isi.edu

RFCs can be obtained via FTP from `ftp.isi.edu`, with the pathname `in-notes/rfcnnnn.txt` (where *nnnn* refers to the number of the RFC). Log in with FTP username `anonymous` and password `guest`.

RFCs can also be obtained via electronic mail from ISI.EDU by using the RFC-INFO service. Address the request to `rfc-info@isi.edu` with a message body of

```
Retrieve: RFC
Doc-ID: RFCnnnn
```

where *nnnn* refers to the number of the RFC. (Always use four digits; the DOC-ID of RFC 822 is RFC0822.) The `RFC-INFO@ISI.EDU` server provides other ways of selecting RFCs based on keywords and such; for more information, send a message to `rfc-info@isi.edu` with the message body `help: help`.

`RFC-Manager@ISI.EDU`

wuarchive.wustl.edu

RFCs can also be obtained via FTP from `wuarchive.wustl.edu`, with the pathname `info/rfc/rfcnnnn.txt.Z` (where *nnnn* refers to the number of the RFC and Z indicates that the document is in compressed form).

At `wuarchive.wustl.edu`, the RFCs are in an archive file system, and various archives can be mounted as part of an NFS file system. Contact Chris Myers (`chris@wugate.wustl.edu`) if you want to mount this file system in your NFS.

`chris@wugate.wustl.edu`

doc.ic.ac.uk

RFCs can be obtained via FTP from `src.doc.ic.ac.uk` with the pathname `rfc/rfcnnnn.txt.Z` or `rfc/rfcnnnn.ps.Z` (where *nnnn* refers to the number of the RFC). Log in with FTP username `anonymous` and password *your-email-address*. To obtain the RFC Index, use the pathname `rfc/rfc-index.txt.Z`. (The trailing `.Z` indicates that the document is in compressed form.)

`src.doc.ic.ac.uk` also provides an automatic mail service for those sites in the UK that cannot use FTP. Address the request to `info-server@doc.ic.ac.uk` with a Subject: line of `wanted` and a message body of

```
request sources
topic path rfc/rfcnnnn.txt.Z
request end
```

where *nnnn* refers to the number of the RFC. Multiple requests may be included in the same message by giving multiple `topic path` commands on separate lines. To request the RFC Index, the command should read

```
topic path rfc/rfc-index.txt.Z
```

The archive is also available using NIFTP and the ISO FTAM system.

```
ukuug-soft@doc.ic.ac.uk
```

ftp.ncren.net

To obtain RFCs from `ftp.ncren.net` via FTP, log in with username anonymous and your Internet e-mail address as the password. The RFCs can be found in the directory `/rfc`, with filenames of the form: `rfcnnnn.txt` or `rfcnnnn.ps`, where *nnnn* refers to the RFC number.

This repository is also accessible via WAIS and the Internet Gopher.

```
rfc-mgr@ncren.net
```

ftp.sesqui.net

RFCs can be obtained via FTP from `ftp.sesqui.net`, with the pathname `pub/rfc/rfcnnnn.xxx` (where *nnnn* refers to the number of the RFC and *xxx* indicates the document form, `txt` for ASCII and `ps` for PostScript).

At `ftp.sesqui.net`, the RFCs are in an archive file system, and various archives can be mounted as part of an NFS file system. Please contact the RFC maintainer (`rfc-maint@sesqui.net`) if you want to mount this file system in your NFS.

```
rfc-maint@sesqui.net
```

nis.garr.it

RFCs can be obtained from `nis.garr.it` FTP archive with the pathname `mirrors/RFC/rfcnnnn.txt` (where *nnnn* refers to the number of the RFC). Log in with FTP, username anonymous and password `guest`.

The following is a summary of ways to get RFC from GARR-NIS FTP archive:

> Via FTP: `ftp.nis.garr.it` directory `mirrors/RFC`
>
> Via gopher: `gopher.nis.garr.it`, folders GARR-NIS; anonymous FTP: `ftp.nis.garr.it` mirrors RFC
>
> Via WWW: `ftp://ftp.nis.garr.it/mirrors/RFC`
>
> Via e-mail: `dbserv@nis.garr.it` whose body contains `get mirrors/RFC/rfc<number>`.

To have an RFC from the FTP archive e-mailed to you, put the `get <fullpathname>` command either in the subject or as a mail body line of a mail message sent to `dbserv@nis.garr.it`. `<fullpathname>` must be the concatenation of two strings: the directory path and the filename.

Remember to use uppercase and lowercase exactly. The directory path is listed at the beginning of each block of files.

For example, to get RFC1004, the command is `get mirrors/RFC/rfc1004.txt`.

Secondary Repositories

Here are other sites that contain the RFC documents.

Sweden

Host	`sunic.sunet.se`
Directory	`rfc`
Host	`chalmers.se`
Directory	`rfc`

Germany

Site	EUnet Germany
Host	`ftp.Germany.EU.net`
Directory	`pub/documents/rfc`

France

Site	Institut National de la Recherche en Informatique et Automatique (INRIA)
Address	`info-server@inria.fr`
Notes	RFCs are available via e-mail to the above address. Info Server manager is Mireille Yamajako (`yamajako@inria.fr`).

France

Site	Centre d'Informatique Scientifique et Medicale (CISM)
Contact	`ftpmaint@univ-lyon1.fr`
Host	`ftp.univ-lyon1.fr`
Directories:	`pub/rfc/*`; classified by hundreds `pub/mirrors/rfc`; mirror of Internic
Notes	Files compressed with gzip. Online decompression done by the FTP server.

Netherlands

Site	EUnet
Host	`mcsun.eu.net`
Directory	`rfc`
Notes	RFCs in compressed format.

Finland

Site	FUNET
Host	`funet.fi`
Directory	`rfc`
Notes	RFCs in compressed format. Also provides e-mail access by sending mail to `archive-server@funet.fi`.

Norway

Host	`ugle.unit.no`
Directory	`pub/rfc`

Denmark

Site	University of Copenhagen
Host	`ftp.denet.dk`
Directory	`rfc`

Australia and Pacific Rim

Site	munnari
Contact	Robert Elz, `kre@cs.mu.OZ.AU`
Host	`munnari.oz.au`
Directory	`rfc`; rfc's in compressed format `rfcNNNN.Z`; PostScript rfc's `rfcNNNN.ps.Z`

South Africa

Site	The Internet Solution
Contact	`ftp-admin@is.co.za`
Host	`ftp.is.co.za`
Directory	`internet/in-notes/rfc`

United States

Site	cerfnet
Contact	`help@cerf.net`
Host	`nic.cerf.net`
Directory	`netinfo/rfc`
Site	NASA NAIC
Contact	`rfc-updates@naic.nasa.gov`
Host	`naic.nasa.gov`
Directory	`files/rfc`
Site	`NIC.DDN.MIL` (DOD users only)
Contact	`NIC@nic.ddn.mil`

Host	NIC.DDN.MIL
Directory	rfc/rfcnnnn.txt. Note DOD users only may obtain RFCs via FTP from NIC.DDN.MIL. Internet users should not use this source (due to inadequate connectivity).
Site	uunet
Contact	James Revell, revell@uunet.uu.net
Host	ftp.uu.net
Directory	inet/rfc

UUNET Archive

UUNET archive, which includes RFCs, various IETF documents, and other information regarding the Internet, is available to the public via anonymous FTP (to ftp.uu.net), anonymous UUCP, and soon via an anonymous kermit server. Get the file/archive/inet/ls-lR.Z for a listing of these documents. Any site in the USA running UUCP may call +1 900 GOT SRCS and use the login uucp. There is no password. The phone company will bill you at $0.50 per minute for the call. The 900 number works only from within the United States.

Requests for special distribution of RFCs should be addressed to either the author of the RFC in question or to nic@internic.net.

Submissions for Requests for Comments should be sent to rfc-editor@isi.edu. Please consult "Instructions to RFC Authors," RFC 1543, for further information.

Requests to be added to or deleted from the RFC distribution list should be sent to RFC-request@nic.ddn.mil.

Changes to this file rfc-retrieval.txt should be sent to rfc-manager@isi.edu.

RFC INDEX

1812 Baker, F.,ed. Requirements for IP Version 4 Routers. 1995, June; 175 p. (Obsoletes 1716, 1009)

1808 Fielding, R. Relative Uniform Resource Locators. 1995, June; 16 p.

1789 Yang, C. INETPhone: Telephone Services and Servers on Internet. 1995, April; 6 p.

1788 Simpson, W. ICMP Domain Name Messages. 1995, April; 7 p.

1780 Postel, J.,ed. INTERNET OFFICIAL PROTOCOL STANDARDS. 1995, March; 39 p. (Obsoletes RFC 1720, RFC 1610, RFC 1540, RFC 1500, RFC 1410, RFC 1360 RFC, 1280, RFC 1250, RFC 1200, RFC 1140, RFC 1130)

1772 Rekhter, Y.; Gross, P.,eds. Application of the Border Gateway Protocol in the Internet. 1995, March; 19 p. (Obsoletes RFC 1655)

1771 Rekhter, Y.; Li, T.,eds. A Border Gateway Protocol 4 (BGP-4). 1995, March; 57 p. (Obsoletes RFC 1654)

1769 Mills, D. Simple Network Time Protocol (SNTP). 1995, March; 14 p. (Obsoletes RFC 1361)

1760 Haller, N. The S/KEY One-Time Password System. 1995, February; 12 p.

1757 Waldbusser, S. Remote Network Monitoring Management Information Base. 1995, February; 91 p. (Obsoletes RFC 1271)

1752 Bradner, S.; Mankin, A. The Recommendation for the IP Next Generation Protocol. January, 1995; 52 p.

1744 Huston, G. Observations on the Management of the Internet Address Space. December 1994; 12 p.

1741 Faltstrom, P.; Crocker, D.; Fair, E. MIME Content Type for BinHex Encoded Files. 1994, December; 6 p.

1739 Kessler, G.; Shepard, S. A Primer On Internet and TCP/IP Tools. 1994, December; 46 p.

1738 Berners-Lee, T.; Masinter, L.; McCahill, M.,eds. Uniform Resource Locators (URL). 1994, December; 25 p.

1737 Sollins, K.; Masinter, L. Functional Requirements for Uniform Resource Names. 1994, December; 7 p.

1736 Kunze, J. Functional Recommendations for Internet Resource Locators. 1995, February; 10 p.

1734 Myers, J. POP3 AUTHentication command. 1994, December; 5 p. (Format: TXT=8499 bytes)

1725 Myers, J.; Rose, M. Post Office Protocol, Version 3. 1994, November; 18 p. (Obsoletes RFC 1460)

1717 Sklower, K.; Lloyd, B.; McGregor, G.; Carr, D. The PPP Multilink Protocol (MP). 1994, November; 21 p.

1713 Romao, A. Tools for DNS debugging. 1994, November; 13 p.

1700 Reynolds, J.; Postel, J. ASSIGNED NUMBERS. 1994, October; 230 p. (Obsoletes RFC 1340)

1663 Rand, D. PPP Reliable Transmission. 1994, July; 8 p.

1661 Simpson, W.,ed. The Point-to-Point Protocol (PPP). 1994, July; 52 p. (Obsoletes RFC 1548)

1651 Freed, N.,ed.; Klensin, J.; Rose, M.; Stefferud, E.; Crocker, D. SMTP Service Extensions. 1994, July; 11 p. (Obsoletes RFC 1425)

1645 Gwinn, A. Simple Network Paging Protocol, Version 2. 1994, July; 15 p. (Obsoletes RFC 1568)

1636 Braden, R.; Clark, D.; Crocker, S.; Huitema, C. Report of IAB Workshop on Security in the Internet Architecture, February 8-10, 1994. 1994, June; 52 p.

1635 Deutsch, P.; Emtage, A.; Marine, A. How to Use Anonymous FTP. 1994, May; 13 p.

1630 Berners-Lee, T. Universal Resource Identifiers in WWW. 1994, June; 28 p.

1618 Simpson, W. PPP over ISDN. 1994, May; 6 p.

1602 Internet Architecture Board; Internet Engineering Steering Group The Internet Standards Process—Revision 2. 1994, March; 37 p.

1601 Huitema, C. Charter of the Internet Architecture Board (IAB). 1994, March; 6 p.

1591 Postel, J. Domain Name System Structure and Delegation. 1994, March; 7 p.

1550 Bradner, S.; Mankin, S. IP: Next Generation (IPng) White Paper Solicitation. 1993, December; 6 p.

1547 Perkins, D. Requirements for an Internet Standard Point-to-Point Protocol. 1993, December; 21 p.

1541 Droms, R. Dynamic Host Configuration Protocol. 1993, October; 39 p. (Obsoletes RFC 1531)

1522 Moore, K. MIME (Multipurpose Internet Mail Extensions) Part Two: Message Header Extensions for Non-ASCII Text. 1993, September; 10 p. (Obsoletes 1342)

1490 Bradley, T.; Brown, C.; Malis, A. Multiprotocol Interconnect over Frame Relay. 1993, July; 35 p.(Obsoletes RFC 1294)

1459 Oikarinen, J.; Reed, D. Internet Relay Chat Protocol. 1993, May; 65 p.

1436 Anklesaria, F.; McCahill, M.; Lindner, P.; Johnson, D.; Torrey, D.; Alberti, B. The Internet Gopher Protocol (a distributed document search and retrieval protocol). 1993, March; 16 p.

1334 Lloyd, B.; Simpson, W. PPP Authentication Protocols. 1992, October; 16 p.

1333 Simpson, W. PPP Link Quality Monitoring. 1992, May; 15 p.

1332 McGregor, G. The PPP Internet Protocol Control Protocol (IPCP). 1992, May; 12 p. (Obsoletes RFC 1172)

1305 Mills, D. Network Time Protocol (Version 3) Specification, Implementation and Analysis. 1992, March; 120 p. (Obsoletes RFC 1119, RFC 1059, RFC 958)

1303 McCloghrie, K.; Rose, M. A Convention for Describing SNMP-based Agents. 1992, February; 12 p.

1301 Armstrong, S.; Freier, A.; Marzullo, K. Multicast Transport Protocol. February, 1992; 38 p.

1296 Lottor, M. Internet Growth (1981-1991). 1992, January; 9 p.

1293 Brown, C. Inverse Address Resolution Protocol. 1992, January; 6 p.

1291 Aggarwal, V. Mid-Level Networks - Potential Technical Services. 1991, December; 10 p.

1288 Zimmerman, D. The Finger User Information Protocol. 1991, December; 12 p. (Obsoletes RFC 1196, RFC 1194, RFC 742)

1282 Kantor, B. BSD Rlogin. 1991, December; 5 p. (Format: TXT=10704 bytes) (Obsoletes RFC 1258)

1281 Pethia, R.; Crocker, S.; Fraser, B. Guidelines for the Secure Operation of the Internet. 1991, November; 10 p.

1277 Hardcastle-Kille, S. Encoding Network Addresses to support operation over non-OSI lower layers. 1991, November; 12 p.

1270 Kastenholz, F.,ed. SNMP communications services. 1991, October; 11 p.

1269 Willis, S.; Burruss, J. Definitions of Managed Objects for the Border Gateway Protocol (version 3). 1991, October; 13 p.

1267 Lougheed, K.; Rekhter, Y. A Border Gateway Protocol 3 (BGP-3). 1991, October; 35 p. (Obsoletes RFC 1105, RFC 1163)

1266 Rekhter, Y.,ed. Experience with the BGP protocol. 1991, Ocober; 9 p.

1265 Rekhter, Y.,ed. BGP protocol analysis. 1991, October; 8 p.

1264 Hinden, R. Internet routing protocol standardization criteria. 1991, October; 8 p.

1261 Williamson, S.; Nobile, L. Transition of NIC services. 1991, September; 3 p.

1256 Deering, S.,ed. ICMP router discovery messages. 1991, September; 19 p.

1254 Mankin, A.; Ramakrishnan, K.,eds. Gateway congestion control survey. 1991, August; 25 p.

1244 Holbrook, J.; Reynolds, J.,eds. Site Security Handbook. 1991, July; 101 p.

1242 Bradner, S.,ed. Benchmarking terminology for network interconnection devices. 1991, July; 12 p.

1240 Shue, C.; Haggerty, W.; Dobbins, K. OSI connectionless transport services on top of UDP: Version 1. 1991, June; 8 p.

1234 Provan, D. Tunneling IPX traffic through IP networks. 1991, June; 6 p.

1221 Edmond, W. Host Access Protocol (HAP) specification: Version 2. 1991, April; 68 p. (Updates RFC 907)

1220 Baker, F.,ed. Point-to-Point Protocol extensions for bridging. 1991, April; 18 p.

1219 Tsuchiya, P. On the assignment of subnet numbers. 1991, April; 13 p.

1215 Rose, M.,ed. Convention for defining traps for use with the SNMP. 1991, March; 9 p.

1211 Westine, A.; Postel, J. Problems with the maintenance of large mailing lists. 1991, March; 54 p.

1209 Piscitello, D.; Lawrence, J. Transmission of IP datagrams over the SMDS Service. 1991, March; 11 p. (Format: TXT=25280 bytes)

1208 Jacobsen, O.; Lynch, D. Glossary of networking terms. 1991, March; 18 p.

1207 Malkin, G.; Marine, A.; Reynolds, J. FYI on Questions and Answers: Answers to commonly asked "experienced Internet user" questions. 1991, February; 15 p.

1205 Chmielewski, P. 5250 Telnet interface. 1991, February; 12 p.

1203 Rice, J. Interactive Mail Access Protocol: Version 3. 1991, February; 49 p. (Obsoletes RFC 1064)

1201 Provan, D. Transmitting IP traffic over ARCNET networks. 1991, February; 7 p. (Obsoletes RFC 1051)

1192 Kahin, B.,ed. Commercialization of the Internet summary report. 1990, November; 13 p.

1191 Mogul, J.; Deering, S. Path MTU discovery. 1990, November; 19 p. (Obsoletes RFC 1063)

1188 Katz, D. Proposed standard for the transmission of IP datagrams over FDDI networks. 1990, October; 11 p. (Obsoletes RFC 1103)

1183 Everhart, C.; Mamakos, L.; Ullmann, R.; Mockapetris, P. New DNS RR definitions. 1990, October; 11 p. (Updates RFC 1034, RFC 1035)

1180 Socolofsky, T.; Kale, C. TCP/IP tutorial. 1991, January; 28 p.

1173 VanBokkelen, J. Responsibilities of host and network managers: A summary of the "oral tradition" of the Internet. 1990, August; 5 p.

1170 Fougner, R. Public key standards and licenses. 1991, January; 2 p.

1166 Kirkpatrick, S.; Stahl, M.; Recker, M. Internet numbers. 1990, July; 182 p. (Obsoletes RFC 1117, RFC 1062, RFC 1020)

1165 Crowcroft, J.; Onions, J. Network Time Protocol (NTP) over the OSI Remote Operations Service. 1990, June; 10 p.

1157 Case, J.; Fedor, M.; Schoffstall, M.; Davin, C. Simple Network Management Protocol (SNMP). 1990, May; 36 p.(Obsoletes RFC 1098)

1144 Jacobson, V. Compressing TCP/IP headers for low-speed serial links. 1990, February; 43 p.

1132 McLaughlin, L. Standard for the transmission of 802.2 packets over IPX networks. 1989, November; 4 p. (Format: TXT=8128 bytes)

1129 Mills, D. Internet time synchronization: The Network Time Protocol. 1989, October; 29 p.

1128 Mills, D. Measured performance of the Network Time Protocol in the Internet system. 1989, October; 20 p.

1125 Estrin, D. Policy requirements for inter Administrative Domain routing. 1989, November; 18 p.

1124 Leiner, B. Policy issues in interconnecting networks. 1989, September; 54 p.

1118 Krol, E. Hitchhikers guide to the Internet. 1989, September; 24 p.

1112 Deering, S. Host extensions for IP multicasting. 1989, August; 17 p. (Obsoletes RFC 988, RFC 1054)

1108 Kent, S. Security Options for the Internet Protocol. 1991, November; 17 p. (Obsoletes RFC 1038)

1101 Mockapetris, P. DNS encoding of network names and other types. 1989, April; 14 p.(Updates RFC 1034, RFC 1035)

1092 Rekhter, J. EGP and policy based routing in the new NSFNET backbone. 1989, February; 5 p.

1089 Schoffstall, M.; Davin, C.; Fedor, M.; Case, J. SNMP over Ethernet. 1989, February; 3 p.

1088 McLaughlin, L. Standard for the transmission of IP datagrams over NetBIOS networks. 1989, February; 3 p.

1087 Defense Advanced Research Projects Agency, Internet Activities Board; DARPA IAB Ethics and the Internet. 1989, January; 2 p.

1082 Rose, M. Post Office Protocol: Version 3: Extended service offerings. 1988, November; 11 p.

1077 Leiner, B.,ed. Critical issues in high-bandwidth networking. 1988, November; 46 p.

1074 Rekhter, J. NSFNET backbone SPF based Interior Gateway Protocol. 1988, October; 5 p.

1056 Lambert, M. PCMAIL: A distributed mail system for personal computers. 1988, June; 38 p. (Obsoletes RFC 993)

1055 Romkey, J. Nonstandard for transmission of IP datagrams over serial lines: SLIP. 1988, June; 6 p.

1049 Sirbu, M. Content-type header field for Internet messages. 1988, March; 8 p.

1042 Postel, J.; Reynolds, J. Standard for the transmission of IP datagrams over IEEE 802 networks. 1988, February; 15 p. (Obsoletes RFC 948)

1033 Lottor, M. Domain administrators operations guide. 1987, November; 22 p.

1032 Stahl, M. Domain administrators guide. 1987, November; 14 p.

1027 Carl-Mitchell, S.; Quarterman, J. Using ARP to implement transparent subnet gateways. 1987, October; 8 p.

1008 McCoy, W. Implementation guide for the ISO Transport Protocol. 1987, June; 73 p.

1007 McCoy, W. Military supplement to the ISO Transport Protocol. 1987, June; 23 p.

1006 Rose, M.; Cass, D. ISO transport services on top of the TCP: Version 3. 1987, May; 17 p. (Obsoletes RFC 983)

Appendix E

Discussions of 36 Internet Robots

This appendix contains basic information about 36 Internet robots.

JumpStation

Maintained by Jonathan Fletcher, e-mail: j.fletcher@stirling.ac.uk.

Jumpstation's purpose is to generate a Resource Discovery database. The HTTP User-agent field is set to JumpStation-Robot, and the From field is also set. Usually run from *.stir.ac.uk. The proposed standard for robot exclusion is supported.

RBSE Spider

Maintained by David Eichmann, e-mail: eichmann@rbse.jsc.nasa.gov.

RBASE Spider's purpose is to generate a Resource Discovery database and generate statistics. The HTTP User-agent field is set to RBSE Spider v. 1.0, and the From field is also set. Usually run from rbse.jsc.nasa.gov (192.88.42.10). The Proposed Standard for Robot Exclusion is supported.

The WebCrawler

Run by Brian Pinkerton, e-mail: `bp@biotech.washington.edu`.

Runs from `webcrawler.cs.washington.edu` and uses WebCrawler/0.00000001 in the HTTP User-agent field.

The NorthStar Robot

Run by Fred Barrie, e-mail: `barrie@unr.edu`, and Billy Barron.

Recent runs will concentrate on textual analysis of the Web versus GopherSpace (from the Veronica data), as well as indexing. Run from `frognot.utdallas.edu`, possibly other sites in `utdallas.edu`, and from `cnidir.org`. Now uses HTTP From fields and sets User-agent to NorthStar.

W4 (the World Wide Web Wanderer)

Run by Matthew Gray `mkgray@mit.edu`.

Run initially in June 1993, its aim is to measure the growth of the Web. W4's purpose is to discover resources on the fly. The HTTP User-agent field is set to Fish-Search-Robot, but the From field isn't set. This is usually run from `www.win.tue.nl`. The HTTP User-agent field is set to WWWWanderer v3.0 by Matthew Gray. The Proposed Standard for Robot Exclusion is not supported.

html_analyzer-0.02

Run by James E. Pitkow `pitkow@aries.colorado.edu`.

`html_analyzer-0.02`'s aim is to check validity of Web servers.

MONspider

Maintained by Roy T. Fielding, `fielding@ics.uci.edu`.

MONspider's purpose is to validate links and generate statistics. The HTTP User-agent field is set to `MOMspider/1.00 libwww-perl/0.40`, and the From field is also set. This is usually run from anywhere. The Proposed Standard for Robot Exclusion is supported.

HTMLgobble

Maintained by Andreas Ley, e-mail: `ley@rz.uni-karlsruhe.de`.

This is a mirroring robot, configured to stay within a directory and sleep between requests. The next version will use HEAD to check if the entire document needs to be retrieved. The HTTP User-Agent is set to HTMLgobble v2.2, and it sets the From field. This is usually run by the author, from `tp70.rz.uni-karlsruhe.de`.

WWWW—the World Wide Web Worm

Maintained by Oliver McBryan, e-mail: `mcbryan@piper.cs.colorado.edu`.

Run from `piper.cs.colorado.edu`.

W3M2

Maintained by Christophe Tronche `tronche@lri.fr`.

W3M2's purpose is to generate a Resource Discovery database, validate links, validate HTML, and generate statistics. The HTTP User-agent field is set to `W3M2/x.xxx`, and the From field is also set. This is usually run from `anyhost.lri.fr`. The Proposed Standard for Robot Exclusion is supported.

Websnarf

Maintained by Charlie Stross `charless@sco.com`.

Websnarf is a WWW mirror designed for off-line browsing of sections of the Web. It is run from `ruddles.london.sco.com`.

The Webfoot Robot

Run by Lee McLoughlin at `L.McLoughlin@doc.ic.ac.uk`.

It was first spotted in mid-February 1994 and is run from `phoenix.doc.ic.ac.uk`.

Lycos

Owned by Dr. Michael L. Mauldin, `fuzzy@cmu.edu` at Carnegie Mellon University.

Lycos is a research program providing information retrieval and discovery in the WWW, using a finite memory model of the Web to guide intelligent, directed searches for specific information needs. The HTTP User-agent is set to `Lycos/x.x`. This is run from `fuzine.mt.cs.cmu.edu`. The Proposed Standard for Robot Exclusion is supported.

ASpider (Associative Spider)

Written and run by Fred Johansen `fred@nvg.unit.no`.

Currently under construction, this spider is a CGI script that searches the Web for keywords given by the user through a form. The HTTP User-agent is set to `ASpider/0.09`, with a From field.

`fredj@nova.pvv.unit.no`

SG-Scout

Introduced by Peter Beebee `ptbb@ai.mit.edu`, `beebee@parc.xerox.com`.

This has run since June 27, 1994, for an internal XEROX research project. The HTTP User-agent is set to `SG-Scout`, with a From field set to the operator. The Proposed Standard for Robot Exclusion is supported. This is run from `beta.xerox.com`.

EIT Link Verifier Robot

Written by Jim McGuire `mcguire@eit.com`.

Announced on July 12, 1994, this is a combination of an HTML form and a CGI script that verifies links from a given starting point (with some controls to prevent it from running with no limits or going off-site). From version 0.2 up, the User-agent is set to `EIT-Link-Verifier-Robot/0.2`. This can be run by anyone from anywhere.

NHSE Web Forager

Maintained by Robert Olson at `olson@mcs.anl.gov`.

Web Forager's purpose is to generate a Resource Discovery database. The HTTP User-agent field is set to `NHSEWalker/3.0`, and the From field is also set. This is usually run from `*.mcs.anl.gov`. The Proposed Standard for Robot Exclusion is supported.

WebLinker

Written and run by James Casey at `jcasey@maths.tcd.ie`.

WebLinker is a tool that traverses a section of Web, doing URN->URL conversion. It will be used as a post-processing tool on documents created by automatic converters such as LaTeX2HTML or WebMaker. The HTTP User-agent is set to `WebLinker/0.0 libwww-perl/0.1`.

Emacs-w3 Search Engine

Maintained by William M. Perry at `wmperry@spry.com`.

Emacs-w3 Search Engine's purpose is to generate a Resource Discovery database. The HTTP User-agent field is set to `Emacs-w3/v[0-9\.]+`, and the From field is also set. This is usually run from a variety of machines. The Proposed Standard for Robot Exclusion is not supported.

Arachnophilia

Run by Vince Taluskie at `taluskie@utpapa.ph.utexas.edu`.

Arachnophilia's purpose is to collect approximately 10 K HTML documents for testing automatic abstract generation. This program will honor the robot exclusion standard and wait one minute between requests to a given server. The HTTP User-agent field is set to `Arachnophilia`. This is run from `halsoft.com`.

Mac WWWWorm

Written by Sebastien Lemieux at `lemieuse@ERE.UMontreal.CA`.

Mac WWWWorm is a French keyword-searching robot for the Mac, written in HyperCard. No other information is currently available.

Churl

Maintained by Justin Yunke at `yunke@umich.edu`.

This is a URL-checking robot that stays within one step of the local server.

Tarspider

Run by Olaf Schreck at `chakl@fu-berlin.de`.

This is a mirroring robot. It sets User-agent to `tarspider version` and From to `chakl@fu-berlin.de`.

The Peregrinator

This is run by Jim Richardson `jimr@maths.su.oz.au`.

This robot, written in Perl V4, commenced operation in August 1994 and is being used to generate an index called MathSearch of documents on Web sites connected with mathematics and statistics. It ignores off-site links, so it does not stray from a list of servers specified initially. The HTTP User-agent field is set to `Peregrinator-Mathematics/0.7`. Peregrinator also sets the From field. The Proposed Standard for Robot Exclusion is supported.

Checkbot

Maintained by Hans de Graaff at `j.j.degraaff@twi.tudelft.nl`.

Checkbot's purpose is to validate links. The HTTP User-agent field is set to `checkbot.pl-x.xx`, and the From field is also set. This is usually run from `dutifp.twi.tudelft.nl`. The Proposed Standard for Robot Exclusion is not supported.

Webwalk

Maintained by Rich Testardi at `rpt@fc.hp.com`.

Its purpose is to generate a Resource Discovery database, validate links, validate HTML, perform mirroring, copy document trees, and generate statistics. The HTTP User-agent field is set to `webwalk`, and the From field is also set. The Proposed Standard for Robot Exclusion is supported.

Harvest

Run by hardy@bruno.cs.colorado.edu.

Harvest is a Resource Discovery Robot, part of the Harvest Project. It runs from bruno.cs.colorado.edu and sets User-agent and From fields.

Katipo

Maintained by Michael Newbery at Michael.Newbery@vuw.ac.nz.

The HTTP User-agent field is set to Katipo/1.0, and the From field is also set. The Proposed Standard for Robot Exclusion is not supported.

InfoSeek Robot 1.0

Maintained by Steve Kirsch at stk@infoseek.com.

InfoSeek's purpose is to generate a Resource Discovery database. The HTTP User-agent field is set to InfoSeek Robot 1.0, and the From field is also set. This is usually run from corp-gw.infoseek.com. The Proposed Standard for Robot Exclusion is supported.

GetURL

Maintained by James Burton at burton@cs.latrobe.edu.au.

GetURL's purpose is to validate links, perform mirroring, and copy document trees. The HTTP User-agent field is set to GetURL.rexx v1.05 by burton@cs.latrobe.edu.au, and the From field is not set. The Proposed Standard for Robot Exclusion is not supported.

Open Text Corporation Robot

Run by Tim Bray at tbray@opentext.com.

This sets User-agent to OMW/0.1 libwww/217. The Proposed Standard for Robot Exclusion is supported.

The TkWWW Robot

Implemented by Scott Spetka at scott@cs.sunyit.edu.

TkWWW is designed to search Web neighborhoods to find pages that might be logically related. The robot returns a list of links that looks like a hot list. The search can be by keyword or all links at a distance of one or two hops may be returned.

A Tcl W3 Robot

Maintained by De-mailly at dl@hplyot.obspm.fr.

Tcl W3's purpose is to validate links and generate statistics. The HTTP User-agent field is set to `dlw3robot/x.y`, and the From field is also set. This is usually run from `hplyot.obspm.fr`. The Proposed Standard for Robot Exclusion is supported.

Titan

Maintained by Yoshihiko Hayashi at `hayashi@nttnly.isl.ntt.jp`.

Titan's purpose is to generate a Resource Discovery database and copy document trees. The primary goal is to develop an advanced method for indexing the WWW documents. The HTTP User-agent field is set to `TITAN/0.1`, and the From field is also set. This is usually run from `nttnly.isl.ntt.jp`. The Proposed Standard for Robot Exclusion is supported.

CS-HKUST WWW Index Server

Maintained by Budi Yuwono at `yuwono-b@cs.ust.hk`.

CS-HKUST's purpose is to generate a Resource Discovery database and validate HTML. The HTTP User-agent field is set to `CS-HKUST-IndexServer/1.0`, and the From field is also set. This is usually run from `dbx.cs.ust.hk`. The Proposed Standard for Robot Exclusion is supported.

WizRobot

Maintained by Spry at `info@spry.com`.

WizRobot's purpose is to generate a Resource Discovery database. Neither User-agent nor From HTTP fields are set. This is usually run from `tiger.spry.com`. The Proposed Standard for Robot Exclusion is not supported.

Appendix F

HTML Encyclopedia

This appendix is a reference to the HTML tags you can use in your documents, according to the HTML 2.0 specification. Tags in common use that are either HTML 3.0 or Netscape extensions are noted as such. Note that some browsers other than Netscape may support the Netscape extensions.

> **Note:** A few of the tags in this section have not been described in the body of the book. If a tag is mentioned here that you haven't seen before, don't worry about it; that means that the tag is not in active use or is for use by HTML-generating and -reading tools, and not for general use in HTML documents.

HTML Tags

The following tags are used to create a basic HTML page with text, headings, and lists.

Comments

`<! ... >`

Creates a comment.

Structure Tags

<HTML>...</HTML>

Encloses the entire HTML document.

Can Include: <HEAD> <BODY>

<HEAD>...</HEAD>

Encloses the head of the HTML document.

Can Include: <TITLE> <ISINDEX> <BASE> <NEXTID> <LINK> <META>

Allowed Inside: <HTML>

<BODY>...</BODY>

Encloses the body (text and tags) of the HTML document.

Attributes:

BACKGROUND="..." (HTML 3.0 only) The name or URL for an image to tile on the page background.

BGCOLOR="..." (Netscape 1.1) The color of the page background.

TEXT="..." (Netscape 1.1) The color of the page's text.

LINK="..." (Netscape 1.1) The color of unfollowed links.

ALINK="..." (Netscape 1.1) The color of activated links.

VLINK="..." (Netscape 1.1) The color of followed links.

Can Include: <H1> <H2> <H3> <H4> <H5> <H6> <P> <OL> <UL> <DIR> <MENU> <DL> <PRE> <BLOCKQUOTE> <FORM> <ISINDEX> <HR> <ADDRESS>

Allowed Inside: <HTML>

<BASE>

Indicates the full URL of the current document.

Attributes: HREF="..."; The full URL of this document.

Allowed Inside: <HEAD>

<ISINDEX>

Indicates that this document is a gateway script that allows searches.

Attributes:

PROMPT="..." (HTML 3.0) The prompt for the search field.

Allowed Inside: <BLOCKQUOTE> <BODY> <DD> <FORM> <HEAD> <LI>

<LINK>

Indicates a link between this document and some other document. Generally used only by HTML-generating tools. <LINK> represents document links to this one as a whole, as opposed to <A> which can create multiple links in the document. Not commonly used.

Attributes:

HREF="..." The URL of the document to be linked to this one.

NAME=... If the document is to be considered an anchor, the name of that anchor.

REL="..." The relationship between the linked-to document and the current document, for example, "TOC" or "Glossary."

REV="..." A reverse relationship between the current document and the linked-to document.

URN="..." A Uniform Resource Number (URN), a unique identifier different from the URL in HREF.

TITLE="..." The title of the linked-to document.

METHODS="..." The method with which the document is to be retrieved; for example, FTP, Gopher, and so on.

Allowed Inside: <HEAD>

<META>

Indicates metainformation about this document (information about the document itself); for example, keywords for search engines, special HTTP headers to be used for retrieveing this document, expiration date, and so on. Metainformation is usually in a key/value pair form.

Attributes:

HTTP-EQUIV="..." Creates a new HTTP header field with the same name as the attributes value, for example HTTP-EQUIV=Expires. The value of that header is specified by CONTENT.

NAME=... If meta data is usually in the form of key/value pairs, NAME indicates the key, for example, Author or ID.

CONTENT=... The content of the key/vaue pair (or of the HTTP header indicated by HTTP-EQUIV).

Allowed Inside: <HEAD>

<NEXTID>

Indicates the "next" document to this one (as might be defined by a tool to manage HTML documents in series). <NEXTID> is considered obsolete.

Headings and Title

All heading tags have the following characteristics:

Attributes:

ALIGN=CENTER: (HTML 3.0 only) Centers the heading.

Can Include: <A> <IMG>
 <EM> <STRONG> <CODE> <SAMP> <KBD> <VAR> <CITE> <TT> <B> <I>

Allowed Inside: <BLOCKQUOTE> <BODY> <PRE> <ADDRESS> <FORM> <TH> <TD>

<H1>...</H1>

A first-level heading.

<H2>...</H2>

A second-level heading.

<H3>...</H3>

A third-level heading.

<H4>...</H4>

A fourth-level heading.

<H5>...</H5>

A fifth-level heading.

<H6>...</H6>

A sixth-level heading.

<TITLE>...</TITLE>

Indicates the title of the document.

Allowed Inside: <HEAD>

Paragraphs
\<P>...\</P>

A plain paragraph. The closing tag (`</P>`) is optional.

Attributes:

`ALIGN=CENTER` (HTML 3.0 only) Centers the paragraph.

Can Include: `<A> <IMG> <BR> <EM> <STRONG> <CODE> <SAMP> <KBD> <VAR> <CITE> <TT> <B> <I>`

Allowed Inside: `<BLOCKQUOTE> <BODY> <DD> <FORM> <LI>`

Links
\<A>...\</A>

With the `HREF` attribute, creates a link to another document or anchor; with the `NAME` attribute, creates an anchor which can be linked to.

Attributes:

`HREF="..."` The URL of the document to be linked to this one.

`NAME=...` The name of the anchor.

`REL="..."` The relationship between the linked-to document and the current document, for example, "TOC" or "Glossary." Not commonly used.

`REV="..."` A reverse relationship between the current document and the linked-to document. Not commonly used.

`URN="..."` A Uniform Resource Number (URN), a unique identifier different from the URL in HREF. Not commonly used.

`TITLE="..."` The title of the linked-to document. Not commonly used.

`METHODS="..."` The method with which the document is to be retrieved; for example, FTP, Gopher, and so on. Not commonly used.

Can Include: `<IMG> <BR> <EM> <STRONG> <CODE> <SAMP> <KBD> <VAR> <CITE> <TT> <B> <I>`

Allowed Inside: `<ADDRESS> <B> <CITE> <CODE> <DD> <DT> <EM> <H1> <H2> <H3> <H4> <H5> <H6> <I> <KBD> <LI> <P> <PRE> <SAMP> <STRONG> <TT> <VAR> <TH> TD>`

Lists

<OL>...</OL>

An ordered (numbered) list.

Attributes:

TYPE="..." (Netscape only) The type of numerals to label the list with. Possible values are A, a, I, i, 1.

START="..." (Netscape) The value to start this list with.

Can Include: <LI>

Allowed Inside: <BLOCKQUOTE> <BODY> <DD> <FORM> <LI> <TH> TD>

<UL>...</UL>

An unordered (bulleted) list.

Attributes:

TYPE="..." (Netscape) The bullet dingbat to use to mark list items. Possible values are DISC, CIRCLE, SQUARE.

Can Include: <LI>

Allowed Inside: <BLOCKQUOTE> <BODY> <DD> <FORM> <LI> <TH> TD>

<MENU>...</MENU>

A menu list of items.

Can Include: <LI>

Allowed Inside: <BLOCKQUOTE> <BODY> <DD> <FORM> <LI> <TH> TD>

<DIR>...</DIR>

A directory listing; items are generally smaller than 20 characters.

Can Include: <LI>

Allowed Inside: <BLOCKQUOTE> <BODY> <DD> <FORM> <LI> <TH> TD>

<LI>

A list item for use with <OL>, <UL>, <MENU>, or <DIR>

Attributes:

TYPE="..." (Netscape) The type of bullet or number to label this item with. Possible values are DISC, CIRCLE, SQUARE, A, a, I, i, 1.

VALUE="..." (Netscape) The numeric value this list item should have (affects this item and all below it in <OL> lists).

Can Include: <A> <IMG>
 <EM> <STRONG> <CODE> <SAMP> <KBD> <VAR> <CITE> <TT> <B> <I> <P> <OL> <UL> <DIR> <MENU> <DL> <PRE> <BLOCKQUOTE>

Allowed Inside: <DIR> <MENU> <OL> <UL>

<DL>...</DL>

A definition or glossary list. The COMPACT attribute specifies a formatting that takes less whitespace to present.

Attributes: COMPACT

Can Include: <DT> <DD>

Allowed Inside: <BLOCKQUOTE> <BODY> <DD> <FORM> <LI> <TH> TD>

<DT>

A definition term, as part of a definition list.

Can Include: <A> <IMG>
 <EM> <STRONG> <CODE> <SAMP> <KBD> <VAR> <CITE> <TT> <B> <I>

Allowed Inside: <DL>

<DD>

The corresponding definition to a definition term, as part of a definition list.

Can Include: <A> <IMG>
 <EM> <STRONG> <CODE> <SAMP> <KBD> <VAR> <CITE> <TT> <B> <I> <P> <OL> <UL> <DIR> <MENU> <DL> <PRE> <BLOCKQUOTE> <FORM> <ISINDEX> <TABLE>

Allowed Inside: <DL>

Character Formatting

All the character formatting tags have these features:

Can Include: <A> <IMG>
 <EM> <STRONG> <CODE> <SAMP> <KBD> <VAR> <CITE> <TT> <B> <I>

Allowed Inside: <A> <ADDRESS> <B> <CITE> <CODE> <DD> <DT> <EM> <H1> <H2> <H3> <H4> <H5> <H6> <I> <KBD> <LI> <P> <PRE> <SAMP> <STRONG> <TT> <VAR> <TH> TD>

<EM>...</EM>

Emphasis (usually italic).

<STRONG>...</STRONG>

Stronger emphasis (usually bold).

<CODE>...</CODE>

Code sample (usually Courier).

<KBD>...</KBD>

Text to be typed (usually Courier).

<VAR>...</VAR>

A variable or placeholder for some other value.

<SAMP>...</SAMP>

Sample text.

<DFN>...<DFN>

(Proposed) A definition of a term.

<CITE>...</CITE>

A citation.

<B>...</B>

Boldface text.

<I>...</I>

Italic text.

<TT>...</TT>

Typewriter font.

Other Elements

<HR>

A horizontal rule line.

Attributes:

SIZE="..." (Netscape) The thickness of the rule, in pixels.

`WIDTH="..."` (Netscape) The width of the rule, in pixels.

`ALIGN="..."` (Netscape) How the rule line will be aligned on the page. Possible values are `LEFT`, `RIGHT`, `CENTER`.

`NOSHADE="..."` (Netscape) Causes the rule line to be drawn as a solid black.

Allowed Inside: `<BLOCKQUOTE>` `<BODY>` `<FORM>` `<PRE>`

*
*
A line break.

Attributes:

`CLEAR="..."` (HTML 3.0) Causes the text to stop flowing around any images. Possible values are `RIGHT`, `LEFT`, `ALL`.

Allowed Inside: `<A>` `<ADDRESS>` `<B>` `<CITE>` `<CODE>` `<DD>` `<DT>` `<EM>` `<H1>` `<H2>` `<H3>` `<H4>` `<H5>` `<H6>` `<I>` `<KBD>` `<LI>` `<P>` `<PRE>` `<SAMP>` `<STRONG>` `<TT>` `<VAR>`

<NOBR>...</NOBR> (Netscape)
Causes the enclosed text not to wrap at the edge of the page.

Allowed Inside: `<A>` `<ADDRESS>` `<B>` `<CITE>` `<CODE>` `<DD>` `<DT>` `<EM>` `<H1>` `<H2>` `<H3>` `<H4>` `<H5>` `<H6>` `<I>` `<KBD>` `<LI>` `<P>` `<PRE>` `<SAMP>` `<STRONG>` `<TT>` `<VAR>`

<WBR> (Netscape)
Wrap the text at this point only if necessary.

Allowed Inside: `<A>` `<ADDRESS>` `<B>` `<CITE>` `<CODE>` `<DD>` `<DT>` `<EM>` `<H1>` `<H2>` `<H3>` `<H4>` `<H5>` `<H6>` `<I>` `<KBD>` `<LI>` `<P>` `<PRE>` `<SAMP>` `<STRONG>` `<TT>` `<VAR>`

<BLOCKQUOTE>... </BLOCKQUOTE>
Used for long quotes or citations.

Can Include: `<H1>` `<H2>` `<H3>` `<H4>` `<H5>` `<H6>` `<P>` `<OL>` `<UL>` `<DIR>` `<MENU>` `<DL>` `<PRE>` `<BLOCKQUOTE>` `<FORM>` `<ISINDEX>` `<HR>` `<ADDRESS>` `<TABLE>`

Allowed Inside: `<BLOCKQUOTE>` `<BODY>` `<DD>` `<FORM>` `<LI>` `<TH>` `TD>`

<CENTER>...</CENTER>
All the content enclosed within these tags is centered.

Can Include: `<A>` `<IMG>` `<BR>` `<EM>` `<STRONG>` `<CODE>` `<SAMP>` `<KBD>` `<VAR>` `<CITE>` `<TT>` `<B>` `<I>`

Allowed Inside: `<BLOCKQUOTE>` `<BODY>` `<DD>` `<FORM>` `<LI>` `<TH>` `TD>`

<ADDRESS>...</ADDRESS>

Used for signatures or general information about a document's author.

Can Include: `<A>` `<IMG>` `<BR>` `<EM>` `<STRONG>` `<CODE>` `<SAMP>` `<KBD>` `<VAR>` `<CITE>` `<TT>` `<B>` `<I>`

Allowed Inside: `<BLOCKQUOTE>` `<BODY>` `<FORM>`

<BLINK>...</BLINK> (Netscape)

Causes the enclosed text to blink irritatingly.

Font Sizes (Netscape)

<FONT>...</FONT>

Changes the size of the font for the enclosed text.

Attributes:

`SIZE="..."` The size of the font, from 1 to 7. Default is 3. Can also be specified as a value relative to the current size, for example, +2.

Can Include: `<A>` `<IMG>` `<BR>` `<EM>` `<STRONG>` `<CODE>` `<SAMP>` `<KBD>` `<VAR>` `<CITE>` `<TT>` `<B>` `<I>`

Allowed Inside: `<A>` `<ADDRESS>` `<B>` `<CITE>` `<CODE>` `<DD>` `<DT>` `<EM>` `<H1>` `<H2>` `<H3>` `<H4>` `<H5>` `<H6>` `<I>` `<KBD>` `<LI>` `<P>` `<PRE>` `<SAMP>` `<STRONG>` `<TT>` `<VAR>`

<BASEFONT>

Sets the default size of the font for the current page.

Attributes:

`SIZE="..."` The default size of the font, from 1 to 7. Default is 3.

Allowed Inside: `<A>` `<ADDRESS>` `<B>` `<CITE>` `<CODE>` `<DD>` `<DT>` `<EM>` `<H1>` `<H2>` `<H3>` `<H4>` `<H5>` `<H6>` `<I>` `<KBD>` `<LI>` `<P>` `<PRE>` `<SAMP>` `<STRONG>` `<TT>` `<VAR>`

Images

<IMG>

Insert an inline image into the document.

Attributes:

`ISMAP` This image is a clickable image map.

SRC="..." The URL of the image.

ALT="..." A text string that will be displayed in browsers that cannot support images.

ALIGN="..." Determines the alignment of the given image. If LEFT or RIGHT (HTML 3.0, Netscape), the image is aligned to the left or right column, and all following text flows beside that image. All other values such as TOP, MIDDLE, BOTTOM, or the Netscape only (TEXTTOP, ABSMIDDLE, BASELINE, ABSBOTTOM), determine the vertical alignment of this image with other items in the same line.

VSPACE="..." The space between the image and the text above or below it.

HSPACE="..." The space between the image and the text to its left or right.

WIDTH="..." (HTML 3.0) The width, in pixels, of the image. If WIDTH is not the actual width, the image is scaled to fit.

HEIGHT="..." (HTML 3.0) The width, in pixels, of the image. If HEIGHT is not the actual height, the image is scaled to fit.

BORDER="..." (Netscape only) Draws a border of the specified value in pixels to be drawn around the image. In the case of images that are also links, BORDER changes the size of the default link border.

LOWSRC="..." (Netscape only) The path or URL of an image that will be loaded first, before the image specified in SRC. The value of LOWSRC is usually a smaller or lower resolution version of the actual image.

Allowed Inside: <A> <ADDRESS> <B> <CITE> <CODE> <DD> <DT> <EM> <H1> <H2> <H3> <H4> <H5> <H6> <I> <KBD> <LI> <P> <SAMP> <STRONG> <TT> <VAR>

Forms

<FORM>...</FORM>

Indicates a form.

Attributes:

ACTION="..." The URL of the script to process this form input.

METHOD="..." How the form input will be sent to the gateway on the server side. Possible values are GET and POST.

ENCTYPE="..." Only one value right now: application/x-www-form-urlencoded.

Can Include: <H1> <H2> <H3> <H4> <H5> <H6> <P> <OL> <UL> <DIR> <MENU> <DL> <PRE> <BLOCKQUOTE> <ISINDEX> <TABLE> <HR> <ADDRESS> <INPUT> <SELECT> <TEXTAREA>

Allowed Inside: <BLOCKQUOTE> <BODY> <DD> <LI> <TH> <TD>

<INPUT>

An input widget for a form.

Attributes:

TYPE="..." The type for this input widget. Possible values are CHECKBOX, HIDDEN, RADIO, RESET, SUBMIT, TEXT, or IMAGE.

NAME="..." The name of this item, as passed to the gateway script as part of a name/value pair.

VALUE="..." For a text or hidden widget, the default value; for a check box or radio button, the value to be submitted with the form; for Reset or Submit buttons, the label for the button itself.

SRC="..." The source file for an image.

CHECKED For checkboxes and radio buttons, indicates that the widget is checked.

SIZE="..." The size, in characters, of a text widget.

MAXLENGTH="..." The maximum number of characters that can be entered into a text widget.

ALIGN="..." For images in forms, determines how the text and image will align (same as with the <IMG> tag).

Allowed Inside: <FORM>

<TEXTAREA>...</TEXTAREA>

Indicates a multiline text entry widget.

Attributes:

NAME="..." The name to be passed to the gateway script as part of the name/value pair.

ROWS="..." The number of rows this text area displays.

COLS="..." The number of columns (characters) this text area displays.

Allowed inside: <FORM>

<SELECT>...</SELECT>

Creates a menu or scrolling list of possible items.

Attributes:

NAME="..." The name that is passed to the gateway script as part of the name/value pair.

SIZE="..." The number of elements to display. If SIZE is indicated, the selection becomes a scrolling list. If no SIZE is given, the selection is a pop-up menu.

MULTIPLE Allows multiple selections from the list.

Can Include: <OPTION>

Allowed Inside: <FORM>

<OPTION>

Indicates a possible item within a <SELECT> widget.

Attributes:

SELECTED With this attribute included, the <OPTION> will be selected by default in the list.

VALUE="..." The value to submit if this <OPTION> is selected when the form is submitted.

Allowed Inside: <SELECT>

<FRAMESET>...<FRAMESET> (Netscape 2.0 and up)

The main container for a frame document.

Attributes:

COLS="column_width_list" The size of the frame's columns in pixels, percentages, or relative scale.

ROWS="row_height_list" The size of the frame's rows in pixels, percentages, or relative scale.

<FRAMES> (Netscape 2.0 and up)

Attributes:

MARGINHEIGHT="value" The height of the frame, in pixels.

MARGINWIDTH="value" The width of the frame, in pixels.

NAME="window_name" Naming the frame enables it for targeting by link in other documents. (Optional)

NORESIZE A flag to denote the frame cannot be resized.

SCROLLING="yes¦no¦auto" Indicates (*yes/no/auto*) whether a frame has scrollbars.

SRC The URL of the document displayed in the frame.

<NOFRAMES>...<NOFRAMES> (Netscape 2.0 and up)

Creates frames that can be viewed by non-frame browsers only. A frames-capable browser ignores the data between the start and end <NOFRAMES> tags.

Tables (HTML 3.0)

<TABLE>...</TABLE>

Creates a table, which can contain a caption (<CAPTION>) and any number of rows (<TR>).

Attributes:

BORDER="..." Indicates whether the table should be drawn with or without a border. In Netscape, BORDER can also have a value indicating the width of the border.

CELLSPACING="..." (Netscape only) The amount of space between the cells in the table.

CELLPADDING="..." (Netscape only) The amount of space between the edges of the cell and its contents.

WIDTH="..." (Netscape only) The width of the table on the page, in either exact pixel values or as a percentage of page width.

Can Include: <CAPTION> <TR>

Allowed Inside: <BLOCKQUOTE> <BODY> <DD> <LI> <FORM>

<CAPTION>...</CAPTION>

The caption for the table.

Attributes:

ALIGN="..." The position of the caption. Possible values are TOP and BOTTOM.

<TR>...</TR>

Defines a table row, containing headings and data (<TR> and <TH> tags).

Attributes:

ALIGN="..." The horizontal alignment of the contents of the cells within this row. Possible values are LEFT, RIGHT, CENTER.

VALIGN="..." The vertical alignment of the contents of the cells within this row. Possible values are TOP, MIDDLE, BOTTOM, and BASELINE (Netscape only).

Can Include: <TH> <TD>

Allowed Inside: <TABLE>

<TH>...</TH>

Defines a table heading cell.

Attributes:

ALIGN="..." The horizontal alignment of the contents of the cell. Possible values are LEFT, RIGHT, CENTER.

VALIGN="..." The vertical alignment of the contents of the cell. Possible values are TOP, MIDDLE, BOTTOM, and BASELINE (Netscape only).

ROWSPAN="..." The number of rows this cell will span.

COLSPAN="..." The number of columns this cell will span.

NOWRAP Do not automatically wrap the contents of this cell.

WIDTH="..." (Netscape only) The width of this column of cells, in exact pixel values or as a percentage of the table width.

Can Include: <H1> <H2> <H3> <H4> <H5> <H6> <P> <OL> <UL> <DIR> <MENU> <DL> <PRE> <BLOCKQUOTE> <FORM> <ISINDEX> <HR> <ADDRESS> <TABLE>

Allowed Inside: <TR>

<TD>...</TD>

Defines a table data cell.

Attributes:

ALIGN="..." The horizontal alignment of the contents of the cell. Possible values are LEFT, RIGHT, CENTER.

VALIGN="..." The vertical alignment of the contents of the cell. Possible values are TOP, MIDDLE, BOTTOM, and BASELINE (Netscape only).

ROWSPAN="..." The number of rows this cell will span.

COLSPAN="..." The number of columns this cell will span.

NOWRAP Do not automatically wrap the contents of this cell.

WIDTH="..." (Netscape only) The width of this column of cells, in exact pixel values or as a percentage of the table width.

Can Include: <H1> <H2> <H3> <H4> <H5> <H6> <P> <OL> <UL> <DIR> <MENU> <DL> <PRE> <BLOCKQUOTE> <FORM> <ISINDEX> <HR> <ADDRESS> <TABLE>

Allowed Inside: <TR>

Internet Explorer 2.0 Tags

<BODY>

You can add `BGPROPERTIES=FIXED` to the `<BODY>` tag to get a nonscrolling background. `<BODY BACKGROUND="`*`mybackground.gif`*`" BGPROPERTIES=FIXED>`

<TABLE>

Internet Explorer 2.0 fully supports tables as specified in the HTML 3.0 draft standard. Using the `ALIGN=RIGHT` or `ALIGN=LEFT` attributes, you can set the alignment of your tables. Using the `BGCOLOR=#`*`nnnnnn`* attribute, you can specify a different color for each cell in a table.

<IMG>

You can add video clips (.AVI files) to your pages with a string of new attributes to the `<IMG>` tag, most notably the dynamic source feature, `DYNSRC=`*`URL`*. You can integrate video clips in such a way as to not exclude viewers without video-enabled browsers. If your browser supports inline clips, you see the video; if not, you see a still image.`<IMG SRC="earth.gif" DYNSRC="spinearht.avi">`

You can use `START=FILEOPEN` or `START=MOUSEOVER` and a variety of `LOOP` commands to gauge when and for how long the clip is played.

<BGSOUND>

You can now use soundtracks for your web pages. Samples or MIDI formats are accepted. `<BGSOUND SRC="whistle.wav">`

You can use `LOOP` features to specify the repetition of the background sound.

<MARQUEE>

As you might guess, this new tag offers your pages a scrolling text marquee. Your text can appear using different attributes, such as `ALIGN=RIGHT` and can have behaviors of `SLIDE`, `SCROLL` (the default), and `ALTERNATE`.`<MARQUEE ALIGN=MIDDLE>Buy Low, Sell High!<MARQUEE>`

Character Entities

Table F.1 contains the possible numeric and character entities for the ISO-Latin-1 (ISO8859-1) character set. Where possible, the character is shown.

Note: Not all browsers can display all characters, and some browsers may even display different characters from those that appear in the table. Newer browsers seem to have a better track record for handling character entities, but be sure and test your HTML files extensively with multiple browsers if you intend to use these entities.

Table F.1. ISO-Latin-1 character set.

Character	Numeric Entity	Character Entity (if any)	Description
	&#00;–&#08;		Unused
				Horizontal tab

	
		Line feed

	&#11;–&#31;		Unused
	 		Space
!	!		Exclamation mark
"	"	"	Quotation mark
#	#		Number sign
$	$		Dollar sign
%	%		Percent sign
&	&	&	Ampersand
'	'		Apostrophe
(	(		Left parenthesis
)	)		Right parenthesis
*	*		Asterisk
+	+		Plus sign
,	,		Comma
-	-		Hyphen
.	.		Period (fullstop)
/	/		Solidus (slash)
0–9	0–9		Digits 0–9
:	:		Colon
;	;		Semi-colon
<	<	<	Less than
=	=		Equals sign

continues

Table F.1. continued

Character	Numeric Entity	Character Entity (if any)	Description
>	&#62;	&gt;	Greater than
?	&#63;		Question mark
@	&#64;		Commercial at
A–Z	A–Z		Letters A–Z
[	&#91;		Left square bracket
\	&#92;		Reverse solidus (backslash)
]	&#93;		Right square bracket
^	&#94;		Caret
—	&#95;		Horizontal bar
`	&#96;		Grave accent
a–z	a–z		Letters a–z
{	&#123;		Left curly brace
|	&#124		Vertical bar
}	&#125;		Right curly brace
~	&#126;		Tilde
	&#127;–		Unused
¡	&#161;		Inverted exclamation
¢	&#162;		Cent sign
£	&#163;		Pound sterling
¤	&#164;		General currency sign
¥	&#165;		Yen sign
¦	&#166;		Broken vertical bar
§	&#167;		Section sign
¨	&#168;		Umlaut (dieresis)
©	&#169;		Copyright
ª	&#170;		Feminine ordinal
‹	&#171;		Left angle quote, guillemet left

Character	Numeric Entity	Character Entity (if any)	Description
¬	&#172;		Not sign
-	&#173;		Soft hyphen
®	&#174;		Registered trade mark
¯	&#175;		Macron accent
°	&#176;		Degree sign
±	&#177;		Plus or minus
²	&#178;		Superscript two
³	&#179;		Superscript three
´	&#180;		Acute accent
µ	&#181;		Micro sign
¶	&#182;		Paragraph sign
·	&#183;		Middle dot
¸	&#184;		Cedilla
¹	&#185;		Superscript one
º	&#186;		Masculine ordinal
›	&#187;		Right angle quote, guillemet right
1/4	&#188;		Fraction one-fourth
1/2	&#189;		Fraction one-half
3/4	&#190;		Fraction three-fourths
¿	&#191;		Inverted question mark
À	&#192;	&Agrave;	Capital A, grave accent
Á	&#193;	&Aacute;	Capital A, acute accent
Â	&#194;	&Acirc;	Capital A, circum flex accent
Ã	&#195;	&Atilde;	Capital A, tilde

continues

Table F.1. continued

Character	Numeric Entity	Character Entity (if any)	Description
Ä	&#196;	&Auml;	Capital A, dieresis or umlaut mark
Å	&#197;	&Aring;	Capital A, ring
Æ	&#198;	&AElig;	Capital AE dipthong (ligature)
Ç	&#199;	&Ccedil;	Capital C, cedilla
È	&#200;	&Egrave;	Capital E, grave accent
É	&#201;	&Eacute;	Capital E, acute accent
Ê	&#202;	&Ecirc;	Capital E, circum flex accent
Ë	&#203;	&Euml;	Capital E, dieresis or umlaut mark
Ì	&#204;	&Igrave;	Capital I, grave accent
Í	&#205;	&Iacute;	Capital I, acute accent
Î	&#206;	&Icirc;	Capital I, circumflex accent
Ï	&#207;	&Iuml;	Capital I, dieresis or umlaut mark
Ð	&#208;	&ETH;	Capital Eth, Icelandic
Ñ	&#209;	&Ntilde;	Capital N, tilde
Ò	&#210;	&Ograve;	Capital O, grave accent
Ó	&#211;	&Oacute;	Capital O, acute accent
Ô	&#212;	&Ocirc;	Capital O, circum flex accent

Character	Numeric Entity	Character Entity (if any)	Description
Õ	&#213;	&Otilde;	Capital O, tilde
Ö	&#214;	&Ouml;	Capital O, dieresis or umlaut mark
×	&#215;		Multiply sign
Ø	&#216;	&Oslash;	Capital O, slash
Ù	&#217;	&Ugrave;	Capital U, grave accent
Ú	&#218;	&Uacute;	Capital U, acute accent
Û	&#219;	&Ucirc;	Capital U, circum flex accent
Ü	&#220;	&Uuml;	Capital U, dieresis or umlaut mark
Ý	&#221;	&Yacute;	Capital Y, acute accent
Þ	&#222;	&THORN;	Capital THORN, Icelandic
β	&#223;	&szlig;	Small sharp s, German (sz ligature)
à	&#224;	&agrave;	Small a, grave accent
á	&#225;	&aacute;	Small a, acute accent
â	&#226;	&acirc;	Small a, circumflex accent
ã	&#227;	&atilde;	Small a, tilde
ä	&#228;	&aauml;	Small a, dieresis or umlaut mark
å	&#229;	&aring;	Small a, ring
æ	&#230;	&aelig;	Small ae dipthong (ligature)

continues

Table F.1. continued

Character	Numeric Entity	Character Entity (if any)	Description
ç	&#231;	&ccedil;	Small c, cedilla
è	&#232;	&egrave;	Small e, grave accent
é	&#233;	&eacute;	Small e, acute accent
ê	&#234;	&ecirc;	Small e, circumflex accent
ë	&#235;	&euml;	Small e, dieresis or umlaut mark
ì	&#236;	&igrave;	Small i, grave accent
í	&#237;	&iacute;	Small i, acute accent
î	&#238;	&icirc;	Small i, circumflex accent
ï	&#239;	&iuml;	Small i, dieresis or umlaut mark
ð	&#240;	&eth;	Small eth, Icelandic
ñ	&#241;	&ntilde;	Small n, tilde
ò	&#242;	&ograve;	Small o, grave accent
ó	&#243;	&oacute;	Small o, acute accent
ô	&#244;	&ocirc;	Small o, circumflex accent
õ	&#245;	&otilde;	Small o, tilde
ö	&#246;	&ouml;	Small o, dieresis or umlaut mark
÷	&#247;		Division sign
ø	&#248;	&oslash;	Small o, slash
ù	&#249;	&ugrave;	Small u, grave accent
ú	&#250;	&uacute;	Small u, acute accent
û	&#251;	&ucirc;	Small u, circumflex accent

Character	Numeric Entity	Character Entity (if any)	Description
ü	&#252;	&uuml;	Small u, dieresis or umlaut mark
ý	&#253;	&yacute;	Small y, acute accent
þ	&#254;	&thorn;	Small thorn, Icelandic
ÿ	&#255;	&yuml;	Small y, dieresis or umlaut mark

Appendix G

Windows CGI 1.2 Interface

- Introduction
- Launching the CGI program
- Command Line
- Launch Method
- CGI Data File
- Example of Form Decoding
- CGI Results Processing
- Reference Code Example

Introduction

This document describes the implementation of CGI support with a typical Windows program (as opposed to running the CGI program in a DOS virtual machine or a console mode shell).

Windows has no native command interpreter. Therefore, any back end must be an executable program. A goal is to keep the interface simple and minimize back-end programming requirements. Therefore, a file-based interface has been chosen (as opposed to DDE or OLE). Request content is placed into a content file, and results must be written to an output file.

It is expected that many of the CGI applications will be developed using Microsoft Visual Basic (VB). VB supports generation of a .EXE file, and supports a wide range of features for accessing data in the Windows environment, such as OLE, DDE, Sockets, and ODBC. The latter permits accessing data in a variety of databases, relational and non-relational. The VB application can be developed without the need for any windows (forms), consisting purely of VB code modules. This makes it possible to meet the recommendation that the CGI program execute invisibly, or at least as an icon.

Eventually, it is hoped that this interface will be standardized among Windows-based HTTP servers. Several other servers in development at this time will be supporting Windows CGI.

Launching the CGI Program

The server uses the `CreateProcess()` service to launch the CGI program. The server maintains synchronization with the CGI program so it can detect when the CGI program exits. This is done using the Win32 `WaitForSingleObject()` service, waiting for the CGI process handle to become signalled, indicating program exit.

Command Line

The server must execute a CGI program request by doing a `CreateProcess()` with a command line in the following form:

```
WinCGI-exe cgi-data-file
```

WinCGI-exe

The complete path to the CGI program executable. The server does not depend on the "current directory" or the PATH environment variable. Note that the "executable" need not be a .EXE file. It may be a document, provided an "association" with a corresponding executable has been established in either WIN.INI or the System Registry (preferred).

```
cgi-data-file
```

The complete path to the CGI data file.

> **Note:** Earlier editions of this specification showed additional command-line arguments (the content and output filenames and any URL arguments). Due to limitations on the length of the command line imposed by the WOW (16-bit emulator) subsystem on Windows NT, and the Windows 95 system itself, it is recommended that servers no longer include these arguments on the command line. These data items are present in the CGI data file, therefore their presence on the command line is redundant.

Launch Method

The server issues the `CreateProcess()` such that the process being launched has its main window hidden.

The launched process itself should not cause the appearance of a window nor a change in the Z-order of the windows on the desktop.

The server supports a CGI program/script debugging mode. If that mode is enabled, the CGI program is launched such that its window shows and is made active. This can assist in debugging CGI applications.

The CGI Data File

The Windows server passes data to its back end via a Windows "private profile" file, in key-value format. The CGI program may then use the standard Windows API services for enumerating and retrieving the key-value pairs in the data file.

The CGI data file contains the following sections:

- [CGI]
- [Accept]
- [System]
- [Extra Headers]
- [Form Literal]
- [Form External]
- [Form Huge]

The [CGI] Section

This section contains most of the CGI data items (accept types, content, and extra headers are defined in separate sections). Each item is provided as a string value. If the value is an empty string, the keyword is omitted. The keywords are listed below:

Request Protocol

The name and revision of the information protocol this request came in with. Format: protocol/revision. Example: "HTTP/1.0."

Request Method

The method with which the request was made. For HTTP, this is GET, HEAD, POST, etc.

Executable Path

The logical path to the CGI program executable, as needed for self-referencing URLs.

Logical Path

A request may specify a path to a resource needed to complete that request. This path may be in a logical pathname space. This item contains the pathname exactly as received by the server, without logical-to-physical translation.

Physical Path

If the request contained logical path information, the server provides the path in physical form, in the native object (e.g., file) access syntax of the operating system.

Query String

The information which follows the ? in the URL that generated the request is the "query" information. The server furnishes this to the back end whenever it is present on the request URL, without any decoding or translation.

Referer

The URL of the document that contained the link pointing to this CGI program. Note that in some browsers the implementation of this is broken, and cannot be relied on.

From

The e-mail address of the browser user. Note that this is in the HTTP specification but is not implemented in some browsers due to privacy concerns.

Content Type

For requests which have attached data this is the MIME content type of that data. Format: type/subtype.

Content Length

For requests that have attached data, this is the length of the content in bytes.

Content File

For requests that have attached data, the server makes the data available to the CGI program by putting it into this file. The value of this item is the complete pathname of that file.

Server Software

The name and version of the information server software answering the request (and running the CGI program). Format: name/version.

Server Name

The network host name or alias of the server, as needed for self-referencing URLs. This (in combination with the ServerPort) could be used to manufacture a full URL to the server for URL fixups.

Server Port

The network port number on which the server is listening. This is also needed for self-referencing URLs.

Server Admin

The e-mail address of the server's administrator. This is used in error messages, and might be used to send MAPI mail to the administrator or to form "mailto:" URLs in generated documents.

CGI Version

The revision of the CGI specification to which this server complies. Format: CGI/revision. For this version, "CGI/1.2 (Win)."

Remote Host

The network host name of the client (requestor) system, if available. This item is used for logging.

Remote Address

The network (IP) address of the client (requestor) system. This item is used for logging if the host name is not available.

Authentication Method

If execution of the CGI program is protected, this is the protocol-specific authentication method used to authenticate the user.

Authentication Realm

If execution of the CGI program is protected, this is the method-specific authentication realm used to authenticate the user. The list of users for the given realm is checked for authentication.

Authenticated Username

If execution of the CGI program is protected, this is the username (in the indicated realm) that the client used to authenticate for access to the CGI program.

The [Accept] Section

This section contains the client's acceptable data types found in the request header as

Accept: type/subtype {parameters}

If the parameters (e.g., "q=0.100") are present, they are passed as the value of the item. If there are no parameters, the value is "Yes."

> **Note:** The accept types may easily be enumerated by the CGI program with a call to `GetPrivateProfileString()` with `NULL` for the key name. This returns all of the keys in the section as a null-delimited string with a double-null terminator.

The [System] Section

This section contains items that are specific to the Windows implementation of CGI. The following keys are used.

GMT Offset

(New in 1.2.) The number of seconds to be added to GMT time to reach local time. For Pacific Standard time, this number is -28,800. Useful for computing GMT times.

Debug Mode

This is "No" unless the server's "CGI/script tracing" mode is enabled, then it is "Yes." Useful for providing conditional tracing within the CGI program.

Output File

The full path/name of the file in which the server expects to receive the CGI program's results.

Content File

The full path/name of the file that contains the content (if any) that came with the request.

The [Extra Headers] Section

This section contains the "extra" headers that were included with the request, in "key=value" form.

> **Note:** The extra headers may easily be enumerated by the CGI program with a call to GetPrivateProfileString() with NULL for the key name. This returns all of the keys in the section as a null-delimited string with a double-null terminator.

The [Form Literal] Section

If the request is an HTTP POST from an HTTP form (with content type of "application/x-www-form-urlencoded"), the server will decode the form data and put it into the [Form Literal] section.

Raw form input is of the form "key=value&key=value&...," with the value parts in url-encoded format. The server splits the "key=value" pairs at the '&', then splits the key and value at the '=', url-decodes the value string and puts the result into "key=(decoded)value" form in the [Form Literal] section.

If the form contains any SELECT MULTIPLE elements, there will be multiple occurrences of the same key. In this case, the server generates a normal "key=value" pair for the first occurrence, and it appends a sequence number to subsequent occurrences. It is up to the CGI program to know about this possibility and to properly recognize the tagged keys.

The [Form External] Section

If the decoded value string is more than 254 characters long, or if the decoded value string contains any control characters or double-quotes, the server puts the decoded value into an external tempfile and lists the field in the [Form External] section as

```
key=pathname length
```

where *pathname* is the path and name of the tempfile containing the decoded value string, and *length* is the length in bytes of the decoded value string.

> **Note:** Be sure to open this file in binary mode unless you are certain that the form data is text!

The [Form Huge] Section

If the raw value string is more than 65,535 bytes long, the server does no decoding, but it does get the keyword and mark the location and size of the value in the Content File. The server lists the huge field in the [Form Huge] section as

```
key=offset length
```

where `offset` is the offset from the beginning of the Content File at which the raw value string for this key is located, and `length` is the length in bytes of the raw value string. You can use the offset to perform a "Seek" to the start of the raw value string, and use the length to know when you have read the entire raw string into your decoder. Note: Be sure to open this file in binary mode unless you are certain that the form data is text!

Example of Form Decoding

In the following sample, the form contains a small field, a SELECT MULTIPLE with 2 small selections, a field with 300 characters in it, one with line breaks (a text area), and a 230KB field.

```
[Form Literal]
smallfield=123 Main St. #122
multiple=first selection
multiple_1=second selection

[Form External]
field300chars=C:\TEMP\HS19AF6C.000 300
fieldwithlinebreaks=C:\TEMP\HS19AF6C.001 43

[Form Huge]
field230K=C:\TEMP\HS19AF6C.002 276920
```

Results Processing

The CGI program returns its results to the server as a data stream representing (directly or indirectly) the goal of the request. The server is responsible for "packaging" the data stream according to HTTP, and for using HTTP to transport the data stream to the requesting client. This means that the server normally adds the needed HTTP headers to the CGI program's results.

The data stream consists of two parts: the header and the body. The header consists of one or more lines of text, and is separated from the body by a blank line. The body contains MIME-conforming data whose content type must be reflected in the header.

The server does not interpret or modify the body in any way. It is essential that the client receive exactly the data that was generated by the back end.

Special Header Lines

The server recognizes the following header lines in the results data stream.

Content-Type:

Indicates that the body contains data of the specified MIME content type. The value must be a MIME content type/subtype.

Status:

Indicates that the server is to return the specified status. The value must be a status indication appropriate for HTTP. Note that the CGI program is responsible for generating a Status value that is legal for that protocol.

If the CGI program's response does not contain a Status: header, the server assumes that the CGI operation succeeded normally, and generates a "200 OK" status.

`URI: <value> (value enclosed in angle brackets)`

The value is either a full URL or a local file reference, either of which points to an object to be returned to the client in lieu of the body (which the server shall ignore in this type of result). If the value is a local file, the server sends it as the results of the request, as though the client issued a GET for that object. If the value is a full URL, the server returns a "401 redirect" to the client to retrieve the specified object directly.

Location:

Same as URI, but this form is now deprecated. The value must not be enclosed in angle brackets with this form.

Other Headers

Any other headers in the result stream are passed (unmodified) by the server to the client. It is the responsibility of the CGI program to avoid including headers that clash with those used by HTTP.

Direct Return

The server provides for the back end to return its results directly to the client, bypassing the server's "packaging" of the data stream for its information protocol. In this case, it is the responsibility of the CGI program to generate a complete message packaged for HTTP.

The server looks at the results in the Output file, and if the first line starts with "HTTP/1.0," it assumes that the results contain a complete HTTP response, and sends the results to the client without packaging.

Examples

■ The following example represents a response made by a CGI program that was invoked by an HTTP server, and consists of an HTML-formatted body:

```
--- BEGIN ---
Content-type: text/html          <== MIME type of body
Status: 200 OK                   <== HTTP status (optional)
                                 <== Header-body separator
<HTML>                           <== Body starts here
<HEAD>
<TITLE>Sample Document</TITLE>
</HEAD>
<BODY>
<H1>Sample Document</H1>
[... etc.]
</BODY>
<HTML>
--- END ---
```

■ This example represents a redirection response, where the server is to direct the client to fetch the object indicated by the URL (using FTP):

```
--- BEGIN ---
Location: ftp://ftp.netcom.com/pub/www/object.dat  <== URL of object
                                                   <== Blank line
--- END ---
```

■ This example represents a direct-return response from a CGI program that was invoked by an HTTP server, where the results contain a complete HTTP response:

```
-- BEGIN ---
HTTP/1.0 200 OK                        <== Start of HTTP Header
Date: Tuesday, 31-May-94 19:04:30 GMT
Server: WebSite 2.0
MIME-version: 1.0
Content-type: text/html
Last-modified: Sunday, 15-May-94 02:12:32 GMT
Content-length: 4109
                                 <== Header-body separator
<HTML> <HEAD>
<TITLE>A document</TITLE>
[... etc.]
--- END ---
```

Reference Code Example

This section contains a reference example that shows, in Visual Basic, how a CGI programmer can enumerate the keys in a CGI Data File section, and get their values.

Enumerating CGI Keys and Values

The following Visual Basic example shows how to enumerate the keys in a section and fetch the key-value pairs into a user-defined structure. Note that the declaration of GetPrivateProfileString() differs from that normally seen in VB programs. The difference is compatible, and allows enumeration by passing NULL for the key name. A '\' at the end of a line indicates continuation. The code must actually be all on one line.

```
Declare Function GetPrivateProfileString Lib "Kernel" \
        (ByVal lpSection As String, \
         ByVal lpKeyName As Any, \          <== This permits NULL key name
         ByVal lpDefault As String, \
         ByVal lpReturnedString As String, \
         ByVal nSize As Integer, \
         ByVal lpFileName As String) As Integer

Type Tuple                      ' Used for Accept: and "extra" headers
    Key As String               ' and for holding POST form key=value pairs
    value As String
End Type

Global CGI_ProfileFile as String                ' Pathname of CGI Data File
Global CGIAcceptTypes(MAX_ACCTYPE) as Tuple     ' Accept: types array
Global CGINumAcceptTypes as Integer             ' Number of Accept: types in array

Const ENUM_BUF_SIZE 8192                         ' Size of key enumeration buffer

'--------------------------------------------------------------------
'
'   GetProfile() - Get a value or enumerate keys in CGI_Data file
'
' Get a value given the section and key, or enumerate keys given the
' section name and "" for the key. If enumerating, the list of keys for
' the given section is returned as a null-separated string, with a
' double null at the end.
'
' VB handles this with flair! I couldn't believe my eyes when I tried this.
'--------------------------------------------------------------------
Private Function GetProfile (sSection As String, sKey As String) As String
    Dim retLen As Integer
    Dim buf As String * ENUM_BUF_SIZE

    If sKey <> "" Then
        retLen = GetPrivateProfileString(sSection, sKey, "", buf, ENUM_BUF_SIZE,
CGI_ProfileFile)
    Else
        retLen = GetPrivateProfileString(sSection, 0&, "", buf, ENUM_BUF_SIZE,
CGI_ProfileFile)
    End If
    If retLen = 0 Then
        GetProfile = ""
    Else
        GetProfile = Left$(buf, retLen)
    End If

End Function

'--------------------------------------------------------------------
'
'   GetAcceptTypes() - Create the array of accept type structs
'
' Enumerate the keys in the [Accept] section of the profile file,
' then get the value for each of the keys.
'--------------------------------------------------------------------
```

```
Private Sub GetAcceptTypes ()
    Dim sList As String
    Dim i As Integer, j As Integer, l As Integer, n As Integer

    sList = GetProfile("Accept", "")        ' Get key list
    l = Len(sList)                          ' Length incl. trailing null
    i = 1                                   ' Start at 1st character
    n = 0                                   ' Index in array
    Do While ((i < l) And (n < MAX_ACCTYPE))' Safety stop here
        j = InStr(i, sList, Chr$(0))        ' J -> next null
        CGI_AcceptTypes(n).Key = Mid$(sList, i, j - i) ' Get Key, then value
        CGI_AcceptTypes(n).value = GetProfile("Accept", CGI_AcceptTypes(n).Key)
        i = j + 1                           ' Bump pointer
        n = n + 1                           ' Bump array index
    Loop
    CGI_NumAcceptTypes = n                  ' Fill in global count

End Sub
```

Appendix H

What's on the CD-ROM

About Shareware

Before telling you about all the great software on the CD, we'll take a moment to tell you how it is possible that software worth hundreds of dollars can be included with a book costing much less than a hundred dollars. This would not be possible without the wonderful concept of shareware.

Anyone who has ever tried to write a computer program knows it is a complex undertaking. This is especially true when you consider all the features that modern software must have before many users will even consider trying it. As if the development process isn't tough enough, packaging, marketing, and distributing the program becomes another roadblock to the success of the software venture.

When you stop and think about it, you realize it is pretty amazing that the shareware concept solves all of these problems. Shareware is a *win-win* deal for both the developer and the user. Developers can concentrate on writing new code (which is what they usually do best), without having to worry about software packaging and distribution issues, and users can try the software for free before they decide if it fits their needs. That's not something you can easily do with shrink-wrap software.

But don't be fooled. Shareware is not free! First of all, if a package is free, it will be clearly labeled as *freeware*, not shareware. Second, if the shareware author has taken time to develop a program, with the hope that others will find it useful, he will have no incentive to enhance the program if nobody agrees to pay the registration fee. In other words, the user will lose out on a lot more than a few dollars because the program will age and cease to be compatible with other new technologies that will inevitably come along.

Shareware registration fees are trivial—frequently between $10 and $60 (much less than commercial software, and often of equal or greater quality). If you decide that a shareware program is convenient, you are expected to follow the registration instructions that come with the package. You will get several benefits in return, depending on what the author states in the license.txt file. It usually includes a printed copy of the user's guide and a new version of the program that doesn't constantly prompt you with the reminder to register.

Unlike many software developers, shareware authors like to hear from their customers directly. You can usually reach them by e-mail, on the Web, or on a relevant listserver or newsgroup. Keep in mind, however, they justifiably like to hear from paying customers the most.

Installation Notes

On the CD you will find all the sample files that have been presented in this book, along with all the applications and utilities needed to set up your site. Although this book is aimed at Windows NT running on the iX86 processor, you will also find versions for the Alpha, MIPS, and Power PC of those applications that support those platforms.

This appendix contains a listing of the files contained on the CD, and their location. Unless other instructions are given in the book, install each application by expanding the file to a temp directory. You will find that some files (the ones with a *.exe extension) are self-extracting archives, whereas others (with a *.zip extension) need an unzip utility for extraction. We have included a shareware application called WinZip.

After a package has been decompressed from the CD to your temp directory, many of the programs include a setup program. You can run the setup program from the temp directory. It will guide you through the steps necessary to finish installing the software. Then you can delete the files in the temp directory. You can always reinstall the software from the CD-ROM if necessary.

\wck\client

14manual.exe	Eudora e-mail client users manual in MS Word format.
Eudor152.exe	Eudora e-mail client.
whois32.zip	32-bit Whois client application.
wsarch08.zip	16-bit Archie client application.
cuteftp3.zip	32-bit GUI application for Ping, Traceroute, and nslookup.

\wck\apps

cfuseval.exe	demo CGI application for 32 bit ODBC database interface.
post_off.exe	SMTP/POP3 Server.
slnet115.exe	Seattle Lab's SLNet, telnet demo.
blat14.zip	Blat 1.3 is an NT send-mail utility program used by PerForm.
cgi2shell	CGI command-line parsing application.
hsi386.zip	The EMWAC Web server.
mpths110.zip	An imagemap utility for creating map files.
psp311.zip	Paint Shop Pro Graphics Editor/Viewer.
redial.zip	Somar Redial for NT keeps your connection while using RAS.
webedit.zip	WebEdit is an HTML editor.
wsi386.zip	EMWAC WAIS Server (Intel).
wti386.zip	EMWAC WAIS Toolkit (Intel).

\wck\apps\alpha

gsalpha.zip	Alpha chip version of the EMWAC Gopher server.
hsalpha.zip	Alpha chip version of the EMWAC Web server.
wtalpha.zip	Alpha chip version of the EMWAC WAIS toolkit.
perform.exe	Alpha chip version of CGI Perform.

\wck\apps\mips

gsmips.zip	MIPS chip version of the EMWAC Gopher server.
hsmips.zip	MIPS chip version of the EMWAC Web server.
wtmips.zip	MIPS chip version of the EMWAC WAIS Toolkit.

\wck\apps\ppc

hsppc.zip	Power PC version of the EMWAC Web server.
wtppc.zip	Power PC version of the EMWAC WAIS Toolkit.

\wck\apps\wordvu

wordvu	Word for Windows Document Viewer.

\wck\cgi\cgi_samp

cgisamp.c	The C source code for a sample CGI application from Chapter 7.

\wck\cgi\cgikit

savedata.c	Source code for the savedata CGI application from Chapter 7.
Cw3211.dll	DLL needed to run the savedata.exe application.
Savedata.exe	Compiled version (Intel) of the savedata.c CGI application.

Feedback.hfo	File that savedata.exe will write to.
Feedback.htm	Sample HTML form that calls the savedata.exe CGI application.
Savedata.mak	Borland C++ makefile for compiling savedata.c.
readme.txt	CGI Kit Readme file.

\wck\cgi\perform

perform.exe	The CGI Perform application.

\wck\cgi\perform\calendar

Sample files for using CGI PerForm to create a Web-based community calendar.

\wck\cgi\perform\catalogue

Sample files for using CGI Perform to create a Web-based catalog.

\wck\cgi\perform\cool_link_list

Sample files for using CGI PerForm to create a Web-based Cool links list.

\wck\cgi\perform\docs

CGI PerForm installation and usage documents.

\wck\cgi\perform\feedback

Sample files for using CGI PerForm to create a Web-based feedback form.

\wck\cgi\perform\gstbook

Sample files for using CGI PerForm to create a Web-based Guest Book.

\wck\cgi\perform\random_image

Sample files for using CGI PerForm to create an HTML page that will load random images.

\wck\cgi\perform\server_push

Sample files for using CGI PerForm to create an HTML page that will load images for animation.

\wck\cgi\perform\topic_list

Sample files for using CGI PerForm to create a Web-based messaging system.

\wck\cgi\vb

All the files from the Visual Basic and C++ database programs in Chapter 15.

\wck\imagemap

Sample files from Chapter 6.

\wck\servers

alint.zip	Alibaba WWW server; 30-day demo version.
folkweb.zip	Folkweb WWW server; demo version.
purvi386.exe	Perveyor WWW Server; 30-day demo version.
pur-read.me	Perveyor read me file.

\wck\site

Sample Web site files from Chapter 10.

\wck\supp

All sample files from Chapter 15 on databases and the Web.

Switch.inf	A sample switch.inf file.
gsi386.zip	EMWAC Gopher server.
he32.zip	HEdit, an Hex editor for Windows NT.
libcgi.zip	ANSI C library for creating CGI applications.

Bibliography

Albitz, Paul and Cricket Liu. *DNS and BIND*. O'Reilly and Associates, Inc., 1994.

Duncan, Ray. "Electronic Publishing on the World Wide Web." *PC Magazine* 11 April 1995: 257-261.

Duncan, Ray. "Publishing Databases on the World-Wide Web." *PC Magazine* August 1995: 403-412.

Duncan, Ray. "Setting Up a Web Server." *PC Magazine* 16 May 1995: 273-280.

Friesenhahn, Bob. "Build Your Own WWW Server." *Byte* April 1995: 83-96.

"HTTP Server Manual" By: Chris Adie of the European Microsoft Windows NT Academic Centre.

"Hypretext Markup Language 2.0" (Internet Draft) by T. Berners-Lee and D. Connolly 1995.

"HyperText Markup Language Specification Version 3.0" (Internet Draft) by Dave Raggett 1995.

"Hypertext Transfer Protocol HTTP 1.0" (Internet Draft) by T Berners-Lee, R. T. Fielding, H. Frystyk Nielsen 1995.

ISDN a Users Guide to Services, Applications and Resources in California, Pacific Bell stock number 9550.

Lemay, Laura. *Teach Yourself Web Publishing with HTML in a Week*. Sams.net Publishing 1995.

Morris, Mary E. S. *HTML for Fun and Profit*. SunSort Press/Prentice Hall 1995.

Resnick, Rosalind and Dave Taylor. *Internet Business Guide*, Second Edition, Sams.net 1995.

Scoggins, Steve. "The SLIP/PPP Route." *Windows NT Magazine* September 1995: 21-25.

Stallings and Van Slyke. *Business Data Communications*. Macmillan Publishing, Second edition, 1994.

Stevens, W. Richard. *TCP/IP Illustrated*, Volumes 1 and 2. Addison-Wesley.

Tropiano, Lenny, and Dinah McNutt. "How to Implement ISDN." *Byte* April 1995: 67-74.

"Virus Scanners," article by Tim Daniels, *Windows NT Magazine*, October 1995: 55-58.

Web Page: "A Beginner's Guide to HTML" By: National Center for Supercomputing Applications pubs@ncsa.uiuc.edu http://www.ncsa.uiuc.edu/demoweb/html-primer.html.

Web Page: Building Internet Servers by CyberGroup, Inc. http://www.charm.net/~cyber/.

Web Page: "Clickable Image Maps" By: Russ Jones http://gnn.com/gnn/bus/ora/features/miis/index.html.

Web Page: "iNformaTion" http://rmm.com/nt/ by Roger Marty.

Web Page: Publishing on the World Wide Web By: Gareth Rees http://www.cl.cam.ac.uk/users/gdr11/publish.html.

Web Page: Rick's Windows NT Info Center by Rick Graesslen http://137.226.92.4/rick/.

Web Page: "Windows NT on the Internet" http://198.105.232.5:80/pages/bussys/internet/in10000.htm

Web Page: The Windows NT Resource Center By: Dave Baker http://www.bhs.com/winnt/.

Web Page: "World Wide Web Robots, Wanderers, and Spiders" By: Martijn Koster e-mail: m.koster@nexor.co.uk http://web.nexor.co.uk/mak/doc/robots/robots.html.

White Paper: "Advanced Internetworking with TCP/IP on Windows NT" by J. Allard 1993 Microsoft Corp.

White Paper: "Microsoft Windows NT 3.5/3.51 TCP/IP Implementation Details" By Steve MacDonald 1995. Microsoft Corp.

Windows NT Resource Kit, Volumes 1 through 4. Microsoft Press.

Glossary

Access A commercial desktop database for Windows developed by Microsoft. A runtime version of the database engine is included with Visual Basic.

American Standard Code for Information Interchange (ASCII) A standard that encodes 128 common English characters by using 7 of the 8 bits in a byte. It also describes the file format of text files.

Application Programming Interface (API) The set of functions that are provided by the operating system as a service to programmers. Using an API is easier than having to develop the capability from scratch and helps to ensure some consistency across all programs that run on a given operating system.

API See *Application Programming Interface.*

Archie This search utility keeps a database of FTP servers and the files that each has available. Actually, the Archie client queries the Archie server that keeps the database. Archie servers can also be queried by e-mail or by Telnet. There are a few dozen Archie servers on the Internet. This tool works best if you have some idea of the filename that you are looking for. It will return a list of domain names of anonymous FTP sites where the string you entered is contained within directory names or filenames.

ASCII See *American Standard Code for Information Interchange.*

Asynchronous Transfer Mode (ATM)   A new data transmission technology that can deliver super-high throughput of 155–622 Mbps.

ATM   See *Asynchronous Transfer Mode.*

Backbone   Nationwide or international connections (usually T3 bandwidth) that provide the basic structure and IP packet routing on the Internet. Regional backbones (usually T1 bandwidth) provide the connections and IP packet routing for several local area ISPs.

Bandwidth   The difference between the highest and lowest sinusoidal frequency signals that can be transmitted across a transmission line or through a network. It is measured in Hertz (Hz) and also defines the maximum information-carrying capacity of the line or network.

Bridge   A network computer or device that contains two-link layer interfaces and listens to all packet traffic on both networks to determine that packets should be allowed to pass between the two.

Byte   See *Random Access Memory.*

C   C is a very popular general-purpose programming language invented in the late 1960s by Dennis Ritchie at AT&T Bell Laboratories.

C++   C++ is a very popular general-purpose and object-oriented programming language invented in the early 1980s by Bjarne Stroustrup at AT&T Bell Laboratories. C++ compilers will also accept most programs written in standard C.

Cairo   Cairo is the code name (made public for marketing reasons) of the next major release of Windows NT, currently expected to be released in late 1996. One major enhancement likely to be included is "Distributed OLE," which will enable programs to function more efficiently and cooperatively on networks.

Canonical Name (CNAME)   See *DNS Alias.*

CCITT   See *Consultative Committee for International Telephone and Telegraph.*

Central Processing Unit (CPU)   The microprocessor, or brain, which performs most of the calculations necessary to run a computer program.

CERN   The European Laboratory for Particle Physics (CERN) invented the World Wide Web to share information among research groups.

CGI   See *Common Gateway Interface.*

Channel Service Unit/Data Service Unit (CSU/DSU)   These are frequently packaged together as one device. A CSU/DSU is used for interfacing with a T1, Frame Relay, or ISDN line. In some cases it is bundled inside of the router, such as the Ascend Pipeline router for ISDN. It serves much the same purpose for high-speed digital lines as a modem does for analog phone lines. (Hmmm, you could call it the digital analog of the modem.) It resides between your computer (or router) and the phone company data line that leaves your building.

CNAME   See *DNS Alias.*

Common Gateway Interface (CGI)   CGI is an interface for external programs to talk to the HTTP server. Programs that are written to use CGI are called CGI programs or CGI scripts. CGI programs are typically used to handle forms or perform output parsing not done by the server. See also WinCGI.

Common Logfile Format   The common logfile format is used by most Web servers to enter information into the access logs. The format is the same among all of the major Web servers, including Netscape Commerce and Communications servers, CERN httpd, and NCSA httpd. The EMWAC HTTPS does not follow the Common Logfile Format.

Consultative Committee for International Telephone and Telegraph (CCITT)   Regulates worldwide data communications standards. Recently renamed the Telecommunications Standards Sector, which is a body of the International Telecommunications Union.

CPU   See *Central Processing Unit.*

CSU/DSU   See *Channel Service Unit/Data Service Unit.*

Daemon   Pronounced *day-mon.* Any program that runs in the background waiting to be used by other programs. Also known as a *server.*

Data Communications Equipment (DCE)   DCE devices most often reside between the computer and an external data source. The most familiar kind of DCE device is the modem. The computer is usually considered a DTE (Data Terminal Equipment) device. Communications software running on the DTE (computer) must activate the DTR (Data Terminal Ready) signal on the DCE (modem) whenever the software and the computer are ready for further data transmission. The DTE and DCE are usually connected through an RS-232C interface and a UART. In a block diagram of a PC/modem configuration, the UART is actually part of the modem.

Data Terminal Equipment (DTE)   See *Data Communications Equipment.*

DCE   See *Data Communications Equipment.*

DHCP   See *Dynamic Host Control Protocol.*

DLL   See *Dynamic Link Library.*

DNS   See *Domain Name System.*

DNS Alias   A DNS alias is a hostname that the DNS server knows points to a different host—specifically a DNS NAME record. Machines always have one real name, but they can have one or more aliases. For example, www.*yourdomain.domain* might be an alias that points to a real machine called realthing.*yourdomain.domain* where the server currently exists. DNS aliases are sometimes referred to as CNAME's or canonical names.

DNS Name Servers   In the DNS client/server model, these are the servers containing information about a portion of the DNS database, which makes computer names available to client resolvers querying for name resolution across the Internet.

Document root   A directory on the server machine that contains the files, images, and data you want to present to users accessing the server.

Domain Name System (DNS)   A DNS is used by machines on a network to associate standard IP addresses (such as `204.252.2.5`) with hostnames (such as `www.FBSolutions.com`). Computers normally get this translated information from a DNS server, or look it up in tables maintained on their systems.

DTE   See *Data Terminal Equipment.*

Dynamic Link Library   A file that contains a collection of subroutines or resources for use by Windows programs or other DLLs. Windows needs to load only one copy of the DLL into memory regardless of how many running programs will take advantage of it. Windows itself consists almost entirely of DLLs.

Environment Variable   A list of variable bindings. When evaluating an expression in some environment, the evaluation of a variable consists of looking up its value in the environment.

Ethernet   Refers to the standard developed by Digital Equipment Corp, Intel Corp, And Xerox Corp. in 1982. It is the predominant standard in Local Area Networks today. Ethernet uses the Carrier Sense, Multiple Access with Collision Detection (CSMA/CD) access method. Ethernet is also covered by the IEEE 802.3 standard.

FAT   See *File Allocation Table.*

FDDI   See *Fiber Distributed Data Interface.*

Fiber Distributed Data Interface (FDDI)   A high-speed (100 MBps) network cabling technology that is immune to Radio Frequency Interference from other electrical sources and protected from the possibility of electronic eavesdropping.

File Allocation Table (FAT)   The file system used by MS-DOS through version 6.22. FAT is famous for the fact that it limits filenames to 8 characters with 3 characters for the file extension. Although the primary file system in Windows NT is NTFS, FAT is also available in NT for backward-compatibility. The file system in Windows 95 is a superset of FAT, called VFAT, which permits long filenames.

FTP   See *File Transfer Protocol.*

File Extension   The last section of a filename that typically defines the type of file (for example, .GIF and .HTML). For example, in the filename index.html the file extension is html. .HTM is also commonly used as the extension for HTML files.

File Transfer Protocol (FTP)   A protocol that governs file transfers between local and remote systems. The programs that use this protocol are referred to as FTP clients and FTP servers. FTP supports several commands that allow bidirectional transfer of binary and ASCII files between systems. The FTP client and server programs on NT are installed with the TCP/IP connectivity utilities. Note that the client that comes with NT is a command-line version.

File Type   The format of a given file. For example, a graphics file doesn't have the same internal representation as a text file. File types are usually identified by the file extension (for example, .GIF or .HTML).

Firewall   A security device placed on a LAN to protect it from Internet intruders. This can be a special kind of hardware router, or a piece of software, or both.

Frame Relay   A data transmission technology becoming more popular as a means of replacing expensive T1 leased-lines in wide-area networks. Frame Relay can be purchased in units more appropriate for anticipated network traffic, it can be scaled up or down over time, and it can be used without predefining multiple point-to-point connections.

FQDN   See *Fully Qualified Domain Name.*

Fully Qualified Domain Name (FQDN)   Hostnames with their domain names appended to them. For example, on a host with hostname `webserv` and DNS domain name `yourco.com`, the FQDN is `webserv.yourco.com`.

Gateway   A gateway is a network computer which is running software for more than one network interface. The gateway manages the flow of data between the two networks according to routing tables.

GIF   See *Graphics Interchange Format.*

Graphics Interchange Format (GIF)   A cross-platform image format originally created by CompuServe. GIF files are usually much smaller in size than other graphic file types (.BMP, .TIFF). GIF is one of the most common interchange formats, and is readily viewable on many platforms.

Gigabyte   See *Random Access Memory.*

Gopher   The Internet program invented at the University of Minnesota for distribution of text files that are selected through character-based menus.

Graphical User Interface (GUI)   This describes the method of interaction that a program offers to its user. A GUI permits mouse and keyboard control, as opposed to a command-line interface, which requires keyboard entry. Most Windows NT programs include a GUI with user-friendly buttons, menus, and scrollbars. Console applications can only be run in the NT Command Prompt window.

GUI   See *Graphical User Interface.*

Home Page   A document that exists on the server and acts as a catalog or entry point for the server's contents. The location of this document is defined within the server's configuration files.

Hostname   A name for a machine of the form `machine.subdomain.domain`, which is translated into an IP address. For example, `www.FBSolutions.com` is considered a hostname or a Fully Qualified Domain Name. This machine, `www` can be either a unique machine (or host) in the subdomain (or network), or it can be an alias (or CNAME) to another machine in the subdomain (or network).

HTML   See *HyperText Markup Language.*

HTTP   See *HyperText Transfer Protocol.*

HTTPD   An abbreviation for the HTTP daemon, a program that serves information using the HTTP protocol. UNIX-based HTTP servers are often called httpd's.

HTTPS   The PC world abbreviation for the HTTP server, a program that serves information using the HTTP protocol.

HyperText Markup Language (HTML)   HTML is a formatting language used for documents on the World Wide Web. HTML files are plain text files with formatting codes that tell browsers, such as Netscape Navigator, how to display text, position graphics and form items, and display hypertext links to other pages.

Hypertext Transfer Protocol (HTTP)   The standard method for exchanging information between HTTP servers and clients on the Web. The HTTP specification lays out the rules of how Web servers and browsers must work together.

IDE   See *Integrated Drive Electronics.*

Imagemapping   A process that enables users to navigate and obtain information by clicking the different regions of the image with a mouse. Imagemap can also refer to a CGI program called *imagemap,* which is used to handle imagemap functionality in UNIX-based httpd implementations.

Industry Standard Architecture (ISA)   Defines the standard IBM PC bus.

Integrated Digital Services Network (ISDN)   Essentially operates as digital phone line. ISDN delivers many benefits over standard analog phone lines, including multiple simultaneous calls and higher-quality data transmissions. ISDN data rates are 56 KBps to 128 KBps.

Integrated Drive Electronics (IDE)   A standard disk drive adapter designed for the PC ISA.

InterNIC   The organization charged with maintaining unique addresses for every computer on the Internet using the domain name system.

Internet Protocol (IP)   The protocol that governs how packets are built and sent over the network. IP does not guarantee packet delivery or the order of delivery. TCP runs on top of IP to provide a reliable, and sequenced internetwork communication stream. See also Transmission Control Protocol/Internet Protocol (TCP/IP).

Internet Service Provider (ISP)   The company that provides you or your company with access to the Internet. ISPs usually have several servers and a high-speed link to the Internet backbone.

Intranet   Most commonly used to describe a corporate network (LAN or WAN) that uses TCP/IP and related application layer protocols such as HTTP, SMTP, POP3. An Intranet doesn't necessarily include a permanent connection to the Internet. Intranets can be used for publishing company documentation internally.

IP   See *Internet Protocol.*

IP Address   An Internet protocol address is a set of four numbers (4 bytes, or 32 bits) separated by dots, which specifies the actual location of a machine on the Internet.

ISA   See *Industry Standard Architecture.*

ISDN   See *Integrated Services Digital Network.*

ISINDEX   Documents can often use a network navigator's capabilities to accept a search string and send it to the server to access a searchable index without using forms. To use ISINDEX, you must create a query handler.

ISMAP   `ISMAP` is an extension to the `IMG SRC` tag used in an HTML document to tell the server that the named image is an imagemap.

ISP   See *Internet Service Provider.*

Key   An entry in the NT Registry Editor that contains a unit of configuration information.

Kilobyte   See *Random Access Memory.*

Megabyte   See *Random Access Memory.*

LAN   See *Local Area Network.*

Local Area Network   A group of computers and peripheral devices that are wired together for the common good of all users. This is usually done in an office environment for the purpose of sharing files and printers. Typical LAN sizes range from 2 to 100 computers.

Listserv or **Listserver**   A server application that allows group members to broadcast e-mail messages amongst themselves. An individual sends a single e-mail message to the server, which in turn sends it to all the other members of the listserv group.

MIME   See *Multi-Purpose Internet Mail Extensions.*

Multi-Purpose Internet Mail Extensions (MIME)   This is an emerging standard for multimedia file transfers on the Internet via e-mail or the Web.

Multi-Threaded   A programming technique that allows for more than one part of a program to be executing simultaneously on an SMP machine. Even on single CPU computers, multi-threaded programs can show the advantage of better responsiveness to user commands while a lengthy background process is running.

National Center for Supercomputing Applications (NCSA)   A research organization at the University of Illinois at Urbana-Champaign. NCSA is credited with the invention of Mosaic, the world's first graphical Web browser. Internet popularity has skyrocketed in the years since 1993 following the availability of Mosaic for desktop computers such as PCs and Macintoshes.

NCSA   See *National Center for Supercomputing Applications.*

Network News Transfer Protocol (NNTP)   This is the protocol Usenet runs to deliver newsgroups. There are thousands of newsgroups on the Internet. Each one is similar to a bulletin board devoted to a particular topic that its readers like to discuss.

NNTP   See *Network News Transfer Protocol.*

NTFS   See *NT File System.*

NT File System (NTFS)   This is the advanced file system that NT provides as an option when formatting hard drives. The advantages of this system are long filenames, reduced file fragmentation, improved fault tolerance, and better recovery performance after a crash (as compared to DOS or OS/2).

Object Linking and Embedding (OLE)   The API developed by Microsoft on which much of the Windows 95 user interface is based. Originally intended only to provide a means of treating documents as objects useable by other documents, it has since been expanded to include cut-and-paste functionality, the capability to program component objects from applications, store files and directories within compound files, and serve as the basis for distributed objects via remote procedure calls in the Cairo version of Windows NT.

ODBC   See *Open Database Connectivity.*

OLE   See *Object Linking and Embedding.*

Open Database Connectivity (ODBC)   The database-independent API developed by Microsoft provides application developers with a portable means of writing database programs. Database vendors supply low-level drivers conforming with the interface to ODBC.DLL. Application programmers make standard calls to ODBC.DLL to access any database regardless of its proprietary format.

PCI   See *Peripheral Component Interconnect.*

PDC   See *Primary Domain Controller.*

Peripheral Component Interconnect (PCI)   PCI is a local bus motherboard design from Intel. It is designed to compete with the industry consortium that developed VESA local bus (VLB.) It runs at half the speed of the main CPU, as opposed to a constant 6 MHz rate for the standard PC ISA bus and the VESA local bus. Its performance outshines VLB in many respects. It is becoming very popular in new Pentium-based systems, despite some early glitches in its career.

PERL   See *Practical Extraction and Report Language.*

Ping   A TCP/IP program that is used to verify network connections between computers and to time how long packets take to traverse the route.

POP, **POP3**   See *Post Office Protocol.*

Post Office Protocol (POP, or POP3)   Defined by RFC 1721, POP3 is an application-level protocol designed to handle the mail at a local level. The POP3 mailbox stores mail received by

SMTP (the routing agent) until it is read by the user. It also passes outgoing messages to the SMTP server for subsequent delivery to the addressee.

PPP   See *Point to Point Protocol.*

Point to Point Protocol (PPP)   An industry standard that is part of Windows NT Remote Access Software (RAS) that allows you to connect to the Internet. Because it offers greater performance, PPP has widely replaced SLIP for remote Internet connections.

Port   A connection or socket used to connect a TCP/IP-based client application to your server. Servers are normally known by their well-known port number as assigned by the Internet Assigned Numbers Authority (IANA). The well-known port for HTTP is 80.

Practical Extraction and Report Language (Perl)   Perl is a programming language designed for scanning arbitrary text files, extracting information, and printing reports. Perl programs are called scripts because they are processed by an interpreter, as opposed to a compiler.

Protocol   A set of rules and conventions by which two computers pass messages across a network.

Proxy Server   A computer program that runs on a server placed between a LAN and its connection to the Internet. The proxy server software will filter all outgoing connections to appear as if they came from only one machine. The purpose for doing this is to prevent external hackers from knowing the structure of your network. The system administrator may also regulate the outside points to which the LAN users may connect.

RAM   See *Random Access Memory.*

Random Access Memory (RAM)   The physical semiconductor-based memory in a computer. One byte of RAM can hold one character, such as the period at the end of this sentence. One kilobyte (KB) holds 1024 characters. One megabyte (MB) of RAM holds one million characters (actually 1024 * 1024). Not counting graphics, this book consists of about 300,000 characters, or 1/3 of a megabyte. One gigabyte (GB) is equal to one thousand megabytes. Yes, that's a lot, and no, it isn't always enough. Terabytes (TB) are not discussed very commonly yet, but just so you know, 1 TB equals 1000 GB.

Redirection   A system by which clients accessing a particular URL are sent to a different location, either on the same server or on a different server.

Registry   The Windows NT system database that holds configuration information for hardware, software, and users.

Resource   As it pertains to HTML, this refers to any document (URL), directory, or program that the server can access and send to a client that asks for it.

Request for Comments (RFCs)   The official documents of the IETF (Internet Engineering Task Force) that specify the details of all the protocols and systems that comprise the Internet.

RFC   See *Request For Comments.*

Robot   For our purposes, we are referring to software robots on the Web. These applications wander the Internet looking for Web servers and return indexing information to their host. Robots are most often used to create databases of Web sites. The Lycos search Web page database is maintained by the Lycos Robot.

Router   This is a special-purpose computer used for connecting two or more networks together. Most routers enable you to create a physical connection between different types of networks such as Ethernet, Token Ring, and FDDI.

SCSI   See *Small Computer Systems Interface.*

Secure Sockets Layer (SSL)   This is a software interface developed by Netscape that provides for encrypted data transfer between client and server applications over the Internet. SSL, STT (from Microsoft and Visa), and S_HTTP (which is a secure version of the HyperText Transfer Protocol) are all means of enabling secure commerce on the Web.

Serial Line Internet Protocol (SLIP)   SLIP is an industry standard protocol that encapsulates IP packets for transmission through modems. It is one of the available protocols when using TCP/IP with RAS.

Server   In general, refers to a computer that provides shared resources to network users. In some specific cases, related to the Internet, server refers to the TCP/IP application layer protocol server, such as HTTPS.

Server Root   A directory on the server machine dedicated to holding the server program, configuration, maintenance, and information files.

Service   A service is an executable object installed in the NT Registry database. A service can be started on demand or started automatically when the system starts up. No more than one instance of a given service can be running at a time.

SGML   See *Standard Generalized Markup Language.*

Simple Mail Transfer Protocol (SMTP)   A standard protocol in TCP/IP that determines how e-mail is transferred on the Internet.

Simple Network Management Protocol (SNMP)   A standard protocol in TCP/IP that determines how networks are monitored for performance.

SLIP   See *Serial Line Internet Protocol.*

Small Computer Systems Interface (SCSI)   Pronounced *scuzzy,* this is a type of hardware interface standard for computers and peripheral devices. It is general-purpose, but most often it is used for hard disk drives, CD-ROM drives, and scanners. SCSI is supported on many platforms. On Windows NT it is the preferred CD-ROM interface. SCSI and IDE drives and controllers can operate together in the same system. Up to seven SCSI devices can be daisy-chained together on one controller card. (But the card itself counts as one device.) Although IDE (or EIDE) remains more popular for PC hard drives because of price, SCSI drives usually offer better performance—especially many of the new varieties of SCSI, such as SCSI II and Fast-Wide SCSI. One Wide SCSI adapter can daisy-chain up to 13 devices.

SMP   See *Symmetric Multi-processor.*

SMTP   See *Simple Mail Transfer Protocol.*

SNMP   See *Simple Network Management Protocol.*

SSL   See *Secure Sockets Layer.*

Standard Generalized Markup Language (SGML)   This is ISO standard 8879:1986 for Information Processing Text and Office Systems. HTML is an application of this standard.

Switched-56   This is a circuit-switched technology with a throughput of 56 KBps. It has been the middle-ground between analog phone lines and dedicated T1 lines prior to the development of ISDN.

Symmetric Multi-Processor (SMP)   A computer architecture in which more than 1 CPU is running and sharing memory simultaneously. Windows NT is designed to take advantage of SMP hardware both inside the operating system and at the application level through the creation of separate threads using the WIN32 API.

T-1   A data transmission medium capable of 1.544 Mbps. Lines can be leased for private or corporate use between two designated points. Some Internet Service Providers offer it.

T-3   A data transmission medium capable of 45 Mbps. It is usually only in the Internet backbone or in large institutions.

TCP   See *Transmission Control Protocol.*

Telnet   A protocol where two machines on the network are connected to each other and support terminal emulation for remote login. A remote computer running a Telnet client application can execute any console based application on an NT Telnet server.

Terabyte   See *Random Access Memory.*

Timeout   A specified time after which a program should give up trying to finish an operation with a remote machine that appears to be non-responsive.

Token Ring   An IBM network arranged in a circular topology in which a circulating electronic token is used to carry the active packet. A node on the network must wait until the empty token passes by before it may insert a message onto the LAN. Token Ring is covered by the IEEE 802.5 standard.

Top-level Domain   The highest category of hostname classification, usually signifying either the type of organization the domain is (for example, .com is a company and .edu is an educational institution) or the country of its origin (for example, .us is the United States and .jp is Japan).

Transmission Control Protocol (TCP)   A connection-based Internet protocol responsible for breaking data into packets, which the Internet Protocol sends over the network. TCP provides a reliable and sequenced internetwork communication stream.

Transmission Control Protocol/Internet Protocol (TCP/IP)   The Internet protocols used to connect a worldwide internetwork of universities, research laboratories, military installations, organizations, and corporations. TCP/IP includes standards for how computers communicate and conventions for connecting networks and routing traffic.

UDP   See *User Datagram Protocol.*

Unicode   A 16-bit character encoding system that covers all the symbols in all the languages of the world and several currency, science, and mathematics symbols. Windows NT uses Unicode internally for all strings and filenames, and provides a set of Unicode APIs so that application developers can more easily build international programs.

Uniform Resource Locator (URL)   Also commonly called a location. This is an addressing system that locates documents on servers. A client uses the URL to request a document to be viewed. The format of a URL is [*protocol*]://[*machine:port*]/[*document*]. An example is `http://www.FBSolutions.com/default.htm`.

Uninterruptible Power Supply (UPS)   See *UPS.*

UPS   A battery-operated power supply connected to a computer to keep the system running during a power failure.

URL   See *Uniform Resource Locator.*

User Datagram Protocol (UDP)   Runs on top of IP to provide more efficient, but less reliable, packet delivery than TCP. UDP is used for certain Internet programs such as Trivial File Transfer Protocol and Ping.

VERONICA   This gets its name from Very Easy Rodent-Oriented Net-wide Index to Computerized Archives. Veronica is a utility for searching gopher databases. It is accessed as a menu item displayed by a gopher server. The data returned by Veronica is displayed as yet another menu of gopher menu items that match the given search topic.

VESA Local Bus (VLB)   This is a popular type of PC local bus defined by the Video Electronics Standards Association. Most VLB machines can support two or three such devices. Peripheral cards in the VLB expansion slots operate with far less overhead than standard cards. It is most frequently used for EIDE hard-drive controllers or VGA display adapters—two devices that are heavily dependent on data throughput rates.

VLB   See *VESA Local Bus.*

Virtual Memory   A software technique, often implemented in the operating system, which uses hard disk space to increase memory capacity beyond the amount of physical RAM present. Windows NT will automatically reload virtual memory from the hard disk into RAM at the instant that an application calls for it. This is not to be confused with a RAM Disk, which is a program that uses RAM to serve as a fast disk drive.

Virtual Reality Markup Language (VRML)   VRML is a draft specification that describes how to implement support for virtual-reality scenes on the Web. It builds on the foundation of HTML, but it is a new language. Like HTML, the language is not binary-restricted to any particular platform. With virtual reality support, clients will be able to traverse 3-D Web pages.

Visual Basic   A point-and-click programming environment from Microsoft for development of Windows programs in the BASIC language. It is popular for its ease of screen design. It includes the Access database engine.

VRML   See *Virtual Reality Markup Language.*

WAIS   WAIS is a subset of the Z39.50-88 protocol that enable remote WAIS clients to conduct searches of server databases that have been prepared using a waisindex tool.

Win16   The 16-bit Windows API that was developed in Windows version 1.0 and extended through Windows For Workgroups version 3.11. It is called 16-bit because it usually uses 2 bytes to represent programming objects such as integers, references to windows, and pointers to memory.

Win32   The 32-bit Windows API that was developed in Windows NT version 3.1 and extended through Windows NT 3.5 and Windows 95. It is called 32-bit because it usually uses 4 bytes to represent programming objects such as integers, references to windows, and pointers to memory. The Win32 API is a much richer and more robust API than Win16. In many cases, programs written for Win16 are very upwardly compatible with Win32.

WinCGI   A new Common Gateway Interface for Windows GUI programs that doesn't require console-mode programs. Many Windows HTTP server packages include a reference implementation in Visual Basic that demonstrates the simple retrieval of CGI environment variables. See also Common Gateway Interface.

Windows 95   The desktop operating system from Microsoft for home and business application software running on PCs. Windows 95 is the all-in-one successor to DOS, Windows 3.1, and Windows for Workgroups 3.11.

Windows NT   The portable, secure, 32-bit, pre-emptive multitasking member of the Microsoft Windows operating system family.

Windows NT Server   As a superset of Windows NT Workstation, Windows NT Server provides better centralized management and security, advanced fault tolerance, and additional connectivity options.

Windows NT Workstation   The less expensive version of Windows NT.

Index

Add to Your Sams.net Library Today
with the Best Books for Internet Technologies

ISBN	Quantity	Description of Item	Unit Cost	Total Cost
1-57521-041-X		Internet Unleashed 1996	$49.99	
1-57521-039-8		Presenting Java	$25.00	
0-672-30745-6		HTML and CGI Unleashed	$49.99	
0-672-30735-9		Teach Yourself the Internet in a Week, Second Edition	$25.00	
1-57521-004-5		Internet Business Guide, Second Edition	$25.00	
0-672-30595-X		Education on the Internet	$25.00	
0-672-30718-9		Navigating the Internet, Third Edition	$25.00	
1-57521-040-1		The World Wide Web Unleashed 1996	$49.99	
1-57521-005-3		Teach Yourself More Web Publishing with HTML in a Week	$29.99	
0-672-30764-2		Teach Yourself Web Publishing with Microsoft Word in a Week	$29.99	
0-672-30669-7		Plug-n-Play Internet	$35.00	
1-57521-010-X		Plug-n-Play Netscape for Windows	$29.99	
0-672-30723-5		Secrets of the MUD Wizards	$25.00	
		Shipping and handling: See information below.		
		TOTAL		

Shipping and handling: $4.00 for the first book, and $1.75 for each additional book. If you need to have it NOW, we can ship product to you in 24 hours for an additional charge of approximately $18.00, and you will receive your item overnight or in two days. Overseas shipping and handling adds $2.00. Prices subject to change. Call between 9:00 a.m. and 5:00 p.m. EST for availability and pricing information on latest editions.

201 W. 103rd Street, Indianapolis, Indiana 46290

1-800-428-5331 — Orders   1-800-835-3202 — FAX   1-800-858-7674 — Customer Service

Book ISBN 1-57521-047-9

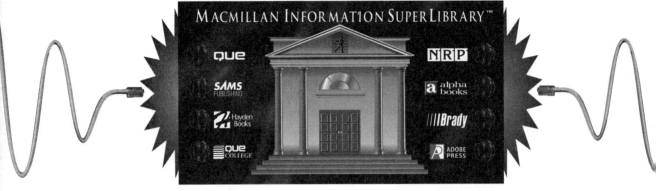

CD-ROM
Installation Page

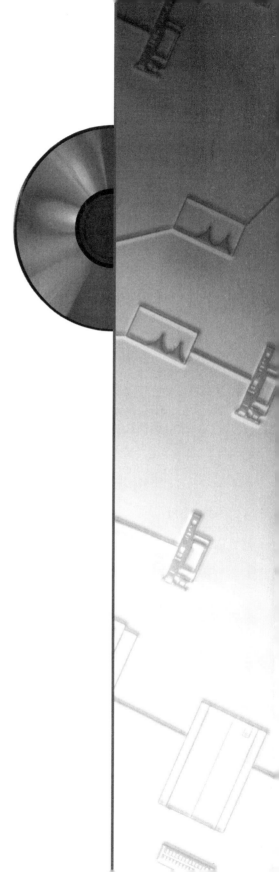

Installing Software from the CD-ROM

The companion CD-ROM contains software distributed under the GNU license, other programs mentioned in the book, and many useful examples. The server software included on this CD-ROM will run only on Windows NT platforms (Intel).

Windows NT Installation Instructions

1. Insert the CD-ROM disc into your CD-ROM drive.
2. From File Manager or Program Manager, choose Run from the File menu.
3. Type *drive*\SETUP and press Enter, where *drive* corresponds to the drive letter of your CD-ROM. For example, if your CD-ROM is drive D:, type D:\SETUP and press Enter.
4. Follow the on-screen instructions in the installation program. Files will be installed to a directory named \WEBCON, unless you choose a different directory during installation.

SETUP creates a Program Manager group called Web Site Kit. An uninstall option is available in the program group that will remove all the source files and software prior to individual installation.

Please refer to Appendix H for a description of the software and location of the directories in which the software can be found.

Technical Support from Macmillan

We can't help you with Windows NT or server problems or software from third parties, but we can assist you if a problem arises with the CD-ROM itself.

E-mail support: Send e-mail to support@mcp.com.

CompuServe: Type GO SAMS to reach the Macmillan Computer Publishing forum. Leave us a message, addressed to SYSOP. If you want the message to be private, address it to *SYSOP.

Telephone: (317) 581-3833

Fax: (317) 581-4773

Mail: Macmillan Computer Publishing
Attention: Support Department
201 West 103rd Street
Indianapolis, IN 46290-1093

World Wide Web (The Macmillan Information SuperLibrary):
http://www.mcp.com/samsnet

Internet FTP:
ftp.mcp.com (/pub/samsnet)